TELEGRAPHIC REALISM

Telegraphic Realism

Victorian Fiction and Other Information Systems

Richard Menke

Stanford University Press

Stanford, California

2008

Stanford University Press
Stanford, California

Printed in the United States of America on acid-free, archival-quality paper

Library of Congress Cataloging-in-Publication Data

Menke, Richard.
   Telegraphic realism : Victorian fiction and other information systems /
Richard Menke.
      p.   cm.
   Includes bibliographical references and index.
   ISBN 978-0-8047-5691-4 (alk. paper)
      1.   English fiction—19th century—History and criticism.
   2. Communication in literature.   3. Technology in literature.
   4. Telecommunication in literature.   5. Telegraph in literature.
   6. Postal service in literature.   7. Realism in literature.   8. Communication
   and technology—Great Britain—History—19th century.   I. Title.

PR878.C636M46 2008
823'.809356—dc22

                                                              2007008106

This book was published with the assistance of the Willson Center for
Humanities and Arts at the University of Georgia.

Contents

Acknowledgments   *vii*

Introduction: Victorian Informatics   1

POST AND TELEGRAPH

1   The New Post Age   31
2   Electric Information   68

EMBODYING INFORMATION

3   Speaking Machines   103
4   Information Unveiled   134
5   The Telegrapher's Tale   163

CABLE AND WIRELESS

6   A Winged Intelligence   191
7   Wireless   217

Coda: Afterlives of Victorian Information   249

Notes   255
Works Cited   286
Index   313

Acknowledgments

My earliest thoughts about this project took shape in the singular media ecology of Stanford University in the 1990s, and I am delighted once again to thank Rob Polhemus, Barbara Gelpi, and Joss Marsh for their inspiration and guidance. I extend thanks to the Stanford Department of English, the Mellon Foundation, and the Mabelle McLeod Lewis Foundation for supporting my work on a dissertation that ended with a chapter on Henry James and the telegraph. For their criticisms, their enthusiasm, and their camaraderie, I am indebted to Diana Maltz and the other members of Stanford's Nineteenth-Century Graduate Group, especially Helen Blythe, Kenneth Brewer, Jason Camlot, Lisa Jenkins, Stephanie Kuduk, Paul Saint-Amour, and Kate Washington.

Hilary Schor has been a constant intellectual presence for me, someone who not only encouraged my first reflections on Victorian media but also helped me see where they might lead. I measured my progress by our brunch meetings, and my trip to the Dickens Universe conference in Santa Cruz a few years ago at her prompting was a turning point for me. A crucial NEH Summer Seminar with Katherine Hayles at UCLA made me believe that a dissertation on embodiment and subjectivity in Victorian fiction should become a book on realism and information, and a later NEH Summer Stipend helped me begin that book, supporting my research at the British Library and the Postal Heritage Trust in London. Obviously, any views, findings, conclusions, or recommendations expressed in this book do not necessarily reflect those of the National Endowment for the Humanities. Most recently, fellowships at the Newberry Library, the Harry Ransom Humanities Research Center at the University of Texas, and the Institute for Advanced Studies in the Humanities at Edinburgh University were greatly helpful in bringing the project to fruition.

At the University of Georgia, the UGA Research Foundation and the Office of the Vice President for Research, the Franklin College of Arts and Sciences, the Center for Teaching and Learning, and the English Department have generously supported my research. In addition to helping me work on this book, Georgia's Willson Center for Humanities and Arts has also supported its publication in the present form. I am greatly indebted to the heads of my department, Anne Williams, Nelson Hilton, Doug Anderson, and Valerie Babb, and I've been most fortunate in my other colleagues and friends in Georgia as well. Some of those who have had the most influence on my understanding of nineteenth-century literature, of the ties between literature and information, or of book-writing, are Kris Boudreau, Alex Brewis, Andrew Cole, Roxanne Eberle, Simon Gatrell, Anne Mallory, Susan Mattern, Adam Parkes, Jed Rasula, Susan Rosenbaum, and Ken Rufo. I'm particularly grateful to Tricia Lootens for her comments on the book, as well as her enthusiasm and guidance. My students at Georgia have also taught me much, especially those who joined my undergraduate and graduate classes on literature and media.

Many people read or heard parts of this work and provided advice and encouragement about, and at, critical points; I'm especially indebted to John Bender, George Dekker, Elaine Freedgood, Lisa Gitelman, Katherine Hayles, Ivan Kreilkamp, J. Hillis Miller, Laura Otis, Sam Pickering, Mary Poovey, Leah Price, and Clifford Siskin. Norris Pope, an expert on this book's subject, has also been its ideal editor at Stanford University Press. I also thank Teresa Mangum and Stanford's other, anonymous reader for their detailed and useful comments on the manuscript.

Finally, I would like to thank my family: my parents, Bruce and Karen Menke; my wife, Sujata Iyengar; and our children, Kavya and Kartik. But perhaps some debts defy expression in any medium.

This book incorporates material that was published elsewhere in different forms. Part of chapter 4 appeared in "Fiction as Vivisection: G. H. Lewes and George Eliot" (*ELH*, 2000), while sections of chapters 2, 5, and 6 draw on my essays "Telegraphic Realism: Henry James's *In the Cage*" (*PMLA*, 2000) and "'Framed and Wired': Teaching 'In the Cage' at the Intersection of Literature and Media" (*The Henry James Review*, 2004). I am grateful to the Johns Hopkins University Press and the Modern Language Association for allowing me to include them here.

Telegraphic Realism

Introduction: Victorian Informatics

[N]either mimetic powers nor mimetic objects remain the same in the course of thousands of years. Rather, we must suppose that the gift of producing similarities . . . and therefore also the gift of recognizing them, have changed with historical development.

— WALTER BENJAMIN, "ON THE MIMETIC FACULTY"

In early 1846, Charles Dickens wrote to the gardener-turned-architect and railway magnate Joseph Paxton with reports on two of their grand ventures. "I can't sleep; and if I fall into a doze I dream of first numbers till my head swims," declares Dickens; sponsored by Paxton and with Dickens as its founding editor, the *Daily News* would launch within days. Dickens's other note concerned a scheme even more ambitious than the founding of a national newspaper, yet one that—in contrast to Dickens's short-lived editorship of the *Daily News*—has not received recognition or comment. For even as Dickens and Paxton founded a new vehicle of daily communication, they also took part in a parallel but more visionary project, sponsoring what was probably the first serious plan to connect England to Europe via an underwater telegraph cable. The electric telegraph had only recently begun to prove itself on land, but for Dickens the prospects of an undersea link from Dover to Calais seemed encouraging: "Captain Taylor writes from Paris this Morning, that his Petition was received with the greatest interest by the Count St. Aulaire [French Ambassador to Britain], and that the idea excited him extremely, as one of most uncommon importance. The Lords of the Admiralty have granted the permission on this side of the Water."[1] Although they received authorization from both governments and began making seaside experiments, Dickens and company never took their plans further; since then, his involvement has remained largely unnoted.[2] Like the *Daily News*, the project of establishing rapid electrical communication across the English Channel would ultimately succeed, but without the involvement of Dickens.

Yet his interest in the scheme represents the translation of recognizably Dickensian concerns into a new medium. The *Daily News* was funded largely by railway money and aligned with railway interests, and during his weeks as editor Dickens was eager to exploit these connections. To make a "preliminary splash," Dickens carefully arranged for its first issue to cover a free trade meeting in Norwich via a special express train, so that "our man or men can come up long before the Mail—write out, on the way—and give us his or their couple of Columns or so, in time for the first Edition."[3] After a similar feat a week later, Dickens would exult that "[t]he Express has done us a World of Good. We are going ahead famously"—aligning the newspaper's progress with the express trains', even as his general interest in editing it was waning.[4]

The first telegraphed news item in a British newspaper had appeared less than a year earlier.[5] But Dickens's enthusiastic involvement in the Anglo-French telegraph scheme, undertaken simultaneously with his work on the *Daily News* and in partnership with its main backer, surely intuits the journalistic possibilities of a communication system even faster and splashier than the railway. At the *Daily News*, observes Peter Ackroyd, Dickens often "seem[ed] more concerned with the speed with which news [wa]s transmitted than the content of the news itself," a parallel for his fiction's emphasis on "images of free flow as opposed to barriers and hindrances, of unimpeded circulation compared to stagnation and blockage"—for instance, in another great enterprise begun later that year, *Dealings with the Firm of Dombey and Son, Wholesale, Retail, and for Exportation* (1846–48).[6] For Dickens, the promise of instantaneous, intangible electric communication might also emphasize the material difference of other vehicles of circulation available in

1846. In *Dombey and Son*, the railway goes ahead, famously, as a bearer not of thrillingly rapid messages but of lethal physical force.

Dickens's period as a would-be telegraph pioneer was brief. But this conjunction of projects in 1846—a newspaper, a telegraph cable, a return to novel-writing after a two-year hiatus—aptly suggests the ties between nineteenth-century fiction and other modes of discourse, both established and emerging. Victorian writing was part of a world of new media, even as those media were just coming into existence.

This book examines British fiction in the age of the Penny Post and the electric telegraph, arguing that imaginative writing responds in crucial and defining ways to the nineteenth century's new media and the ideas they encouraged about information, communication, and language. While I discuss many media, my detailed examinations of Victorian information technologies focus chiefly on transmission systems that directly incorporate or adapt *writing*—the post, electric telegraph, and wireless telegraphy—as opposed to photography, the telephone, the gramophone, or cinema. In particular, I highlight relationships between these new methods of transcoding and transmitting the data of real life and Victorian fiction's modes of mimesis. Examining these technical systems of alphabetic dissemination, and what fiction had to say about them, can help us read the changing nature of textuality in the nineteenth century—of the kind of existence written language seemed to have, its link to human minds and bodies, its connection to an author, its relationship to an audience. The age of the postage stamp and the electric telegraph decisively altered the meaning of the old technologies of writing and print. One powerful expression of these media shifts just behind the ink and paper of the era's written record, I am arguing, is Victorian fictional realism.

To that end, I intend this book as not simply a thematic study of new media technologies in fiction but an examination of how fiction could begin imagining itself as a medium and information system in an age of new media. Accordingly, the point of this study is not only to discuss fiction that weaves plots around particular Victorian media technologies, although several of the following chapters do just that. Rather, I have sought to delineate the deep ways in which new technologies, and the wider understandings that a culture could derive from them, register in literature's ways of imagining and representing the real. I find this connection especially strong in nineteenth-century fiction, where it helps illuminate the logic and fortunes of realism. And in contrast to the era's poetry, fiction minimizes the formal markers that might separate it from a larger world of everyday printed information. My pages trace a changing informatic orientation through (for instance) Trollope's postal order, Charlotte Brontë's long-distance intimacies, Dickens's and George Eliot's mediumistic characters, Henry James's fictional telegraphy, and Kipling's intuition of a culture gone wireless.

Conversely, if more tentatively, I also point out ways in which imaginative writing anticipated and helped to shape these larger cultural understandings, how fiction could offer a forum for exploring a real world that had come to seem laden with information, or even constituted by it. In this light, a sprawling Victorian triple-decker looks like both a treatment of a world as information, and an affirmation that such a mass of information could be arranged and made meaningful while still remaining true. The multivolume novel with its intertwined plots; the historical romance; the detective story; the tightly drawn, consciously literary turn-of-the-century tale—these Victorian fictional forms and genres all have their own informational economies. But across literary works of many kinds, we can also see the outlines of a new idea emerging: the concept of *information* itself. An informatic history of literature also offers a literary history of information.

Even a cursory list of the new media devices and information systems developed during the latter two-thirds of the nineteenth century helps indicate the scope of the Victorian information revolution: the photograph (from daguerreotype and William Henry Fox Talbot's calotype to celluloid film), Rowland Hill's new Penny Post and the ubiquitous postage stamp, the electric telegraph, electric lighting, the telephone, the phonograph and gramophone, the typewriter, the electrotype process, the linotype machine, the motion picture, wireless telegraphy. Over the course of this period, the arrival of astonishing new media technologies, and the progression of each from marvel of the age to daily use, became familiar, as late-Victorian reviews of the century's technical achievements suggested.[7] Great Britain could claim a central role in the history of many of the century's new media, whether in their invention, development, commercialization, or all three, especially when it came to the innovations that offered primarily communication rather than data storage. "England has stood in the foreground"

of cable telegraphy, exulted the brother and collaborator of the great engineer Sir Charles Bright in 1867.[8] "London . . . is the principal centre of
the Telegraphic enterprise in the world," noted another telegraphic brother
in 1873, the naturalized Briton William Siemens, representative of Werner
Siemens's famous electrical firm in the United Kingdom.[9] British boasting
could also apply to postal reform a generation earlier or wireless telegraphy
thirty years later. Even the telephone, invented in the United States, was
developed by a Scotsman.

And yet the cross-pollination between imaginative writing and media innovation in nineteenth-century Britain still remains underexplored in literary and media history alike. This is surprising, especially given the fascination with which Victorian authors often viewed new media and information systems. It's not hard to picture Dickens coming to Hampstead for a
convivial dinner spent quizzing Roland Hill on the new postal system. Or
to envision Kipling chatting knowingly with Marconi about wireless telegraphy over lunch; they would have had much to talk about, these two young
technophiles who would go on to win Nobel prizes—and to become notorious for their reactionary politics. Either encounter is easy to imagine; both
of them actually happened.

Inspired in part by our own contemporary experiences with new media,
literary scholars have recently begun to emphasize the rich connections between the Victorians' media and their literature.[10] The following chapters
will attest to my indebtedness to such scholarship, as well as to Friedrich
Kittler's poststructuralist media history, and Katherine Hayles's work on
twentieth-century literature and informatics. In its attempts to approach a
culture through its media, this book also takes inspiration from the classic
media theories of Marshall McLuhan and Walter Ong, and from Jay David
Bolter and Richard Grusin's more recent analysis of the reciprocal "remediation" between old and new media. Yet I have also tried to take up a challenge
suggested by Alexander Welsh's groundbreaking *George Eliot and Blackmail*
(1985): to read Victorian texts in relation not merely to particular media but
more broadly to an emergent "culture of information," to the growing importance of the large-scale production and rapid circulation of information
in the nineteenth century—a culture that both reflected and inspired the
creation of new media.[11] Welsh explores the blackmail plot as a lens through
which fiction could view the passage from a culture of shared knowledge to

a new world of fungible information. In contrast to Welsh's emphasis on secrecy, publicity, law, and psychology, however, this book argues that Victorian literature registers the presence of new forms of information exchange most crucially in the complex of literary realism itself.

Again and again, the new ways in which real things could become information intersect with the ways in which fictitious stories treated a world of real things. Yet fiction also responded keenly to new information systems when it came to representing things we never see: for instance, the inner thoughts of others, or the structure of relations that makes for social coherence and meaning. The universalizing Penny Post, the lightning-fast electric telegraph, and the mystical and all-pervading wireless: as they increased the speed, ubiquity, and ineffableness of telecommunication, these instruments offered figures for the connections of interest and intersubjectivity that linked the members of a society, and for the multifarious networks of relation often postulated by Victorian literary realisms. Influential critics have found in such modes of realism both "a massive confidence as to what the nature of Reality actually was," with an assurance that it "lay in the material world," and a shaping self-consciousness and skepticism about what reality was and how fiction could represent it.[12] Viewing realism as part of a world of new media, accelerated knowledge production, and complex information systems clarifies why the elaboration of a recognizable fictional reality in prose could seem both excitingly possible and inherently dubious or tentative.

Victorian fiction obviously owes much to older literary forms, especially to the British and European novels that preceded it, texts that took shape as part of their own distinctive media environments. Scholars as diverse as Ong, Benedict Anderson, and Lennard Davis have emphasized the relationship between the British novel's development and the flood of print that began in the eighteenth century. While Ong argues for the connections between print, linear narrative, and closure, Anderson suggests the historical affiliation between novels, vernacular "print capitalism," and modern nationalism.[13] In greater detail, Davis traces the genealogy of the English novel—including the "constitutive ambivalence towards fact and fiction" that he identifies as realism—through its slow differentiation in the eighteenth century's surge of prose narrative.[14]

But over the course of the nineteenth century, new media and information systems offered inspiration for reimagining how the world might register in prose. For instance, from the beginning of electric telegraphy in the 1830s and 1840s, accounts of the technology celebrate it for allowing "the instantaneous transmission of thought": by "dissolving a few pieces of metal connected with a long wire, we can develope [*sic*] instantaneously, a thousand miles off, a force which will speak for us, write for us, print for us, and, so far as the conveyance of our thoughts is concerned, annihilate space and time."[15] By the time Alfred Russel Wallace looked back on the century's achievements, he could use the same description to celebrate the telephone and wireless as well, all of them new devices for the "conveyance of thought."[16] Such language is more conventional than accurate, since the telegraph conveyed not raw "thought" but messages sent for someone to read—not mentalese but signals, coded characters, language. Yet this attention to how "thought" was transmitted in the flows of an electric network could inspire new considerations of what consciousness might look like outside the human mind and in prose, just as thinking about how visible things appeared in a photograph could encourage new interest in how words might render a frozen, repeatable image that was also a true impression.

As my emphasis on the realistic treatment of things unseen hints, this book will sometimes proceed by examining the discourse of the real even where fiction subtly or sensationally exceeds the bounds of everyday verisimilitude. For often it is in these leaps between an imagined reality and a more orthodox realism that fiction registers the force of information systems or the power of new media. George Levine provides a pattern for such a move when he takes Mary Shelley's *Frankenstein* (1818) as a starting point for *The Realistic Imagination* (1981); for Levine, Frankenstein's creature offers a paradigm for fiction's ability to create a simulacrum of the real and to animate it with the force of imagination.

But, in keeping with the focus of this book, we might also describe the creature as a headily powerful blend of inscription and technology that takes on a life of its own, a walking discourse network, to borrow the phrase used to translate Friedrich Kittler's *Aufschreibesysteme*, or inscription systems. For Kittler, a *discourse network* "designate[s] the networks of technologies and institutions that allow a given culture to select, store, and process relevant data."[17] In these terms, Frankenstein's creature represents Shelley's astonishing experiment upon what Kittler calls the discourse network of 1800.

In his account, this Romantic-era system domesticated writing by treating it as "a virtual orality" linked to nature and desire through the figure of the mother.[18] Using masculine science to eliminate maternity from this network, *Frankenstein* unravels the system—and fatally destabilizes the Romantic alignment of writing, speech, and nature. The creature learns speech and writing together; he studies both the "godlike science" of "articulate sounds" and "the science of letters" by spying on the De Laceys as they integrate a foreign bride into their self-contained familial and linguistic circle.[19] But his hideous artificial construction and wavering creator turn the creature's own domestic desires into rage and murder. With his rhetorical skill, powerful enough to elicit Frankenstein's warnings to Walton and to ensure that those warnings fail, the creature achieves the status not simply of a realized idea but of something like autonomous language—haunting, defying, and outliving its producer. Placed outside of nature, and where mothers are absent, the creature becomes the unnatural, technological, contumacious side of writing itself.

Like Kittler, and like *Frankenstein*, this book is concerned not merely with new technologies but with how they could form *systems* for setting down, processing, and circulating discourse, systems that linked media to each other as well as to the bodies and minds of their users. After analyzing such systems in the age of Goethe, Kittler takes up their history again at the nineteenth century's end, when an array of new media (*Gramophone, Film, Typewriter*, as another of his book titles puts it) encourages attention to the properties of alphabetic writing as one medium among many. Kittler emphasizes the epistemological distance between these media moments. But thinking about the midcentury media that he hardly mentions (photography, penny postage, telegraphy) provides a starting point for considering what we could call the discourse networks of 1850.[20] As we examine their relationship to imaginative literature, writing appears neither purely as a form of natural speech (as in Kittler's 1800 discourse network) nor as a disenchanted, combinatory technology (his 1900). For if nineteenth-century realism partakes of a Romantic belief in the integrative power of written language, it also reflects and could encourage an emergent understanding of writing as a specific technology.

What is true of nineteenth-century realism applies more broadly: writing in 1850 is neither the song of the bard nor the stimulus of the psycholinguist.

A similarly intermediate understanding characterizes mid-Victorian treatments of the age's new information technologies. For instance, in the 1840s and 1850s, even experts wrote about transmission on the electric telegraph as an experience of virtual orality—a paradigm echoed in *Jane Eyre* (1847)—yet they also treated it as a form of neutral truth-telling that achieved the impartiality of a machine. My object in this book is not only to explore one aspect of Victorian life as treated in novels, but ultimately to recognize nineteenth-century realism as part of a world of new media and industrialized information.[21]

Fictional Writing in the Victorian Media Ecology

Perhaps the Victorian period deserves the title of "The First Information Age"—unless, as various writers have declared, that designation belongs to the Gutenberg era, to the time of Diderot's *Encyclopédie*, or to the mid-twentieth century that turned information into mathematics and made its study a science.[22] Inevitably, such a retrodescriptive label undercuts the claim toward which it gestures, the fact that the concept of information, and not just specific technologies or media, has a history. But whatever its claims for the title of information epoch, the nineteenth century saw not only astonishing technological advances in the transmission and storage of information but also crucial developments in the history of information as an idea.

For one thing, the century witnessed a continuing explosion in the amount of information available, a primitive accumulation permitted by developments such as imperial expansion, a rapidly growing and increasingly literate populace, the professionalization of science and other knowledge-work, an immense acceleration in invention, and a transport revolution (from mail coaches and canals to railways and steamers—all of which appear in the following pages).[23] In *When Information Came of Age*, Daniel Headrick analyzes many of the new systems for information management which developed in the eighteenth and early nineteenth centuries—scientific taxonomies, statistics, graphs, dictionaries and encyclopedias, postal and semaphore communication—but concedes that his survey offers only "a sampling."[24] From 1840 to 1901, while the population of the United Kingdom increased from 26.5 million to 41.5 million, the annual number of letters handled by the

Post Office rose from 169 million to 2,323 million, now in addition to 419 million postcards and 566 million telegrams.[25]

This growth in the quantity of information was accompanied by technical innovations in publishing such as the stereotype printing and steam press of the century's first decades and the cheap wood-pulp paper and machine typesetting of its second half.[26] Over the period, but with increasing urgency in its final decades, the cultural emphasis moves from the raw accretion and static organization of information to the use of tools for managing its flows. The publication of government papers and bluebooks "seemed to explode" from the 1830s on, garnering widespread complaints "that the public was inundated with excessive factual material"—an important backdrop for the selective use of such material, for instance, in the social problem fiction of the 1840s.[27] By the end of the century, *Dracula* (1897) stanches the gothic predations of the Count with a bureaucratic romance of information management.

It was not only new technologies that helped this information super-railway pick up steam; books and other printed materials fully participated in the era's information explosion. But the appearance of newer media helped alter the meaning of print textuality in the nineteenth century's media environment. As a technology, writing combines the functions of transmission and data storage. Print publication makes this arrangement especially clear, for the mass production of identical texts creates both the possibility of wide dissemination and a supply of backup copies. As long as writing and print held a comparative monopoly on communication across time and space, storage and transmission remained united. But the new media technologies invented and popularized in the Victorian era decoupled that alliance. One way to explore the textual implications of this change is by considering the question of the embodiment of writing, an issue that arises in many of the chapters ahead.

In comparison to the new technologies that *stored* data without writing, written texts might seem disembodied, might generate a Derridean sense of absence where we look for a producer or an origin. Photography or sound recording could well seem ghostly; they arrested the moment, kept it hauntingly available in a technologically altered and alienated form. But compared to printed writing, the photograph and phonograph bespeak a presence at their origins, a physical contiguity between the recorded object and the medium of representation. After all, photographs were—in a phrase often used to describe them at midcentury—"painted by the sun," the chemical result of light that glanced off objects themselves. Early technologies for direct, one-of-a-kind recording, such as daguerreotypy or Edison's phonography, make that sense of presence clearest, as the metal plate or wax cylinder memorializes its former proximity to the sight or a sound whose marks it bears. But even the arrival of photographic negatives and pressed gramophone discs would not altogether dispel that lingering sense of physical connection. By the end of the century, moreover, technologies such as the typewriter and linotype had attenuated the traditional roles of the author's or compositor's body in the production of texts—placing bodies at a further remove from the scene of printed writing.

Yet if nineteenth-century technologies of storage could make print textuality seem abstract and disembodied, the century's new technologies of real-time *transmission* could make texts seem material and embodied by comparison. The electric telegraph used codes that referred to the written alphabet, but it replaced physical marks on paper with fugitive pulses of current from afar, on-off rhythms distinct from any particular way of writing them down. Wireless telegraphy went a step further, sending its tattoo of Morse into the void via an undetectable medium, the luminiferous ether, that would turn out not to exist at all. Alongside these media, print textuality seems tangible, material, and embodied. Like a photograph or a phonograph cylinder, a written text was at least a physical object, not just a fleeting electrical or ethereal pattern.

The new media ecology of the nineteenth century tended to align storage with materiality, transmission with immateriality, so that writing—with its dual capacity for storage and transmission—occupied a shifting and ambiguous ground between the two. Along these lines, we should think of Victorian realism itself as an exploration of the power and the limits of written textuality in an age busy producing alternatives to it. These alternatives did not replace print and writing in any simple way but changed them, remediated them, counterpointed or reaffirmed their various potentials. Like telegraphy, photography, or early motion pictures, fictional realism sets out from the attraction and advantages of transposing daily discourse to a powerful medium with its own principles of order.

In order to consider the multiple relationships of fiction to other media forms, this book draws on the idea of a media ecology. This concept emphasizes that a culture's range of technologies and codes of communication dramatically shape and are shaped by human experiences, thoughts, and values. Recognizing that media are not simply technological but social, it suggests the rich possibilities of studying media within the cultures that employ them and of reading cultures in terms of the media they employ. As a label, *media ecology* is hardly perfect; it may sound too naturalistic, wrongly implying a static world in which media spontaneously find their destined niches. Yet the concept can help plot a course between social contingency and technological determinism, emphasizing how a society understands itself through its media and understands its media in relation to the rest of its culture.

For a media-rich society such as nineteenth-century Britain, the sum of the media ecology would come close to the whole of its culture, especially when we add the term *information* and consider the era's practices of organization and taxonomy. Major components of the Victorians' changing media ecology would include printed books, pamphlets, and periodicals; new technologies of recording (photograph, phonograph, stereoscope, moving picture) and transmission (Penny Post, electric telegraph, telephone—even electric lights); orations and sermons; dramatic and musical performances; lectures and exhibitions (for instance, panoramas, dioramas, and the magic-lantern shows that helped inspire fictional effects from Dickensian phantasmagoria to Proustian reverie). Furthermore, a thorough account of these media should consider their production, distribution, and reception. Such a survey might exceed the scope of any study; it certainly lies beyond this one. Rather, by focusing specifically on the relationship of fictional realism to new communication systems and the ideas about information they encouraged, this book treats Victorian fiction as a critical part of the shifting media ecology in which it arose, circulated, and had meaning and value.

Reading the histories of media and literature together helps us understand literary forms in relation to cultural history. By sketching out a particular history of Victorian fiction from the Penny Post to wireless, this book indicates what media studies might bring to literary studies, and vice versa. But in a larger sense it should also suggest that neither media nor literature are so self-contained. Many of my chapters highlight the electric telegraph, the medium that makes the informatic orientation of the century's new media technologies clearest—and one with direct implications for the status of textuality. Yet in literature, the broader informatic awareness encouraged by the telegraph or photograph lets fiction examine, and sometimes prefigure, a realm of newer technologies that would turn our time- and space-bound experience of reality into a stream of analog information: the telephone, the phonograph, the motion picture, broadcast. As realistic fiction not only responds to existing technologies but also hints at potential ones, it comes to exemplify Walter Benjamin's art form that "aspires to effects which could be fully obtained only with a changed technical standard."[28] This may seem uncanny, but—like the uncanny in Freud's analysis—it also comes as no surprise; part of the point of realism is imagining how the real world might be channeled.

Like David Thorburn and Henry Jenkins, I believe that in order to understand media transitions, "we must resist notions of media purity, recognizing that each medium is touched by and in turn touches its neighbors and rivals," a recognition with implications for literary history.[29] Clifford Siskin's *The Work of Writing* analyzes the consolidation of print culture in Britain over the long eighteenth century, a process leading to what he calls "the modern . . . fully 'naturalized' . . . world of print" by the 1830s.[30] This world might seem to contrast with our own media multiplicity; however, even in the 1830s, the world of print was not a world of print alone. Likewise, Ong's *Orality and Literacy* treats realistic fiction—with its norms of character development, structured plotlines, and the quest for closure—as the quintessential application of the norms of print literacy to storytelling.[31] Yet this book challenges and broadens that formula, locating Victorian realism in relation to a specific, changing media ecology, one that includes not just the dominance of print but the emergence of newer media. By the final third of the century, fiction explicitly comes to register the presence of the technologies that redefined print. But as I show, these developments could also shape works that hardly cite new media by name.

It is not only writing that changes with developments in the information ecology. As the oldest of electric media, the telegraph helps to change the character of print and writing, and later the telephone and radio shift the place of the telegraph. Media are not hermetic but hybrid. Most readers' earliest experience of telegraphic discourse would have been in newspapers of the late 1840s and early 1850s, which made strong claims for the status of electric information. A few decades later, when personal telegrams had become common, receiving one of them might give a Victorian a first glimpse of typescript.[32] Likewise, photography enters this study chiefly as it becomes part of a combined technology for the reproduction and distribution of images by printing, a development that coincides with the photographic visions of Eliot's "The Lifted Veil."

Furthermore, the impurity and complexity of media arise not only among them but also within them—a state of affairs writ large by the novel and its freewheeling engagements with other forms of print and writing, from letters, journals, and travelogues to newspapers, legal documents, parliamentary bluebooks, and advertisements. My account of fiction in the era of Penny Post, telegraph, and early wireless highlights the implications of these systems as ideas, but it also attends to practical developments within them, especially as they become publicly apparent. A telegraph isn't just a telegraph. It is private or state-owned, printing or signaling, visual or acoustic, manual or automatic, simplex or duplex or quadruplex; it registers signals in Morse's code or Cooke and Wheatstone's, on a needle, a register tape, an alphabetic dial, ringing bells, or a clacking magnetic lever.

The literary field of course has its own, more familiar, differentiations. Although the main point of this study is to place Victorian fictional realism in the context of the nineteenth-century information revolution, it regularly tracks fictional realism by stalking it across contrasting genres, modes, and techniques: nonfiction narratives that turn to fiction's methods to represent the real; tales of adventure or sensation; naturalism; modernism. The point of this strategy isn't to imply that realism has no limits—although the best accounts of it have long recognized its flexibility and pragmatism—but to examine realism by thinking about its imprint on other texts as they imagine reality. This approach has an eminently Victorian precedent. Shortly before Marian Evans became George Eliot, essays such as "Silly Novels by Lady Novelists" and "The Natural History of German Life" (1856)—the first about fiction that was not realistic, the second shaped around nonfiction that essentially was—helped her map the bounds of a realism that her novels would soon fill in.

Network, Information, Flow

To help understand the distinctiveness of the Victorian media environment, its connections to fiction, and its relationship to later developments in informatics, this study will often recur to three terms: the figure of the *network*, the concept of *information*, and the idea of *flow* that often links them. Armand Mattelart's *Networking the World, 1794–2000* demonstrates the origins of communication networks in post-Enlightenment thought and nineteenth-century liberalism, as well as exploring the material embodiment of the world-as-network in technologies such as the railway and electric telegraph. For Victorian scientists, sages, and novelists alike, the network becomes a figure that organizes the real interchanges, the unseen or imperfectly visible systems of connections and disconnections, that underlie the everyday world. Consider Walter Bagehot's 1856 reflections on the "difficulty" of governing—or even envisioning—a modern, liberal society:

> Any body can understand a rough despotic community;—a small buying class of nobles, a small selling class of traders, a large producing class of serfs, are much the same in all quarters of the globe; but a free intellectual community is a complicated network of ramified relations, interlacing and passing hither and thither, old and new. . . . You are never sure what effect any force or any change may produce on a frame work so exquisite and so involved.[33]

Such a network of relations justified literary forms such as the "multiplot novel," a work whose storylines link an entire range of characters, and one of the distinctive forms of nineteenth-century fiction.[34] Perhaps the most famous Victorian network is the image of the web in Eliot's *Middlemarch* (1871–72), an image that represents the organized linkage of person to person, story to story—and also one that, as a recurrent connective metaphor within the text, itself helps enact that linkage. As *Middlemarch* reminds us, for the Victorians, the idea of the network related the natural structures of bodies to technological structures for communication. The parallels universally drawn between the electric telegraph and the electrochemistry of the nervous system—an analogy that Laura Otis has analyzed in nineteenth-century biology, engineering, and fiction—only reinforced the connection.[35]

If *Middlemarch* offers Victorian fiction's most resonant invocation of the network, its most notorious response to what we would call information is the attack on "facts" in Dickens's *Hard Times* (1854). *Hard Times* plays abstract fact against "fancy," the life of the imagination that allows us to escape from brute existence into sympathy and play. But what is perhaps most revealing about the discourse of fact in *Hard Times* is that it opposes factuality not only to airy fancy but also to embodied experience and lived knowledge. On her deathbed, Mrs. Gradgrind articulates the separation between impersonal information and bodily experience in its most outrageously schematic form. When Louisa asks whether she is in pain, her mother can only reply, "I think there's a pain somewhere in the room, . . . but I couldn't positively say that I have got it."[36] In this line whose pathos is inextricable from its sublime epistemological dizziness, Mrs. Gradgrind's very pain—the most subjective and inward of bodily states—circulates in the room as an external, disembodied fact. The moment offers an arresting image of what linguist Geoffrey Nunberg identifies as the core, modern sense of information: "a kind of abstract stuff present in the world, disconnected from the situations that it is *about*."[37]

The irascible, self-aggrandizing Josiah Bounderby is no repressed utilitarian, but he shares the Gradgrindian disavowal of lived experience, abjuring the real history embodied by his mother in favor of mythical disconnection and self-generation—even after death. His "vain-glorious will" calls for the legal fabrication of twenty-five more Josiah Bounderbys, a crop of middle-aged replicas who will "for ever dine in Bounderby Hall, for ever lodge in Bounderby Buildings, for ever attend a Bounderby chapel" as they emit "a vast amount of Bounderby balderdash and bluster."[38] It's almost as if Bounderby wished to become pure information, that cultural form that assumes that one can separate facts from their living contexts, the better to arrange them and manage their propagation, while still retaining their utility and truth. Bounderby's desire may seem eccentric, but a comparable if more somber vision of an informatic afterlife will also emerge in a later Dickens novel, *A Tale of Two Cities* (1859).

As the "facts" of *Hard Times* indicate, the Victorians did not invariably use the word *information* where we might. But across a variety of their discourses we can see the norms of modern information emerging and being examined. Indeed, Nunberg traces the modern, "abstract sense" of *information* to "the mid-nineteenth century."[39] The putative autonomy of information distinguishes it from related concepts that were becoming distinct from it, concepts represented by words such as *intelligence* and *knowledge*.[40] *Intel-*

ligence "refers both to signals received from without and the capacity to register and interpret these signals," seamlessly aligning facts with the mind's ability to manage them.[41] In *Bleak House* (1852–53), for instance, the "fashionable intelligence," which follows Lady Dedlock's behavior, names a set of facts that is conflated with a set of persons, the social group in which those facts circulate and have significance.[42] Like intelligence, *knowledge* "usually entails a knower"; "given this personal attachment, knowledge seems harder to detach than information" from subjectivity and experience.[43] Knowledge requires effort to assimilate; it is "something we digest rather than merely hold."[44]

In the early nineteenth century, this conception of knowledge contributes to the Whiggish belief that producing and spreading it would bring not simply material but moral progress. The most direct attempt to put this faith in the "march of intellect" into practice was the Society for the Diffusion of Useful Knowledge (1826–1846), an organization created not to sponsor research but purely to disseminate knowledge via print.[45] The S.D.U.K.'s brief lifespan and much-ridiculed name belie its influence and its distillation of general cultural concerns; I will note the connections of Rowland Hill's penny postage to the S.D.U.K. As evidence of the century's knowledge culture, Alan Rauch points to its outpouring of "*knowledge texts* (encyclopedias, instruction manuals, and didactic works for children)," to the founding of museums, libraries, and lecture halls, and even to "the very emergence of realism as a dominant genre for nineteenth-century fiction."[46]

The early Victorians' emphasis on the morality of diffused knowledge led to successful campaigns against the fees that Leigh Hunt's *Examiner* called the "taxes on knowledge." Promoted by Radicals in Parliament and by Anti-Corn-Law-style tactics, the campaign against these taxes urged a freer trade in words for the sake not only of economics but of social harmony and stability.[47] Even by 1839, the Tory *Quarterly Review*'s denunciation of cheap postage as "*Sedition made easy*" must have seemed quaint.[48] The duties on newspapers, paper, and advertising were reduced in the 1830s and eliminated between 1853 and 1861. If the Enlightenment first intimated that "information wants to be free," in the words of Stewart Brand's famous modern mantra, it took the Victorians to start turning something like that sentiment into public policy. Brand's slogan depends on the ambiguities of that "free" state, a slippage between economic and political liberty exploited by Internet-era cyberliberationists as much as by the Victorian Radicals who were their distant forebears.[49] The catchphrase awards an uncanny, machinic volition to airy information; likewise, a spectral, reified agency can emerge in the imagined life of Victorian information as well.

Early Victorian beliefs in the moral power of disseminating knowledge tend to treat knowledge as something unifying, coherent, and communal. But this assumption was coming under pressure even by the time the S.D.U.K. dissolved, thanks in part to the growing rift between science and religion.[50] A generation later, the always-contrarian J. A. Froude could draw on the emerging overtones of *information* to challenge the conventional association between factual learning and morality: "The mind expands, we are told; larger information generates larger and nobler thoughts. Is it so?"[51] Froude plays up the idea of information as something abstract and removed from ordinary life, although he hopes that "[t]he evils caused by a smattering of *information*, sounder *knowledge* may eventually cure" (my emphasis).[52]

But new modes of rapid communication and ramped-up data collection threatened to exceed any capacity for diffusion, assimilation, or use. Thomas Richards notes that the Victorians

> found themselves in the midst of the first knowledge explosion. If today we call this the "information explosion," it was because by the century's end many people had stopped using the word "knowledge," which always had something about it of a prospective unity emerging, and started using the word "information," with its contemporary overtones of scattered disjunct fragments of fact.[53]

As Christopher Keep elaborates the problem, while new communication technologies encouraged "a greater sense of proximity" between distant places, "they also brought with them such an outpouring of facts without adequate context that the world seemed increasingly remote and unknowable."[54] "Information" in the modern sense "is a consequence of the dematerialization of the sign" into "electronic impulses or sonic vibrations," Keep concludes.[55] Information becomes fact that has lost its context, signs that have lost their matter, intelligence that has lost its faculties.[56] The very act of diffusion might make for useless knowledge.

Realistic fiction offered a forum for exploring the possibilities of such losses and disjunctions within an existing medium, for imagining whether dislocated, dematerialized information about reality might register as real knowledge. After all, this problem—the question of how well we can know what we don't experience directly—touches on the very project of social realism itself. Victorian realism signals an awareness of both the possibilities and the dangers of the putative overcoming of space, time, context, matter, and medium that made for modern information. This book takes up Mark Seltzer's suggestion that realism might be better understood "in relation to . . . technologies of registration than reduced to the self-evidently dismissible desire, frequently attributed to realist writing, to ignore the medium of representation and to claim an unmediated access or 'reference' to the real."[57] But it also recognizes that those very registration technologies, and cultural attitudes toward them, could promote the belief that media might be ignored. Even when Victorian writing shapes itself around other media, this may not dispel the temptation to write media off.

The vision of information without accouterments connects modern media, with their ability to disperse electric data or detain the fugitive evidence of the senses, to deep habits of language and thought. The English language's central paradigm for communication has been identified as a "conduit metaphor," a framework that treats words and other signs as vehicles for content carried over to a recipient—and a model that views media, and the bodies that use them, as "mere 'channels'" for disembodied meaning.[58] The idea of information consolidates the conduit metaphor for an age of new media technologies. Imaginatively abstracted from the material of any particular medium, *information* offers an apposite notion of what such a conduit is moving along. In their imaginary separation from each other, conduit and content could emphasize different sides of communication. While thinking about the network (a conduit) emphasizes an embedded structure of relations, focusing on information (its content) treats data as an entity that remains real even apart from any substrate of context or matter. In this way, for instance, electric telegraphy could be both hailed as an instrument of humanizing interconnection and celebrated for its ability to transmit neutral, disembodied discourse.

Defined partly by its independence from context, information might well seem fragmented and disjointed. One of the quieter jabs against "fact" in *Hard Times* is Sissy Jupe's confusion between "statistics" and "stutterings"—discourse so fitful and obstructed that it blocks communication and meaning.[59] Such choked-off, atomized discourse befits the classroom of M'Choakumchild and his star pupil Bitzer. Even the famous Barthesian "reality effect," in which apparently superfluous details actually function to convey a sense of "what is commonly called 'concrete reality,'" may be largely a product of this era and its management of fractured, detached information.[60] Contrasting the reality effect with older descriptive rhetorics, Barthes provides examples from the nineteenth-century historian Michelet and from Flaubert—although in the second instance, a barometer, the detail seems to speak more directly of the kind of informatic device that can turn a single detail into a reading of the entire fictional atmosphere.[61]

But information's supposedly nonmaterial status also created other possibilities. Once the world became bodiless information, it could be collected, managed, or processed systematically, and could enter the network as a *flow*. The treatment of information as a fluid drew on the traditional ideas about communication-as-conduit but gave them a Victorian inflection. Wolfgang Schivelbusch's *The Railway Journey* identifies a nineteenth-century ideology that exalted "circulation . . . as healthy, progressive, constructive"; as an idea, he notes, "circulation" drew on contemporary physiology but also mirrored the "actual traffic conditions" of an accelerating movement of goods, people, and knowledge.[62] By the century's second half, the ideology of circulation found new expression in techno-social practices. James Beniger's *The Control Revolution* traces the origins of the modern information society to the crisis of information within nineteenth-century industrialism, a crisis *Hard Times* translates into novelistic terms. Emphasizing the discovery of "*flow*" as "the essential problem in control of [mass] production," Beniger outlines the revolutionary reorganization of production, distribution, consumption—of modern society itself—along the lines of controlled flow.[63] For Beniger, the practical techno-bureaucratic management of information flows is what makes this control revolution possible in the first place. On the theoretical side, in the decade after Dickens denounced industrialized information as so many "stutterings," James Clerk Maxwell published the first mathematical analysis of continuous control systems in "On Governors" (1868), a paper hailed in the twentieth century as the beginning of cybernetics.

For the Victorians, thinking of information as a flow—a model I will examine from Hill's Penny Post to the wireless, and from Dickens and Trollope to Kipling—permitted exploration of its movements via the hydraulic or fluvial language used to describe the physiology of the body, the emanations of the spirit, or the invisible motions of electricity or ether. Again and again fiction writers use figures of flow to represent not simply the Heraclitean flux of reality but the management of information about it: an inundation of newspapers at the central post office, a canal that figures a novel's own movements, the measurable pulse of bodily life, a river arrested in a mental photograph, a sea of telegraphic words, an ocean of messages on the airwaves. Furthermore, I will argue that the alignment of information flows and the intangible "liquid" of electricity has left a distinctly Victorian legacy in present-day assumptions about information.

Accounts of modernism often contrast a nineteenth-century enshrinement of continuity (expressed as development, evolution, or organicism) with a modernist emphasis on discontinuity, a contrast highlighted by works as divergent as William Everdell's *The First Moderns* and Kittler's *Discourse Networks*. Both authors cast their lot with modern discontinuity, an affiliation expressed by Everdell's celebration of heroic geniuses breaking from the past as much as by Kittler's impersonal treatment of epistemological rupture. But in the paradigm of the information network, continuity or discontinuity depends on your perspective. A continuous network relies on discrete points as nodes of interconnection, and disconnected facts could circulate as information flows within the right systems. Given the relationships between Victorian realism and informatics, we should not be surprised to see fiction playing out a set of antinomies between disjunction and connection, autonomy and embeddedness, idiosyncrasy and order.

Being Analog

If issues of information shape Victorian culture and fiction so critically, why haven't we heard the message more clearly before now? Perhaps because it took our own experiences with information anxiety and rapid media transitions over the past decades to make us ready to listen. But perhaps also because the ideologies of our own information age can divide us from its Victorian antecedents. If we look for information in the nineteenth century, we may see something different from what we expect. Just as this book resists collapsing literature into some generic category of information transfer, it seeks to avoid hastily assimilating the Victorian experience of information into ours. Recognizing the difference does greater justice to the Victorians' information systems, but it also allows us to recognize how Victorian informatics, and the fictions that arose alongside it, might offer challenges to our own.

In the mid-twentieth century, Claude Shannon's epoch-making article "A Mathematical Theory of Communication" described information in terms of binary digits—and began with the gesture of freeing information from questions of signification. "Frequently . . . messages have *meaning*," recognizes Shannon, "that is they refer to or are correlated according to some system with certain physical or conceptual entities." But "[t]hese semantic aspects of communication are irrelevant" to information theory.[64] Shannon's research helped initiate the age of digital computing, an age in which information has come to mean binary bits and bytes, numerical patterns awaiting the transformation and transmission that mathematics makes possible. Under this regime, information becomes "a probability function with no dimensions, no materiality and no necessary connection with meaning."[65] As this book indicates, the emerging Victorian understandings of information anticipate this vision in important respects. In fact, "the simple . . . phenomenon" of Morse telegraphy lies at "the roots" of Shannon's communication theory, as well as providing his paper's paradigmatic example.[66] But before the rise of information theory and digital computers, understandings of information also diverged from modern ideas in ways that help us historicize them both.

For one thing, the Victorian concept of information itself—like realism, or the novel—was heuristic and miscellaneous, partly because the idea of information was still new, but more importantly because there was no equivalent of the universal digitization that now promises to represent everything as fungible bits. The electric telegraph might use a quasi-digital code, but this does not seem to trouble Victorian writers with the prospect of an unbridgeable ontological gap between its discrete data and an organic world of analog continuities—perhaps because discourse about electricity often portrayed it as a living thing. Moreover, electric signals were still produced by human operators, and the conduits on which they circulated seemed similar to nerves. "Man has been defined as a laughing, a cooking, a naked animal, but never, so far as I know, as a Telegraphic one," joked one writer in 1858, but forty years later another could declare that "[o]f all the inventions which man has called into existence . . . none so closely resembles man himself in his dual quality of body and soul as the telegraph."[67] Even George Boole's mathematical logic, which thanks to Shannon became the foundation for electronic switches and digital programming in the twentieth century, was developed by the Victorian mathematician in order to generate "some probable intimations concerning the nature and constitution of the human mind."[68] Nineteenth-century information was not automatically imagined as separate from the reality of embodied subjects and material objects. In Victorian fictions, any such separation usually seems perilous and temporary; the conversion of life to information is often represented as estranging and violent, and information often returns to haunt the world of matter and bodies.

In Victorian information systems, and the Victorians' responses to them, we can locate not merely a genealogy but often a critique of our own. Comparing the informatic outlooks of a recent digital futurist and the nineteenth century's computer visionary suggests some of the differences between postmodern and early Victorian informatics. Nicholas Negroponte's *Being Digital* (1995), once the breathless prophecy of a millennial cyberfuture, now reads like a prospectus for the high-tech investment bubble that would soon follow it. But its central conceit of the confrontation between an old universe of atoms and a new one of bits remains provocative. For Negroponte the "global movement of weightless bits at the speed of light" will soon push aside the lumbering world of "atom-based businesses" and the hoary economic, political, and social systems that developed alongside them.[69] Negroponte disregards the fact that these shimmering bits would be worth little if they could not be stored, manipulated, and circulated via devices made of atoms; for that matter, these bits will surely be worth less to persons who lack the necessary atoms to feed, clothe, and shelter themselves. With its opposition between lightness and encumbrance, celerity and sloth, data and matter, Negroponte's formulation encodes an old fantasy—ultimately a theological one—of liberation from material existence.

But for the Victorians, information did not come in mathematical "bits," a shortening of *binary digits* endorsed by Shannon and company. Nor was it conceivable as essentially digital, an adjective that still referred not to numbers but fingers. What, then, was information in an *analog* epoch—a term that seems to have arisen during the early nineteenth century, and one that centers on the systematic correlations between physical or conceptual entities (as Shannon might put it)? Charles Babbage's *Ninth Bridgewater Treatise* (1837) offers us one view. Published in the year that Victoria's reign began— also the year of Hill's pamphlet on postal reform and of Cooke and Wheatstone's electric telegraph—this technologist's work of theology upholds the possibility of miracles in an age of mechanism. Yet, in contrast to Thomas Carlyle's contemporary defenses of the miraculous against the mechanical, Babbage uses an advanced Victorian technology to affirm the existence of marvels in the very programming of the universe.[70]

For Babbage, physical reality was fully mechanistic yet capable of miracles, thanks to its unknowable original algorithms. Indeed, the entire universe amounted to a device resembling Babbage's own Calculating Engine, which he could program to count by ones up to 100,000,001, and then— once the sequence seemed redundantly clear to onlookers—abruptly to begin counting by steps of 10,000 without any reprogramming.[71] The change appeared sudden, marvelous, a transgression of the only rule the device's observers could formulate from what they had seen previously, yet the miracle was there all along, encoded in the program long beforehand. As an "engine," affirms Babbage, the universe "embodie[s] in its mechanical structure . . . a law so complicated, that analysis itself, in its present state, can scarcely grasp the whole question."[72]

In Babbage's vision of a miraculous, mechanical universe set in motion by an ingenious celestial programmer, atoms represent not only the output of the divine algorithm but also the storage mechanism for all the data of eternity:

> Thus considered, what a strange chaos is this wide atmosphere we breathe! Every atom, impressed with good and with ill, retains at once the motions which philosophers and sages have imparted to it, mixed and combined in ten thousand ways with all that is worthless and base. The air itself is one vast library, on whose pages are forever written all that man has ever said or woman whispered. There, in their mutable but unerring characters, mixed with the earliest, as well as with the latest sighs of mortality, stand for ever recorded, vows unredeemed, promises unfulfilled, perpetuating in the united movements of each particle, the testimony of man's changeful will.
>
> But if the air we breathe is the never-failing historian of the sentiments we have uttered, earth, air, and ocean, are the eternal witnesses of the acts

we have done. . . . No motion impressed by natural causes, or by human agency, is ever obliterated.[73]

In this passage, which his friend Dickens would cite years later in a speech, Babbage offers not simply a vision of a material world overflowing with the evidence of human words and actions, but a world that itself *constituted* that human record—a "vast library" not just embedded in the universe but embodied by it.[74] For computing's Victorian patriarch, one could say, the atoms *were* the bits; after all, the computing machines he designed were also mechanical mills or engines. When atoms act as bits for Babbage, they contain a different sort of information from the kind that we digital beings might expect: not numbers or coded electric pulses (Babbage's text just precedes Cooke and Wheatstone's first telegraph patent) but the infinitesimal imprints of human actions and the echoes of our "sentiments." With its "pages" of broken "vows," female "whisper[s]" and mortal sighs by individual human beings, Babbage's imaginary catalog of this real-world "library" turns the physical universe into a massive databank that is also a book, an immense history, a work of Victorian multiplot fiction.

The formulation of a universe that records everybody's story supports the association of Babbage with the panopticism—expressed in grand fantasies and less impressive practices—of Bentham and his followers.[75] And the notion of a library that is also the universe may offer an inkling of the late-Victorian fear of a world that threatens to overwhelm with data. But Babbage's informatic atoms differ crucially from Negroponte's disembodied bits. Rather than being detached from context and history, Babbage's atoms record them. They call for a different kind of information management, a project of using the library of reality, of deciphering and organizing this vast world of information. To "read" this universe that vibrates with human data, Babbage conjures up a "Being" with limitless skill at "mathematical analysis," who can "trace" each atom's quivers to their causes as well as foretell the "future history" of every particle. This spirit of material insight would not be God, however; "[s]uch a Being, however far exalted above our race, would still be immeasurably below even our conception of infinite intelligence."[76]

The presiding spirit at work in Victorian realism lacks the mathematical acumen of Babbage's Being but seems to share many of its features: the project of tracing out the causes and effects of human actions and sentiments, the assumption of the entwining of persons and environments, the view of a world composed of human stories to be discovered and told. As with Babbage's Being, realism's vision is crucially material, its elevated viewpoint nonetheless terrestrial, its miracles as secular as the programming of the Calculating Engine. However "judgmental" the project of Victorian fiction, even its all-seeing narrators stop short of any vision into an otherworldly afterlife—in contrast to the "Heavenly spectators" of contemporary evangelical epics.[77]

Following Babbage, I would understand Victorian fictional realism as part of an analog library initiative, a project to translate and reimagine the data composing the world, in a medium that maintained a sense of potential connection to that world. Nineteenth-century realism itself might represent an analog cultural form, purporting to provide not naively transparent representations of referents in the outside world so much as a system of analogies within the text that, like a perspectival drawing, simulates the relations writers found in the world. Such a conception helps to harmonize the insights of several competing views of realism: Elizabeth Ermarth's recognition of the ties between literary realism and visual art, Levine's focus on realism's *via media*, and even Michael Riffaterre's semiotic approach, which analyzes realism as a text's constrained variations on what it has already said. Thinking about fictional realities along the lines of trope and medium, not just reference, confirms the self-consciousness of novelists and the need to keep track of figures even as one charts relationships between Victorian fiction and the other discourse systems that offered subjects and subtexts.

Nineteenth-century realism bespeaks a world producing, and becoming, information in more and more ways, a situation that both supported the ambitions of fiction and began to underscore the limits of written textuality. In that light, even a work as dark as *Bleak House* begins to look less like an expression of wry pessimism at a universe of proliferating textuality and interpretation—a view familiar from J. Hillis Miller's celebrated reading of the novel—than like a cautiously existential tale about navigating a world of information.[78] Victorian fiction, with its tendencies toward extended narrative, multiple plotlines, and experiments in serialization, was well suited for the enterprise of imagining a course through the vast Babel-like, Babbage-esque library of a world that was also information. Indeed, in many ways it seems to have been created for the task.

The first section of *Telegraphic Realism*, "Post and Telegraph," concentrates on the early Victorian period, examining its epochal innovations in communication alongside the literary reference points from which they could be addressed. Many histories of modern communication or information begin with the telegraph, electrified by its status as Victorian high technology. Yet Hill's contemporary plan for the Penny Post is equally revealing, especially since it relies not on technological innovation but on a dramatic reconsideration of postal service in informatic terms. Chapter 1, "The New Post Age," brings the Penny Post within the circuit of the new systems that would shape modern information, while also charting some of its connections to both Dickens and the postal bureaucrat and arch-realist Anthony Trollope. "Electric Information," my second chapter, discusses the electric telegraph and its promise to annihilate distance with instant communication. Ideas about the marvelous immediacy of electric writing had particular currency when the prospects of telegraphy outpaced most people's actual experience of it—as invocations of the telegraph by Charlotte Brontë, Gaskell, and Dickens suggest. Yet something of these early views would survive in modern-day treatments of information as a kind of intangible fluid moving at lightning speed.

New media and information systems suggested new possibilities for representing the real. "Embodying Information," the book's next section, analyzes how mid-Victorian fiction responded to such suggestions, sometimes even in works that might seem otherwise unconcerned with information technology. "Speaking Machines," my third chapter, finds in Dickens's *A Tale of Two Cities* an emphasis on the break between the media environment of the mid-nineteenth century and that of the past. This split poses Madame Defarge's Revolution-era optical telegraphy against the overthrow of time, space, and history in Carton's final, headless vision. "Information Unveiled" analyzes George Eliot's contemporary "The Lifted Veil" (1859) as a parallel story of the power and the costs of disembodied information. With its searing photographic visions and gruesome science, the tale offers a gothic gloss on Eliot's usual realism, but it also presages the informatic dimensions of her later works. The last chapter of this section, "The Telegrapher's Tale," considers a wave of telegraphic fiction by mainstream authors. When writers such as Dickens, Trollope, R. M. Ballantyne, and Bracebridge Hemyng begin tackling telegraphy as a specific subject, they find themselves drawn to the figure of the telegrapher as manipulator or victim of information. As they explore the telegrapher's position, these fictions align telegraphy with narration. But they also raise new questions about the materiality of information and the nature of information work, especially when information's web stretches across differences of nationality, class, gender—or technical orientation.

The book's last section, "Cable and Wireless," follows up these themes in a pair of chapters about turn-of-the-century texts centered on electric communication: "A Winged Intelligence," on Henry James's *In the Cage* (1898); "Wireless," on Kipling's 1902 tale named for that medium. These works make the parallel between fiction and information technology elaborate and explicit. As a literary attempt to order reality's connections and disjunctions, realism now comes to suggest the limitations and biases of any information system. In aesthetic terms, this could provide a starting point for a modernism that foregrounds the force of representation over its reference to the thing represented. But the tendency is also wholly in keeping with Beniger's control revolution, with its growing attention to the mechanisms of information transmission and systematic control.

Print literature is the original technologically reproducible art form, and imaginative writing from the nineteenth-century print explosion would join the cultural pool for the twentieth century's mass media. Kipling's "'Wireless'" vividly encapsulates the situation, liquidating realism into a sea of broadcast information. Communication modes as fugitive as telegraphy or wireless can only enter the archive via a medium for storing serial data. But with their ability to leave multiple, instant, coded traces of communication on a user's consciousness, they offer late-Victorian writers a prototype for the phenomenology of mass culture under modernity. By the turn of the century, realistic fiction finds itself, like Kipling, on the cusp between mass culture and modernism—two strategies of cultural production in an age of multimedia dissemination. Yet even in an altered media ecology, the encounter between realism and information continues to shape printed writing's dreams of the real.

Post and Telegraph

Chapter 1

The New Post Age

Thomas Carlyle had little affection for novels. But novelists' elaboration of his arguments, images, and themes surely makes him the patron sage of mid-century fiction—from Dickens, Gaskell, and Kingsley to Eliot.[1] "Signs of the Times" (1829) and "Chartism" (1839) shaped fictional responses to the condition-of-England problem, *Past and Present* (1843) raised the cultural stakes for historical narrative, and *The French Revolution* (1837) provided Dickens with material for the most enduringly popular Victorian historical novel. Yet it is *Sartor Resartus* (1833–34), a dazzling patchwork of spiritual autobiography and satire, German philosophy and political prophecy, that most explicitly makes the connections between technologies of communication and the structure of reality, connections that will present a framework for realist fiction.

In *Sartor*'s "Organic Filaments" chapter, Carlyle fabricates a controlling image of the strands of social change "mysteriously spinning themselves" out of the old order.[2] The image of fibers strangely spun out in a pattern we cannot yet discern is also *Sartor's* figure for the emergence of narrative and argument from its own disparate threads. Carlyle's summary of the chapter, added to the text years later (as if to corroborate his model of slow emergence), confirms that these filaments are textual ones: "Organic filaments of the New Religion: Newspapers and Literature" (*SR*, 247). If "filaments" of writing link past to present and future, permitting "[w]onderful connection[s]" across time, they also work synchronically, weaving together a society (*SR*, 247). "Wondrous truly are the bonds that unite us one and all," muses Diogenes Teufelsdröckh (*SR*, 186).

In keeping with *Sartor's* teasing claim to view its topics under the "Torch of Science," Teufelsdröckh delineates these ties by a quasi-scientific thought experiment (*SR*, 3):

> More than once, have I said to myself, of some perhaps whimsically strutting Figure, such as provokes whimsical thoughts: "Wert thou, my little Brotherkin, suddenly covered up with even the largest imaginable Glassbell,—what a thing it were, not for thyself only, but for the world! Post Letters, more or fewer, from all the four winds, impinge against thy Glass walls, but must drop unread: neither from within comes there question or response into any Post-bag; thy Thoughts fall into no friendly ear or heart, thy Manufacture into no purchasing hand; thou art no longer a circulating venous-arterial Heart, that, taking and giving, circulatest through all Space and all Time: there has a Hole fallen out in the immeasurable, universal World-tissue, which must be darned up again!" (*SR*, 185–86)

Mentally placing his unsuspecting everyman under glass, Teufelsdröckh cuts him off from the network of social, textual, and material flows, and finds that the very fabric of reality must be rewoven. Carlyle figures an individual's disconnection in the strangely poignant image of dead letters knocking against the glass, the sign of removal from the vital system circulating "[t]houghts" and goods. In the space of a single sentence, the imaginary experiment moves from the postal isolation of a single person to its cosmic consequence: if your letters can't reach you, a "Hole" opens in the universe.

Carlyle might scorn machinery and system-building, but he exalts the postal order. For all its facetiousness and willful eccentricity, *Sartor Resartus* suggests the imaginative stakes of playing post office. As an everyday network for moving texts between persons (there was no parcel service yet), a public agency that provided a medium for private relations, and a system

that seemed to promise universality and inclusiveness, the Post Office could readily stand for larger but less tangible social structures. In the debate over Rowland Hill's proposals for a new, national penny postage, it often did just that. Hill's pamphlet *Post Office Reform: Its Importance and Practicability* (1837) grew out of the reformist discourses of the 1830s, the impulse toward practical improvement and social progress which Carlyle's contemporary works both reflect and deflect. But the seriousness, the acrimony, and the rhetoric of the debate over Hill's plan all suggest that it meant far more to the reformers and their opponents than simply a revised schedule of postage fees. Ultimately, Teufelsdröckh's thought experiment helps us understand how a subject as apparently prosaic as postal reform could figure as a wholesale reweaving of the social fabric.

Once they came into effect in 1840, Hill's reforms would bring all England within the same postal zone, would inspire the invention of the postage stamp out of an ideal of social inclusiveness, and would encourage the postal and authorial creativity of Anthony Trollope. The success of Uniform Penny Postage would lead to a vastly expanded Post Office and even—via Parliament's later decision to nationalize the electric telegraph industry in the name of low, uniform Hill-style charges—to the office's future responsibilities for telephony and broadcast. As it was put into effect, Hill's plan emphasized the workaday ability of the Post Office to subsume the structure of an entire society into its own information network—an ability that resonates with both the ambition and the everyday interests of realist narratives. More immediately, as if in response to the Carlylean danger that addressees might find themselves hermetically shut from their letters, it compelled Londoners to cut holes in their front doors, as sure a material sign of interconnection as the electric wires that would begin entering houses by the century's end.

After reviewing the practical and ideological justifications for postal reform, and their imaginative expression upon the earliest vehicles of penny postage, this chapter will turn to two narratives from the new postal era. Charles Dickens's "Valentine's Day at the Post-Office" (1850), an essay written for the first issue of *Household Words*, uses a visit to the Post Office's headquarters as a model for the journal's observation of everyday life, as well as for the fusion of fact and fancy Dickens cited in the 1850s as his writing's aesthetic basis and social value. Trollope's *The Three Clerks* (1858), the novel most obviously indebted to his years as clerk for the Post Office, critiques

Hill's vision of bureaucratic machinery but recognizes the mechanisms of the reformed postal system as a paradigm for fiction.

Emancipating the Postage

At times this chapter will need to tease out the relationship between Victorian fiction and postal reform. But sometimes it appears right on the page. As the original readers of *Nicholas Nickleby* (1838–39) flipped through its thirteenth number—dated April 1, 1839—they found a peculiar text on the last printed sheet. In place of the usual advertisements for "Godfrey's Extract of Elder Flower for Softening the Skin" (the last page of the previous number) or "Kirby's . . . Ne Plus Ultra Needles" (next month's final sheet) appeared a two-page dramatic vignette entitled "Queen Victoria and the Uniform Penny Postage; a Scene at Windsor Castle." Uniquely within the run of *Nickleby,* here was an advertisement that was also an appended story and an overt fiction, a work of satire and self-conscious invention about a social issue even timelier than the Yorkshire schools.

No reader would have been such an April Fool as to mistake this text for Dickens, yet it might have taken a moment, and perhaps a turn of the page, to figure out exactly what it was. For the work's final tag line makes its point clear: "REMEMBER the 4,000 petitions last year [that] emancipated the slaves. Let there be the same number this year to emancipate the POSTAGE."[3] This "Scene" was the work of the civil servant and reformer Henry Cole, the man responsible for *The Post Circular,* a propaganda sheet that championed Hill's postal reforms (and which, to Cole's delight, circulated free in the post as a newspaper under the Stamp Act, co-opting the mechanics of the existing postal system to work against it).[4] Cole and his associates sent two thousand pamphlets with this dialogue on penny postage to members of Parliament and distributed nearly one hundred thousand more around the country— not including the forty or fifty thousand copies delivered via *Nickleby.*[5]

Cole's dramatic sketch not only fuses the topicality of a Dickensian satire with the tendentiousness of any solicitation for pins or patent medicine ("REFORM YOUR TAILORS' BILLS!" urges an adjacent advertisement in *Nickleby*); it recruits Queen Victoria herself as the agent of social reform. If Victorian political fictions require heroines, as Ruth Bernard Yeazell argues, this piece goes straight to the top. Cole's Victoria does not have time to participate in the courtship plots Yeazell analyzes, and she never has to restrain male "political violence," but her firm impartiality and inquisitiveness amount to a regal version of the maidenly "innocence" that Yeazell finds central to her heroines.[6] With its opening stage-direction, Cole's "Scene" presents the twenty-year-old Queen as a bluebook boffin, alert to the calls for postal reform but not yet persuaded: "*Council Chamber in Windsor Castle—Her Majesty is sitting at a large table, on which are lying the* [Parliamentary] *Reports on Postage; Copies of the Post Circular; Annual Reports of the French and American Post-Offices—Her Majesty is in deep study over 'Post-Office Reform,' by Rowland Hill. . . .*"

   In a royal bid for fairness that corroborates the sketch's dramatic form, Cole's queen summons both Hill, to explain his suggested reforms, and the Postmaster General, Lord Lichfield, to refute them with his real-life comments—including his infamous dismissal: "Of all the wild and visionary schemes which I have ever heard or read of, it is the most extravagant." After quizzing them about postal rates and costs, Her Majesty adjudicates the matter decisively in Hill's favor, threatening to replace not only Lichfield but the entire Whig government if it fails to reform the postal system. The final section of the advertisement urges its readers to "SUPPORT YOUR QUEEN . . . with your Petitions for a UNIFORM PENNY POST." In real life, ratifying and implementing postal reform would not prove so effortless.

   For more than two centuries after King Charles I had opened the governmental Post Office to public use, postal service was largely treated as "a source of revenue to the Government," a tax.[7] Parliament had repeatedly raised postal rates along with other taxes during the Napoleonic wars and had been reluctant to lower them afterward. By the 1830s, many British letter-writers evaded postal charges by exploiting the franking privilege of a member of Parliament or other eminent person, by hiding letters in stamped newspapers (or marking the newspapers up), or by having their letters smuggled by a coachman or traveler. Most large cities had an inexpensive local service modeled on London's old Penny Post (now the Twopenny Post, thanks to rate hikes), but these urban services were separate from both the Inland Post Office in charge of the national letters and the Foreign Post Office for international ones; in London, each office had its own bureaucracy, sorters, and letter carriers.[8] In Britain, *Sartor's* treatment of postal circulation as a smooth, unbroken network was more fantasy than reality. It is not surprising that Cole later recalled Carlyle as a "strong advocate" of postal reform.[9]

The complexities of the Post Office's structure were exceeded by the elaborate system of postal charges (even London's so-called Twopenny Post charged threepence for outer districts). Each letter was assessed according to an elaborate tariff schedule based on the distance it traveled, but this charge could be modified by charges for road tolls or shipboard transit, or other transport costs. Furthermore, letters were charged according to the number of sheets of paper they included, so postal workers had to "candle" letters by holding them up to a light, a practice that both slowed the assessment of postage and tempted unscrupulous clerks to steal any banknotes or other items they saw. Finally, the letters had to be delivered and postage collected from the recipients, a practice that made distribution excruciatingly slow, as the carriers knocked on doors, requested payment, made change, and kept accounts. The practice of collecting postage on delivery ensured that many letters that reached their destination would never be paid for or delivered, either because the addressee could not be found or could not pay, or because the letter's sender and recipient had agreed to use the delivery attempt itself as a code. In that case, returned to its sender, the unpaid letter could do "double duty for nothing, telling . . . the sender that it had been seen."[10] In essence, from start to finish, the Post Office handled each letter in a highly "individual . . . manner," as a unique object: ascertaining the rate between its origin and destination, determining its physical composition, assessing its particular charge, and trying to collect its fee at delivery.[11]

In *Post Office Reform*, Hill took on the existing postal system not in the name of emancipation (as Cole's drama would put it) so much as transparency, utility, and efficiency. Hill came to social reform as a sort of family business. His father, a progressive schoolmaster, invented the first system of proportional representation with a single transferable vote.[12] Rowland Hill began teaching at his father's school as a boy and later directed it. Always interested in efficient modes of dissemination, and addicted to planning and tinkering, he invented a device for sending messages pneumatically as well as a high-speed rotary printing press that was only derailed by the government's insistence that the Stamp Act required paper to be cut into sheets and painstakingly hand-stamped.[13]

Pursuing his concerns along another line, Hill became a founding member of the Society for the Diffusion of Useful Knowledge (S.D.U.K.), best known for publishing the popular *Penny Magazine* (1832–45) and the *Penny Cyclopaedia* (1833–46). If Hill needed an example of how to plan, and to price, a universalizing innovation that used economies of scale to distribute information on the cheap, he had one at hand. By the mid-1830s, as secretary of the South Australian Colonisation Committee, Hill was directing his attention to diffusing people; his father's son, he organized the first public election to incorporate proportional representation, in Adelaide.[14] Thanks to his work with other reformers, Hill was well poised to begin a drive to reform one of the government's most visible departments, a campaign launched with the publication of his pamphlet in early 1837 by the S.D.U.K.'s Charles Knight.

Schemes for postal reform made an appealing exercise for intellectuals in the 1820s and 1830s; Babbage's *Economy of Machinery and Manufactures* (1832) suggests a network of ropes on which local letters could move by pulley, as well as a parcel post.[15] But Hill's suggestions were simple, dramatic, and unique. Hill's pamphlet begins by juxtaposing the United Kingdom's population growth with the stagnation of postal revenues; rates are so arbitrarily high, he concludes, that they are effectively reducing Post Office returns in an era of demographic expansion and increased mobility and literacy. How then should postal rates be determined? Hill's fundamental insight was to realize that the actual cost of transporting an individual letter, the only expense that actually varied with distance, was vanishingly low, just a fraction of a penny—for instance, "about one thirty-sixth of a penny" for an average-sized letter from London to Edinburgh.[16] Under the present scheme, most of the postal fees in effect paid for the "complex arrangements" of the system itself: for franks and frauds, and for the elaborate calculation and collection of each letter's postage (*POR*, 27).

Hill starts out not from an abstract principle of uniform pricing but from the idea that prices should be a more accurate representation of costs.[17] But since most real postal costs are fixed and hardly vary from letter to letter, Hill's pursuit of transparency arrives at low, uniform postage as a pragmatic solution—"unless it can be shown how we are to collect so small a sum as the thirty-sixth part of a penny" (*POR*, 11). From being an individualized assessment and a tax, postage in Hill's plan now becomes a minimal, universal tariff for entering the system. Prepayment and uniform postage, like the standardized street addresses Hill also promoted, would operate as forms of "preprocessing," the crucial task of reducing information "in order to facilitate its processing."[18] The scheme would transform the treatment of the mail from a handling of unique objects to a management of the postal flow. It is precisely such shifts that characterize what James Beniger calls the "control revolution," the modernization of processing and control that would turn the industrial era into a nascent information age.

The other reforms Hill recommends elaborate this model and its stress upon efficiency and economies of scale. To promote "frequent and rapid communication," he proposes adding facilities for letter collection, improving the speed of the post (for instance, by weighing large letters rather than candling them), and increasing the number of daily urban deliveries and rural areas covered by free delivery (*POR*, 24). On the same grounds, Hill urges the prepayment of postage, either by money paid at a receiving house or via prepaid stationery or envelopes, a proposal inspired by Knight's earlier suggestion that rather than stamping every sheet of newspapers, it would be simpler to post them in stamped wrappers (*POR*, 19). The adhesive postage stamp, Hill's most famous legacy, was only an afterthought. In a few lines added to the pamphlet's second edition, Hill offered it as a solution to the problem of customers "unaccustomed" to the postal system who arrive at a Post Office without a prepaid envelope but who cannot simply buy one and recopy the address because they are "unable to write" (*POR*, 20). The postage stamp arises as an expedient for those who are illiterate yet bearing letters, a means of including in the postal system even persons who cannot read or write. Small wonder that the Penny Black, the first adhesive stamp, should end up as the icon of postal reform, of the system's uniformity, simplicity, and aspirations to social comprehensiveness.

Post Office Reform presents its plan as a benefit for "all sects in politics and religion; and all classes from the highest to the lowest"; "[f]ortunately this is not a party question," Hill concludes, predicting hopefully that his reforms should "not meet with opposition" (*POR*, 28). But in the political atmosphere of the 1830s, postal reform would prove a party question. In Parliament, the reformer Robert Wallace was already involved in efforts to reduce postal rates. Wallace assisted Hill's work by offering him all the information on postal procedures and costs that the department's haphazard internal data collection permitted, adding "some hundred weight of raw material" to the "heavy blue books, in which invaluable matter too often lies hidden amidst heaps of rubbish" and which had been Hill's "only source of information."[19] No wonder Cole's Queen Victoria reaches the same conclusions as Hill; she has retraced his steps. As Hill found, planning a new government scheme was an informational enterprise of its own.

For reform-minded Victorians, Hill's scheme promised "another great reform, not unlike the recent revision of parliamentary representation or the abolition of slavery"; radical leaders recognized his plan as not only a move toward rationalization and regularity but also a tool for cheaply spreading information and coordinating political action.[20] Promoting his plan, the utilitarian Hill tended to highlight its economic efficiency, "simplicity," and "abstract fairness," as he put it in testimony to a parliamentary committee chaired by Wallace.[21] But other advocates of penny postage emphasized its capacity to sustain ties of commerce and affection across the kingdom—another version of Carlyle's extrapolation from the postal network to the social fabric.[22] George Birkbeck testified that the Post Office was "the intellectual railroad of society."[23] More expansively, the science writer Dionysius Lardner called high postal rates "a most iniquitous tax upon the affections, the morals, upon every social good."[24] The "stream of facts" must have "its free course," asserted a pamphleteer, offering a Victorian version of Stewart Brand's catchphrase.[25] By assisting this flow, cheap postage would even reduce class conflict, since workers' strikes "result from causes which would not have existed if the men could have communicated freely with each other, so as to have ascertained the rates of wages at different localities."[26]

Postal reform saw social progress in the improvement of private communication; like contemporary condition-of-England fiction, it located communal value in expanding personal relations. As Asa Briggs points out, G. R. Porter's compendious *Progress of the Nation* (1847, 2nd ed.) places its chapter on "Postage &c." not under the rubric of "Interchange" or "Public Revenue and Expenses" but of "Moral Progress."[27] Furthermore, reformers attested to the salutary effects of cheap postage on literature. It would provide "a cheap system of distribution" (testified Hill), allow closer correspondence between authors and publishers (Knight), and support "the easy inter-communication of minds" on which literature depends (Lardner).[28] The agitation for reform itself demonstrated the unifying power of cheap postage.

Proposing the uniform penny postage to Parliament, the chancellor of the exchequer singled out the petitions submitted to the government as "the most extraordinary combination I ever saw of representations to one purpose from all classes . . . from persons of all shades of opinion, political and religious, . . . in all parts of the kingdom."[29]

After several years of committee reports, agitation, and governmental inertia, in 1839 Parliament passed a bill enacting the Penny Post as an appeal to reformist voters. The real Queen Victoria followed her fictional double as a postal heroine, voluntarily surrendering her franking privilege to pay her penny postage along with members of Parliament and everyone else in the British Isles.[30] When she opened Parliament in January 1840, less than a week after the Uniform Penny Post came into force, she proclaimed, "I have lost no time in carrying into effect the intentions of Parliament by the reduction of duties on postage, and I trust that the beneficial effects of this measure will be felt throughout all classes of the community."[31] In predicting the Penny Post's cross-class benefits, the Queen echoes the reformers' boldest claim, that the universality and uniformity of its rates would help to deliver a nation united by shared facts and feelings.

Penny postage had won, but Hill's postal battles had not ended. Awarded a temporary position in the Treasury to implement his plan, Hill found himself an outsider to the postal bureaucracy. In 1846, his anomalous place was institutionalized when he was appointed to the special position of secretary to the postmaster general, awkwardly sandwiched between the politician responsible for the department (the postmaster general) and the civil servant who managed it (the secretary to the Post Office). Bureaucratic conservatism and Hill's oversensitivity made for perpetual conflict—to some extent, even after Hill himself became secretary to the Post Office in 1854.[32] Hill's prospects were bound with the financial success or failure of penny postage, and as it took years to become remunerative, Hill became virtually obsessed with the efficiency and regularity of the postal system. Afflicted with what his most ardent modern admirer calls an "almost morbid passion" for statistics and exactitude, Hill became a stickler for order, pushing for rationalized street names and house numbers as well as creating the familiar division of London into postal districts and beginning a campaign for the installation of letter-slits and delivery boxes on the doors of private houses.[33] Hill also knew that part of regulating the system had to be making it ever more accessible and inclusive. Adding more deliveries and access points would extend the spatial and temporal reach of the network and increase its use even by those it already served well—a classic network situation. By the time Hill retired in 1864, profits from the Penny Post subsidized most of the Post Office's other services.

In the meantime, Hill's battles with the government and postal bureaucracy became notorious. When the jurist and bureaucrat James Fitzjames Stephen attacked Dickens's depiction of the Circumlocution Office in *Little Dorrit* (1855–57), pointing to Hill's reforms as a refutation of governmental obstructionism and lassitude, a gleeful Dickens countered by mockingly treating Stephen's example as itself a mistaken transmission, a set of letters gone awry, "a curious misprint" in the pages of the *Edinburgh Review*. Indeed, Dickens treats Hill as a less fatalistic Daniel Doyce and produces a detailed narrative of Hill's twenty-year war against "his natural enemy," the Circumlocution Office.[34]

Little Dorrit is vague about Doyce's invention, but we can be quite clear about Hill's postal innovations. In the existing system, Hill realized, the high rates of postage expressed only the conventions of the system itself. Clearing away these cumbersome practices would allow not only a cheaper system, one in which nearly everyone might participate, but a more transparent one. Hill recognized even the unreformed Post Office as "abstractedly considered, a wonderful machine" but found it so obscured by a sense of "mystery" that it seemed "beyond the comprehension of the profane vulgar"—or the reach of rational reform.[35] Cutting through such opacity, Hill's postal reforms began from a determination to pass on a truer representation of costs and reached uniformity out of pragmatism. Yet it was uniformity that became the watchword for those who sought to revise government fees for communication and transport in the wake of postal reform.[36]

Transparency, inclusiveness, regularity, and a certain pragmatism, all bound up with ideas about the power of private communication to express and strengthen the structure of social relations: a similar set of loose and possibly contradictory principles stands behind postal reform and literary realism. Like realism too, the new postal paradigm worked to reconcile uniformity, universality, and order with a sense of openness to life itself, an assumption that the flows of life were orderly yet unbounded. The prepayment system sold stamps for letters that had not been written, and Victorian advice to letter-writers called for the keeping of extra stamps for letters not yet even contemplated.[37] Hill had been vague about the mechanics of pre-payment, but now its vehicle would become the signifier of the Penny Post itself, the universal sign of a system that promised to deliver a textual like-ness of the social order in every postbag.

Postal Representations

Postal reformers were hardly alone in hailing the Penny Post as a vast, in-clusive system that would extend communication to new classes.[38] William Waverton's *The People's Letter Bag and Penny Post Companion* (1840) seizes on penny postage as a marketing opportunity, directing itself "especially [to] those persons, to whom the New Postage Bill has afforded the same fa-cilities for the frequent exchange of sentiments as have hitherto been in the enjoyment of those only whose means were ample."[39] Priced at a shilling (postage for a dozen letters), Waverton's book includes scores of sample let-ters for tradesmen, farmers, and especially servants, letters about business, courtship, and family life. Intriguingly, all include names, dates in 1840, and street addresses, as if they had been taken from a real letter bag. Miniature epistolary narratives, they simultaneously proffer model letters and solicit the prurient interest of reading a note from a young man seeking to court a woman (with replies that granted or denied permission) or from a dismissed servant contritely requesting a reference.

The genre of the letter guide was hardly new, nor was its potential to become an epistolary fiction. A century earlier, Samuel Richardson's idea for a new letter-writing guide that included moral advice had produced *Letters Written to and for Particular Friends, On the Most Important Occasions* (1741)—but not before it inspired that more famous series of familiar letters, *Pamela* (1740).[40] But in 1840, the mail suddenly came to offer a figure for a com-prehensive society, with a multiplicity of classes and voices—voices that *The People's Letter Bag* both individualizes with names and addresses, and flattens out with its aspiration to provide generic letters. Obviously, the democracy of the letter bag was a fiction, since it entitled no one to equal representation. As cynics remarked, penny postage offered the greatest boon to people who already sent many letters, like the tradesmen who made up Cole's committee. But the connection between the mass of letters and the national body—a representation of society in every postbag—became a Victorian commonplace. As a *Blackwood's* writer exulted in 1885,

> If ever there was a democratic community, it is that of letters. For some hours peer and peasant—even her Majesty and the village cobbler—are thrown together in the letter-bag, and arrive the same hour at their destination. In no other department of the public service is there so entire an absence of any social distinction of rank or wealth. The sorter cares little whether he handles the coronet of the earl or the thimble-wax impression of John Smith . . . all are tossed together into the bag in close companionship until they arrive at their final destination.
>
> This equality was not, however, fully developed until Sir Rowland Hill introduced that great change—greater than any preceding social change—the penny postage.[41]

"[T]he reformed Post Office invited" all "household[s] and citizen[s], regardless of class, to imagine themselves as connected to each other and as part of a national discourse network," notes Katie-Louise Thomas.[42] In every postbag lay a republic of letters.

Whether or not the "social change" of penny postage was "greater" than any other, it was certainly popular. The number of paid letters handled annually by the Post Office more than doubled from 1839 to 1840 (and would double several more times by the century's end).[43] It is less clear how well the system served the nearly one-third of men and one-half of women who (according to Victorian estimates) were not literate,[44] much less whether the Penny Post increased national or cosmic unity. But for several months in 1840, it did lead to a strange situation: that Britons of all conditions were sending their messages under a cover that graphically proclaimed the reach of the postal system—but which its users recognized as a dead ringer for the monthly wrapper of a Dickens novel.

Hill had commissioned the artist William Mulready to design the new prepaid letter covers and envelopes, and Mulready had responded with an elaborate composition that took up nearly half the envelope's face. In the upper center, a seated Britannia sends off four winged messengers as the British lion lies at her feet. Toward the top corners are clusters of figures from East and West: on the left, merchant ships sail toward Chinese traders, Arabs with camels, and Indians on elephants; on the right, confusingly,

Figure 1.1. *The Mulready envelope* (1840). R. and G. B. Hill, *The Life of Sir Rowland Hill and the History of Penny Postage.*

a reindeer guides the eye to a group of Native Americans greeting a band of Europeans, as well as workers packing up casks. Along the sides of the "Mulready" we see the recipients of letters: an infirm woman clasps her hands as another looks at a letter; children gather excitedly around their mother to see the letter she is reading. Dispatching its figures to the four corners of the envelope, the "crowded," "inclusive," and "imperial" design typifies the outsized ambitions of the reforms that produced it—never mind the fact that with its penny postage, the envelope could only circulate in the British Isles.[45] As Mary Favret observes, the Victorian Post Office glorified the postal system above letters themselves; this system represented the entire nation as "primarily a network of communication and exchange"—and thus also provided a "model for the British Empire."[46]

Hill found the Mulreadies "really beautiful," but others strongly disagreed.[47] Comic writers such as Thomas Hood composed verses about them. Newspapers called the design "Mulled-it-already" or "Mullheaded" and published elaborate mock-epic descriptions of it.[48] The *Times* found the design "ludicrous"; "Cruikshank could scarcely produce anything so laughable."[49] Another London paper concurred, sarcastically admiring the Mulready as "a wondrous combination of pictorial genius, after which Phiz and Cruikshank must hide their diminished heads."[50] The Mulready's critics saw it as an uncomfortably close relative of work by the most popular caricaturists and book illustrators, for a number of reasons. In particular, Mulready's balanced, multipartite, engraved design, created to frame the words of a textual inscription, resembles not Cruikshank's stand-alone engravings or Phiz's plates so much as their designs for publications' title pages or paper covers. With their uniform design in the service of varied contents, the Mulready especially echoes the wrappers for Dickens's serial novels such as the recent *Nicholas Nickleby*.

The covert affiliation between the Mulready and Dickens's covers makes sense not just because critics saw the Mulready as inadvertently hilarious, or because Phiz's wrapper was also a kind of illustrated envelope, but because the freewheeling plots of Dickens's early novels meant that the design chosen at the outset had to be both meaningful and vague. With the astonishing success of *The Pickwick Papers* (1836–37), Dickens and his publishers hit upon the distinctive format in which he would publish most of his novels: monthly issues in a colored wrapper with a uniform illustrated cover.[51] Like Mulreadies, a Dickens wrapper had to appear general enough to cover texts that had yet to be written, texts that might bring sadness or cheer. (Dickens asked readers of *Nicholas Nickleby* to consider the novel as the monthly "correspondence of one who wished their happiness, and contributed to their amusement."[52]) Yet the Dickens wrapper and Mulready cover also had to look distinctive enough to be instantly recognizable—and to discourage counterfeits. Boz's novels faced competition with crudely illustrated impostors such as "Bos's" *Oliver Twiss* and *Nickelas Nickelbery*; likewise, the Mulready design "was elaborate in order to prevent forgery," as well as to "portray the blessings of cheap postal communication."[53] Enclosed in a Mulready, any letter could travel under a uniform cover like the ones that enfolded *Pickwick* or *Nicholas Nickleby*. It was as if for one strange cultural moment, Mulready's wrappers enclosed thousands of parts making up the biggest novel in history, and every letter could become part of an immense serial available throughout the British Isles, an endless epistolary narrative—with fresh installments in every sorting slot and postbag—that no one could possibly read in full.

Phiz and company didn't hide their heads for long. Within weeks, gen-

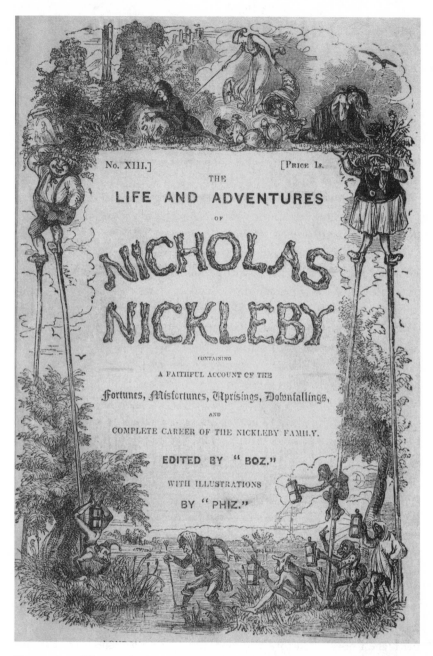

eral ridicule of the Mulready spurred Dickens's illustrators past, present, and future to produce their own parodic versions.[54] John Leech's versions proved especially popular; Dickens's friend George Augustus Sala credited Leech's work as laughing the Mulready "into extinction."[55] In Phiz's rendition, Britannia becomes "a kind of jovial Mrs. Jarley"—hardly surprising, since Phiz was just then illustrating *The Old Curiosity Shop* (1840–41) in the pages of *Master Humphrey's Clock*.[56] Her messengers' feathers have become pens, and their caps are inkstands. On the left, Phiz's Chinese group is about to receive a letter via a cannonball fired from the merchant ship—a visually comic but chillingly accurate summary of the Opium War in progress. As often happens with Dickens, the real comes in under the cover of caricature; by minimally distorting Mulready's idealized representation of global goodwill, Phiz graphically registers the truth that the official version excludes. Strapping their cannonades to the government's envelopes, the Mulready parodies ridiculed not only the individual elements of the original but also its logic of juxtaposition and its fantasy of benign imperial breadth.

Hill had assumed that prepaid envelopes and stationery would be the usual vehicles for penny postage, but he was wrong. A special furnace had to be invented to destroy all the unwanted Mulready envelopes.[57] Their uncontroversial replacements bore simply an embossed image of the queen—the same figure used on stamps. Although journalists also ridiculed the first adhesive stamp (the Penny Black was a bit of "sticking plaster" with an image "much too vulgar of expression" to resemble the real queen), the postage stamp stuck.[58] A figure of the head of state would now circulate as the representation of the reformed postal network, a sign not just of prepayment but of the system's unity, ubiquity, and reach.

Narrating the Postal Order

A decade later, Dickens too would seek a unifying scheme for a project he presented as his contribution to the cheap diffusion of stories and useful knowledge: the journal that would become *Household Words*. Like the Post Office, Dickens worked from a flamboyant plan to a subtler one; moreover, from the journal's first issue, he found not only an ideal subject but an analogue for his editorial and authorial projects in the Post Office itself. When

FIGURE 1.3. Phiz's Mulready parody (1840). Evans, *A Description of the Mulready Envelope.* © British Library Board, All Rights Reserved (8247.DE.30).

he first imagined a presiding spirit and a unifying frame for a new weekly journal, Dickens conceived of a relative of Babbage's informatic Being, a shadowy demon who could appear anywhere:

> to bind all this together, and to get a character established as it were which any of the writers may maintain without difficulty, I want to suppose a certain SHADOW, which may go into any place . . . and be in all homes, and all nooks and corners, and be supposed to be cognisant of everything, and go everywhere, without the least difficulty. Which may be in the Theatre, the Palace, the House of Commons, the Prisons, the Unions, the Churches, on the Railroad, on the Sea, abroad and at home: a kind of semi-omniscient, omnipresent, intangible creature. . . . a sort of previously unthought-of Power going about.[59]

Although this creature would give "warnings from time to time, that he is going to fall on such a subject; or to expose such and such a piece of humbug; or that he may be expected shortly in such and such a place," Dickens imagines him not as an intrusive sentinel but as "a cheerful, useful, and always welcome Shadow."[60] He would be "the Thing at everybody's elbow, and in everybody's footsteps. At the window, by the fire, in the street, in the house. . . . "[61]

Dickens soon dropped this organizing fiction for his journal, turning to a tone (a contributor called it "Dickensese") and a single name as unifying devices[62]; *Household Words* did not identify its contributors, but every page proclaimed it "conducted by Charles Dickens"—like an orchestra, a train, or an electric current. But the spirit of the Shadow haunts other quarters of Dickens's work. Harry Stone identifies the shadowy persona of Dickens's Uncommercial Traveller as one later version.[63] And in a deft analysis of Dickensian "semi-omniscience," Audrey Jaffe highlights the connections between this passage and Dickensian characters and narrators who embody similar fantasies of Asmodeus-like mobility, ubiquity, and knowledge.[64] But in *Household Words* too the ghost of this Shadow materializes, although in forms quite different from Dickens's original framework. For one thing, the point of the scheme wasn't just editorial aggrandizement—the Shadow as omnipresent angel—but impersonality and standardization; under the cover of anonymity, "any" of the journal's writers could stand behind the Shadow. Moreover, the Shadow's power of "going about" and poking into curious corners would be exercised in the nonfiction articles about contemporary society that made up much of *Household Words*, especially in what Dickens called its "process" articles, that is, informative "accounts, often highly individualized and imaginative, of business and manufacturing processes."[65]

Such pieces would become a staple of the journal. Treating their true-life subjects with humor and "fancy," they exemplify the aspiration proclaimed by Dickens's "Preliminary Word" to the first issue of *Household Words* (1850): "To show to all, that in all familiar things . . . there is Romance enough, if we will find it out."[66] The goal anticipates the aims as well as the language of *Bleak House* and *Hard Times*, Dickens's other great projects of the early 1850s (the latter appearing in the journal's pages). Indeed, more thoroughly and flexibly than *Hard Times*, the "process" articles of *Household Words* infuse fact with fancy, information with imagination, as they aim for a lively apprehension of real things. Often written collaboratively by Dickens himself, they turn real processes into imaginative narratives, typically combining fancy with statistics (supplied by Dickens and his co-writers, respectively) to produce a semi-omniscience that could make the Shadow proud. In a world of proliferating information, storytelling and imagination distinguish even nonfiction literature from the aridity of mere fact.

In the first issue of *Household Words*, after Dickens's "Preliminary Word" and a chapter of fiction by Elizabeth Gaskell, appears "Valentine's Day at the Post-Office," a piece Dickens wrote in collaboration with the journal's subeditor, W. H. Wills. Stone calls this article "the prototype" for all the future process articles in *Household Words* and its successor *All the Year Round*.[67] The postal subject of this inaugural essay hardly seems arbitrary. Christopher Keirstead observes that "[t]hroughout his career, Dickens was deeply interested in postal matters," and John Bowen identifies a postal subtext as far back as *The Pickwick Papers*.[68] Moreover, if the Victorian Post Office was "the bureaucracy of bureaucracies,"[69] then "Valentine's Day at the Post-Office" seems like the process article of process articles, since it details the mechanics by which *Household Words* itself would often be "conducted" by its itinerant editor and would reach many of its readers. As early handbills announced, the journal would cost twopence, or threepence if "stamped for post."[70] For a penny, a (newspaper) stamp would send the journal on its way.

The authors had carefully researched and planned "Valentine's Day at the Post-Office"; Wills, a friend of Rowland Hill, had even brought Dickens to Hill's house "to be dined and 'crammed'" one evening.[71] In the piece's first lines, "an individual who bore not the slightest resemblance to a despairing lover," is "seen" to drop two letters in bright envelopes into the box of a receiving-house on Fleet Street before entering the shop itself to leave a "suspicious" green envelope and a penny (*VD*, 70). The opening of Dickens's first essay for *Household Words* reenacts his primal scene of publication, as he had described it just a few years earlier. In an 1847 preface to *Pickwick*, Dickens recalls buying a copy of the first journal to publish one of his sketches, and the dazzling effect of seeing that "my first effusion—dropped stealthily one evening at twilight, with fear and trembling, into a dark letter-box, in a dark office, up a dark court in Fleet Street—appeared in all the glory of print."[72]

Having dispatched his three letters, the postal customer of "Valentine's Day at the Post-Office" "coolly" walks east to St. Martin's-le-Grand to meet his accomplice. Together these literary versions of Dickens and Wills pass into the "the Great National Post-Office," the center of the British postal system and a Victorian landmark, where "huge slits gape for letters" and "wooden panes open for clerks to frame their large faces, like giant visages in the slides of a Magic Lanthorn," Dickens's favorite figure for phantas-magoria (*VD*, 70). After navigating a dark "maze of offices and passages," our subjects emerge "like knights-errant in a fairy tale—in an enormous hall, illumined by myriads of lights" where a "Legion" of men floats about "in an enchanted state of idleness" (*VD*, 73). Entering the communication network, the travelers interpret its mysterious topography as a domain of magic and romance; as Jay Clayton wryly puts it, "[t]his is how it feels to enter cyberspace, nineteenth-century style."[73]

While the visitors watch, "an immense train" of London letter-carriers appears and begins to "slaughter" letter bags. The idlers suddenly become "human ants" picking at the entrails: letters of every kind, addressed to ev-erywhere, from all over London (*VD*, 73). Now the plan of the piece comes into focus: not to mystify the post but to plot it out via the gaudy envelopes; they will operate as tracers for mapping a network, one made more evocative by the four hundred thousand extra letters posted on Valentine's Day (*VD*, 75). One clerk "count[s] the stamped letters like lightning, and a flash of red gleaming past" shows the path of one of their letters (*VD*, 74). A glimpse of the green envelope draws attention to the disposition of unstamped letters paid with coins. And the yellow envelope pops up in a small group of unpaid letters, which will have to be charged to their recipients, a throwback to the older regime. The scheme not only allows the essay to narrate the system but also permits a comparison among the three letters' varied paths. While the stamped red letter "gleam[s] past like a meteor," the "money-paid" green and unpaid yellow must be examined and assessed more slowly (*VD*, 74). Their different treatment by the postal system has a moral. Unstamped letters "cause a great complication," a postal official explains; if "the public would put stamps on *all* letters, it would save us, and therefore *itself*, some thousands a year" (*VD*, 74).

This is a real-life story of the wonders of Victorian "data processing," as Francis Spufford notes of a similar 1850 essay perhaps inspired by this one.[74] At the sorting table, the colored letters reemerge "as magically as a conjurer causes any card . . . to fly out of the whole pack" and pass underground to the Inland Office, which handled letters from London to the rest of the kingdom (*VD*, 76). All of them are bound for Scotland, tracing the classic, system-spanning journey taken by postal samples, from Hill's London-to-Edinburgh letter that cost one thirty-sixth of a penny, to the letters in the famous documentary film *Night Mail* (1936) and the poem Auden wrote for it.

The visitors prepare to follow their letters to the Inland Office but are caught in "a thunder-cloud of newspapers" being posted just before the six o'clock deadline, a sight that inspires the piece's most sustained and Dickensian description (*VD*, 77). The "drizzling" becomes a "storm," which produces a torrent, a "fountain," and "[w]aterspouts" of newspapers that swallow up the clerks behind the newspaper window (*VD*, 77).[75] The news appears as an undifferentiated, natural flow to be channeled, a paradigm that conveys a slight erotic charge on Valentine's Day. "All the boys in London seemed to have gone mad, and to be besieging the Post-Office with newspapers" in such tumult that the observer wonders how the boys avoid "post[ing] themselves . . . with the newspapers" and being "delivered all over the world" (*VD*, 77).

At six, the windows shut and the outer hall suddenly empties. "But what a chaos within" as clerks rake up newspapers, dig among them, gather and sort this "Niagara of language," an immense surge of textual information whose Babbage-like flow must be directed by the postal network: "All the history of the time, all chronicles of births, deaths, and marriages, all the crimes, all the accidents, all the vanities, all the changes, all the realities, of all the civilised earth" (*VD*, 77, 78). As the news begins its postal journey, "all the realities" fit to print become part of the immense informatic stream. Levine has noted a similar logic in Victorian realist fiction, in which the "bric-à-brac density" of the real "frequently threatens to run away with the form" that arranges it.[76] On the floor of the General Post Office, the day's post seems like "an apparently interminable and hopeless confusion," yet it is "really in a system of admirable order"; "Which of us, after this, shall find fault with the rather more extensive system of good and evil, when we don't quite understand it at a glance" (*VD*, 78)? A wondrous yet explicable ordering of the flows that record reality, the postal process stands in for more comprehensive systems. By the end of the article, the observers have seen every aspect of letter handling at the General Post Office, save its supervision by the "invisible individual" who in panoptic style may or may not watch behind a screen of ground glass to prevent theft—semi-omniscient, present even when he is not there, intangible (*VD*, 84). As with the "system of good and evil," there are parts of the postal system that lie beyond our purview.

Hill's cheap postage, multiple deliveries, and letter slots helped lovers get their messages through the door, as opponents of penny postage had predicted. "Will clerks write only to their fathers, and girls to their mothers?" one attack on penny postage had asked; "Will not letters of romance or love, intrigue or mischief, increase in at least equal proportion?"[77] Despite the surge of letters, the number of refused or undeliverable valentines ("dead valentines") had fallen by fifty thousand a year under Hill's prepayment system.[78] But in the last line of "Valentine's Day at the Post-Office," the narrator, who has now merged with the two postal visitors, dryly begs to state that the "experimental" letters they posted to trace out the system were not love letters (*VD*, 84). Of course not—why should they be? The wonders beheld by the visitors, the system's floods and flows, happen all the time. The 400,000—or 400,003—extra letters posted today are duly sorted and counted but otherwise pass without note: at the post office, every day is Valentine's Day.

With its infusion of fact with fancy, "Valentine's Day at the Post-Office" provided a model for any number of *Household Words* essays yet to come. For example, Dickens and Wills's "Postal Money Orders" (1852), a sort of sequel, simply extends its perspective to a different section of the office. Another expression of semi-omniscience, it describes the history of the postal money order and imagines some of the stories that would emerge if only "Clairvoyance" could "get a postman's place, and read the sealed letters as well as deliver them."[79] But in a larger sense the narrative logic and themes of "Valentine's Day" correspond with those of realist fiction at midcentury: the use of fact as a scaffolding for fancy, and fancy to condense the realities expressed more diffusely by facts; the technique of tracking a set of parallel entities in order both to illumine or moralize their differences and to map out the larger system in which they circulate. For example, we might reimagine the three letters starting on their journeys as three parallel figures getting on in the world—say, as three young men working at similar jobs in London, trying to make their personal and professional ways. Following them along the paths assigned them by virtue of their goals and the characters they bear, we would gain a semi-omniscient understanding of the system in which they move. The process article would become a realist narrative. Indeed, it would become something like Anthony Trollope's *The Three Clerks*, a novel that builds upon and transforms Trollope's more extensive experiences behind the scenes of the postal system.

From Letters to Characters

Shadowing forth his new journal, Dickens imagined a creature who could investigate "humbug" anywhere. But what if such inspections had been undertaken by a more earthbound figure, if such routine exposures constituted his day job? Such a creature could be a midlevel functionary. He might even work for the Post Office, overseeing its operations like a permanent, authorized version of the Valentine's Day visitors. This is how Trollope described his work of the early 1850s:

> I began in Devonshire; and visited, I think I may say, every nook in that county, in Cornwall, Somersetshire, the greater part of Dorsetshire, the Channel Islands, part of Oxfordshire, Wiltshire, Gloucestershire, Worcestershire, Herefordshire, Monmouthshire, and the six southern Welsh counties. In this way, I had an opportunity of seeing a considerable portion of Great Britain, with a minuteness which few have enjoyed. . . . I saw almost every house—I think I may say every house of importance—in this large district. The object was to create a postal network which should catch all recipients of letters.[80]

Reinvigorating the metaphor of the "postal network," Trollope treats it as a net to "catch" everyone who might receive something. Carlyle hailed the postal system as the sign of a coherent social fabric, a world-tissue rent by anyone's exclusion, but Trollope and his colleagues put that vision into practice. As a postal surveyor in Ireland and England, Trollope devoted himself to making sure that the postal system was consistent and that it minimized the number of persons who would slip through.[81]

Inspecting rural posts and falling on the humbug of the private fees imposed by some country postmen ("in my eyes, at that time, the one sin for which there was no pardon"), Trollope became "a beneficent angel to the public," a sort of postal Shadow, "bringing everywhere with me an earlier, cheaper, and much more regular delivery of letters" (*A*, 90). "It is amusing to watch how a passion will grow upon a man," he recalled; "During those two years it was the ambition of my life to cover the country with rural let-ter-carriers" (*A*, 89). In fact, for this period Trollope found himself "so com-pletely absorbed" in the task that the novelist who would become famous for his prolific output was "able to write nothing" (*A*, 87). His everyday ingenu-ity went instead into his postal work; it was during these years that Trollope suggested the use of public letter-boxes on the Channel Islands.[82] A famous and enduring postal innovation, and one that perfectly complemented Hill's prepayment system, Trollope's pillar-boxes proved immediately popular, and the Post Office soon introduced them across Britain.[83] Now the pillar-box and postage stamp could "make the sender's presence at the postal counter just as superfluous as the recipient's presence at delivery," notes Bernhard Siegert.[84] Letters arrived and letters went out, courtesy of a network with built-in, impersonal nodes on any front door or street corner.

Part of Trollope's amusement at his postal passion may stem from the fact that in those years his ambitions for the network coincided with those of his nemesis, Rowland Hill. In his autobiography, Trollope proudly de-clared himself "always an anti-Hillite" (*A*, 283). "In figures and facts he was most accurate," he conceded, "but I never came across any one who so little understood the ways of men"; in Trollope's view, the utilitarian Hill treated "the servants of the Post Office" as if they "were so many machines who could be counted on for their exact work without deviation" (*A*, 133). Trol-lope didn't like Hill's management, and Hill didn't approve of Trollope's literary work, regarding it as a distraction from his duties. The most famous postal official *cum* man-of-letters (the editor and novelist Edmund Yates, of the Missing Letter Department, ran a distant second), Trollope had a postal career that bookended Hill's. In 1834 he joined the department at the age of nineteen, nearly three years before Hill's *Post Office Reform*, and he would resign from it in 1867, three years after Hill's retirement. After his early, aimless days as a clerk in St. Martin's-le-Grand, Trollope became first a surveyor's clerk in Ireland and then a surveyor—as well as a novelist. Trollope suspected he had especially "given official offence" with *The Three Clerks*, the novel that most obviously draws on his experiences in the Post Office, and one written and published during Hill's tenure as Post Office secretary (*A*, 134).

If postal employees were machinery, Hill recognized the surveyors as crucial mechanisms for reform. Often described as "the eyes" of the Post Office, the dozen-odd surveyors inspected and ordered the workings of the postal system in their districts.[85] They were critical to Hill's plan to make the system more accessible and regular, for instance, by streamlining collection and expanding rural delivery. As Hill wrote in an 1847 directive to them, the success of his reforms would "depend greatly on" their "zeal, activity, and intelligence" in carrying out their assignments.[86] Before he rose to head the Post Office, Hill often complained about his inability to communicate directly with the surveyors so central to his plans.[87] Against Hill's express wishes, even the directive above went out without his name on it, and the responses it solicited from the surveyors only reached him indirectly.

Once Hill came to power, he reissued his instructions to the surveyors, only—according to Post Office lore—to face complaints by Trollope over not their "tenor" but their "literary composition."[88] Characteristically, Trollope accepted Hill's goals but not his style.[89] While rural deliveries were supposed to be strictly regulated by a "law as to expense," Trollope found himself inclined to "be sanguine in his figures" in order to justify new routes; "I did not prepare false accounts; but I fear . . . that I was anxious for good results" (*A*, 89). Surveying the postal system meant squaring particular conditions with a general framework, and it inevitably involved individual biases, self-delusion, self-justification, and mixed motives. In these respects, it was much like a Trollope novel.

As R. H. Super notes in his study of Trollope's postal work, "[n]ovel after novel shows his pride in the Post Office, his knowledge of its practices, his amusement at the eccentricities of its patrons."[90] Yet for the most part, Trollope's forty-seven novels seldom include more than a glimpse behind the scenes at the Post Office; his late works *John Caldigate* (1878–79), which hinges on a diligent clerk's discovery of a forged postmark, and *Marion Fay* (1881–82), in which a postal clerk discovers that he is an Italian duke (and a corrupt clergyman threatens blackmail via "the penny-post"), probably offer the clearest exceptions.[91] But—perhaps because his experiences with the Post Office's bureaucracy were on his mind as he fictionalized his early years there—*The Three Clerks* proves an acutely postal fiction as well as one that suggests more general connections between Trollope's work as postal officer and as novelist.

Trollope gives us glimpses of the clerks' duties with little of Dickens's phantasmagoria, but *The Three Clerks* as much as "Valentine's Day at the Post-Office" uses the Post Office as a scheme for organizing the representation of real life. In fact, *The Three Clerks* runs surprisingly parallel to "Valentine's Day"; it is the story of a threesome who enter a system with different characters and undertake different modes of advancement—and whose divergent paths through the system map its spaces and sketch its workings. Moreover, the novel's most sustained social critique explicitly attacks an alternative system of sorting persons: the practice of civil service examinations and promotion by merit instead of by seniority, as recommended by the recent Northcote-Trevelyan Report (1854).[92]

The novel's three clerks, Harry Norman, Alaric Tudor, and Charley Tudor are carefully individualized protagonists with distinct histories, capacities, perspectives, and failings. But more schematically, they also become three articles placed into the machinery of the bureaucracy and the novel to be sorted, figures whose journeys are traced diachronically by the action of their plots and synchronically by the comparisons between them that help organize the narrative. The scheme creates "a book more obviously planned in structure" than most of Trollope's,[93] but also one that helps delineate the logic of his fictional realism. Realism demands a balance of design and contingency, openness and determination, as it unravels the patterns that structure reality but have a local expression (as Lukács argues); this balance is part of realism's allegiance to consensus (Ermarth), compromise (Kearns), or the middle term (Levine).[94] Trollope learned about the mesh of general rule and particular circumstances as a postal clerk and surveyor. "He was for many years concerned in the management of the Post-Office; and we can imagine no experience more fitted to impress a man with the diversity of human relations," wrote Henry James.[95] But in the reformed postal system as well as the Trollope novel, those diverse relations were carried by a larger system of correspondence.

The novel posts the three clerks in various manners. Harry and Alaric join the exemplary Office of Weights and Measures ("exactly antipodistic of the Circumlocution Office"), while Charley begins working at the dissipated Internal Navigation.[96] All enter at least partly through patronage, and then Alaric advances by both examination and favoritism. *The Three Clerks* represents the statistical apogee of Trollope's jocularly transparent naming, one of his characteristic forms of novelistic preprocessing[97]: the reformer Sir Gregory Hardlines (who wishes to bring "political economy into the Post Office" and achieves power after "publish[ing] a pamphlet"); the mining speculator Mr. Manylodes; the moneylender M'Ruen; the examination candidates Uppinall, A. Minusex, and Alphabet Precis (whose name, in a miniature tour de force, sums up the very principle of synoptic nomenclature) (*TC*, 58, 59). In this context, even the names borne by the protagonists suggest their paths and functions. Introduced first, Harry Norman combines a squirearchical pedigree with rectitude and normativity (*norm* and *normal* both enter common use in the early Victorian period), while Alaric's name suggests the threat posed by his Visigothic ambitions and his readiness to compromise the system that has so far rewarded them.

Their official lives place the clerks in parallel, and their romantic destinies make the paradigm even clearer. In the novel's logic, each clerk must find a Valentine among one of Harry's three cousins; for instance, rejected by Gertrude Woodward, who marries Alaric, Harry must come to love her sister Linda. Ensconced in leafy Hampton, the novel's suburban refuge from the male world of the office (or, for their bachelor Uncle Bat, of the Navy), the Woodward sisters provide the novel's standardized romantic destination—again, despite their methodical differentiation by means of sororal comparisons. Yet from the sequence of its first three chapters—"Weights and Measures," "The Internal Navigation," "The Woodwards"—*The Three Clerks* treats the domestic space of Mrs. Woodward and her daughters as another division in the novel's bureaucratic system, the office assigned to provide respectable weekends and suitable brides to the young clerks of London. In a book filled with committees and reports, Mrs. Woodward even describes a domestic recitation of Charley's first published story as its reading "in full committee" (*TC*, 232).

The name *Woodward*, with its amalgam of rural biome and directional suffix, suggests the status of Gertrude, Linda, and Katie as the trajectories for the novel's marital plots; after all, each will shed this name once she and her clerk reach their wedded state. The logic of the scheme is so overpowering that it seems to dispatch the youngest daughter, Katie, from childhood to bridehood so that she may save Charley from the dissolution encapsulated by his affair with a barmaid. This necessary leap takes place at the cost of a queasiness that registers in various ways: tonally in the sickly sentimentality of this subplot (at odds with a novel that includes an inset parody of sentimental romance by the budding author Charley) and mimetically in the extended illness that both forestalls and enacts Katie's transition. But as the last chapter of the novel puts it, "[i]t need hardly be told in so many words to an habitual novel-reader that Charley did get his bride at last" (*TC*, 540–41). Trollope's plots too involve a certain level of preprocessing.

Cheap letters to and from the city, collected and delivered many times a day, coordinate this system of clerkly leisure and romantic circulation via "the Hampton Court five p.m. train" (*TC*, 25). Moving people was never that different from moving letters, as Dickens's vision of posted newsboys hints; a decade earlier, while Hill worked for the London and Brighton Railway Company during a period of postal exile, the former colonization commissioner became a pioneer of both the railway commute and the cheap weekend excursion fare.[98] The Woodwards' house, Surbiton Cottage, takes its name from a village across the Thames that was becoming a byword for commuter life, thanks to a convenient railway connection.[99] Whereas Alaric's early establishment in the West End suggests his desire to rise quickly, as the only one of the clerks still in the civil service, Charley expands Surbiton Cottage and sets up house in suburbia at the novel's end.

Ever since Henry James's claim that "[n]o contemporary story-teller deals so much in letters," critics have noted the quality and frequency of letters in Trollope's fiction.[100] David Pearson calls him "the most epistolary of non-epistolary novelists," and Ellen Moody argues that "epistolarity" is a distinguishing trait of "Trollope's story-telling art."[101] Moreover, Moody points to *The Three Clerks* as signaling Trollope's development of a characteristic free-indirect epistolarity, a mode that mixes quotation, paraphrase, and summary to present a compressed letter in a way that weaves together the perspectives of its writer, its reader, and the novel's narrator.[102] If the Victorian postbag offered an image of social polyphony, Trollope finds a way to deliver such coherent multiplicity in a single letter. In Moody's example, the consoling letter Mrs. Woodward sends to Harry after Alaric wins promotion over him, the novel interleaves the note's message with Harry's response and a narratorial tribute to Mrs. Woodward—along with the narrator's warning that she and Harry are mistaken to assume that Gertrude will accept his marriage offer (*TC*, 134–35). Letters offer a potential convergence point between characters, narrator, and audience, as all focus upon the same text. Separating and recombining these perspectives, Trollope's letters reconcile realism's drives to explicate particular characters in detail and to place them within larger frameworks of narrative structure and moral judgment—even as they reassert the ties between fiction and daily discourse.

As a surveyor, Trollope worked to ensure the rapidity and ubiquity of the postal system. In his novels, these features give letters the systematic power to warp the general lines of the story into the narrative presentation of the plot. As with other Trollope works, the narrative of *The Three Clerks* regularly sends letters in advance of its characters' movements: when Alaric leaves the Woodwards with a promise to write, we read of the letter he sends a week later, and Gertrude's reply, *before* we learn the things he does earlier "[o]n his return to town" (*TC*, 151). A chapter later, we follow the letters to the rejected Norman that announce the coming marriage of Alaric and Gertrude. First comes a note from Mrs. Woodward, then letters from Gertrude and Alaric—three messages whose different arrivals and effects the text traces, but which are anything but valentines. Gertrude's Dear-John letter receives a line-by-line critique from Harry, rendered in a mixture of citation and free indirect discourse containing his thoughts: "Dearest Harry!—Why should it begin with a lie? He was not dearest!" (*TC*, 164). But Alaric's is returned unread; "By return of post it went back under a blank cover" (*TC*, 164). The grammar here captures Harry's frame of mind, passively awarding agency to the letter. For the rest of the book, Harry will remain estranged from Alaric, as if powerless to forgive him. The career of an unread letter encapsulates the story of the onetime "Damon and Pythias" of the office (*TC*, 170).

While *The Three Clerks* uses more than a dozen letters to pace its storytelling and weave together its perspectives, the novel carefully distinguishes its two government departments from the real Post Office. Structurally, Trollope divides his fictional bureaucracy, and apportions the scenes of his own clerical life, between Harry and Alaric's exalted Weights and Measures and Charley's seedy Internal Navigation. While the Weights and Measures inhabits a "handsome edifice" on Downing Street, the "Infernal Navigation" occupies a warren of dark rooms at Somerset House—unfashionable, but "not so decidedly plebeian as the Custom House, Excise, and Post Office" (*TC*, 1, 11, 10). As N. John Hall points out, Trollope has made the dissolute office an imaginary one, while the model Weights and Measures was "very real."[103] The apportionment is politic, but the combination also makes an apt figure for the novel's meshing of fact and imagination, its fusion of the kind of youthful experiences Trollope later recounted in his autobiography and the mental "castle-building" of those years, which he came to see as preparation for writing novels (*A*, 42).

But the division between Weights and Measures and Internal Navigation also schematizes the novel's own work as it assesses characters, sorts them out, and charts their paths through the novel's plotlines and social geography. Coral Lansbury claims that throughout Trollope's fiction, "[t]he critical mode of enquiry [i]s the discovery of the truth by means of comparison."[104] In *The Three Clerks*, with its trios of clerks and sisters, comparison becomes a dominant mode of characterization and a principle of narrative organization. "Each character is built up through careful contrasts," contrasts so sustained that they come to form the novel's "basic structure."[105] Again and again, the narrative gauges characters both against each other and in light of other characters' precepts. The clerks' prospects and progress, or the Woodward sisters' looks and personalities, register in a network of comparisons between them. But the method also permits juxtapositions between members of different groups; long before they become each other's second love, the first alignment of Harry and Linda contrasts his sulks with her quiet fortitude as they react to Alaric and Gertrude's engagement (*TC*, 165). Meanwhile, a range of characters—the Machiavellian Undy Scott, the reformer Hardlines, or more comically the disappointed Uncle Bat or the bureaucratic stickler Fidus Neverbend—supply conflicting canons for conduct and advancement, guidelines they offer as explicit commentary on the clerks' progress in the system. Like the parliamentarian Mr. Whip Vigil, the narrative may "know the proverbial character of a comparison," but it diligently takes up the odious task since various characters have "instituted this comparison" anyway (*TC*, 537).

In order for comparison to provide such structure, the objects of comparison themselves must remain stable, and the novel must treat character as unchanging more than unfolding. As critics have noted of Trollope's fiction more broadly, its "point of departure is a presumption that personality is essentially monolithic" and solid; "though many of Trollope's characters might be said to mature, their characteristics are already established, often firmly so, when the novels begin."[106] In *The Three Clerks*, even the "malleable" Charley, who accepts "the full impression of the stamp to which he [i]s subjected" at the Infernal Navigation, confirms such a system of character, both because his pliancy is innate and because it is essentially external (*TC*,

17). His moral peril lies not in the possibility that he will abandon a pretty barmaid after flirting with her but that he will feel compelled to marry her as the honorable thing. The stamp's impression marks the wrapper, not its contents.

While the stable material of characters is weighed and measured in various ways, it becomes ultimately the system of judgment as much as the characters themselves that are reckoned. This scheme too is amply Trollopian. Whether in the equable *The Warden* (1855) or the astringent *The Way We Live Now* (1875), Trollope's social novels emphasize the conflict not only between characters but between systems of judgment and evaluation. In Ruth apRoberts's formulation, Trollope's "realism" operates via the "sharp juxtaposition of different perspectives," viewpoints held together by his novels' polyvalent irony and "pluralism."[107] As the first page of *The Three Clerks* carefully informs us, the proper name of the Weights and Measures is "the 'Office of the Board of Commissioners for *Regulating* Weights and Measures'" (*TC*, 1, emphasis added). "All material intercourse between man and man must be regulated, either justly or unjustly, by weights and measures," but it is the rules for measuring, more than measurements themselves, that are at stake as the narrative and the clerks go about their business (*TC*, 2). A classic form of preprocessing, weights and measures abstract certain properties of objects to represent them as information, in order that they may circulate, exchange, or combine with other assessable objects. Questions about measuring systems are questions of information and exchange; the ideal driving rational, standardized measures in the eighteenth and nineteenth centuries was nothing less than "universal communication."[108]

If the Weights and Measures corresponds with the novel's constant comparison and assessment of characters, the Internal Navigation figures their vicissitudes of fortune and their movements about the spaces of the novel, from London to Hampton, from clerkship to courtship, from transgression to redemption—or emigration to Australia. With its responsibility for canals and locks, the fictitious Internal Navigation models the narrative's superimposition of narratives of inexorable movement with stories of rising and falling. The novel summarizes Alaric's confusion between advancing and rising in just such terms: "thinking . . . of the career before him, he had ever tempted himself to spring onwards,—upwards he would have said himself" (*TC*, 585).[109] *The Three Clerks* passes the Longfellovian slogan

"Excelsior!"—"higher!"—from a narratorial assessment of Alaric to Alaric's own thoughts, then to Charley's motto as recalled by Harry—and ruefully by Charley himself (*TC*, 131, 169, 215).[110] By the final volume of the novel the word has returned to Alaric with increasing irony: "Ah! he had fatally mistaken the meaning of the word which he had so often used. There had been the error of his life. 'Excelsior!' When he took such a watchword for his use, he should surely have taught himself the meaning of it" (*TC*, 546). Or at least he could have learned its grammar. Longfellow misused a comparative Latin adjective as an adverbial interjection (a mistake that Trollope, "a fair Latin scholar," might have noted); Alaric ignores the need to value higher things in his haste to mount higher and higher (*A*, 18).

Images of rivers, water journeys, and flows saturate the novel: Harry's hobby of rowing on the Thames, Bat Cuttwater's naval career, the boating accident that changes the course of Katie's life ("We'll put it all down at the Navigation," jokes Charley)—and even the "current of her thoughts" after Charley rescues her and sets in motion their love story (*TC*, 238, 239). When they are separated, Katie begins "sinking deep, deep in waters which were to go near to drown her warm heart," while Charley is "left to drift before the wind without the ballast of any woman's love," floating "about the gulfs and straits of the London ocean without compass or rudder" (*TC*, 297, 379). In order to speculate on a bridge-building project, Alaric appropriates money he holds in trust, promising himself he will repay it after selling his shares; "[e]xpediency is the dangerous wind by which so many of us have wrecked our little boats," the narrator warns (*TC*, 346). Later, facing a rising tide of suspicion and surges of conscience, Alaric tries to believe that he will "still run out his course with full sails, and bring his vessel into port" (*TC*, 433). But his mind betrays him all the while: "His thoughts would run off from him, not into the happy outer world, but into a multitude of noisy, unpleasant paths, all intimately connected with his present misery, but none of which led him at all towards the conclusions at which he would fain arrive" (*TC*, 432). As it steers him from the "outer world" toward conclusions he would rather not reach, his consciousness becomes the ultimate internal navigation.

Analyzing the novel's "Dickensian" use of imagery and motif to create unity and resonance, Tony Bareham recognizes the river in particular as "a central linking emblem" in *The Three Clerks*, nearly a precursor to the

Thames in *Our Mutual Friend* (1864–65).[111] Even if the technique is unusual for Trollope, the river image—with its combination of permanence and transience, inexorable movement and Heraclitean change—seems appropriate for a novelist attempting to lend a provisional stability to "the blurring flux of life."[112] In fact, the Internal Navigation office actually deals with canals, artificial or manipulated rivers. That image epitomizes the channeling of flows in a large-scale structure for communication and commerce; moreover, it naturalizes this paradigm, making social channels into part of the landscape.

As offices, the Internal Navigation and Weights and Measures provide Trollope's poles of bureaucratic waste and proficiency, but as metaphors they form two parts of a coherent novelistic system. For one thing, their division corresponds to the "dialectic" Lansbury notes in Trollope's fiction "between the necessity for narrative" (novels' internal navigations) "and the authority of expository characterization" (their weights and measures).[113] Lansbury finds that the latter usually wins out. And appropriately, as *The Three Clerks* reaches its conclusion and its characters complete their journeys into marriage and maturity, the Internal Navigation is permanently shuttered, "officially obliterated" in a "flood" of reform (*TC*, 528). Forgiven his incompetence at that defunct office, Charley rises to the Weights and Measures on the basis of his innate disposition.

Yet together the Internal Navigation and Weights and Measures also suggest another system that Trollope knew intimately. Individually, neither of these bureaucracies is the Post Office, as the novel makes clear. But place them together and you get a practical outline of what the reformed Post Office does: it weighs and measures letters (without trying to shine a light into them) and directs their navigation around Britain. In more theoretical terms, the post-Hill system considers objects as comparable items in an information flow and briskly directs them to their ends via an everyday network. Abstracting his civil service experiences as a subject for a novel, Trollope maps their highs and lows onto the tales of his fictional clerks; his autobiography will "refer" us to Charley's haphazard admission into the Internal Navigation as the story of the author's own entry to the Post Office, "given accurately" (*A*, 36, 35). But in a larger sense, Trollope has remapped the Post Office itself onto the offices of his novel, representing a real institution in the form of a lucid fictional system.

Gertrude complains that "a man" in the civil service must "sacrifice his individuality" and "become body and soul a part of a lumbering old machine," but as the narrator points out, she is wrong (*TC*, 513). While the text itself uses the word *system* principally to mark the misguided plans of the civil service hard-liners, the novel's own schemata balance consistency with flexibility, in Trollopian fashion. James Kincaid finds a productive tension between "closed" and "open" fictional forms in his novels, especially between the traditional closures of his romantic comedy and the subplots, narratorial intrusions, and (in *The Three Clerks*) parodies that undercut them and expose their construction.[114] In literary terms, Trollope could find a predecessor in Jane Austen when it came to such a balance, points out Kincaid. Yet Trollope would have found much the same thing when he surveyed the postal system: not Hill's fantasies of a perfectible "machine"—a vision that would have maddened Trollope and Carlyle alike—but a cohesive system sustained by the postal surveyors' attention to individual conditions and capacities. It was on just such a basis that Trollope had justified the trial introduction of letter-boxes in Jersey and Guernsey.

From the viewpoint of a utilitarian reformer, or perhaps a customer, the postal system might seem like a perfectible machine. Any postal surveyor or realist novelist would know better. As Kincaid says of the competitive examinations Trollope so vigorously rejected, Hill's approach offers "a symbol for the simple-minded belief in ordered, patterned life."[115] Trollope's clerks follow different paths, but none of their lives disclose the simple order promised by such systems of meritorious advancement: Alaric's crimes, and the proud Gertrude's fiercer devotion to him because of them; Harry's marriage to his second-favorite cousin and retreat from London clerk to country squire; Charley's rescue by the grace of the civil service and the love of a good adolescent. Many of Trollope's best-known novels express just this interest in individuals within complex social and institutional systems governed by a mixture of tradition and pragmatism—which is why there's so much "politicking" but so little politics in the parliamentary Palliser novels, or why the church schisms in Barchester should be so wholeheartedly secular.[116] In such novels, an "institution" appears as "a wide, highly variegated network, with multiple and mutually correcting jurisdictions."[117] The resulting flexibility opens novels up to the sort of Foucault-inspired analysis in which whatever might challenge norms is recaptured as what energizes them. As a consequence, a critic such as D. A. Miller can use realism's own claims of verisimilitude to respond to its textual economy of representation, its commitments to both particularity and pattern, with what is a bracing literary analysis of realism but would be a misleading social critique.[118]

Trollope's autobiography would immodestly cite Nathaniel Hawthorne's praise as exemplifying the kind of realism he hoped to achieve, a mode of fiction that seemed "just as real as if some giant had hewn a great lump out of the earth and put it under a glass case, with all its inhabitants going about their daily business, and not suspecting that they were being made a show of" (Quoted in *A*, 144). Hawthorne's comments expand Carlyle's glass-bell isolation of a man from his letters into a terrarium of the actual. Clearly, this "figure of a world under glass, is the relation of the real world to the Trollopian novel—a metonymic rather than a metaphoric relation."[119] Yet hewing a chunk of reality and placing it under glass is also separating it from that world, and thus severing the connection that made it a metonym to begin with. Celebrating the metonymic relation between text and reality, Hawthorne's comments subtly convert the relationship into something closer to metaphor—a characteristic move of realist fiction.

Figural play marks Victorian understandings of the relationships between material networks and the larger social fabric. As Carlyle acknowledges, *Sartor*'s postbag contains only the literal expression, the outward mantle, of a system of interchange invisible to human sight. After claiming that to cut off a man from his letters would open a "Hole" in the universe, Teufelsdröckh steps back to explain:

> Such venous-arterial circulation, of Letters, verbal Messages, paper and other Packages, going out from him and coming in, are a blood-circulation, visible to the eye: but the finer nervous circulation, by which all things, the minutest that he does, minutely influence all men, and the very look of his face blesses or curses whomso it lights on, and so generates ever new blessing or new cursing: all this you cannot see, but only imagine. (*SR*, 186)

As the body's cardiovascular network presents a more scrutable analogue for the nervous system, so does the flow of material communication via "verbal messages" on "paper" offer a parallel for less tangible modes of transmission. The double analogy hints at the links between information transfer and the mind-body nexus, links that will only become more complex and compelling when, thanks to electrical communication, information seems to lose its material body.

This chapter has examined how the reformed post office could offer a parallel for the multifarious correspondence Victorian fiction carried out with life. With its theoretical inclusiveness and its ability to connect any sender to any recipient, the postal network provided Victorians as disparate as Carlyle, Mulready, Dickens, and Trollope—as well as advocates of postal reform—with a material figure for social interconnection. For Dickens, the postal system models the wonder of the everyday; for Trollope, Hill's Post Office offers a principle of narrative organization. But Victorian writers would also respond to an even more revolutionary change in communication and information systems: the patenting and introduction of the electric telegraph. Postal reform changed the ideology, the ubiquity, and the agency of the letter. Going further, the electric telegraph transformed basic understandings not only of the possibilities of communication but of textuality itself. Fiction would have to be trapped in a glass-bell not to register the change.

CHAPTER 2

Electric Information

In addition to bringing a queen's coronation and Hill's dream of a new post age, "1837 was the year of the telegraph the world over."[1] An exact contemporary of Hill's postal plan, the electric telegraph of William Fothergill Cooke and Charles Wheatstone represented a far more striking innovation. With their new patents, Cooke and Wheatstone in England, like their contemporaries Samuel Morse and Alfred Vail in the United States, would become the most famous inventors of electric telegraphy. Yet they were hardly the first to conceive of electric telegraphs, or even to produce working models. From the time Alessandro Volta described his "voltaic pile" (an early electric battery) to the Royal Society in 1800, the electric telegraph was invented again and again, with increasing frequency; one late-Victorian writer devoted an entire book to the history of electric telegraphy before 1837.[2] As a critic of Cooke and Wheatstone's originality noted, "during the year 1837, several individuals in different parts of the world"—England, Scotland, North America, and especially Germany—"were actively engaged in working out the suggestions which had been often previously made for the application of the subtle agency of electricity to the purposes of rapid and distant communication."[3] Cooke and Wheatstone's models clearly built on German prototypes.[4] (Even so, they would soon end up bitterly at odds over the question of their contributions to the telegraph, a dispute that even formal arbitration did not resolve—an inauspicious beginning for a device that would be hailed as a tool of social harmony.[5])

In effect, Cooke and Wheatstone, along with Morse and Vail, were the *last* to invent the electric telegraph. For after their work—their promotion and patents as much as their experiments and machines—the electric telegraph could no longer be invented, although it would be endlessly improved and adapted. Well into the 1840s, the telegraph could still be treated as a "novelty" and meet with incomprehension and skepticism, perhaps most notably in the United States Congress's debate over whether to fund Morse's work.[6] But the lasting establishment of electric telegraphy at this time—like the convergence of British, American, and European work on the subject, and the parallel abolition of distance in Hill's proposed postal reform—suggests that in the 1830s and 1840s the telegraph sent a message that the world was now prepared to hear.

A technology does not become adopted simply because it exists; it requires a social framework that will make its establishment seem worthwhile, feasible, and thinkable. In the practical realm, the railway scramble of the 1830s had created experience with financing similar enterprises, as well as securing a thin network of land on which single companies held right-of-way—and establishing the industry that became the telegraph's first customer. For railway companies, the telegraph would increase safety and efficiency at once, allowing more trains to use a single track. By the mid-1840s, the telegraph was on its way to becoming a critical part of the railway, a "nervous system" by which "the whole line is kept throbbing with intelligence."[7] In the view of one engineer and writer, "as the muscle of a human body without the nerve flashing through it would be a mere lifeless hunk of flesh," so were the railway's "flying muscles" "animated by the guiding thought imperiously flashing through the nerves of the telegraph wires."[8]

"By the end of 1845 the telegraph had arrived; the vital creative phase was complete."[9] But as with penny postage, many practical aspects of telegraphy remained to be determined after its adoption. While the principle of electric telegraphy was dramatic, the social impact of its advent was comparatively unobtrusive and slow. In contrast to the rapid enactment and popularity of the Penny Post, electric telegraphy would remain better known in outline than in ordinary life for many years. "By 1848, telegraph lines crisscrossed the British Isles," but a generation of critics would complain that high rates and a patchwork system run by private companies hampered the popular use of telegrams in Britain.[10] Telegrams would only become common in everyday private life, and in fiction, after the Post Office took over the British telegraph network in the 1870s in order to build a cheaper and more consistent system. Yet the *idea* of the electric telegraph was abroad after 1837, and as an idea as well as an eventual reality, the telegraph soon became "not just a new tool of commerce but also a thing to think with, an agency for the alteration of ideas," as James Carey puts it.[11] The work of Carey and others will help identify the place of the telegraph in the history of communication. But I will also make a case for the crucial role of electric telegraphy in the invention of modern information, a role with continuing implications for present-day informatics.

This chapter explores the thinking that early Victorian culture could do with the electric telegraph, and the new ideas about communication and information it helped to inspire and shape. These concepts will appear in a number of discourses, from telegraph manuals to journalism and history, but I will analyze them at greatest length in the work of novelists: in Charlotte Brontë's *Jane Eyre*, and in writers' reflections on the telegraphic art of fiction. Juxtaposing Victorian fictional and telegraphic discourse, I will argue for, and analyze, the similar logic sustaining fictional realism and electric telegraphy at midcentury. For authors as disparate as Brontë, Elizabeth Gaskell, and Charles Dickens, telegraphy offered a means of thinking about the juncture of reality, materiality, and textuality in fiction—a means of considering what critics since the late nineteenth century have called realism— even before many telegrams began arriving in novels.

The demand for railway travel drove the establishment of telegraph networks in Britain, yet in a less tangible way, a new technology must also prove compatible with the ways that people imagine, or would like to imagine, their world. When, in *The Electric Telegraph Popularised* (1855), the science writer Dionysius Lardner attempts to express the wonder of inventions such as the telegraph, his touchstone for the capacity of modern technology to outstrip belief is a novelist's defense of his realism:

The author of some of the most popular fictions of the day has affirmed, that in adapting to his purpose the results of his personal observations on men and manners, he has not unfrequently found himself compelled to mitigate the real in order to bring it within the limits of the probable. No observer of the progress of the arts of life, at the present time, can fail to be struck with the prevalence of the same character in their results as that which compelled this writer to suppress the most wonderful of what had fallen under his eye, in order to bring his descriptions within the bounds of credibility.[12]

Lardner knew Dickens (who called him the "prince of humbugs"), and here perhaps he recalls the novelist's protestation in his preface to *Nicholas Nickleby* that "Mr Squeers and his school are faint and feeble pictures of an existing reality, purposely subdued and kept down lest they should be deemed impossible."[13] If the telegraph could offer a parallel for realism, as I will argue, the realism of the "fictions of the day" could also offer a figure for the reality of the telegraph.

Another early writer on the telegraph suggests how telegraphic discourse seemed to offer an analogue for real life, a translation of it into another medium, in the same way that realist writing could. Thinking about the telegraph wires running under London between the central telegraph office in Lothbury and the railway stations, Francis Bond Head finds it "almost impossible for any ruminating being to walk the streets without occasionally pausing to reflect not only on the busy bustling scenes which glide before his eyes, but on those which, at very different rates, are at the same moment flowing beneath his feet."[14] A hypothetical yet representative "being" wanders through the real streets, picturing something just as real but not actually visible in real life. This is close to the outlook of fiction writers; in fact, the sentence sounds like an excerpt from an updated *Sketches by Boz* (1836–39). Revealingly, the passage envisions not discrete, cryptic telegrams flashing along the line, but a textual flow forming "scenes" that resemble the real cityscape outside and above, only in a condensed and accelerated form.

In contrast to the jumbled simultaneity of the stories jostling against each other in every postbag, the scenes on the wire must go seriatim, in the kind of sequence that a keen imagination might elaborate into a narrative. All we would need is a Boz to imagine those invisible scenes and bring them to life. Lothbury is not so far from Monmouth Street, the "true and real emporium for second-hand . . . apparel" that inspires Boz to imagine a whole life-story wrapped up in a rack of used clothes, the *Sketches'* most elaborate conjuration of real life from a mantle of everyday signs.[15] As our "ruminating being" meditates upon the daily dramas flowing though London's telegraph wires, he is envisaging electrified novels.

Imagining Information

The electric telegraph represents "a watershed" in the history of communication because it decisively decoupled data transmission from transportation, relieving the circulation of messages from the constraints of physical movement.[16] That is, the telegraph made possible the idea of communication in its modern sense, overriding any residual equation of communication with proximity (the implication that survives when we speak of rooms that *communicate* with each other). As Raymond Williams notes, during "the main period of development of roads, canals, and railways" in the first half of the nineteenth century, "*communications* was often the abstract general term for these physical facilities" for transportation and commerce.[17] When Porter's *Progress of the Nation* boasts in 1847 that England has "done more than any other nation of Europe, for facilitating *communications* from and to every nook and corner of the land," the "cheap and easy communication" that it celebrates means transport (emphasis added).[18] Over the next decades, under the influence of the telegraph and its progeny, the idea of communication left transport behind. By 1898, Alfred Wallace recognizes the independence of "communication" from "locomotion" as a distinctive feature of "the present century."[19]

A few earlier forms of transmission had offered an occasional, limited version of such rapid long-distance communication—signal fires and smoke signals, or the optical telegraph stations of the late eighteenth century, in which flags or paddles were mounted on hilltop towers (an earlier form of telegraphy which the next chapter explores at greater length).[20] But the electric telegraph overcame the limitations of visual transmission and established a permanent, growing network that gradually became more and more significant in daily life: for coordinating railway traffic, for transacting government or private business nationally and then internationally, and finally for personal communication. Electric telegraphy redefined communication as the essential means of overcoming geographic space. In 1838, Rudolf Steinheil made the astonishing discovery that a full telegraphic circuit could be made even when only a single wire ran between stations. As long as each end of the wire was placed in the ground, the earth would mysteriously function as a return wire and instantly complete the connection—no matter how distant the stations. Bernhard Siegert wittily observes that Hill disconnected the postal system from "the earth" in 1837, whereas a year later Steinheil reconnected the telegraph to the earth.[21] But in truth the telegraph uncouples communication from geography far more profoundly than the Penny Post. All that matters is sinking the ends of its wires into an undifferentiated piece of "moist earth" to make the "*earth itself*" serve as "one-half of the circuit."[22] The discovery of how to "ground" or "earth" wires not only simplified the telegraph system and reduced the cost of expanding it but suggested that somehow the entire globe participated in every transmission.

"The telegraph is the real communications revolution," argues McKenzie Wark, for by letting messages outrun matter, telegraphy and its successors created a world in which far-flung persons and things could be methodically coordinated and monitored.[23] In this light, it becomes less surprising that the much-publicized early use of Cooke and Wheatstone's five-needle telegraph to capture the murderer John Tawell as he fled from Slough to Paddington in 1845 should be so faithfully replicated in the famous employment of the wireless to apprehend Dr. Hawley Harvey Crippen in 1910. Tawell left on a train and was dressed as a "KWAKER" (this early telegraph omitted the letter *Q*); after poisoning his wife, Crippen shaved his mustache, dressed his lover Ethel as a boy, and absconded to Canada on the SS *Montrose*. On board, Crippen voiced his naive admiration for wireless telegraphy, but he failed to understand its potential to turn every transmission into an all points bulletin.[24] With its weightless, instant travel on the wire or in the ether, an electric message can outrun any murderer.

The telegraph dramatically altered understandings not only of communication but of textuality itself, of the status and power of externalized language. Early accounts make the search for new ways of talking about telegraphic discourse especially clear. In an 1840 article for *Chambers's Edinburgh Journal*, a writer visits Wheatstone's laboratory to view his new alphabetic telegraph, which presented sender and recipient with a circle of letters rather than using a code. Turning the machine's capstan creates an electric impulse that shoots across miles of wire instantly to reveal the appropriate letter on the dial of a case. The author is delighted but seeks the right terms for understanding the electrical and textual connection between the ends of the wire: "there is a sympathy, as I may call it, between the letters in the case and the letters on the capstan."

So when, thanks to this sympathy, alphabetic language moves instantly from point to point as pulses of electricity, which aspect of the text actually goes down the line? The author's answer is surprising. "A lady, turning the capstan with her finger, brought into view the word L o n d o n, in the time it could be uttered letter by letter, although the idea had to travel through four miles of wire."[25] In one of its earliest treatments in print, electric textuality ("L o n d o n") already seems to point us toward a "secondary orality," Ong's term for the renewed ascendancy of the spoken word thanks to new technologies in a literate age.[26] But no sooner are these letters spoken than they are thoroughly outstripped. Not simply the six letters of a word but the "*idea*" of London flashes through the wire. Telegraphic discourse begins and ends with the carefully spelled-out signifier, the outward expression of the perfect sympathy between its transmitter and receiver. Yet during its instantaneous electrical journey, the message travels as something more transcendent and elusive: as pure electrical signified.

For several decades, most accounts of the electric telegraph converge on a specific formula to discuss its new ability to transmit written content without transporting its medium. Books and articles about the device inevitably furnish anecdotes about servants, laborers, rustics, or oldsters who fail to understand the logic of transmission without physical movement. These apocryphal innocents may wish to send parcels via telegraph, or they may subscribe to some supposed folk belief: that the telegraph wires are hollow tubes for moving tiny notes, that one can hear the messages whistling along the wires, that the wires "are pulled like bell wires"—or even that a little "man run[s] along the wires with letter bags," a postal pixie.[27] Tidily mapping the surprise of a technology for intangible information transfer onto stereotyped figures of amusing ignorance, such recurrent stories constitute a mini-genre in early writing on telegraphy. Given the similar structure of these technological folktales, we can identify them as Victorian mythemes about telegraphic textuality that deal with (to adapt Lévi-Strauss) the overrating and underrating of textual materiality.[28] However dubious the provenance of these tales, and however clear their ideological function of displacing bewilderment at modern communication onto stock figures of nonmodernity, they confirm the strangeness of a system that transmitted the content of messages while their stable, material form stayed behind.

The fact that electric telegraphy was universally celebrated as the first practical use of electricity—an invisible spirit that moved the body, and whose animating power crossed the divide between organism and mechanism—only increased this sense of the new medium's power and mystery. Yet long after we have become accustomed to electrical communication— even after the recent abandonment of Morse code—Victorian telegraphy still lends a certain charge to our own informatic imaginary.[29] Writing about twentieth-century understandings of information, Katherine Hayles has criticized the modern tendency "to think of information as a kind of immaterial fluid that circulates effortlessly around the globe while still retaining the solidity of a reified concept."[30] Hayles convincingly traces this idea of "information . . . as a disembodied medium" back to the early history of cybernetics and information theory.[31] But we can follow it further. For in the nineteenth century we can precisely identify the lightning-fast, immaterial liquid that becomes modern information: it is Victorian electricity, which was almost universally discussed in precisely those terms—and which had just begun to flash informatic signals around the globe on the telegraph network. Not only did the electric telegraph help generate the modern concept of information, but the subsequent history of information still bears the impress of this heritage.

As the chemist and professor of technology George Wilson put it in 1849, electricity was an "imponderable fluid"; it could "be assumed to be a highly attenuated substance,—analogous to an elastic fluid, such as hydrogen gas, but infinitely lighter; in truth, not sensibly heavy at all."[32] Even the turn-of-the-century physicist Oliver Lodge, a far more sophisticated authority, found this understanding of electricity unavoidable, although he recommended treating it with caution. "It may be advisable carefully to guard oneself against becoming too strongly imbued with the notion that because electricity obeys the laws of a liquid therefore it is one," he writes; however, until a "discrepancy" appears, "we are justified in pursuing the analogy—more than justified, we are impelled."[33] So even Lodge largely adopts the hydraulic and fluvial language that follows from the metaphor. And if late-Victorian physics begins to suspect that electricity itself is not really a fluid, then there is always the mysterious ether, the putative medium for all electromagnetic phenomena: "Ether is often called a fluid, or a liquid"—unless it is "called a solid and likened to a jelly . . . but none of these names are very much good."[34] (Chapter 7 will examine Lodge's views of the ether in more detail, when the flow of electrical information goes wireless.)

The vision of imponderable flows runs from mid-Victorian electricity to the turn-of-the-century ether to contemporary, computerized information. Furthermore, Hayles's critique of modern information's propensity to lose its material body, and to encourage fantasies that its users might do the same, elaborates a tendency in Victorian accounts of the telegraph and electricity itself. As Jeffrey Sconce points out, while "the technology of the telegraph physically linked states and nations, the concept of telegraphy made possible a fantastic splitting of mind and body in the cultural imagination."[35] Electricity's discourse of ineffable fluids shifted easily into talk of a spirit that could be opposed to mere matter. The "electric fluid" was more like "a spiritual than a material force"; a eulogy on Samuel Morse hailed the telegraph as offering a "body" and "voice" for the "mighty spirit" of electricity—for its fluid but also its soul.[36] The workings of the telegraph "resemble the operations of a spiritual, rather than of a material agency," making it a perfect vehicle for the "silent revolution" wrought by modern technology.[37]

With its ability to stimulate animal matter and to charge lifeless wires with pulses of human thought, electricity ran a circuit between the organic and inorganic worlds and animated both, becoming an impersonal, secular spirit invisibly permeating the world. In the same speech in which he hailed Babbage's idea of the universe as a library of human word and action, Dickens cited the electric telegraph and railway as rebuttals to Victorian handwringing about the materiality of the times:

> I confess . . . that I do not understand this much-used and much-abused phrase, a "material age". . . . For instance: has electricity become more material in the mind of any sane, or moderately insane [*laughter*] man, woman, or child, because of the discovery that in the good providence of God it was made available for the service and use of man to an immeasurably greater extent than for his destruction? Do I make a more material journey to the bedside of my dying parents or my dying child, when I travel there at the

rate of sixty miles an hour, than when I travel thither at the rate of six?

"What is the materiality of the cable or the wire, compared with the immateriality of the spark?"; it is the nature of electricity itself that finally gainsays those who see the march of invention as merely material progress.[38] Sending sparks down the line, every telegraphic impulse turned mere letters and numbers into links between spirit and matter.

Electric telegraphy "changed the fundamental ways in which communication was thought about."[39] As it infused the emerging concept of information with Victorian ideas about the electric spirit, the telegraph encouraged an understanding of information as something essentially removed from its material markers. If writing by its nature wriggles free of what deconstruction called the metaphysics of presence, the telegraph and its successors took the disconnection a step further; electrified writing seemed to decouple the content of the message from any material instantiation, and the text from inscription by any body. By the end of the century, after telegrams had become familiar in daily life, it would become clear that this apparent power was based on a multiply mediated network of senders and wires, recipients and relays, and that this network had powerful effects of its own. But as a way of talking about long-distance truth-telling, the idea of the electric telegraph registered in fiction long before many authors became its customers.

A Shock of Recognition

At the famous climax of *Jane Eyre* (1847), separated from her beloved Mr. Rochester by distance, and by her rejection of bigamy, Jane faces the demand of St. John Rivers that she consent to a loveless marriage and accompany him as a missionary to India. Aware that her cousin wants to martyr her to his work but half-convinced that such a sacrifice may be her duty, Jane begs for a sign of divine will. In response, she receives something strangely like one of the electric messages just beginning to reach public consciousness in the 1840s—or even like an unexpected telephone call, all the more astonishing since the patenting of that later device (by a man who came into the world in the same year as *Jane Eyre*) still lay three decades in the future. As the natural rhythms of her body break off, Jane's sensorium awaits some impulse sent along other lines:

My heart beat fast and thick: I heard its throb. Suddenly it stood still to an inexpressible feeling that thrilled it through, and passed at once to my head and extremities. The feeling was not like an electric shock; but it was quite as sharp, as strange, as startling: it acted on my senses as if their utmost activity hitherto had been but torpor; from which they were now summoned, and forced to wake. They rose expectant: eye and ear waited, while the flesh quivered on my bones.[40]

The rhythm of her own heartbeat breaks off for a moment as Jane awaits some perception on a different channel—perhaps a bit like the preliminary bell that (as contemporary accounts described) rang to summon a telegraph operator before a message began.[41] With a sudden, indescribable thrill that recalls an "electric shock" without quite being one, her senses awaken to a world of true impressions hitherto beyond their reach.

From Jane's first appearance as a forlorn stranger on his doorstep, the sharp-eyed St. John has scrutinized her every response, seemingly able "to read [her] face, as if its features and lines were characters on a page"—a typical Brontëan comparison that turns a stern, interpreting male character into a stand-in for the reader (*JE*, 354). Once St. John discovers her true identity, this reader of Jane becomes a writer: he recites Jane's own story to her as if it were "the sequel of a tale," "assuming the narrator's part, and converting [her] into a listener"—a noteworthy turnabout in a novel that gains much of its power from its insistent first-person narrative (*JE*, 379). Given his acute observation of Jane, and his willingness to take over her tale, St. John cannot fail to notice now that her senses have momentarily opened to a thing he cannot perceive, to something that lies outside his power to read Jane like a book or to recite her story:

"What have you heard? What do you see?" asked St. John. I saw nothing: but I heard a voice somewhere cry—

"Jane! Jane! Jane!" Nothing more.

"O God! what is it?" I gasped.

I might have said, "Where is it?" for it did not seem in the room—nor in the house—nor in the garden: it did not come out of the air—nor from under the earth—nor from overhead. I had heard it—where, or whence, for ever impossible to know! And it was the voice of a human being—a known, loved, well-remembered voice—that of Edward Fairfax Rochester; and it spoke in pain and woe wildly, eerily, urgently.

"I am coming!" I cried. "Wait for me! . . . " (*JE*, 419–20)

In response to her plea for a heavenly signal, Jane hears not God but the "human" words of her far-off lover, something external and real that has made an astonishing, invisible, instantaneous journey. Not from anywhere near her, or even from the air around her—but Jane somehow hears Rochester's words, his voice.

The moment reenacts and rehabilitates Jane's primal scene of haunted solitude, a recurrence in keeping with the novel's riot of psychological transference. As a child locked in the red room, Jane feared that her "violent grief might awaken a preternatural voice to comfort me," an "idea, consolatory in theory" but "terrible if realized" (*JE*, 17). An unexpected gleam of light made her "heart beat thick" in anticipation of "some coming vision from another world; then "a sound filled [her] ears which [she] deemed the rushing of wings," and Jane breaks down with a cry of fear and sobs of anguish (*JE*, 17). Hundreds of pages later, the adult Jane has had a similarly heart-stopping, ear-filling experience, in which she finally hears a preternatural voice. But now it is one that she recognizes, one that travels on silent wings or none at all, and one whose reality Jane will go out of her way to confirm.

When Jane leaves St. John to find her love again, she learns that Rochester actually spoke these words as she heard them, in an anguished midnight prayer. For his part, an unsuspecting Rochester spontaneously mentions his impression of having heard Jane's reply across the miles that separated them: "I am coming: wait for me" (*JE*, 447). Rochester confesses his "superstitious" belief that the two of them must have met "[i]n spirit" at that moment, even though he assumes that Jane was "no doubt . . . at that hour, in unconscious sleep" (*JE*, 447). "Reader, it was on Monday night—near midnight—that I too had received the mysterious summons," the narrating Jane breaks in, and "those were the very words by which I replied to it" (*JE*, 448). The simultaneity of their cries and the transmission of their voices remain eerie, but the content of the transmission is perfectly accurate.

Some of the book's first readers instantly recognized the subtext telegraphed by the incident's conception and language. In an 1848 review for *Tait's Edinburgh Magazine*, George Troup praises *Jane Eyre* as "undoubtedly the best novel of the season" but takes this moment of psychic telegraphy to task as not simply improbable but technically mistaken:

> This supernatural call, heard by her at the distance of at least fifty miles, is the only objectionable thing, in our estimation, to be found in the work. Although very poetical and pathetic, it has no feature of the real about it, and

nothing of the probable. The mere force of sympathy could not produce such a result. Imagination inwardly, and mesmerism from outside influences, may do great feats, no doubt, and cause people to believe anything; but the voice has not got a telegraphic communication direct to the ear at fifty miles distance, although intelligence by the magnetic wire may travel hundreds and thousands "in no time." In this case it is not time, but sound, that makes the difference.[42]

Significantly, Troup rejects the episode not because there are no telegraphs or wires in evidence but because a "magnetic wire" cannot transmit voices. The problem is not that Brontë has extended the concept of telegraphy to a communication mode that mystically eliminates the hardware but that she has stretched the idea of telegraphy too far. Yet in fact, even early telegraphers who used Cooke and Wheatstone's needle telegraph rather than the acoustic devices that later became popular often treated the telegraph as a speaking machine. A handbook from the same year as *Jane Eyre* calls the device a "lightning-tongued messenger of thought" and refers to telegraphic communication as "speaking."[43] Other works from the period look forward to undersea cables that will bring England "within 'ear shot'" of Europe or even "speaking distance" of America.[44] The "quivering magnetic needle" is the "tongue of the Electric Telegraph, and already engineers talk of it as speaking," confirms George Wilson in 1859.[45] The peculiar immediacy of the needle telegraph, which operated in real time and left no written record, made it resemble something more direct than writing, something like electric speech.

Exploring the mystery of "Rochester's celestial telegram," John Sutherland concedes that "early reviewers" considered it a telegraphic allusion, but bizarrely—in defiance of Troup's contemporary testimony—he rejects the association because "1847 is too early for this."[46] Instead, Sutherland takes up Troup's other suggestion and points to mesmerism as a possible foundation for the incident and for Brontë's defense of its reality ("But it is a true thing; it really happened").[47] Yet the discourses of telegraphy and mesmerism were not necessarily far apart in the 1840s, when the electric telegraph remained an exciting idea more than a common experience; Troup's review separates them by only a semicolon. As Alison Winter notes in *Mesmerized*, telegraphy and mesmerism shared a discourse of fluids, sympathy, and magnetic influence. Wheatstone himself began experimenting with mesmerism, or "animal magnetism," soon after he patented the telegraph, and his part-ner in the enterprise, Dionysius Lardner, believed that mesmeric trances had an "electric or magnetic character."[48] In a larger sense, telegraphy—like Winter's mesmerism—allowed Victorians to explore issues of influence at a distance, consensus, and control.[49]

Telegraphy, mesmerism, or some amalgam of the two could serve as a device for imagining spiritual connection in a novel as anxious to proclaim its realism (it is "a plain tale" filled with the taste of burnt porridge, the story of "a Governess, disconnected, poor, and plain") as it is to reveal a world of Gothic intensity behind, below, or in the attic above the real (*JE*, 3, 161).[50] The moment when Jane hears Rochester's cry is a mystical commu-nion between two souls, and the most extravagant point in the novel's infu-sion of external events with psychomachy. "The mechanism which enables Jane to hear Rochester's cry remains mysterious," observes Ruth Yeazell, "but the psychic reason is not."[51] Yet the not-quite-electric-shock of Roch-ester's words also represents a spiritualized version of a real technology that promised to transmit human words instantly across the distance. As with the capstan telegraph that involved language at either end of the wire but an invisible "idea" in between, there is a sympathy between Jane and Rochester. Telegraphs didn't actually administer electric shocks either, although one of the earliest schemes for electrical communication had pictured an array of wires running from city to city, connecting a row of charged Leyden jars to a band of servants—each assigned to shout out a particular letter when he felt a jolt.[52]

The affiliation between the technological and literary imagination may be headiest and most revealing when a technology is new and unfamiliar; *Jane Eyre*'s fantasy of telecommunication outstrips and transforms the real information systems of 1847. But electric telegraphy itself was often treated as a mystical phenomenon in the 1840s and 1850s, in part because the "mys-terious principle" of electricity itself was not yet well understood.[53] "So wonderful a discovery as the means of conveying information silently and invisibly from place to place, is a subject of such supernatural interest, that we might readily expect some strange effects," muses a book on the tele-graph published the same year as Brontë's novel.[54] As Morse himself put it in the message that formally inaugurated American long-distance telegraphy in 1844—and which might stand as a comment on Jane's answered prayer three years later—"What hath God wrought"?

For that matter, the words of Alexander Graham Bell's impromptu first telephone call to his assistant—"Come here, I want you"—could have been spoken by Rochester. Strikingly, both Brontë's fictional message and Bell's real one demand corporeal propinquity, as if the fundamental yearning at work in such primal telephonic contact were to obviate the very need for telephony, to realize physically the closeness being simulated mystically or electrically. Sconce's summary of the telegraph's power makes clear the ways in which it sets the terms for Jane's experience. His description of telegraphy's psychodynamics sounds like a clinical gloss on the incident: "[t]he simultaneity of this new medium allowed for temporal immediacy amid spatial isolation and brought psychical connection in spite of physical separation."[55] As Sconce and Roger Luckhurst have both shown, nineteenth-century telepathy owes much of its logic and even the Greek word roots in its name to the new media technologies of its era. When the spirits materialized in 1840s America, home of Morse's new telegraph and its dot-dash code as well as the birthplace of Modern Spiritualism, they sent their messages by rapping and tapping. *Jane Eyre* would seem to be several steps ahead of midcentury technology and spiritualism alike; its imagination of a far-off voice audible only to a single person in the room anticipates both telephony and the turn-of-the-century séance.

At *Jane Eyre*'s climax, print surpasses the capabilities of then-existent new media, but it does so precisely by pursuing the implications of those media in order to imagine an experience of silent speech across the miles. Yet if the novel builds on the contemporary discourse and logic of the telegraph to anticipate the "new and useful Improvements in Telegraphy" Bell would patent as well as what Luckhurst calls the invention of telepathy, it also speaks to more timely matters. In carefully confirming not only the content of Rochester's messages but also their timing, Jane addresses an urgent, practical issue raised by new systems of communication in the 1840s: with their ability to synchronize distant points, they seemed to demand a universal standard for timekeeping, a practice that until then had been employed only by seafarers and by the Post Office.[56] Traditionally, each city or town had its own local time based on the calculation of noon at its longitude. The coming of the railway made this system unwieldy; timetables had to include elaborate information about time conversions, and travelers had to set and reset their watches, or to perform constant calculations.

The railway first raised this issue, but the "establishment of the Electric Telegraph" in Britain "increased a hundred fold" the "urgency" to institute a *"uniformity of Time*," as the rail pioneer Henry Booth argued in a pamphlet from the same year as *Jane Eyre*.[57] In early 1846, the board of Booth's London and North Western Railway discussed the problem and recommended adopting London time in its major stations, a practice soon extended to its entire line, and one quickly copied by other railways.[58] Wheatstone invented "telegraph clocks," which were electrically linked to a central chronometer, for just such a purpose.[59] The justification for standardized time might be practical, but its imaginary effects would hardly be mundane. In an expansive passage, Booth conjures up a "panoramic view" of the entire island under uniform time: "There is sublimity in the idea of a whole nation stirred by one impulse; in every arrangement, one common signal regulating the movements of a mighty people!"[60] Compare this synchronic vision to Benedict Anderson's description of the traditional novel as "a complex gloss upon the word 'meanwhile,'" in which a "homogeneous" sense of time links the stories of characters within a society.[61]

Furthermore, as *Jane Eyre* attests, long-distance simultaneity could become the stuff of romance, a romance that now seemed threatened by the possibility of instant communication without uniform time. As Booth remarks more facetiously, "when the fair one is far away from her *intended*, what so natural as the mutual request to 'think of me at such an hour?' And so, at the appointed time, they do, or think to do; but it is no such thing. The longitude has put all wrong! and the anachronism once proclaimed, the charm is dissolved, and farewell, for the future, all such imaginings!"[62] Courtesy of modern technology, standard time would keep far-off lovers' secret thoughts in sync. Similarly, Sir Francis Bond Head observes in 1849 that electric telegraphy could offer a boon for romance, but he suggests that any young women who used it would have to be as careful about romantic timekeeping as Jane. To be sure, "young people who form imprudent attachments, instead of being effectually separated, as in old-fashioned times, by distance, can now-a-days, though four or five hundred miles apart, at any moment, by daylight or by moonlight, electrically converse with each other—in short, ask questions and give answers."[63] But Head warns his "young readers, especially those of the fairer sex," that without a uniform British standard time, a lover must take note of any local difference lest she accidentally accept a marriage proposal "before, according to local clocks, it had actually been proposed to her in London!"[64] Despite the efforts of Booth and others, such dangers would persist until the 1880 extension of Greenwich Mean Time from the British postal and railway networks to the entire country.

Like Head's vision of instant messaging between young lovers, *Jane Eyre* imagines the kind of knowledge-at-a-distance permitted by the telegraph as not a product of multiple mediations but the ultimate expression of intimacy—first between lover and beloved, but finally between narrator and reader. The novel's fusion of realism with something that exceeds it might well encourage this concurrent affirmation and denial of the power of a mediating framework, part of what critics such as Levine have recognized as realism's complex attitude toward its own medium of written language. In one of the novel's most celebrated speeches, the character Jane disclaims all media, even the very speech with which she now addresses Rochester: "I am not talking to you now through the medium of custom, conventionalities, nor even of mortal flesh:—it is my spirit that addresses your spirit" (*JE*, 253). As if in reward for casting off such terrestrial channels of communication, she immediately receives a marriage proposal—although, pointedly, this too-early proposal will lead to their disastrous, abortive first wedding.

As the narrating Jane herself recognizes in a different context, expressing her polarized impulses toward "submission" and "revolt," "I know no medium: I never in my life have known any medium" (*JE*, 400). Such self-proclaimed extremism by its title character encapsulates some of the complications the novel presents for a realistic mode defined in part by a "refusal of extremes" in favor of consensus, pragmatism, or compromise.[65] Jane's narrative carefully authenticates telecommunication with Rochester without inquiring very closely into its mechanism; here is another refusal to know a medium. But in fact Jane's extremism and the novel's extension of communication beyond the abilities of real media ultimately test and confirm the power of its distinctive mode of realism—as with Dickens's animism or Thackeray's union of irony and sentimentalism. For the use to which the novel's narrator puts the cosmic telegraph—as a device for realizing long-distance intimacy, and a climax to *Jane Eyre*'s discourse of communication—

suggests that the novel's most brazen violation of the laws of reality also draws on a new medium of communication to help confirm its paradoxical realism.[66]

Questions of communication permeate *Jane Eyre*; as Brontë's letters to Constantin Heger suggest, the author herself knew about the torments of distance.[67] From its opening chapters, the novel has presented a story in which Jane pragmatically learns how to tell her story: to the apothecary who instructs the loathsome Reeds to send her to school; to Helen Burns and Miss Temple, who offers careful advice about how to narrate her own tale; to Rochester. From all of them, Jane learns that she may gain sympathy and love by telling her tale aright.[68] Throughout the novel, the narrating Jane has used versions of the word *communicate* many times, especially to express the psychological desideratum of an intimacy that maintains independence. *Communication* describes how Miss Temple offers Helen Burns the "information" she values (*JE*, 57), what Jane and Rochester do as they fall in love (*JE*, 143, 199), what Jane seeks from companionable "minds" once she goes beyond "conventional reserve" (*JE*, 374), and even what she could retain if she accompanied St. John to India without marrying him ("my natural unenslaved feelings with which to communicate in moments of loneliness") (*JE*, 407). Jane first meets Rochester when his sudden arrival forestalls a more conventional communication, interrupting her trip from Thornfield to post a letter.

In contrast, hearing Rochester's far-off cry proves a mode of communication too sublime for the character Jane to communicate to any other figure in the story, including Rochester. In fact, Rochester would have seemed well prepared for any corroboration of his impression of spiritual contact. Hundreds of pages earlier he has explained to Jane his "queer feeling" that a something binds them like a "string somewhere under [their] left ribs," warning "that if . . . two hundred miles or so of land come broad between us, I am afraid that cord of communion will be snapt" (*JE*, 252). Jane soon goes him one better, meeting this avowal with her denial of the media of custom or flesh between them. Yet Jane chooses not to confirm Rochester's final impression of messages tugging at these heartstrings, not to authenticate the reality of their communion, not to complete the final circuit of this communication. In place of the fantasy of communication as an impossible, utopian mingling of the spirit, John Durham Peters urges us to treat it as a pragmatic activity defined by ordinary blockages and contingent on the everyday otherness of our interlocutors.[69] One more astonishing thing about *Jane Eyre*'s scene of cosmic telephony is its paradoxical affirmation of this state of affairs—the impossibility of full communication—through a strange reversal, as Jane pragmatically chooses not to communicate to Rochester the fact that she has momentarily achieved transcendent communion with him.

Jane agrees again to marry Rochester, but she refuses to share with him her experience of psychic exchange. For as the narrating Jane avers, "[t]he coincidence struck me as too awful and inexplicable to be communicated or discussed"—except when it comes to the "[r]eader" she addresses by name (*JE*, 448).[70] It is as if the character Jane had momentarily experienced the privileges of a third-person narrator to ignore distance and to read another character's thoughts, a power that authors from Dickens and Eliot to James will align with new information systems, and is unwilling to share this dispensation with another character. Only the narrating Jane can "communicate" the incident, and only to the reader who stands outside.[71] The moment marks a split in Jane between a character's silence and a narrator's disclosure; moreover, it neatly redirects the tale's most intimate message from a lover to a reader, making the novel's diegesis into the ultimate long-distance communication to an absent, unseen person. Much more than the writers who imagined love affairs conducted on the wires, Brontë seems to intuit and exploit the ambiguous semi-privacy that would come to seem a defining trait of telegraphic discourse.

Lisa Sternlieb notes that "Jane is most likely to share intimacies with her reader . . . when she is most loath to tell her story to anyone else in the narrative," but one can view the narrative's channeling of intimacy even more schematically.[72] For Jane's secret telepathy with Rochester heightens her emotionally intimate yet structurally distant connection to the "reader" she hails. Only half a page after the narrating Jane confirms to the reader what the character declines to reveal to her lover, the novel's last chapter opens with the best-known readerly address in English literature. And once again, this sentence—"Reader, I married him"—supports narratorial intimacy through the narration of intimacy (*JE*, 448). Writing *"Reader, we married"* would have emphasized Jane and Rochester's joint action and the new bond between them; announcing *"Reader, I was married to him"* would have awarded agency in the deed to a husband or a clergyman. But "Reader, I married him" makes a wedding announcement into an act of self-assertion and the consummation of a different intimacy. Brontë has craftily supplanted the vows of fidelity the character would have addressed to her husband in favor of a report from a narrator to an audience. In place of the marriage oath, which enacts what it declares, comes an avowal that announces the act to a "reader" in a famous effort to consolidate this textual bond. With only four words, the line economically reuses the telegraphic circuit *Jane Eyre* has just established from a charged-up erotic communion to the anonymous, invisibly mediated intimacies of fiction.

Ivan Kreilkamp has persuasively argued that *Jane Eyre* and *Villette* (1853) resist the equation "between writing and speech," a conflation Brontë would have found above all in contemporary public performances by male authors such as Dickens and Thackeray, in favor of a print-based "publicity obtained without showing one's face or raising one's voice."[73] Kreilkamp explores this refusal to speak as an alternative figure for professional authorship. But, building on his analysis, we can recognize how *Jane Eyre* makes hearing voices a textual experience. Ever since she feared awakening a preternatural voice in the red room, Jane has often heard them. Most notably there have been her inner voice ("the secret voice which talks to us in our own hearts") and the mysterious laughter at Thornfield, a disembodied voice disturbingly difficult to associate with the person of Grace Poole (*JE*, 157). But now hearing voices, like the withholding of speech noted by Kreilkamp and Sternlieb, becomes a way of managing what Levine calls "the realist's traditional self-consciousness about [her] medium and [her] audience."[74] As the ghostliness of a disembodied voice confirms the communicational bond between narrator and reader, the incorporeal speaking that haunts Jane becomes the impression of hearing voices whose non-oral transmission makes them not voices of the "mortal flesh" at all, a *mise en abîme* of the experience of reading this first-person novel.

"Only writing can define the new kind of powerful interiority, abstract justice, and appeal to a mass audience that Brontë seeks," concludes Kreilkamp.[75] But what I would add is that the writing that can do this has been charged with the spirit of electric telegraphy, a spirit that accounts from the late 1840s associate with the sympathy and synchronicity between separated lovers. By narrating the experience of telecommunication only to the reader, *Jane Eyre*'s narrator creates the novel's highest form of commu-

nication, an almost electric mode of narrative closeness and fictional truth-
telling for an emerging age of long-distance intimacy.

The Electric Telegraph and the Logic of Realism

The telegraph brought a sense that the links between reality, materiality,
and text were shifting and realigning, a sense well suited to *Jane Eyre's* romantic realism; the novel's mimetic and narrative telegraphy brings the disconnected governess her ultimate connections to a husband and a reader.
When Gaskell and Dickens consider the electric telegraph as a model for
fiction, they treat it in similar ways: as a vehicle of narrative truth-telling,
a figure of fictional connectivity, and a confirmation of the meaningful ties
that wire together the world.

Elizabeth Gaskell left few pronouncements on the art of the novel,
fictional realism, or the author's obligations. One of her rare statements
comes in an 1859 letter to a young writer who had asked her opinion of his
manuscript:

> I believe in spite of yr objection to the term "novel" you do wish to "nar-
> rate,"—and I believe you can do it if you try,—but I think you must ob-
> serve what is *out* of you, instead of examining what is *in* you. It is always an
> unhealthy sign when we are too conscious of any of the physical processes
> that go on within us; & I believe in like manner that we ought not to be too
> cognizant of our mental proceedings, only taking note of the results. But
> certainly—whether introspection be morbid or not,—it is not a safe training
> for a novelist. It is a weakening of the art which has crept in of late years.
> Just read a few pages of De Foe &c—and you will see the healthy way in
> which he sets *objects* not *feelings* before you. I am sure the right way is this.
> You are an Electric telegraph something or other,—[76]

Gaskell's words are sometimes cited as evidence of her solid, no-nonsense
approach to novel-writing, but critics have largely failed to note the strange
terms in which she couches her advice.[77] Narration, claims Gaskell, should
grow from looking outward and not inward, for being too conscious of our
minds' inner workings is as "unhealthy" as being too aware of our bodies';
"introspection" resembles indigestion—or worse. As a curative measure,

and a healthy example of fiction that eschews emotion in favor of "objects," she prescribes Defoe.

Gaskell's stance on the need to avoid too much emotion or self-expression in fiction may seem naive. But McLuhan characterized printed, alphabetic literature along similar lines a century later, identifying it as a "hot medium," one that worked in high definition and therefore had to avoid cultivating too much audience "empathy or participation."[78] "The content of writing is speech, just as the written word is the content of print, and print is the content of the telegraph," McLuhan also observed.[79] Yet with its lower definition (the puzzling description of Tawell the "KWAKER" was repeatedly queried until someone at the receiving office realized its meaning), the electric telegraph might offer an inspiration for cooled-down print, for writing that left the audience more to do by telling less.

Telegraphy, associated with neutral, abstract information, offers an up-to-date figure for what Gaskell claims novels do best. "You are an Electric telegraph something or other,—" Gaskell pronounces with a combination of the oblique and the oracular reminiscent of the characters in her novel *Cranford*: that is, a device that instantly relays bodiless information from point to point. Like many Cranfordian declarations, Gaskell's metaphor is shrewder than it might appear. Since telegraphs both send and receive messages, they offer an apposite figure for the claims of realism and imagination in Victorian fiction; the electric telegraph is the passive transmission of the message as well as its active production—simultaneously the mirror and the lamp. The ambiguous "you" adds to the equivocation. Is the electric telegraph an image of the novelist who "sets objects" out with a crisp, dot-dash clarity? Is it the reader, who receives the images?

As Levine remarks, nineteenth-century realist writers self-consciously assume "a special role as mediator," with duties both to an increasingly problematic "reality" and to an "audience" whom other literary modes may have misled.[80] Gaskell uses the telegraphic metaphor to capture that sense of mediation and render it neutral, impersonal, objective in a literal sense. A telegraph something-or-other, "—*not an x-ray thingamajig*," she might have added had she been living forty years later. For Gaskell, the metaphor of telegraphy both diminishes the distortion involved in the novelist's mediations and provides a safeguard against the queasy possibilities of an inward, psychologized fiction. It's an unhealthy sign when we are too aware of the corporeal processes within us, but the telegraph signifies electric information that lacks a material body, and that seems identifiable with no body in particular. Coming down the line from points unknown, it seems to bring the kind of "view from nowhere" that characterizes objectivity.[81]

Writing in his private memoranda book a few years later, Dickens offers another vision of narration as telegraphy: "Open the story by bringing two strongly contrasted places and strongly contrasted sets of people, into the connexion necessary for the story, by means of an electric message. Describe the message—*be* the message—flashing along through space—over the earth, and under the sea."[82] The medium of electric telegraphy is the metaphor, and the story's narrative voice *is* "the message—flashing along through space." Pulsing between disparate characters and settings, the telegraphic narrator becomes the thing that connects them. The idea of following a letter through the postal system would have been familiar from process articles such as "Valentine's Day at the Post-Office" or "Right through the Post" (1859). In the latter piece, written by John Hollingshead for Dickens's *All the Year Round*, a human narrator is granted the privilege of becoming a letter—a "registered letter," naturally, since his movements will be tracked—left in one of Trollope's new pillar boxes and then processed aboard the Travelling Post Office.[83] Dickens's note adapts such narrative schemes as a possible technique for fiction, following an electric message down the wires.

But the telegraphic memorandum suggests special parallels between the medium of telegraphy and the principles of Dickens's art. His scheme for this unwritten story encapsulates in the image of the "electric message" what his fiction elsewhere delineates by other means. For one thing, the idea of building fiction on contrasted settings and groups of people that come together characterizes novels such as *Little Dorrit* and *A Tale of Two Cities*. Moreover, the memorandum's principle and even its language recall a famous narrative pause in *Bleak House*: "What connexion can there be, between the place in Lincolnshire, the house in town, the Mercury in powder, and the whereabout [*sic*] of Jo the outlaw with the broom . . . ? What connexion can there have been between many people in the innumerable histories of this world, who, from opposite sides of great gulfs, have, nevertheless, been very curiously brought together!"[84] Like the shift from the question mark of the first sentence to the exclamation point of the second, the telegraphic message confirms that a coherent structure of unseen connections is already in place.

Running overhead and underwater, the telegraph wire actualizes the imaginary links that Dickens highlights in his novels, especially in the fiction of his "mature" period from the late 1840s onward, the years that also saw the explosive growth and spread of telegraphy.

In *Realism and Consensus in the English Novel,* Elizabeth Ermarth argues that from quattrocento painting to nineteenth-century fiction, "realism" in its various forms depends on a notion of collective, coordinated space that itself grows from an idea of time as continuous and uniform. Citing a version of Dickens's telegraphic memorandum, Ermarth notes the ways in which the figure of the telegraph message describes Dickens's strategies for creating narrative perspective.[85] For Ermarth, his novels ultimately reveal a "commanding structure [that] comes into view slowly, emerging from all parts of the world and grounded in them. Each point is a relay for the electric messages that connect them."[86] This fundamental "structure of significance, uniting various worlds of experience into one," underlies—and is tested by—the caricature and stylization in Dickens's fiction; for Ermarth, this unifying system of "consensus" finally constitutes his realism.[87]

Although he describes realism not in consensual but in dialectical terms, Georg Lukács comes to a similar conclusion about the project of realist fiction. Championing realism as a political aesthetic, Lukács identifies and exalts the primary "goal" of the realist novelist: "to penetrate the laws governing objective reality and to uncover the deeper, hidden, mediated, not immediately perceptible network of relationships that go to make up society"—a network that readers, like characters, only experience in a partial, local, subjective way.[88] If realist fiction works to uncover a coherent but not directly observable network of real connections, then by the time of Dickens, the parallel between fiction and telegraphy might have been irresistible. For, although Ermarth does not note it, both Dickens's telegraphic memo and his emphasis on a system of "connexion" resonate with mid-nineteenth-century accounts of the telegraphic network that was beginning to interconnect "the world with its vast network of communicating fibres."[89] A Victorian technologist could even view the telegraph network as "a sentient connexion between" far-off places.[90]

As the places it linked became more distant, claims for the telegraph's global significance could become extravagant. Probably written in 1862, Dickens's notebook entry alludes to contemporary efforts to lay telegraphic

cables across empires and oceans ("over the earth, and under the sea"), especially the immense project of creating a transatlantic connection between
Britain and North America. The plan of Dickens, Paxton, and company to
build a cable under the English Channel in the 1840s had never reached
fruition, but just a few years afterward, a rival group succeeded in the task,
confirming the possibility of submarine telegraphy and inspiring schemes
for intercontinental communication. Understanding of underwater electrical transmission was still rudimentary, as the confusion attending the short-
lived first Atlantic cable in 1858 attests. But after a hiatus during the American Civil War, and new consultation with the physicist William Thomson
(soon created Baron Kelvin for his work), the effort to lay a transatlantic
cable produced a permanent link eight years later.[91]

From the telegraph's earliest days, accounts of it had predicted "great
social benefits": diffused knowledge, collective amity, even the prevention
of crimes ("[c]rime, to a great extent, must cease, from the impossibility of
commission without detection").[92] Now, as international and intercontinental telegraphy became a possibility and then a profitable reality, the power
of the electric telegraph to unite a geopolitical world of varied experience
and conflicting interests became a commonplace in Whiggish accounts of
human advancement. News accounts took the establishment of the Anglo-
French cable as a sign of "the progress of our race" (*The Spectator*) and the
coming "'brotherhood of nations'—that long Utopian dream" (*The London
Illustrated News*): "All Europe ought to hold together; but it is unluckily in
pieces, and some pieces are perpetually falling out," wrote *The Examiner*;
"The safest joining is copper wire."[93] *Household Words* paid lavish poetic tribute to "The Great Peace-Maker."[94] For Charles Briggs and Augustus Maverick, writing in the wake of the laying of the first transatlantic cable ("the
greatest event in the present century"), it was now "impossible that old prej-
udices and hostilities should longer exist, while such an instrument has been
created for an exchange of thought." Indeed, they predict that "now the
great work is complete, the whole earth will be belted with the electric current, palpitating with human thoughts and emotions." The telegraph would
"forestall the flight of Time, and inaugurate new realizations of human powers and possibilities."[95] Harnessing "a spirit like Ariel to carry our thoughts
with the speed of thought to the uttermost ends of the earth," the electric

telegraph was widely acclaimed as a "step towards realizing the dream of the poet, to 'Put a girdle round about the earth/In forty minutes.'"[96]

Like mid-Victorian realism in Ermarth's account, then, mid-Victorian telegraphy promised to bring together disparate worlds and viewpoints by means of an encompassing framework of discourse, a "vast inter-connected system" of communication.[97] In 1881, a *Scientific American* article on the "moral influence of the telegraph" claimed that "the touch of the telegraph key . . . welded human sympathy and made possible its manifestation in a common, universal, simultaneous heart throb," a burst conveyed by "electric pulsations" that passed "over the continents and under the seas." Indeed, the recent outpouring of telegraphic sympathy after President Garfield's assassination presaged "a day when science shall have so blended, interwoven, and unified human thoughts and interests that the feeling of universal kinship shall be, not a spasmodic outburst of occasional emotion, but constant and controlling."[98]

The comments of Gaskell and Dickens suggest the similar cultural logic behind understandings of realist fiction and the electric telegraph during the initial decades of Victorian realism and commercial telegraphy—chronologically twinned technologies that grow in tandem from experimentation in the 1830s and early 1840s, to standardization in the late 1840s, and to a certain triumphant audacity by the late 1850s and 1860s. In the formulations of Gaskell and Dickens, the figure of electric telegraphy helps crystallize the assumptions and evasions of Victorian realism, its claims to neutrally transmit a domain of shared meaning, its evocations of a many-sided but coherent world palpitating with thought and sentiment, its desire to be a message that invisibly connects a reality of contrasts. Flashing through space, realism and electric telegraphy would become tools for intersubjectivity, affirming the ties of sympathy and interest between each node of their networks. The British telegraph industry remained in private hands until 1870, but its machines had to remain universally available as a matter of law. As the Telegraph Act of 1863 ordered, "Every telegraph . . . shall be open for the messages of all persons alike, without favour or preference"—or at least anyone who could afford the charges.[99]

The telegraph rewired the material and discursive connections tying the contemporary world together. An 1850 book by the railway telegraph chief Charles Walker juxtaposes the rail map of southeast England with a "plan"

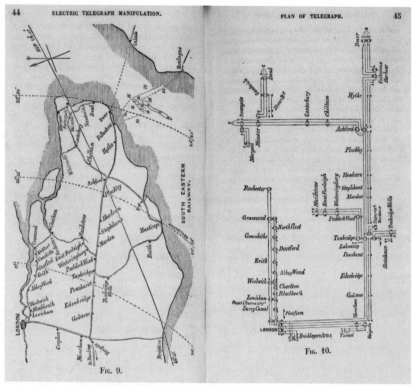

FIGURE 2.1.   Southeastern England by railway and by telegraph. C. Walker, *Electric Telegraph Manipulation* (1850). © British Library Board, All Rights Reserved (787. c.31).

of its telegraph stations. The telegraph chart turns the railway's already schematized topography into network topology, carefully replacing the curves of a map with the right angles of a circuit diagram. Here is a graphic harbinger of the modern "world market" system in which, as McKenzie Wark puts it, our "partially abstracted territory requires a fully abstracted information landscape."[100] On Walker's telegraph chart, even the names and distances of the stations appear more tightly locked to the grid of the network, marking the movement from physical geography to modern, homogenous, "abstract space."[101] As long as the wires are working, the stations on the line are virtually adjacent and electrically equidistant.

Victorian information networks encouraged a wider sense of new contiguities and expanding interconnection. While this impression might have

only a dubious application to society, it was only the most prosaic description of the growing network itself, a fact that might have implications for
novels. In Roman Jakobson's analysis, realist fiction relies on a "predomi-
nance of metonymy" to structure its narrative movements from "plot" to
"atmosphere," from "characters" to "setting," from external detail to thematic meaning.[102] Metonymy depends on the associations between things
that are already closely associated, but what happens when the telegraph
promises to bring the world into a state of total connection?

To borrow a term from Bakhtin, we might think of the telegraph as a
chronotope for realist fiction in the period, a figure that unites representations of space and of time.[103] The telegraph, after all, would bring the world
closer by instantaneous communication, would materialize the connections
of *Bleak House* and the web of *Middlemarch*. To this end, Dickens and Gaskell
assume the transparency of the electric telegraph as a medium. For Gaskell,
such transparency seems to underwrite the neutral connection between author and subject, or author and reader; the telegraphic comparison exalts the
ideal of communication but minimizes the involvement of human interiority
and subjectivity ("introspection . . . morbid or not") in the process.

Objectivity and Electric Language

These beliefs in the telegraph's technological neutrality may seem unsophis-
ticated, but they also characterize the discourse of telegraphic journalism,
perhaps the most public use of the device, as well as its directest connection to print. By the late 1840s, a telegraphic dateline could function as
a token of "objectivity" and "authenticity" in newspapers—even when the
news had actually traveled via mail, sea, or courier for much of the way.[104]
Neither extension of the network nor growing familiarity with the medium
dispelled such overtones. As the telegraph came to link Britain to Europe,
North America, and the Empire, ideas about the putative transparency and
neutrality of the electromagnetic medium became deeply bound up with
evolving ideas about objective reporting. By the end of the century, the journalistic distinction between fact and opinion could even be mapped onto
the difference between media. As a reporter for the *Times* was admonished
in 1894, "telegraphs are for facts; appreciation and political comment can

come by post."[105] The terms differ from Gaskell's, but the logic is similar: the telegraph represents directness, clarity, facts and objects rather than feelings and opinions.

To this day, newspaper historians often identify "[t]he introduction of the electric telegraph in the 1840s . . . as a crucial contributory factor" in "the emergence of journalistic 'objectivity' as a professional ideal."[106] Nineteenth-century journalists and modern historians attempt to explain the alignment between telegraphy and objectivity in a number of ways. For one thing, the technology brought the rise of telegraphic news agencies, such as Reuters in Britain and the Associated Press in America, which sold subscriptions to a range of papers, as well as to businesses more concerned with accuracy than with political spin. In 1854, the manager of the New York Associated Press directed reporters to send only "bare matter of fact" on the wires.[107] An internal memo issued by Reuters in 1883 made the connection between telegraphic speed and unembellished factuality into company policy, instructing that when it came to unexpected events "the bare fact be first telegraphed with the utmost promptitude," followed afterward by "a descriptive account."[108] Maybe this protocol arose when the telegraph lines were unstable, as during the American Civil War.[109] Or perhaps telegraphy was simply too expensive for anything more elaborate than facts (although this argument hardly applies to journalistic telegrams within Britain after 1870, which went by a special cheap rate). Or the preference for unvarnished facts might come about because material submitted by a far-off correspondent had to be quickly assembled and refashioned by a newsroom "stringer" who had no special familiarity with the story.[110]

Such multiple explanations for the overdetermined connection between electric telegraphy and objective reportage suggest that the convention of associating them may be largely just that, an expression of ideology as much as technology.[111] Perhaps electric information simply seemed more difficult to identify with any specific body, and therefore with any individual point of view. The connection between telegraphy and objectivity might seem consolidated by the telegraph's conjunction of technology, distance, and dialogism; clearly, there exists a "close connection between objectivity and intersubjectivity."[112] To the extent that Victorian journalism sought to collect and present untouched "information," rather than overtly "collating or interpreting it" as modern journalism generally does, columns of virtually unedited telegrams soon became a hallmark of this effort.[113] By the end of the period, the Reuters editor who took credit for instituting "the present service of sober, naked statements of facts" back in the 1850s now complained of the "dull skeleton telegrams" that still circulated despite the vastly reduced cost of telegraphy.[114]

In an 1865 speech, a famous editor and former journalist played on the impersonality of telegraph journalism in order to envisage the effects of a news-sellers' strike in amusingly incongruous terms:

> Why, even Mr. Reuter, the great Reuter whom I am always glad to imagine slumbering at night by the side of Mrs. Reuter, with a galvanic battery under the bolster, telegraph wires to the head of the bed, and an electric bell at each ear [*roars of laughter*] even he would click and flash those wondrous dispatches of his to little purpose, if it were not for the humble . . . activity, which gathers up the stitches of the electric needle, and scatters them over the land. [*Cheers.*][115]

The Reuters' domestic arrangements are suitably absurd, but some of Dickens's comedy in the passage comes from imagining Mr. Reuter—an actual human being between the electric bells and wires—at all. "Who is Mr. Reuter?" asked an 1861 essay. "All the world is asking this question"—is he "an institution or a myth," "or is he a man like ourselves," this figure whose name was now synonymous with a "system" that stood for "impartiality and accuracy" as well as speed?[116]

As Dickens's words suggest, the mechanics of Cooke and Wheatstone's "needle" telegraphs could enhance the association between the telegraphic network, the stitching together of disparate stories into a multifarious text, and the complex, interwoven fabric of reality. The telegraph encapsulated not only daily journalism's claims to speed and trustworthiness but also a new idea of "covering" events, in a sense of the word first applied to newspaper reporting at the end of the century. If newspapers increasingly seemed to cover the contemporary world—a project that echoes the ambitions of realist fiction—this was largely because the telegraph wires already did. Even before the newspapers or the wires could claim such thorough coverage, electric telegraphy offered a topos that linked individual stories to a coherent, widespread framework for organizing and disseminating information.

Without mentioning the telegraph, the opening chapter of Macaulay's

History of England (1848) invokes this topos when it contrasts a modern age of publicity with medieval society:

> We live in a highly civilised society, through which *intelligence is so rapidly diffused by means of the press and of the post office* that any gross act of oppression committed in any part of our island is, in a few hours, discussed by millions. If the sovereign were now to immure a subject in defiance of the writ of Habeas Corpus, or to put a conspirator to the torture, the whole nation would be *instantly electrified* by the news. In the middle ages the state of society was widely different. Rarely and with great difficulty did the wrongs of individuals come to the knowledge of the public.[117] (emphases added)

Thanks to nineteenth-century communication systems, asserts the famously Whiggish historian, individual wrongs will immediately electrify the public; modern information seems to circulate effortlessly, instantly, truthfully, automatically. Writing his *History*, Macaulay hoped to combine accuracy and thoroughness with the excitement of "the last fashionable novel"; this passage indicates his affiliations with contemporary social fiction.[118] As Brontë, Gaskell, and Dickens suggest, Victorian novels too presuppose—and are part of—the modern information systems that effectively diffuse personal stories as public intelligence.

Electric information might seem bodiless—able to stand for the sympathetic connections between Jane and her distant communicants, for Gaskell's evasion of morbid interiority in fiction, for Dickens's weightless movement between connected stories, for the telegraph press's claims to neutrality and objectivity. But new media technologies hardly transcend the body and leave it behind—as media scholars from McLuhan to Hayles and Kittler have richly shown, and as a new medium's users quickly discover. Rather, new media modify bodies' capabilities and create different connections to what lies outside them. Media give bodies different ways of registering the world and of registering in it; they entail new skills and disciplines; they change the relationships of bodies to discourse, to culture, and to other bodies.

To explore a sustained expression of such changes, the rest of this book examines the ways in which fiction both embodied information and treated the body as an informatic text. "Ideas live in culture not disembodied, but as actions, attitudes, assumptions, moral imperatives," and this description applies even to a concept as abstract as the emerging idea of information.[119]

In the quest to locate this idea in nineteenth-century writing, few cultural fields seem more promising than realist fiction, with its dual allegiances to imagination and actuality, postulation and perception. The streetscape of London offers a way of imagining the scenes played out on the telegraph, just as the network of electric wires presents a material analogue for the structures that interconnect the world.

"Information Embodied," the next section of this book, looks at the interchange between mid-Victorian fiction and information. Even before the telegraph becomes a part of daily life, fiction suggests the electric effects of modern information systems, as writers imagine the interplay of texts, bodies, and the registration of reality. One predominant version of this interplay treats texts and characters as channels that register the flows of reality—that is, as something like modern media devices. As *Jane Eyre* shows, this paradigm can result in the temporary advance of characters to the status of realist narrators—a fictional parallel, perhaps, for the sense of simultaneous intellectual power and epistemological unease produced by new media such as the telegraph and photography at midcentury. Dickens's *A Tale of Two Cities* and Eliot's "The Lifted Veil" seldom invoke modern media by name, yet both works will embody information in just such slippage from character to narrator. The ambiguous movement between characters and narrators brings unseen realities into visibility, as informatic visions overcome the bounds of space and time (the universal promise of new media in the period).[120] But in these texts, imaginatively replacing the body of a character with a body of neutral information also exacts a ghastly cost.

Following McLuhan's analyses of typographic literacy, Ong treats the classic novel as the ultimate literary expression of the "fixed point of view" encouraged by the culture of print.[121] But McLuhan's work actually suggests that by the mid-nineteenth century the situation is more complex. "The Gutenberg Galaxy was theoretically dissolved in 1905 with the discovery of curved space," he writes, "but in practice it had been invaded by the telegraph two generations before that."[122] In many of the fictions considered in the following chapters, the unfixing of point of view—shifts in the status of a character or the perspective of the narrator—suggests the mediation between the dispositions of print and the pressure of newer media.[123] Such works bear out the possibility that "before the material means and the conceptual modes of new media have become fixed, when such new media are not yet accepted as natural," they may challenge the "ritualized conventions of existing media."[124]

As Levine points out, "the realistic method proceeds to what is not visible . . . through the visible."[125] But sometimes new things come into visibility—and modern media may extend our perceptions to things that never attain visibility at all. By the 1860s and 1870s a new awareness of the telegraph as a medium, and of the roles of the bodies that actually carry on the telegraphic interchange, would alter the kinds of relationships that authors could draw between fiction and the modern information systems typified by the telegraph. The electric telegraph would still offer a thing for novelists to think with, but it also became a thing for them to think about, a new subject for fiction. What if telegraphers, with their special access to information, became semi-omniscient narrators? Such possibilities would first emerge in works primed to test the assumptions of realism—ghost stories, railway fiction, adventure tales—as well as in Trollope's imaginative return to a Post Office that now included telegraph clerks.

Embodying Information

CHAPTER 3

Speaking Machines

Nineteenth-century fictional realism registers the changing position of print and writing in an age of information and new media. But these media themselves do not often become the subjects of explicit, sustained fictional attention until the 1860s and 1870s, when this focus first appears most commonly in genre fiction constructed around the excitement of what was still high technology. Yet even before then, novels begin to display new media effects as authors negotiate the power of textuality, and as realistic fiction imagines ways of materializing things to which we can never really have direct access: the consciousness of others, the flow of scenes that are distant in space or time, the network of affiliations that gives coherence to social life or to the plots of realist novels.

These responses represent a complex form of "remediation," to borrow Jay David Bolter and Richard Grusin's suggestive term for the appropriation and rivalry between media in a particular media ecology. Remediation comes about as newer media are understood in terms of the ones they purport to improve or surpass, and as those older media react to the presence of new ones. Bolter and Grusin analyze the dynamics of remediation as a dialectic between the evocation of "immediacy" (downplaying the presence of a medium in order to focus on its content) and "hypermediacy" (foregrounding the presence of the medium itself, of mediation). They associate realism, or at least realism in the visual media from which they draw most of their examples, with a straightforward quest for transparency and immediacy.[1]

But I have already noted some of the ways in which Victorian novelists diverge from that model of refusing to know media, even beyond such potential anomalies as intrusive narrators. Trollope can map three clerks' stories via a scheme that corresponds to the Victorian postal system, just as Gaskell can use the model of the electric telegraph as a figure for fiction that presents objects at a careful remove from emotions. Fictional realism doesn't merely seek immediacy in any simple way. Indeed, Lukács applauds nineteenth-century realism for avoiding the seductions of descriptive detail and immersion in raw experience, traits he associates instead with his bêtes noires of naturalism and modernism.[2] Likewise, Levine emphasizes realism's allegiance not to the immediate but to the middle ground.

In Bolter and Grusin's terms, rather than a search for untrammeled immediacy, literary realism entails something more like a pragmatic effort to stabilize the claims of immediacy and hypermediacy in fiction. As a literary mode, realism self-consciously recalls the language, style, and narrativity of extraliterary texts. And in its balance of immediacy and hypermediacy too, realism reflects its readers' encounters with daily discourse. The great age of fictional realism was also the era of the explosion of print, the rise of journalism, and the birth of new technological media; in the media ecologies of the eighteenth and nineteenth centuries, readers' own awareness of the real, social world itself fused direct experience and mediated knowledge in a new and heightened way. Such a media and cognitive context suggests that we might think of realism not so much in terms of transparency as of *translucence*—not of a simple desire to disregard mediation but of an emphasis on the way in which mediations make certain real aspects of represented things shine through.[3]

Drawing on the history of Victorian information, this chapter and the one that follows will argue for particular modes of translucence in two works of fiction published in 1859: Charles Dickens's *A Tale of Two Cities* and George

Eliot's "The Lifted Veil." In many respects, the two would seem an unlikely pair, the first a swift-moving historical novel and the second a strange tale of prevision and gothic science. Yet I will argue that the texts respond to the claims of mid-Victorian technological media and information in parallel ways. The telegraph seemed to promise transcendent discourse, while the photograph promised to remove the bodily experience of vision from space and time. By turning language or visual experience into information, such technologies seemed to offer a kind of objectivity that paralleled but could also challenge the claims of fictional realism. *A Tale of Two Cities* and "The Lifted Veil" suggest the power and the price of such informatic promises. Extending the real powers of the human sensorium, both texts imagine the possibility of objective access to real things unavailable to bodily perception, the kind of access promised by modern media and information systems. And both also vividly imagine the sacrifice of the living, human body in the name of disembodied information.

As a work of historical fiction, *A Tale of Two Cities* may at first seem an improbable vehicle for reflections on modern information. Indeed, it offers a significant test to my claims about nineteenth-century informatics, realism, and textuality, since one might expect this novel's historical setting to rule out depictions of a specifically Victorian information ecology. Yet information systems can shape even a work whose subject might appear to have little intrinsic connection to them. In its outlook, its representational strategies, and its most insistent themes, *A Tale of Two Cities* reveals an informatic orientation notably different from the novels of Walter Scott or from *Barnaby Rudge* (1841), Dickens's previous foray into historical fiction. With early nineteenth-century historical novels, claims Lukács, fiction comes to view past events, social conditions, and characters as fundamentally enmeshed in the movements of history.[4] But *A Tale of Two Cities* suggests something more: that for the sake of realism historical fiction now must historicize communication systems as part of the relationship between past and present. In the era of the French Revolution, *A Tale of Two Cities* recognizes not only the genealogy of its own era, as in the "classical" historical fiction Lukács discusses, but the origins of the modern age of speed and information.

Scott, whose work stands behind all of the century's historical fiction, can certainly acknowledge the modern growth of communication. He does so for instance in the inventive and invented narrative of *Redgauntlet* (1824) when Alan Fairford's posting of a letter inspires a discussion of Edinburgh postal habits, and a complaint: "pray, what the devil have the people of Auld Reekie to do with London correspondents?"[5] In the 1832 "Magnum" edition, Scott added a personal note in keeping with his now-acknowledged authorship: "Not much in those days, for within my recollection the London post was brought north in a small mail-cart; and men are yet alive who recollect when it came down with only one single letter for Edinburgh, addressed to the manager of the British Linen Company."[6]

From *Waverley* (1814) to *Redgauntlet*, Scott's novels may themselves form the age's ultimate Scottish-English literary correspondence. But even as Scott offhandedly expresses a sense of media change, the form of *Redgauntlet* turns back to the period of its action. As a semi-epistolary "tale of the eighteenth century" (in the words of its subtitle), it offers a kind of formal pastiche just as its central historical event (the return of Charles Stuart decades after the Battle of Culloden) is hypothetical, a simulated history.[7] *Redgauntlet* readily concedes epistolarity's longueurs, the "various prolixities and redundancies . . . in the course of an interchange of letters, which must hang as a dead weight on the progress of the narrative," but even once it abandons this old-fashioned mode, it does not map this phenomenon onto any contrast between contemporary speed and bygone sloth.[8] Celeste Langan has demonstrated Scott's media consciousness in *The Lay of the Last Minstrel* (1805), a poem she reads as a reflection on the properties of (printed) writing in the early nineteenth-century media ecology.[9] But in *Redgauntlet*, set not in the Middle Ages but in the recent past, the novel's sporadic media awareness seems largely separate from its historical consciousness.

In contrast, *A Tale of Two Cities* suggests a recognition of media change as an inescapable feature of modern history. From its opening incidents aboard the fastest mode of transportation and communication eighteenth-century Britain had to offer, the novel deeply concerns itself with the speed and mobility of persons and information. While it evokes the promise of such rapid circulation, *A Tale of Two Cities* emphasizes how the age's social and political conflicts place that potential under encumbrance and violence. Furthermore, the novel locates the media ecology of Revolution-era France and England at the origin of an information revolution that also helps define the work of modern fiction. In *A Tale of Two Cities*, the Revolutionary era generates modern subjectivity, but it is the task of fiction to convert that subjectivity into information—a paradigm mirrored by the themes and techniques of the novel itself.

Thinking about an information revolution as part of Dickens's historical awareness in the 1850s is no anachronism. For one implication of the mid-Victorian rhetoric of technological revolution was to reclassify even the recent past as a technical ancien régime. In 1852, for instance, Michael Angelo Garvey published *The Silent Revolution,* an entire book celebrating the social implications of electricity, steam, and other forces as they came to be applied not simply to industrial production but to transport and communication. And Dickens was fascinated by modern information flows. In its impulse to historicize media systems, its focus on the movement of texts and persons, and its vision of how reality might register as information, *A Tale of Two Cities* is a historical novel for a new information epoch. From a focus on the former dependence of communication upon transport, aligned with the opacity of the embodied mind, the book moves to a Revolution impatient to breach the integrity of bodies and communications alike. By its climactic scene of self-sacrifice, *A Tale of Two Cities* has come to treat fiction itself as one of the new media that divide the Revolutionary era from informatic modernity—from the promise that a communication revolution would overcome the constraints of materiality.

Problems with the Mail

Critics have long tagged *A Tale of Two Cities* as the best of Dickens and the worst of him, a novel with unusually careful pacing and a unity of tone exceeded only by *Great Expectations* (1860–61), but also one with little of the humor or memorable characterization invariably dubbed "Dickensian." If it has become conventional to borrow the opening lines of *A Tale of Two Cities* as a critical account of the novel itself, that is altogether appropriate. For the lines are not unselfconsciously supplying a descriptive formula but parodying such authoritative pronouncements, as the sentence itself reveals, once it breaks from those ponderous contrasts to the summary that dismisses them:

> It was the best of times, it was the worst of times, it was the age of wisdom, it was the age of foolishness, it was the epoch of belief, it was the epoch of

incredulity, it was the season of Light, it was the season of Darkness, it was the spring of hope, it was the winter of despair, we had everything before us, we had nothing before us, we were all going direct to Heaven, we were all going direct the other way—in short, the period was so far like the present period, that some of its noisiest authorities insisted on its being received, for good or for evil, in the superlative degree of comparison only.[10]

Merging a Carlylean critique of ossified language with a Dickensian alertness to the linguistic riches of humbug, the lines present such a successful parody of deadening, formulaic language that they have themselves become a formula.

Yet even amid the passage's hyperbolic rhetoric emerges the ambivalence about history and historical narrative that will characterize the novel, with its troubled fusion of Whiggishness (we are all going direct toward human progress) and a sense of history as merciless, brutal, and blind (we are going direct the other way—or at least we are not going direct at all).[11] The phrase that signifies our motion, "going direct," efficiently conflates the course and the temporality of our journey, providing the first token of the novel's concern with travel and speed. Such topics befit a novel that tackles the relationship between history and information transfer—and a work first issued in what Carlyle called "the 'tea-spoon-full' form" of short, rapid-fire installments in *All the Year Round*.[12] With its swift action, small cast, meticulous plotting, and sustained tone, *A Tale of Two Cities* is clearly a novel in which Dickens has learned to use the vehicle of tight weekly episodes successfully, a claim that would be harder to make for his earlier assays at the form, even the information-haunted *Hard Times*.

In addition to its recourse to hyperbole, the late eighteenth century resembles Dickens's present in its attention to the "messages" of "the spirits," the rapping of Dr. Johnson's "Cock-lane ghost" setting the pattern for the modern "spirits of this very year last past (supernaturally deficient in originality)" (*TTC*, 5). The novel's first reference to revolution materializes as a contrast to such dubious emanations: "Mere messages in the earthly order of events had lately come . . . from a congress of British subjects in America: which, strange to relate, have proved more important to the human race than any communications yet received through any of the chickens of the Cock-lane brood" (*TTC*, 5–6). In *A Tale of Two Cities*, the most portentous events, including revolutions themselves, begin as long-distance messages.

But if the novel's opening paragraphs highlight the parallels between past and present, the next ones make much of their divergences; the cruelty of the old order in France finds a parallel to an eighteenth-century England beset by daily murders and nightly highway robberies. "Thus did the year one thousand seven hundred and seventy-five conduct their Greatnesses"—the kings and queens of France and England—"and myriads of small creatures—the creatures of this chronicle among the rest—along the roads that lay before them" (*TTC*, 7). So ends the first chapter of the novel.

The "roads" here may sound metaphorical, the travels merely figurative. On the contrary, they announce the novel's fascination with transport and transmission, with direct goings and divagations—even beyond the Paris-London axis that organizes the narrative with its circulation of persons and messages. Now that the brief first chapter ("The Period") has set the historical scene, the next ("The Mail") conducts us to the plot, or rather bogs us down in it. For we begin by meeting on "the Dover road . . . on a Friday night late in November, . . . the first of the persons with whom this history has business": the repressed but good-hearted banker, Jarvis Lorry, as he tramps beside the Dover mail coach on a nighttime journey to Paris, forced with the other passengers to alight so that the mired horses can pull the "heavy" mail across the mud (*TTC*, 8). Dickens had supported one of the first attempts to run a telegraph cable from Dover to Calais, to allow weightless information to make the same London-to-Paris trip on which Lorry is bound. The maps included in the last chapter showed how the railway and telegraphic circuits between London and Dover looked in 1850. In contrast, the first scene of *A Tale of Two Cities* makes it clear that there is no question yet of the separation of communication from physical transport and its messy, material hindrances. What is the past like? To begin with: grimy, slow, obstructed.[13]

This opening scene approaches historical accuracy in strenuously negative terms, a tactic exemplified by Dickens's refusal here to sentimentalize the early days of his warmly remembered mail coaches. This seems surprising, and deliberate. In reality, in addition to offering "the most important advance in postal service during the latter part of the [eighteenth] century," "almost as important an innovation" as Hill's Penny Post, the adoption of the mail coach "marked a new era in postal facilities; it became the 'last word' in travel and in the carriage of mail until the railway, in its turn, displaced the horsed coach."[14] The coaching era reached its zenith in the 1830s, on the eve of the railways' arrival, and the telegraph's; "[w]hen mail-coaches began to fade away, the electric telegraph boldly raised its head."[15] A sort of monument to the coaching days that would end so soon, *The Pickwick Papers* (1836–37) includes a proleptic vision of ghostly mail coaches in the inset "Story of the Bagman's Uncle." In fact, the picaresque *Pickwick* names its protagonist, and itself, after a real Bath coach company bearing "the magic name of PICKWICK," as Sam Weller helpfully points out.[16]

The age of the coach and the turnpike roads offered mid-Victorians—elsewhere including Dickens—a forum for nostalgia for a kind of obsolete modernity, an age whose once impressive magnificence and speed had been superseded by the railway's release of subterranean energy. "The modern modes of travelling cannot compare with the mail-coach system in grandeur and power," claims De Quincey in "The English Mail-Coach, or the Glory of Motion" (1849), since we experience the railway's great velocity only as a form of "lifeless knowledge," mere external information about time and distance. "But seated on the old mail-coach," "we heard our speed, we saw it, we felt it."[17] In keeping with this focus on the phantasmagoria of bodily transport, De Quincey develops his essay's subject—recollections of riding as an outside passenger on the mail coaches—into an astonishing and complex "dream-fugue": on state power, on the force of news in the Napoleonic era, on the horror of collisions, on sudden death.[18] When "The English Mail-Coach" builds to an apocalyptic vision of a thundering car hurtling toward catastrophe and renewal, the sublime power of the careering mail coach merges with the resistless movements of the essay itself as it races away with the transfixed reader as its bewildered outside passenger.

In contrast, the first scene of *A Tale of Two Cities* approaches the mail coach as a system whose shortcomings are far more evident than its power; there is little glorious motion here, and any sense of terrifying speed will be transferred to the "furious recklessness" of the wicked Marquis's carriage as it careens down Paris's crowded streets (*TTC*, 113). This too is noteworthy. In reality, the English mail coaches had doubled the speed of the post almost as soon as they appeared; by the late eighteenth century, their velocity was regarded as so remarkable that some considered riding them "highly dangerous to the head, independently of the perils of an overturn."[19] Their punctuality became proverbial, for the mail coaches' adherence to tight schedules was not just a convenience but a "safeguard, the non-arrival at a stage at the appointed time being of itself a signal for raising a hue and cry."[20] And unlike the regular private stagecoaches, the mail coaches "could be relied upon to run to a close schedule in all weathers."[21] In the age of the mail coach, "[c]oaching became almost a science," exults Garvey's panegyric on modern innovation.[22]

Yet such regularity and speed enter the novel only negatively, via the coachman's keen frustration at not having topped Shooter's Hill by "[t]en minutes . . . past eleven" (*TTC*, 9). Galloping on horseback, Jerry Cruncher readily catches a mail coach expressly devised to outpace single riders bearing messages—the kind of system that had made "the post about the slowest conveyance in the country" before the days of the mail coach.[23] The century-long improvement of British roads appears in a similarly contrary fashion, as the intractable problem of road drainage in the age before Telford and McAdam. And the most prominent safety feature of the mail coaches— the provision of a guard in "his own particular perch behind the mail, . . . keeping an eye and a hand on the arm-chest before him, where a loaded blunderbuss lay at the top of six or eight loaded horse-pistols, deposited on a substratum of cutlass"—in the novel suggests only fear, unsafety, and the prospect of sudden violence (*TTC*, 9).

Moreover, for all the attention to these details, precise down to the strata of the guard's weapons case, there are two striking, and structuring, anachronisms here. First of all, on a wet November night in 1775 there simply could have been no "lumbering old mail-coach" making its way to Dover (*TTC*, 15). John Palmer only established the first of his "Mail Machines" in August 1784, with expansion from the Bath Road to other major routes (including Dover) the next year; before then, mail in England traveled via mounted post-boy, or occasionally on a slow cart.[24] For all Dickens's methodical setting of the historical scene, he has begun the action of *A Tale of Two Cities* by dispatching the Dover mail back in time by nearly a decade.

Dickens's second anachronism is equally significant. In his treatment of the late eighteenth-century mail coach, everyone aboard—especially the well-armed guard—trembles with fear of murderous highway robbers, haunted by the suspicion that the other travelers may be in league with them. To be sure, Palmer's mail coach system responded not just to a growing desire for speed but to the reality that robbers plagued both the post-boys and

conventional stagecoaches.[25] Shooter's Hill "bore for long years a particularly bad name as being the lurking-place of ferocious footpads, cutpurses,
[and] highwaymen . . . who rushed out from [its] leafy coverts and took liberal toll from wayfarers."[26] Yet in fact, with their speed and guards, the mail
coaches largely *ended* robbery of the mails; "no mail coach was robbed for
some years after their introduction."[27] While the coach was stopped for food
and drink or fresh horses, a guard might be distracted and letters or parcels
stolen, yet in practice armed bandits now presented little threat.[28] No doubt,
a lingering sense of "real danger from highwaymen" persisted during "the
early days of the mail-coach," but as De Quincey suggests, serious road accidents were the real risk of the coaches.[29]

Dickens has introduced the mail coach a decade before its time only
systematically to negate all of its benefits. In both historical and thematic
terms, then, the opening scene of *A Tale of Two Cities* points to an actuality
beyond what it depicts, a coming reality of expanded, streamlined intercommunication.[30] In this way, the scene's strategic anachronism expresses both
the novel's informatic consciousness and the theme of blocked communication that the text will soon proclaim. For it is not only the Dover road that
is miry and obstructed as Jarvis Lorry—whose name identifies him with a
country wagon or Victorian railway truck—trudges beside the coach:

> There was a steaming mist in all the hollows, and it had roamed in its
> forlornness up the hill, like an evil spirit, seeking rest and finding none.
> A clammy and intensely cold mist, it made its slow way through the air in
> ripples that visibly followed and overspread one another, as the waves of
> an unwholesome sea might do. It was dense enough to shut out everything
> from the light of the coach-lamps but these its own workings, and a few
> yards of road, and the reek of the labouring horses steamed into it, as if they
> had made it all. (*TTC*, 8)

The turbid sea will soon provide Dickens with a recurring figure for the
"black ocean" of the Revolutionary mob (*TTC*, 242). Here, the simile aids
the striking condensation of the moral atmosphere into the physical environment. The result is something more encompassing and disconcerting
than Ruskin's pathetic fallacy: a setting enfolded and circumfused by a metaphor, something one might with literary and meteorological accuracy call
troposphere.

The sealike mist shuts out nearly everything except the rippling transmission of its own mistiness, a property with characterological corollaries and narrative ramifications. For the social and psychological milieu of this scene turns out to be as foggy and obstructed as the weather and terrain. As if merely by way of illustrating the age's savagery, "The Period" has described the burglaries and highway robberies that took place "every night" in the England of 1775 (*TTC*, 6). With a deductive narrative logic so direct it is almost disorienting, "The Mail" moves us from the historical general to the fictional specific, presenting the atmosphere of mutual suspicion and self-enclosure among the guard, driver, and riders of the Dover mail. "Not one of the three" passengers, swaddled with heavy clothes and shod in "jackboots," "could have said, from anything he saw, what either of the other two was like," for each one's head is "wrapped to the cheekbones and over the ears" (*TTC*, 9). Again, the physical shrouding crystallizes the psychological: "each was hidden under almost as many wrappers from the eyes of the mind, as from the eyes of the body, of his two companions" (*TTC*, 9).

In this scene, the narrative carefully neglects to penetrate either the physical mist or the clothed concealment, as if it too were another suspicious character aboard the Dover mail, equally constrained by the corporeal limits of vision and knowledge. The simulated embodiment of the narrative limits readers' perceptions as well; like the coach's anxious passengers and guard, we have no reason not to imagine that the approaching Jerry Cruncher comes to raid the coach or that Jarvis Lorry, the particular "passenger booked by this history," is part of the scheme (*TTC*, 10). Technically and thematically, the novel emphasizes the potential for suspicion and misunderstanding in a world mired in matter, a world in which communication is heavily encumbered by the body's material movements and limited perceptions. As the novel's opening lines suggest, such a world may include a proliferation of discourse but also entail a grave lack of real knowledge.

Unspeakable Subjects

The scene's murky atmosphere helps prepare us for the startling declaration that opens the next chapter, "The Night Shadows," the end of the novel's initial installment: "A wonderful fact to reflect upon, that every human creature is constituted to be that profound secret and mystery to every other"

(*TTC*, 14). In contrast to Victorian novels' familiar calls for a rapprochement between characters, between classes, between readership and represented subject—part of what Ermarth identifies as their realism—this passage proclaims that human beings are essentially unknowable. People are simply "so constituted"; what we have here is more than a failure to communicate. The unmoored deictic *that* in "that profound secret and mystery" underscores the point, pointing us toward a referent that is nowhere to be found.

To emphasize its claim, the next lines of the novel even introduce the first-person into the narration, the first and last time *A Tale of Two Cities* will employ this narrative mode. It is as if the shadowy, pensive third-person narrator of "The Mail" has stepped out of the fog and, confirming the virtual personhood that constrained his observations, now reveals himself in the forlorn flesh. In a broad sense this sort of play with the status of the narrator, the kind of shift that energized *Jane Eyre*'s spiritual telegraphy, appears regularly in Dickens's work. Audrey Jaffe's study of Dickens and narrative omniscience argues that enigmatic, semi-omniscient narrators and focal figures such as Boz, Master Humphrey, and Florence Dombey grant the reader the comfort of identification with their superior position, since they know the other characters but remain somehow invisible. Yet in *A Tale of Two Cities*, a novel Jaffe does not discuss, the passage immediately following the "wonderful fact" inserts the first-person pronoun into the narration in order to *deny* the possibility of knowing other people.

If the passage's sentiment and rhetoric occasionally echo Carlyle,[31] the narrative voice is a recognizable descendant of the Boz who wandered London as an alternately sardonic and meditative flaneur. Yet the Boz who revels in his ability to read life from its external signs has been replaced by a more chastened narrative persona:

> A solemn consideration, when I enter a great city by night, that every one
> of those darkly clustered houses encloses its own secret; that every room in
> every one of them encloses its own secret; that every beating heart in the
> hundreds of thousands of breasts there, is, in some of its imaginings, a secret
> to the heart nearest it! Something of the awfulness, even of Death itself,
> is referable to this. No more can I turn the leaves of this dear book that I
> loved, and vainly hope in time to read it all. No more can I look into the
> depths of this unfathomable water, wherein, as momentary lights glanced
> into it, I have had glimpses of buried treasure and other things submerged.

It was appointed that the book should shut with a spring, for ever and for ever, when I had read but a page. It was appointed that the water should be locked in an eternal frost, when the light was playing on its surface, and I stood in ignorance on the shore. My friend is dead, my neighbour is dead, my love, the darling of my soul, is dead; it is the inexorable consolidation and perpetuation of the secret that was always in that individuality, and which I shall carry in mine to my life's end. (*TTC*, 14–15)

It is a radically diminished Boz who delivers the "Night Shadows" threnody, or an Asmodean Shadow whose vision is obstructed and whose wings are clipped.

In this "Night Shadows" passage, the essential unknowability of human beings makes death absolute and terrifying, since it is the termination of a story we never knew; it brings to an end the tantalizing glimpses of others' interiority we have caught during life. The passage makes it sound as if it is "only death which really fulfills what the person always was"—but this subjective essence still remains out of sight.[32] Human beings are books that can only be read in fragments, inland seas that offer glimpses of submerged treasure but are fated to congeal into permafrost. The metaphor of the book turns people into cryptic texts (like the tightly bound Jarvis Lorry who is "booked by" the novel), while the image of people as bodies of water will be dramatically redeployed by the novel's treatment of the Revolution, during which individual people with their secret hearts become potential tributaries to the rising flood of mob.[33]

J. M. Rignall points out that in some sense the novel's statement of the "metaphysical mystery of individuality" goes too far, since Dickens's "imperious command of his characters is never subject to epistemological uncertainty, and even the most estranged figures, like Dr. Manette and Carton, are in the end not mysterious but knowable and known."[34] Rignall is surely right that the passage fails as a credible description of the characters within the novel itself. Moreover, notes Catherine Gallagher, it offers a paradoxical "reassurance that the private will always be there and yet will always be just beyond our full comprehension"—and therefore that we need novels to help give us access to private life.[35] We hear regularly about characters' mysteriousness to each other, and about the secrecy their selves enfold: Lorry and Lucie Manette are invisible to each other even when they are in the same room (*TTC*, 34); Lorry cannot identify a fellow passenger from the Mail in court (*TTC*, 71); Dr. Manette warns an amorous Darnay that Lucie's heart remains a cipher even to him, since "mysteries arise out of close love, as well as out of wide division" (*TTC*, 140); Carton can scarcely explicate himself for Darnay ("Upon my life," he exclaims, prophetically) but uses his "inscrutability" to unnerve Barsad the spy (*TTC*, 214, 314). The ambience of the novel makes Carton's life-saving resemblance to Darnay—especially in an age before photography could help stabilize the lineaments of visual identity—less miraculous than skeptical readers often take it to be.

The characters may be perplexing to each other, but they can hardly be that to their readers. Yet what the opening of the early "Night Shadows" chapter does offer is a plausible indication of the reasons why *A Tale of Two Cities* works as it does, of the apprehensions and assumptions that underlie its project of narrating fictional selves. The novel's treatment of individuals as dead to each other, locked in a sarcophagus of subjectivity, accords with its emphasis on inanimate and violated bodies as well as with its focus on the explosion of subjects into violent Revolution. Even the *Tale*'s endlessly reiterated resurrection-motif provides no comforting harbinger of rebirth but orchestrates a grotesque reciprocal movement between life and death. While dead bodies may leave their graves, as with Jerry's body-snatching or the recalling of Manette to life, living ones may house something deadened automatized, out of reach.[36]

Treating the interplay between subjectivity and the death of the subject, the novel turns private life and self-expression into a realm of mediation and media effects. Take for instance the first character with whom *A Tale of Two Cities* "has business," Jarvis Lorry. The novel has business with him because Lorry presents himself as all business, mechanically reiterating his putative status as impassive "man of business" and deputy of Tellson's bank in Paris and London. "I have been a man of business, ever since I have been a man," meditates Lorry after many pages of adverting to that state; "indeed, I may say that I was a man of business when a boy" (*TTC*, 322). Even his physiognomy records his condition, once the narrative unwraps it: "A face, habitually suppressed and quieted, was still lighted up . . . by a pair of moist bright eyes that it must have cost their owner, in years gone by, some pains to drill to the composed and reserved expression of Tellson's Bank" (*TTC*, 20). "Drilling" himself over the course of years, Lorry has both learned the correct countenance through bodily discipline and bored this visage onto

his face. The Frenchman who writes of Tellson's as "the great bank of Til-
son" gets it right, for the bank itself—"very small, very dark, very ugly, very
incommodious"—is a prisonlike till, and Lorry is indisputably its son (*TTC*,
250, 55). As sympathetic as he is, he will refuse to harbor the Manettes with
him at Tellson's in Revolutionary Paris, lest they compromise the House
through their connection to the jailed Darnay; it is "[o]ne of the first considerations" of his "business mind" (*TTC*, 274).

The point is not merely that bachelorhood and business life are supposed
to have instilled in Lorry a habitual repression that Dickens may sentimen-
tally belie with "bright eyes" and an affectionate disposition, making Lorry a
kind of pallid study for the glorious Wemmick in *Great Expectations*. Rather,
they allow for a set of technologies of the self, including "quiet business
confidence," that "business mind," the "business eye" (*TTC*, 12, 274, 311).
In fact, as Lorry himself puts it, they permit the conversion of the self into
nothing more than a technology, a medium. Revealing to Lucie Manette the
existence of the father she had long assumed dead, Lorry declares himself
only a businessman going about his work, and urges her to regard him as "a
mere machine" (*TTC*, 25). By a similar logic, he tries to report her father's
story as if it were the story of someone else, or as if it were not a story at
all but simply a mass of business information presented by an automaton or
conveyed via one-way transmission:

> "Miss Manette, I am a man of business. I have a business charge to acquit
> myself of. In your reception of it, don't heed me any more than if I was a
> speaking machine—truly, I am not much else. I will, with your leave, relate
> to you, miss, the story of one of our customers."
>
> "Story!"
>
> He seemed wilfully to mistake the word she had repeated, when he
> added, in a hurry, "Yes, customers; in the banking business we usually call
> our connexion our customers." (*TTC*, 25)

Twenty years before the invention of the phonograph, Lorry presents
himself in dictaphonic terms, as an international business machine. In the
context of the novel, Dickens has appropriated another aspect of the late
eighteenth-century media ecology, a fascination with articulate automata.
"Between 1770 and 1790, four persons in Europe built working speaking
machines, apparently without knowledge of each other"—projects that

would help inspire the mid-nineteenth century's very different technologies of sound reproduction.[37]

Or we could say that Lorry presents himself as that predecessor of the Dictaphone, *writing*—in its aspect as the original mechanism for simulating speech in the absence of a living, present speaker. Machinically conveying the story of Dr. Manette, he offers it as a story that is not Dr. Manette's at all, the secret history of no one:

> if Monsieur Manette had not died; if he had suddenly and silently disappeared; if he had been spirited away; if it had not been difficult to guess to what dreadful place, though no art could trace him; if he had an enemy in some compatriot who could exercise a privilege . . . for instance, the privilege of filling up blank forms for the consignment of any one to the oblivion of a prison for any length of time; . . . —then the history of your father would have been the history of this unfortunate gentleman, the Doctor of Beauvais. (*TTC*, 26–27)

Both Lorry's mechanical pose and his impersonal discourse are meant to moderate Lucie's shock upon learning that her father is alive—or to give her space for a brief fit of catatonia as abstract information becomes daughterly knowledge. But the techniques also permit a unexpectedly incisive reflection on the workings of fiction itself, as Lorry offers himself as a vehicle, a virtual medium. A character insists that he is only a contrivance that gives the rough effect of producing speech, a device that can only simulate a conversational position ("Story!"—"Yes, customers . . . "); meanwhile, stripped of a speaking subject, dislodged from a distinct individual character, and minimized as any kind of private "story" at all, Lorry's disclosure of the fate of a supposititious Manette poses itself as repeatable, hypothetical, automated language. Strictly speaking, all of this is perfectly correct, since it is precisely the case when it comes to a character's written dialogue and to a story in realist fiction.

Dr. Manette, the nonsubject of the nonstory Lorry isn't really there to recite to Lucie, turns out to be Lorry's counterpart. "[B]uried alive for eighteen years" in the Bastille, the unresponsive Manette upon his release seems to be an automatized subject, an unspeaking machine (*TTC*, 19). His "perception" grown "dull" and "mechanical," his words bereft of "the life and resonance of the human voice" and hollowed out "like a voice underground," Manette is speech turned to a "feeble echo," the very shade of a night shadow (*TTC*, 42). "No human intelligence could have read the mysteries of his mind, in the scared blank wonder of his face," the narrator concludes (*TTC*, 51). Manette eventually returns to himself, but imprisonment has made him into an extreme example of the general case, of a subjectivity that cannot be spoken, a book that cannot be opened. Gingerly discussing the matter with Lorry, who in businesslike fashion introduces the topic of Manette's obsessive shoemaking as a "case" of automatized blacksmithing by a "friend of mine" (*TTC*, 207), Manette admits—holding to the third-person—that he would like to impart his silent suffering and "secret brooding" but avers that such a thing would be "quite impossible" (*TTC*, 209). In this novel, even the behavior of the most blandly sane character may have something incommunicable and automatic to it. Charles Darnay longs to return to France even before he receives the letter from Postmaster Gabelle that gives him the excuse of aristocratic duty; Paris draws him like a "Loadstone Rock" (*TTC*, 252). If the characters in *A Tale of Two Cities* never quite bear out its statement of the fundamental mystery of the self, they at least allow the novel to remind us of it again and again—and to express the depth of that mystery, paradoxically, through the very automatism that even Victorian critics could treat as a mark of the supposed superficiality of Dickensian characterization.[38]

Memory Devices

According to *A Tale of Two Cities*, the fact that we can never know the people around us makes them like books we cannot read, seas we cannot plumb, and like the dead in their graves; from our vantage point, the living seem buried alive. This framework for the self adds new significance to the portentous message Jarvis Lorry gives Jerry Cruncher at the end of the misty second chapter: "RECALLED TO LIFE" (*TTC*, 12). As Jerry recognizes, the note struck by "recalled to life" intersects with the resurrection images that the novel will propagate in a range of registers: from the release of Dr. Manette and the double rescues of Darnay, to Jerry's anatomical body-snatching and the reappearance of John Barsad/Solomon Pross/Roger Cly after his riotous funeral. But in addition to suggesting the novel's tirelessly repeated resurrection motif, the phrase "recalled to life" betokens not simply a reentry but a recollection into existence. Manette, long forgotten and forgetful, is remembered into life by the "golden thread" of Lucie, his link from the present to a past and a future (*TTC*, 83).

The ambitious barrister Stryver nicknames his aide-de-camp "Memory" Carton for his prodigious ability to master the facts of a case, even in the midst of his rather hazy dissipations (*TTC*, 92). But for the novel's readers, the name "Memory Carton" is meant to evoke "The Golden Thread" of loving remembrance. Before hitting upon "A Tale of Two Cities," Dickens had considered both phrases as possible titles for the novel; memory seems always to have been central in his designs. And other designs too attest to the centrality of this strand of the *Tale*. On Phiz's triptychlike cover for the novel's monthly parts, the thread of Lucie's needlework winds from her own panel on the center-right, around the lattice of scenes from the novel, connecting a shoemaking Dr. Manette, a figure of Liberty, an execution scene, a murderous rioter, the robbery of a grave. Both the cover's symmetrical organization and Lucie's thread mark out counterparts among the panels: Manette buried alive and Jerry's resurrection-work, Liberty and riot. The thread that begins with Lucie's needle ends its long-distance connections by merging into the knitting of her parallel in the arrangement: Madame Defarge.[39]

For Sydney and Lucie are not the novel's only figures of memory. The intently remembering Madame Defarge trumps both of them; already armed with a memory to rival Carton's, she knits up her knowledge into a more permanent form. As her husband brags,

> if madame my wife undertook to keep the register in her memory alone, she would not lose a word of it—not a syllable of it. Knitted, in her own stitches and her own symbols, it will always be as plain to her as the sun. Confide in Madame Defarge. It would be easier for the weakest poltroon that lives, to erase himself from existence, than to erase one letter of his name or crimes from the knitted register of Madame Defarge. (*TTC*, 179)

In his night thoughts, the novel's mournful Boz lamented the unknowability of every individual, a condition that made the specter of death more terrible. Here, in contrast, Defarge exults in his wife's ability to collect information that will long outlast its subjects. Like Carton, Madame Defarge has an unerring memory; unlike him, she recognizes that turning memory into history calls for a firmer medium. Since she knows that writing is history in the making, Madame Defarge sticks to her knitting and never drops a stitch. The novel's carefully devised plot confirms the Defarges' sense of the inexorable power of texts. For, like Lorry's fantasy of existence as a "speaking machine" whose inconvenient physical presence may be disregarded, writing in *A Tale of Two Cities* has the marked power to overtake and displace the body and psychology of the writer. The ever-practical Lorry is prudent to carry "not a scrap of writing" when he goes to France (*TTC*, 29).

Although the darkness of the image makes it difficult to tell, the incarcerated, solitary, engrossed Dr. Manette on the title page of the novel's volume edition is not at work making shoes but busy writing his story. In the Bastille, long before the first scene of the novel, he is making his secret declaration of the aristocratic Evrémondes' acts of rape and murder, the crimes committed against Madame Defarge's family. Manette should have learned from experience, for he owes his very imprisonment to the perils of letter-writing. Having composed a private letter of complaint about the deeds of the Evrémonde brothers, he returns home from hand-delivering the letter to a Minister only to be apprehended that very night by the Marquis St. Evrémonde, who burns Manette's letter in his face and sends him to the Bastille for nearly twenty years. His imprisonment for sending a letter alludes to the notorious "*cabinet noir*," the semi-secret "black chamber" of the French post office in which letters were read by authorities of the ancien régime.[40] Although postal spying and censorship became one of the official grievances of 1789, Robespierre's Committee of Public Safety made the violation of private correspondence an official policy, and a new black chamber long survived both Robespierre and the Revolution.[41]

Manette's prison letter is composed under very different circumstances, etched on bits of paper "in scrapings of soot and charcoal . . . mixed with blood" and hidden in a wall, but it will meet with a similar fate (*TTC*, 331). During the storming of the Bastille, Defarge liberates this second letter; Manette's direction of it to "[s]ome pitying hand" who "may find it . . . when I and my sorrows are dust" determines neither its audience nor the use to which it will be put (*TTC*, 331). At the tribunal that will sentence Darnay to be executed, Dr. Manette now hears the text of his own letter, which was excavated without his knowledge, read into evidence against his will. "[H]is eyes fixed on the reader," he watches as his words issue from another's mouth, from a juridical speaking machine whose particular identity is unimportant and never mentioned (*TTC*, 330). The eyes of the courtroom are "intent upon the Doctor, who saw none of them," become in his rapt attention like the text that now reifies his buried, automated subjectivity—able to be read in public but not to vary or respond (*TTC*, 330).

Written a decade into his imprisonment, Manette's letter repeatedly proclaims the fidelity of his remembrance down to the smallest particular: "my memory is exact and circumstantial"; "[m]y memory is circumstantial and unshaken[:] I try it with these details, and I see them all . . . as I saw them all that night"; "[t]here is no confusion or failure in my memory; it can recal [*sic*], and could detail, every word that was ever spoken between me and those brothers" (*TTC*, 331, 335, 340). Drawing on the legal formula of a will to make his testament, Manette "solemnly declare[s] that [he is] at this time in the possession of [his] right mind," and the details he provides demonstrate his mental balance and sustain the truthfulness of his account of what happened "[o]ne cloudy moonlight night, in the first week of December (I think the twenty-second of the month)" (*TTC*, 331).

Yet the doctor's notes also correctly diagnose the imminent loss of his faculties, inferring "from terrible warnings I have noted in myself that my reason will not long remain unimpaired" (*TTC*, 331). Ostensibly, Manette writes in the first place because he knows that his mind will soon fail, but his symptoms remain wholly vague. In the novel's timeline, it seems more as if, having externalized his thoughts and experience in the medium of the letter, Manette drains his subjectivity to the point of vacancy, repressing or forgetting what the letter takes such pains to detail. With Madame Defarge's total recall and Manette's recovered memory, *A Tale of Two Cities* treats the inability to forget as the main cause of revolutionary violence.[42]

The novel's action commenced with an instance of the slowness of the mail, a phenomenon that merged into the refusal of other minds to deliver their secret thoughts from "The Night Shadows." Now these factors come together again still more forcefully. Buried in the dirt more deeply than the Dover mail's wheels, Manette's letter takes a quarter century to be delivered. But when it does, the Revolutionary tribunal brings to light "The Substance of the Shadow"—the name of the chapter composed almost wholly of the uninterrupted reading of the letter. The logic of Jerry Cruncher's peculiar double career now becomes clear. "What have you been, besides a messenger?" asks Lorry once his suspicions are aroused (*TTC*, 318). To be "Jerry the messenger," a medium bearing others' information, is also to be some-thing else: a grave-digger, a body-snatcher (*TTC*, 61). Thanks to Manette's exteriorized memories, Darnay is recalled to death. "The Prisoners!" chant the revolutionaries as they take the Bastille, "The Records!" (*TTC*, 225). The illustration of Manette in his cell turns out to be the image of a man authoring himself into oblivion as he scribbles out his son-in-law's death warrant.

If in the "Night Shadows" passage it is a melancholy thing not to be known, it may be a worse thing to be known. Perhaps Madame Defarge is right to record her intelligence in the private code of her knitting; that me-dium is the functional equivalent of her flawless but self-enclosed personal memory, a recording web that no one else will ever be able to unravel. But against the mechanization of selves, the frozen sea of imprisoned interiority, and the violent agency of the belated letter, *A Tale of Two Cities* has appre-hended and will execute its narrative project. It will deliver its final message by means of a special narrative device, a speaking machine assembled from the remains of a character and his inaccessible subjectivity. This medium will go beyond the fiction of the novel to convey history's information as Madame Defarge's knitting never does. But before climbing the scaffold to arrive at the sudden informatic transformation of Sydney Carton, we must consider a device that embodies the Revolutionary age's propensity at once to foreshadow and to forestall the world of modern information: a textual technology that visibly separated alphabetic transmission from storage, and the first machine to bear the name *télégraphe*.

A Tale of Two Telegraphs

Victorian invocations of the electric telegraph often treat it as simultane-ously objective and eerie, wholly truthful yet utterly mysterious. Not only the vehicle of electricity but also the genealogy of telegraphy as a concept would have encouraged a particular sense of the ghostliness of the electric telegraph. For the machines of Cooke and Wheatstone or Morse were nei-ther the first to offer a systematic framework for the conveyance of messages far faster than they could have been materially transported, nor the first textual network to decouple information storage from transfer, nor even the first communication devices called "telegraphs." McLuhan's "laws" of media specify that new media forms retrieve, enhance, and obsolesce earlier ones.[43] Strangely, the first medium reclaimed, amplified, and superseded by electric telegraphy was the "telegraph"—that is, the optical telegraph system of the late eighteenth century.

The optical telegraph "was one of the most important technological innovations to have been spawned by the French Revolution"—"[a]long with the guillotine."[44] In 1793, Claude Chappe had presented France's National Convention with his new plan for transmitting messages via a network of hilltop semaphore stations, a system he came to call the *télégraphe*, for distance-writing. Perhaps the most noteworthy aspect of Chappe's invention is that, as with Hill's Uniform Penny Post four decades later, none of its elements were truly new. Chappe's system might readily have been invented thousands of years before. The only new thing was the "demand" for such a telecommunication system in the late eighteenth century—and specifically, within a large, centralized state uncommonly anxious about enemies within and without.[45]

Carlyle's *French Revolution* (1837), warmly cited in Dickens's preface to *A Tale of Two Cities* as the novel's main historical source, introduces Chappe's telegraph as part of a sequence about technological progress and savagery in the Revolution, a "flame-picture" in which the wonders of decimal weights and measures or hot-air balloons appear alongside new tanning techniques for the skins of guillotine victims:

> What . . . is this that Engineer Chappe is doing, in the Park of Vincennes? . . . [H]e has scaffolding set up, has posts driven in; wooden arms with elbow joints are jerking and fugling in the air, in the most rapid mysterious manner! Citoyens ran up, suspicious. Yes, O Citoyens, we are signaling: it is a device this, worthy of the Republic; a thing for what we will call *Far-writing* without the aid of postbags; in Greek, it shall be named Telegraph.—*Télégraphe sacré*! answers Citoyenism. . . . [46]

As Carlyle notes, the first response of the French citizenry to the cryptic messages of the telegraph was to demolish it and chase down Chappe as a spy—a real-life example of the era's ability to simultaneously instigate and impede the flow of information. In Carlyle, this glimpse of the telegraph also seems to prompt the puzzled observation, soon afterward, that "*La Révolution* is but so many Alphabetic Letters; a thing nowhere to be laid hands on, to be clapped under lock and key: where is it? what is it?" (*FR,* 2:376). Revolution is a word but circulates like an impalpable idea.

The Republic tested and adopted Chappe's system, Napoleon extended it, and soon other countries including England produced their own versions, most using the optical telegraph chiefly for official military and governmental communication. In England, the Admiralty built and maintained telegraph stations, although they never coalesced into a unified network.[47] These telegraphs were impressive enough to begin lending their name to newspapers and fast coaches almost immediately as a byword for speed. But their shortcomings soon became clear, including their helplessness against the darkness of the night and the vagaries of the weather, especially in wet, foggy England (the same conditions Dickens imagines hindering the Dover mail). As one early plan for an electric telegraph network had pointed out in 1837, "existing . . . [optical] Telegraphic communication has . . . been limited by the extent of human vision"; a new power was needed to overcome the limits of our physical senses.[48] Only in France was optical telegraphy well enough established to delay the development of an electric telegraph network.[49] Yet their shared name and function meant that the rise of electric telegraphy replaced a technology of large-scale, public transmission with something far less tangible, something that supplanted brute visibility with invisible pulses of electricity. The two telegraphs shared a basic purpose, but their methods were so different that the disparity might help encourage a sense of something sublime, of inscrutable signals rushing under the threshold of human perception, once the electric telegraph superseded the earlier system but retained its name.

When as early as *Sketches by Boz* and *The Pickwick Papers* Dickens invokes the telegraph as a favorite metaphor for people communicating via look and gesture rather than by words, he means the optical telegraph. Mr. Pickwick dislikes the "telegraphic answer" given him when he asks what will happen if he loses the case of *Bardell v. Pickwick* (his solicitor "smiled, took a very long pinch of snuff, stirred the fire, shrugged his shoulders, and remained expressively silent"); Bob Sawyer engages in "various telegraphic communications" with the laughing crowd outside the carriage; Sam Weller and his father "exchanged a complete code of telegraph nods and gestures" as they conspire to place Sam in the Fleet Prison with Pickwick.[50] These examples translate the semaphore of optical telegraphs, with their mounted flags, arms, or shutters, into a comically stylized language of bodily gesture, a coded communication that sidesteps speech or writing. Dickens casually refers to this sort of visual "telegraphy" in many works, generally treating it as either absurdly obvious or ludicrously cryptic. With its basic fusion of hilltop visibility and elaborate coding—Chappe's system for instance used not alphabetic signals but long codebooks to translate thousands of different words and phrases—the optical telegraph could readily offer a figure for both.

As a favorite metaphor, such gestural telegraphy appears throughout the Dickens corpus; it is not surprising to find it invoked as a momentary reference point in *A Tale of Two Cities*. But the novel's setting and thematic concerns place Dickens's optical telegraph in a new framework, one that connects the telegraph to the text's fascination with speed and transmission, with the machinery of communication, with secrecy and bodily expression. It also identifies the telegraph with the power of the novel's principal villain and embodiment of Revolutionary violence, its figure for fatal recording and merciless retribution, Madame Defarge. After the profiteer Foulon, having faked his death, is recalled to official custody, the news spreads with the speed of that crucial Revolutionary information system, the Parisian street. "As if a train of powder laid from the outermost bound of the Saint Antoine Quarter to the wine-shop door, had been suddenly fired, a fast-spreading murmur came rushing along" (*TTC*, 231). And when the Defarges lead their neighbors to the Hall of Examination to view Foulon's questioning, Madame Defarge transcends her function as recorder to become the center of an optical telegraph system that transmits her sentiments and attitudes to the crowd:

> The people immediately behind Madame Defarge, explaining the cause of her satisfaction to those behind them, and those again explaining to others, and those to others, the neighbouring streets resounded with the clapping of hands. Similarly, during two or three hours of drawl, and the winnowing of many bushels of words, Madame Defarge's frequent expressions of impatience were taken up, with marvellous quickness, at a distance: the more readily, because certain men who had by some wonderful exercise of agility climbed up the external architecture to look in from the windows, knew Madame Defarge well, and acted as a telegraph between her and the crowd outside the building. (*TTC*, 233)

In the real history of the French Revolution, the arrest and brutal murder of Foulon, which occurred a little more than a week after the triumphant storming of the Bastille, was an ominous moment in the conflict's initial phase. Going further, *A Tale of Two Cities* makes it not merely a token of mob violence but a critical event in the rapid dissemination of revolution. With "marvellous" swiftness, Madame Defarge's visual telegraph registers "at a distance" the impatient desire for greater speed.[51] And so, in a telegraphic trice, Foulon is seized by the Defarges—an abduction "known directly, to the furthest confines of the crowd"—and promptly but clumsily lynched by the mob that "take[s] up" Madame Defarge's "expressions" and unspoken desires (*TTC*, 234). In McLuhan's terms, we can identify this system as a "cool medium," one that operates in low definition—and demands the most frenzied form of audience participation.[52] Where is *La Révolution*? Carlyle locates it in the "Madness that dwells in the hearts of men" (*FR*, 2:376), but Dickens in this passage finds it in a virtual telegraph based on the external expressions of a character's body.

In a novel that conflates the difficulties of communication with living death, little distance would seem to separate the Revolutionary telegraph from "a certain movable framework with a sack and a knife in it," another new machine that promised speed and consistency (*TTC*, 6). Only a few chapters earlier, Madame Defarge had reassured her husband that the time for revenge was approaching more reliably than the Dover mail: "although it is a long time on the road, it is on the road and coming" (*TTC*, 185). Now the telegraph becomes the ultimate tool for visually disseminating the violent, theatrical self-expression that English commentators since Edmund Burke associated with the revolution. With its "ripples that visibly followed and overspread one another," the heavy mist of the "Night Shadows" becomes the optical telegraph's antitype, a system that radiates opacity and nontransmission—but one that might have protected against the marriage of disinterred knowledge, mass public dissemination, and sudden violence the novel links with the machinery of revolution. In its climactic final scene, the novel will offer an alternative mechanism, a virtual device that turns a character's self-sacrifice into a device for the transmission of disembodied information.

Memory Carton, Recalled to Life

Having witnessed the excesses of the Revolution, especially its disastrous deflation of the price fetched by corpses, the former resurrection-man Jerry proclaims his contrition: "A man don't see all this here a goin' on dreadful round him, in the way of Subjects without heads, dear me, plentiful enough fur to bring the price down to porterage and hardly that, without havin' his serious thoughts of things" (*TTC*, 337). When subjects lose their heads, bodies become worth nothing more than "porterage," mere physical conveyance. As if in response to Jerry's renunciation of resurrection-work, the end of the novel provides its own version of the raising and reuse of the dead. The plot of *A Tale of Two Cities*, the motifs of living death and revivification, the recognition of the machinic possibilities of characters and their stories, and the emphasis on information transfer as ideal or anxiety or impossibility, all come together in the famous death scene of Sydney Carton, the realization of what Dickens's preface calls the "main idea" of the tale (*TTC*, 397).[53] For the Victorians, a "carton" is not a cardboard box, but a paper target, a bulls-eye, dead center. Or, more generally, a carton is transformed paper, "layers" of it "pressed until they have attained the sturdiness of cardboard or pasteboard . . . a kind of papier-mâché" created to present the illusion of solidity.[54]

Carton's surname may even offer a Lorry-like hint of his final mode of transport, "the death-carts" that deliver the day's victims to the guillotine (*TTC*, 384). These are the novel's infamous "tumbrils"; thanks to *A Tale of Two Cities*, observed Orwell, "the very word 'tumbril' has a murderous sound; one forgets that a tumbril is only a sort of farm-cart."[55] In a phantasmagoric flight of historical fancy, the novel imagines the inexorable tumbrils turned back into "what they were": "the carriages of absolute monarchs, the equipages of feudal nobles, the toilettes of flaring Jezebels . . . " (*TTC*, 385). But such a reversal of history would be impossible. "Changeless and hopeless, the tumbrils roll along," and history keeps pace with them (*TTC*, 385). In this novel obsessed with transport, the character who represents the inescapability of the Revolution and the dark innocence of its peasant partakers is a humble "mender of roads" (*TTC*, 181).

Purchasing the drugs that allow him to stupefy Darnay and take his place on the tumbril, Carton possesses "the settled manner of a tired man, who had wandered and struggled and got lost, but who at length struck into his road and saw its end" (*TTC*, 325). What helps to clear that road is the Manette-like fracture of writing between authorship and material inscription. As he drugs his double, Carton makes him take dictation, enacting their exchange of identity by recruiting the fading Darnay to inscribe Carton's last letter, a suicide note without a "date" and addressed "[t]o no one" (*TTC*, 365). Darnay complies, even as "his memory" becomes "impaired, or his faculties disordered"; as the scene presents it, the act of dictation itself seems to evacuate Darnay's subjectivity and leave him unconscious (*TTC*, 366). Passing as Darnay, Carton remains as unidentifiable as a passenger on the Dover mail decades earlier, but now there is no question of a message of recall to stop his journey in its tracks.

From the Dover mail to the tumbrils, the novel's conveyances take us to "the foot of the same scaffold" with Carton, where "[o]ne of the most remarkable sufferers by the same axe—a woman—had asked . . . not long before, to be allowed to write down the thoughts that were inspiring her" (*TTC*, 389). It is an impulse far more authentic and intriguing, the novel implies, than the behavior of those prisoners fixated on outward mien and gesture even at their last moments, "so heedful of their looks that they cast upon the multitude such glances as they have seen in theatres, and in pictures" (*TTC*, 385). *A Tale of Two Cities* rejects the outwardness of drama and bodily expression in favor of a different mode of communication.[56]

With the novel's mention of the sufferer who sought to transcribe her dying thoughts comes a final reminder that Carlyle was here first. *The French Revolution* records that on 8 November 1793 the Girondin Jeanne-Marie Phlipon Roland asked "at the foot of the scaffold . . . for pen and paper, 'to write the strange thoughts that were rising in her': a remarkable request; which was refused" (*FR*, 2:339–40). Astounded by the audacity and strange grace of her petition, Carlyle imagines it as the sanctified death scene of a converted rationalist: "Biography will long remember that trait of asking for a pen 'to write the strange thoughts that were rising in her.' It is as a little light-beam, shedding softness, and a kind of sacredness, over all that preceded: so in her too there was an Unnameable; she too was a Daughter of the Infinite; there were mysteries which Philosophism had not dreamt of!" (*FR*, 2:340). For our part, we might view Madame Roland, an avid prison writer, as an autobiographical Scheherazade hoping to document her last moment, an act which in turn will have to be recorded. The task would be potentially endless, since it is impossible to narrate the moments of one's own death, at least outside the pages of Eliot's "The Lifted Veil." But Madame Roland's request is rejected. Never written down, her final reflections are forever lost to history, yet they allow Carlyle to fill in the gap with the thoughts that the incident raises in him.

Citing her petition, this example of unwritten writing, Dickens introduces the novel's final passage, breaking off from the action just *after* the moment at which Carton becomes victim number twenty-three of the guillotine that day: "If he had given any utterance to his [thoughts], and they were prophetic, they would have been these" (*TTC*, 389). Placed in quotation marks, the vision that follows is a disembodied, imaginary monologue on the scaffold—a speech that the novel describes as unuttered, a vision that like Madame Roland's memoir remains invisible to history. In it, the (non)speaker sees the fortunes of friends and enemies, of characters and nations, of an England and France "at peace," at last (*TTC*, 389). Since the beginning of the novel, we have had few passages juxtaposing the tale's two cities, and only a single chapter set in both (the chapter devoted to the world-historic events of July 1789). But as a subject without a head, Carton achieves a "prophetic" simultaneous vision of nineteenth-century London and Paris that transcends mere narrative porterage. This seems appropriate for two capitals that would be in permanent contact via electric telegraph from 1851 onward, a development that was itself treated, not altogether inaccurately, as a harbinger of continued peace between the two nations.[57]

Given over to this visionary retrospective, the last pages of the novel surmount the boundaries of space and time to include everybody's story, the kind of total view elsewhere found in a postbag or running through the electric wires. Each of the fourteen sentences that compose the vision begins with the same phrase, "I see . . . " (*TTC*, 398). And this extended, incantatory anaphora ("I see . . . I see . . . I see . . . ") produces a sense of serene, neutral transcendence by making the first-person pronoun and verb of each sentence paradoxically *im*personal because they are so minimized, changeless, and automatic. The passage exhibits precisely the putative "perspective neutrality" that Nunberg finds in the idea and rhetoric of modern information, a "view from nowhere" produced by "the suppression of self-reference, personal voice, and obviously subjective terms in favor of the 'neutral' presentation of observable fact that represents itself as mere 'reporting.'"[58] Here is a paradigm for Levine's "epistemology of dying to know," the notion that objective knowledge requires an absolute relinquishment of the self.[59]

As Sydney Carton's surname associates him with thickened paper, with a target, and with transport, his first name—an alteration of "St. Denis" (or, appropriately for a reformed drunkard, "St. Dionysius")—identifies him as the latter-day avatar of a Parisian martyr legendary for his flow of fresh discourse after being decapitated. While St. Denis is supposed to have preached a headless sermon to the crowd, Sydney's sacrifice transforms him more thoroughly. No longer a particularized character, he now becomes a medium for storytelling, a disembodied channel for speech that is not speech, a vehicle for moving from a novel's plots and characters to the neutral facts of history. If Madame Defarge develops into the center of an optical telegraph network that like any cool medium calls for participation, Carton becomes a hotter medium, one that creates sensory immersion but brings exclusion—including the exclusion of Carton himself as much of a participant in this vision. At the last moment of this historical novel, Carton even comes to transcend the very "times," for good or ill. The end of his vision is also the famous last sentence of the novel, which recalls and recasts the empty best/worst rhetoric of its opening line: "'It is a far, far better thing that I do, than I have ever done; it is a far, far better rest that I go to, than I have ever known'" (*TTC*, 390).

Sydney Carton dies as a character to become a speaking machine for modern information: neutral, bodiless, swift, communal, transcendent. Indeed, in contrast to the opaque, gesturing bodies that transmit or obstruct the flow of information in the rest of the narrative, Carton *becomes* information that has lost its body, news from nowhere. For Nunberg, information's "perspectival objectivity" and "detachment from individual speech acts" make it—in contrast to knowledge—"something that can exist in the absence of a subject."[60] Going further, *A Tale of Two Cities* locates information precisely at the annihilation of the subject as either material body or fictional character. The final scene of his vision foresees a son of Lucie and Darnay who bears Carton's name telling Carton's story to another child who bears Carton's name. Generated not out of the presence of a progenitor's body but out of its absence, this potentially endless line of Sydneys faithfully transmits the lineaments of his story, the story of *A Tale of Two Cities*.

A Tale of Two Cities begins by silently dragging the Dover mail and Lorry a decade back in time; it ends by hurling something of Sydney Carton sixty years ahead.[61] The novel first cancels out the revolutionary promise of new information systems—speed, communication, the annihilation of space and time—in order finally to resurrect them with Carton's death. At that moment, the novel represents the separation between information and materiality, between Carton's neutralized awareness and his dead and objectified body, as the redemptive passage from the frenzies of the Revolution to serenity and detachment (a place where "there is no Time . . . and no trouble")—and to the promise of Victorian modernity (*TTC*, 388). Letter-writing has sealed Carton's fate in the novel, so how else should he surmount that fate but by becoming a form of information that rises above the letter? Relinquishing his fictional person to become an informatic text, Carton reverses the process by which Dr. Manette was forced to surrender his person, as a punishment for sending his first letter or a corollary of writing his second. A headless subject, Carton prophetically glimpses a future in which he has escaped from both embodiment and history to survive in the facts of his own story: Memory Carton, recalled to life (*TTC*, 320).

A Tale of Two Cities recollects the remains of Carton as the hot medium of fictional writing itself. "If he had given any utterance to his [thoughts], and they were prophetic . . . ": how much of this is subjunctive, how much conditional? It remains syntactically ambiguous whether the *if* that has introduced Carton's visions refers only to the muteness of his thoughts or extends to their premonitory dimension—whether these oracular thoughts would have been these *if* they were spoken, or only *if* they happened to be his thoughts, a wholly circular assertion. The first possibility would mean that what follows will be pure writing, the second that it will be sheer fiction.[62] As he loses his head, Carton becomes a sea that reveals its buried treasure, a book to be read to the final page. Indeed, he *becomes* the final page of *A Tale of Two Cities*. He is no longer an inscrutable text that other characters try to read but a translucent text that the novel's audience has read through.

Sydney Carton overcomes the constraints of time, space, matter, and personality to become a channel for information. At the cost of his fictional life, he becomes the sanctified double no longer merely of Charles Darnay but of realist writing, those words on a page that at once assert their uncanny truthfulness and their manifest fictionality, that envision a small array of imaginary stories and characters as a synecdoche for more general realities. At this climax, *A Tale of Two Cities* displaces a simulated subjectivity with the rhetoric of objectivity, supplementing inexpressible consciousness with unspoken language. Realism sometimes stands accused of plotting an imaginary escape from the limitations of textuality, but the end of the novel reveals instead the power of Dickens's unruly realism to exploit print's sense of reified, detached, reproducible intimacy. Fiction here recapitulates the impartiality and directness promised by new media at midcentury without capitulating to a fantasy of eluding its own medium.

Perhaps Carton's death scene is really no death scene at all but a promotion of a fictional character to the status of an omniscient narrator, the novel's ultimate medium for presenting information. In *A Tale of Two Cities*, it takes the momentary rebirth of a character as an informatic fiction to accommodate the kinds of powers associated with modern information. But what if a story treated the complex and disturbing interplay between information, the body, and the machinery of fiction not as a climax announcing the passage from history to modernity but as the story's very premise? Carton dies in order to become a device for disembodied information, but what if he had lived? As the next chapter will demonstrate, this is just the sort of possibility investigated by an experimental novella published in *Blackwood's Magazine* as *A Tale of Two Cities* was appearing in *All the Year Round*: George Eliot's "The Lifted Veil."

CHAPTER 4

Information Unveiled

At a blow, Carton's posthumous vision moves us from the eighteenth century to the nineteenth, from the Place de la Révolution to a view that comprehends France and England alike, from visual transmission or recording to less tangible modes of dissemination. My previous chapter followed the tracks of modern information in a novel set in the age of the mail coach and semaphore telegraph; now this chapter will read the imprint of realism on a fantastic tale by Victorian fiction's most self-conscious realist. The end of *A Tale of Two Cities* takes us from the death of a character to the psychic life of information—the same route traced, in a more agonizing fashion, by George Eliot's strange early novella "The Lifted Veil" (1859).

Writing a hundred years later, McLuhan claims that modern media, and above all "a century of electric technology," have "extended our central nervous system" in directions that take us far from the Gutenberg galaxy.[1] In "The Lifted Veil," Eliot imagines a protagonist whose sensorium has been extended in McLuhan-esque fashion. In contrast to McLuhan's analysis of modern culture, the plot of "The Lifted Veil" does not attribute the clair-voyant Latimer's abilities to technology—or to anything else, for that matter. Yet to convey her character's experience of eerie access of everyday realities, Eliot invokes and adapts two highly up-to-date ways of turning the flows of life into detached information: *photography* in its recent alliance with the press, and a new *physiology* that read and recorded changes in the living body—the kind of science practiced by Eliot's companion, George Henry Lewes.

Information's Networks

In the media ecology of the mid-nineteenth century, neither of these informatic subjects takes us very far from the telegraph. For one thing, even outside the pages of Dickens and Eliot, the mechanics of cerebration and communication were already coming together. Laura Otis's *Networking: Communicating with Bodies and Machines in the Nineteenth Century* traces the idea of the network during the period, from telegraph engineering and physiology to fiction. "[T]he telegraph and the nervous system appeared to be doing the same things, and for the same reasons," she notes; "[t]heir common purpose was the transmission of information, and they both conveyed information as alterations in electrical signals."[2] Mesmerists and scientists alike could even treat the brain as a "*galvanic battery*" radiating an electrical force through "the medium of the nerves" and blood.[3] Indeed, in *Electro-Biology* (1849), the great electrophysiologist, ophthalmic surgeon, and inventor Alfred Smee not only traces all physiological sensation to electrical impulses but views the brain as a "combination battery" that allows impulses traveling from the somatic nerves to be "simply repeated" in the cerebrum by means of electric brainpower.[4] Very precisely, Smee describes the link between body and brain as a telegraphic repeater or relay, the essential device that permitted long-distance electric signaling.

If the telegraph became a thing for the Victorians to think with, one of the main topics they used it to think about was thinking itself. For the physiologist closest to Eliot, the standard comparisons between the nerves and the wires could go too far. In *The Physiology of Common Life* (1859–60), G. H. Lewes argues that the prevailing association between nerves and telegraph wires is acceptable only "as a loose and superficial analogy," for it treats nerves as passive transmitters of a "force" from one point to another.[5] On the contrary, he contends, the nerves are no mere electrical wires but have a power of their own; with increasing insistence, Lewes's work over the following decades would make the case for the distribution of mental functions, possibly even including consciousness, across the nervous system. Yet in describing consciousness as dispersed across separate but interconnected nodes of perception and control, Lewes effectively replaces a cursory comparison between nerves and telegraph wires with a deeper parallel between consciousness and the entire network.[6]

Later, in his ambitious five-volume *Problems of Life and Mind* (1874–80), Lewes would rely on an electrical figure to represent the necessary "union of the physiological with the psychological investigation"—one of the main points of his entire project.[7] As in *Jane Eyre* and early telegraphic discourse, electricity represents the translation of subjective experience into more objective form:

> If, then, it is indispensable that Psychology should formulate the laws of the human mind, and not simply classify the individual states, the feelings and thoughts of others must be accessible; and if these are not accessible on their subjective side, access must be sought on their objective side. We must quit Introspection for Observation. *We must study the mind's operations in its expressions, as we study electrical operations in their effects.* We must vary our observations of the actions of men and animals by experiment, filling up the gaps of observation with hypothesis.[8] (emphasis added)

Lewes argues that "Literature and Art" offer one source of "objective" understanding of thoughts and emotions outside of our own minds.[9] A properly experimental psychology would offer another, as observation and experiment give us admittance into "the feelings and thoughts of others." The fiction of George Eliot would imaginatively fuse the two—art and experiment.

The electric telegraph and the nerves were connected not only by their apparent structure and function but by the history of scientific discovery and invention. In the late eighteenth century, Luigi Galvani found that the legs of a dissected frog jerked under electric stimulation. Impressed by the phenomenon but not by Galvani's claims for a special "animal electricity" in the muscles and nerves, Alessandro Volta invented the voltaic-pile battery, which used metal plates to create the first source of steady electric current. "Who could have thought that the accidental contraction of the muscles of a frog would ever have paved the way to such brilliant results as have already appeared!" rejoiced a Victorian science writer and inventor, exulting in the ultimate consequences of Galvani's experiments; he means the telegraph.[10]

In a similar manner, photography and telegraphy were also linked by both contemporary discourse and their intertwined histories. As Nancy Armstrong has noted, the two contemporary technologies were "frequently compared"; an 1859 article in *The National Review* celebrated the era in typical fashion as "the age of the electric telegraph and of photography."[11] In addition to his work on electricity and acoustics, Wheatstone invented the stereoscope, which would become one of the century's most popular media for photographic images.[12] Morse had failed in his own early attempts to fix images on paper with silver nitrate, but after meeting Daguerre in Paris in 1839, he provided the American press with its first eyewitness account of photography, and helped produce some of the first daguerreotype portraits of living people.[13] (As one of his country's first daguerreotypists, Morse taught photography to Mathew Brady, whose portraits and Civil War images would make him the era's preeminent American photographer.) Latimer Clark, a pioneer of submarine telegraphy in the 1850s (and a namesake of the protagonist of "The Lifted Veil"), also created a stereoscopic camera. In a formulation that recalls descriptions of the Penny Post or telegraph, Lady Elizabeth Eastlake described photography as a "new form of communication between man and man—neither letter, message, nor picture—which now happily fills up the space between them"—and fills it with "cheap, prompt, and correct facts."[14] If information can't quite be free, at least new media might make it "cheap."

Victorian photography and physiology both promised to capture the flows of life, to make the ephemeral into something permanently legible. They joined telegraphy as models of the era's new informatics in their promise to place subjective experiences—vision, sensation, living embodiment—into an apparently more objective form. Photography arrests the flux of outward reality, fixing it in a portable, visual medium; courtesy of new instruments for continuously measuring and recording the interior life of the organism, Victorian physiology renders the hidden flows of the body as serial information.[15] As "The Lifted Veil" imagines the implications of an objectified subjectivity, it invokes both of these as figures for fiction's power to capture something of the complexity of life in alienated, repeatable form. Moreover,

Eliot parallels such state-of-the-art informatics with a set of uncanny textual effects made possible by print itself—highlighting potentials in print textuality which Victorian fiction usually manages less obtrusively.

Photo-realism, physiology, and the properties of print as a medium—in "The Lifted Veil" these modes of storage, inquiry, and dissemination form a miniature, mid-Victorian discourse network. Bringing the dynamics of this network into fiction, the story offers a parable of the powers and limitations of depersonalized perception; a horror tale helps unveil the hidden logic, and the suppressed alienation or violence, of realism's fantasies of information. Although the tone and technique of "The Lifted Veil" make it unique in Eliot's oeuvre, its outlook will also presage developments in her great final novels, *Middlemarch* (1871–72) and *Daniel Deronda* (1876).

The Accuracy of a Sun-Picture

In "The Natural History of German Life" (1856), an essay composed shortly before her own entry into fiction-writing, Marian Evans invoked the photograph to measure the promise of aesthetic realism against the achievements of science. The potential of realistic representation is great, she argues, for "Art is the nearest thing to life; it is a mode of amplifying experience and extending our contact with our fellow-men beyond the bounds of our personal lot."[16] After citing Teniers's and Murillo's paintings of the poor as models from the visual arts, Evans affirms that "[w]e have one great novelist who is gifted with the utmost power of rendering the external traits of our town population" (*NH*, 271). But she immediately qualifies that praise, forbearing to name Dickens yet referring to his novel in progress:

> if he could give us their psychological character—their conceptions of life, and their emotions—with the same truth as their idiom and manners, his books would be the greatest contribution Art has ever made to the awakening of social sympathies. But while he can copy Mrs Plornish's colloquial style with the delicate accuracy of a sun-picture . . . he scarcely ever passes from the humorous and external to the emotional and tragic, without becoming as transcendent in his unreality as he was a moment before in his artistic truthfulness. (*NH*, 271)

As a copyist of appearances, Dickens approaches photography—perhaps nowhere more closely than in *Little Dorrit* (1855–57), a novel not only blessed with the comic presence of Mrs. Plornish but also structured by explicit perspective shifts and sun-and-shadow contrasts. By the 1850s, laudatory comparisons of Dickens to "a taker of daguerreotypes, sun-pictures, [or] photographs" were common in reviews of his work.[17] But here the "sun-picture" image only reinforces the complaint about Dickens's superficiality, his unreal rendering of character, his presentation of exterior appearances without inner life. The "psychology" offered by Dickens is "frequently false," Evans claims (*NH*, 271). While conceding the "delicate accuracy" of the medium, and of Dickens's art, "The Natural History of German Life" treats photography as a figure for precise outward mimicry without deep human resonance, a mode of copying without the power of "awakening . . . sympathies."

Following up on her earlier praise of Teniers and company, Eliot would declare the homely realism of Dutch genre painting a model for her fiction in *Adam Bede* (1859), the humane and conventionally realistic novel she wrote just before "The Lifted Veil." In a famous "pause" in its seventeenth chapter, *Adam Bede* hails "Dutch paintings" for their "rare, precious quality of truthfulness"; such "faithful pictures of a monotonously homely existence" allow the "delicious" experience of "deep human sympathy."[18] Yet as Eliot's comments on Dickens indicate, modern technology offered newer models for imagining how fiction might turn real life into pictures, reality into fictional information. And the traits of photography that encapsulate Dickens's limitations might threaten to unsettle the alliance between accuracy, commonality, and fellow-feeling on which Eliot bases her theory of realism.

Like genre painting, photography promised truthful images of the everyday, but as "light-writing," it did so in a way that seemed to remove human agency—and, for Eliot, human sympathy—from the machinery of representation. More than a decade earlier, the photographic pioneer William Henry Fox Talbot had justified photography's potential for humble realism in precisely the same terms as Eliot in *Adam Bede*.[19] Talbot invented the calotype, which used a two-step negative/positive process to place images on paper, allowing the production of multiple prints, in contrast to the uniqueness of the metal daguerreotype. His *The Pencil of Nature* (1844–46), the first book illustrated by photographs, includes a picture of a rustic broom slanted against the open door of a rural stable, an image that would become perhaps his most famous.[20] Compared to *The Pencil of Nature*'s photographs of classical busts or the cloisters of Talbot's Lacock Abbey, the ordinary scene captured in "The Open Door" might seem unworthy of memorializing, but Talbot defends it as art: "We have sufficient authority in the Dutch school of art, for taking as subjects of representation scenes of daily and familiar occurrence. A painter's eye will often be arrested where ordinary people see nothing remarkable."[21]

An 1845 review approvingly took up Talbot's comparison; "[w]ith this broom the famous broom of [the seventeenth-century Dutch painter] Wouverman must never be compared: it becomes at once a clumsy imitation."[22] But for all such invocations of painting by photographers such as Talbot, photography remained "mysterious" for the Victorians, "a hybrid difficult to situate. It resulted in . . . pictures which resembled those of the Dutch school; yet . . . these pictures came into being 'naturally.'"[23] Despite Talbot's treatment of the camera lens as the artist's eye, Victorians came to see "the photograph . . . as an automatic recording device," largely equivalent to "what the average person would have seen standing in the same spot at the same time."[24] "The relay of truthful information, however insignificant, was central to the larger cultural importance of photography," finds Jennifer Green-Lewis, and "photography's potential for detail, for verisimilitude, and for stasis became a standard in other forms of realism."[25] Against the hallucinatory accuracy of the mid-Victorian photograph, the truthful ordinariness of Dutch painting might seem nostalgic or outmoded—commonplace indeed.

"The Lifted Veil" challenges or inverts so much of Eliot's early theory and practice of fiction that it seems appropriate for it to draw upon an alternative model of visual realism. The tale mixes psychology, science, and sensation fiction to set forth the dark tale of the narrator, a delicate young man cursed with the power of prevision and the ability to read—really, the inability to screen out—the thoughts of those around him. That is, Latimer gets precisely what Eliot had missed in Dickens, the "psychological character" of others, "their conceptions of life, and their emotions," rendered with the immediacy of direct observation. His powers bring him the amplified experience and contact beyond his individual lot that Eliot craved from the highest art—and this development produces not sympathetic understanding but alienation and horror. Recounting the story of his life, Latimer tells us that its happiest period was a time in boyhood when his mother had to tend to him because an illness made him temporarily blind. But in his early adulthood, this experience is reversed and transformed: another illness permanently alters his powers of perception, extending them far beyond ordinary vision into "incessant insight and foresight."[26] Only the mind of the beautiful and haughty Bertha, his brother's fiancée and Latimer's own future wife, initially remains veiled to him, making her an "oasis of mystery in the dreary desert" of certainty (*LV*, 18).

Latimer's first and most elaborately presented prophetic vision arrives "like the new images in a dissolving view" (the fading of one magic-lantern image into another) when he hears the name of a city mentioned as a destination for his future travels (*LV*, 10). "My father was called away before he had finished his sentence, and he left my mind resting on the word *Prague*"; suddenly, as if completing the sentence in another register, Latimer envisions "a new and wondrous scene":

> a city under the broad sunshine, that seemed to me as if it were the summer sunshine of a long-past century arrested in its course—unrefreshed for ages by dews of night, or the rushing rain-cloud; scorching the dusty, weary, time-eaten grandeur of a people doomed to live on in the stale repetition of memories. . . . The city looked so thirsty that the broad river seemed to me a sheet of metal; and the blackened statues, as I passed under their blank gaze, along the unending bridge, . . . seemed to me the real inhabitants and owners of this place, while the busy, trivial men and women, hurrying to and fro, were a swarm of ephemeral visitants infesting it for a day. (*LV*, 9)

Julian Wolfreys recognizes the elaborate "textual-optical machinery" of "The Lifted Veil," a tale that seems to suggest some "ill-defined . . . new means of tele-technological communication."[27] But in fact, as the reference to a magic lantern show hints, we can be much more specific in defining the textual-optical technology involved. Eliot had traveled to Prague with Lewes in the summer of 1858.[28] In contrast, Latimer has never visited the city and has "seen no picture" of it (*LV*, 9). But this image of a Prague in "perpetual midday, without the repose of night or the new birth of morning" precisely mimics a very particular kind of picture indeed (*LV*, 9): the cityscapes of early Victorian photography, that technology with the power to detain the light of the past in a perpetual repetition of memory, to arrest the flow of time in its course.

In nearly every detail, Latimer's vision incorporates the traits of an early photographic view: the sense it conveys of a changeless scene etched by sunlight (in the standard phrase, photography meant "printing pictures by means of the sun")[29]; the dead, metallic appearance of a body of water when its flows are petrified in silver nitrate on paper or upon the actual "sheet of metal" that made up a daguerreotype; the impression that a place's "real inhabitants" are its stationary objects, which obligingly hold their poses for even the longest exposure time, while its living, moving populace becomes a "swarm" of hazy, transient ghosts. A Victorian photograph even begins with the act of lifting an opaque veil or cover in order to set a new scene before a sensitized medium. Although Latimer assures us he has never seen an image of Prague, this scene precisely describes the view of the Prague Bridge which was starting to become one of the city's signature photographic images.

Eliot could have viewed one of these pictures—indeed, she could have seen a photograph of Prague produced specifically to mark photography's attainment of the technical reproducibility of print. In late 1858, a few months before Eliot wrote "The Lifted Veil," the London-based *Photographic News* distributed hundreds of copies of "Bridge over the River Moldau, at Prague, Bohemia" as the first in a series of prints created to demonstrate Talbot's new "photoglyphic process" for engraving photographs on metal plates so that they could be "printed off . . . with the usual printer's ink" just like any written text.[30] The predecessor of modern photogravure processes, this "immensely important invention" turned photographs into printable plates.[31] Perhaps the ultimate textual-optical technology of the 1850s, Talbot's photomechanical system "inaugurated a vast new field offering rapid, mass visual communication of graphic information."[32] As one historian of photography gushes, such an ample distribution of photographic images via printed paper was a tribute to "the significance of photoreproduction" and "[q]uite a novelty for the year 1858!"[33]

The art historian Carol Armstrong has recently urged us to rethink the history of photography on paper, treating it not alongside painting but in relation to the original reproducible "paper art," printed writing; moreover, she finds the intersection of photography and the book in mid-Victorian Britain "particularly rich and peculiar."[34] Convinced that the iterability of

FIGURE 4.1. William Henry Fox Talbot, photoglyphic engraving of Prague. *The Photographic News* (1858). Photography Collection, Harry Ransom Humanities Research Center, The University of Texas at Austin.

the paper photograph was the defining advantage of his "English process" over the higher-definition daguerreotype, Talbot promoted his techniques in terms of print as early as the 1840s; one of his patents includes a proposal for composing lines of type to be copied onto paper via photography instead of with a printing press.[35] Talbot's "photoglyphic" process and its successors confirmed photography's importance as a technology not just for recording or representing reality but for disseminating it. The technique greatly reduced the cost of printing from photographs; photoglyphy would soon place photographic reproductions within the reach of "the masses," predicted the inevitable process article in *All the Year Round*.[36] It also brought greater detail and permanence to the reproduced image, a special concern of Talbot, since some of his early attempts at photographic publishing had failed when the images pasted into *The Pencil of Nature* and other books proved chemically unstable.[37]

Talbot's reproduction of "Bridge over the River Moldau," originally half of a stereoscope image by the French photographers Clouzard and Soulier, circulated widely as one of the first testaments to the accuracy and above all the permanence of photoglyphy, a new way to register reality in printer's ink. We might be tempted to speculate that Talbot selected the image as not simply an example but an icon of his techniques. The photoglyphic process lends photography the endurance of print, if not quite of statuary; the bridge between Prague's Old and New Towns becomes an endless connection between the past and the future, between an old textual medium and a modern visual technology. Arresting and reproducing the world's Heraclitean flux, photographic printing gives us the same river any number of times.

Talbot and *The Photographic News* printed hundreds of copies of "Bridge on the River Moldau" and a series of similar images. I know of no evidence that Eliot saw these particular images, but in a real sense, she didn't need to. For all its promise as a photoglyphic icon, the dissemination of this image and its fellows makes it clear that they ultimately offered not aesthetic originality but purposely generic testaments to the accuracy of a new media innovation. As with Latimer's vision, which also functions as both the icon of a visual mode and general proof of concept, the medium of "Bridge on the River Moldau" is extraordinary, but its actual pictorial content is perfectly standard—a detailed, well-composed image entirely typical of contemporary photographic cityscapes: the sense of an arrested midday, the scorched river, the black statues, the bridge disappearing into the horizon, the blurry figures made by real human beings (one of whom is barely visible as a ghost, just to the left of the lamp in the central foreground). If Victorian realism represents the intersection of novelistic representation with modern, standardized forms of mass visuality, as Nancy Armstrong claims, then Talbot's image of Prague, or Latimer's, might betoken a new scene in that conjunction. In terms of nineteenth-century printed writing, the photoglyphic process recalls not handset text so much as stereotype, the casting of an entire plate upon a single piece of metal.

Overwhelmed by the clarity and force of his unexpected vision, Latimer wonders at first whether "illness ha[s] wrought some happy change in my organisation—given a firmer tension to my nerves"; could it be a sudden stirring of his latent poetic genius (*LV*, 10)? "Surely it was in this way that Homer saw the plain of Troy, that Dante saw the abodes of the departed, that Milton saw the earthward flight of the Tempter" (*LV*, 10). The awkward coupling of bardic vision with the language of nervous psychology suggests the implausibility of the theory. As an experiment, Latimer tries to envision Venice, hoping that "the same sort of result would follow," the same sense of a real scene rising before him (*LV*, 10). But no; for his pains, Latimer receives not the "vivid images" he seeks, no lifelike "accident of form or shadow," but only scattered memories of "Canaletto engravings" (*LV*, 10). Compared to the mental sun-picture of Prague, the mass visuality of landscape painting seems a feeble and secondhand experience. Like Latimer's visions, a photograph preempts the work of memory with a stable image taken out of the flux of contingency and time.

Latimer's new power might strike us as nearly godlike. Yet the very force of his visions makes Latimer submissive before them. In an essay on the relationship of Victorian photography to a growing consciousness of forgetting and oblivion, Green-Lewis points out that photography does not change the past but "changes . . . the relationship we have with it."[38] Altering the word *past* to *future* would summarize Latimer's relationship to his photograph-like visions of the static, evacuated landscape of his own destiny. As he begins to suspect that they are no artist's fancies but alienated glimpses of his own coming experience, Latimer becomes as passive as the sensitized surface of a photographic plate, treating them as scenes that have already been photographed or texts that have already been printed. Even a vision of his conjugal misery with Bertha—a vision he fully credits—does not dissuade him from marrying her. This might seem puzzling, but, as Thomas Nagel observes, viewing our own actions from "an objective or external standpoint" can make us seem "helpless" before them.[39]

This passivity too may be a corollary of the uncanny photorealism of the sun-picture in 1859. It is no great leap from the stability hailed by *The Photographic News* and *All the Year Round* to the disturbing sense of stasis expressed in Eliot's passage. Perhaps the possibility of such representational deadness inheres in all descriptive realisms, even Dutch genre painting, but here Latimer's photographic vision makes the rift between teleperception and lived experience inescapable. Only the image of "a patch of rainbow light on the pavement, transmitted through a coloured lamp in the shape of a star" seems to escape the pictorial desiccation of Latimer's visionary Prague (*LV*, 9). The single spot of color dabbed on a monochromatic scene, this feature fuses Old and New Testament signs of hope with the Barthesian impression of random, haphazard detail. But hope and hap both disappear when Latimer arrives in Prague and verifies that the images he saw were indeed his own future perceptions, temporarily disconnected from embodied experience as well as from the normal chronology of his life. The rainbow light becomes the confirmation of his vision's accurate reproduction, a sign of narrative foreclosure. And Barthes's reality effect turns into his *punctum*, the "element which rises from the scene" of a photograph to pierce the beholder with its truth, "that accident which pricks me."[40]

For the Victorians, photographic technology seemed to exemplify the registration of appearances without an intervening subjectivity.[41] Lady Eastlake's "Photography" (1857), the age's best-known essay on the topic, credits the photograph with "the accuracy and the insensibility of a machine"; what could better represent the divorce of experience from perception, embodied knowledge from abstract information?[42] Just as Latimer ruefully discovers that his visions are not poetry, so Eastlake determines that photography is not art. Art requires "whatever appertains to the free-will of the intelligent being, as opposed to the obedience of the machine," but photography's "business is to give evidence of facts, as minutely and as impartially as, to our shame, only an unreasoning machine can give."[43] Devices that impartially and exhaustively disconnect facts from intelligence and reason, with no question of free will: Latimer, and the camera, produce information at the expense of human subjectivity. Both Talbot's and Eliot's images of Prague mark the changelessness of the scene by turning real human passersby into half-absent ghosts. Eliot herself would soon admit that her experience with a photographic portrait in 1858 had given her "rather a horror of photography."[44]

In Elizabeth Ermarth's account, visual and literary realisms alike assert the possibility of a shared perspective and common understanding. The Victorian photograph may support the idea of turning an individual field of vision into a viewpoint that anyone might occupy, but it also hints that what we see may bring us something less than understanding or knowledge. After the burst of his initial vision, Latimer tries to renew the experience by thinking about what he actually knows for himself: "I sent my thoughts ranging over my world of knowledge, in the hope that they would find some object which would send a reawakening vibration through my slumbering genius. But no; my world remained as dim as ever, and that flash of strange light refused to come again" (*LV*, 11). As his knowledge does not provoke visions, so his visions never become useful knowledge; moments of experience freed from time and space, stripped of any context, they are real but never realized. This may be the quiet chill behind the showier horrors of "The Lifted Veil": its dark suggestion that even as it amplifies our experience of the world and extends our contact with others, fiction may cast our most intimate knowledge—of places, of individuals, of embodied life—as information.[45] In this respect, fiction resembles not only photography but also nineteenth-century physiology. As the first appears the objective recorder of external appearances, so the second could play the same part for inner life.

A Microscopic Vision

As a supplement to the outward truth of the sun-picture, its metaphor for the external accuracy of Dickens's copying, Evans's essay cites natural history. This wide-ranging predecessor field for disciplines such as modern biology and ecology provides a paradigm for social and fictional inquiry. Indeed, Sally Shuttleworth has found this science, with its emphasis on the description of natural objects in stable relationships, central to Eliot's early novels. Moreover, Eliot's invocations of natural history parallel Lewes's work in the mid-1850s, as he transformed himself from belletrist to biologist; the dual reinventions of Lewes as a man of science and of Eliot as a novelist mirror each other as much as the chronology of his serial publication of *Sea-Side Studies* (*Blackwood's Magazine*, beginning August 1856) and hers of *Scenes of Clerical Life* (*Blackwood's*, beginning January 1857) would suggest. But Lewes had more than mollusks on his mind. By the end of the 1850s, his work was beginning to explore the physiology of the nerves and brain—the principal subject in the second volume of *The Physiology of Common Life*. To this end, Lewes performed, described, and promoted research involving animal ex-

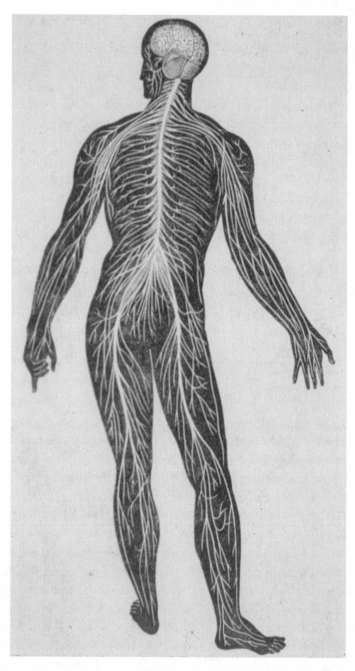

FIGURE 4.2. The nervous system as information network. G. H. Lewes, *The Physiology of Common Life* (1859-60).

periments and vivisection, eventually becoming a public advocate for such practices amid growing controversy about them.[46]

Lewes's shift from static natural history to a dynamic, experimental physiology—a shift Shuttleworth finds echoed in Eliot's fiction—reflects larger movements in scientific thought. In *The Birth of the Clinic*, Michel Foucault analyzes the early nineteenth-century rise of pathological anatomy as medicine's central model. For the first time, argues Foucault, medical knowledge now meant knowing "the individual."[47] Under the Romantic-era regime of pathological anatomy, dissection became the essential tool for research; whereas life seemed to conceal the body's truth, Foucault argues, death revealed "to the light of day the black coffer of the body."[48] But during the course of the nineteenth century, scientists such as the great French physiologist Claude Bernard developed the research program and laboratory techniques of a new, experimental biology. The knowable body now became not merely internal and individual but alive, accessible, and responsive to the outside world. In disciplinary terms, these innovations amounted to a movement from Foucault's pathological anatomy to experimental physiology; in practical terms, they presented a movement from employing dissection as the basis for understanding the body to using vivisection and other investigations of living bodies. The scalpel had been the principal tool of the old anatomy, but now it would be joined by new inventions such as the sphygmograph and kymograph, devices to measure the body's inner pulsations and flows, and to transcribe them as a mode of writing.[49] Such biomedical media devices dispassionately rendered the living body as graphic information, registering the invisible and internal as photography did the visible and external.

Lewes believed that art and literature could parallel scientific experimentation, and "The Lifted Veil" suggests an experiment in combining a pathology of the sun-picture with a vivisectory physiology of the psyche. As Kate Flint observes, "Eliot's novella would have been impossible without Lewes's physiological researches."[50] Flint cites a fantasy of scientific vision in *The Physiology of Common Life* that seems particularly apposite: "If for a moment we could with the bodily eye see into the frame of man, as with the microscope we see into the transparent frames of some simpler animals, what a spectacle would be unveiled!"[51] As photography provides the unspoken topos for Latimer's prevision, neurophysiology plays a more explicit role in his mind-reading. Although we are assured that Latimer was a poor student, his narrative describes the experience of reading thoughts in the terms of the scientific education Eliot cannily places in his past and of the experimental medicine studied by his only friend, Charles Meunier:

> [T]his superadded consciousness . . . became an intense pain and grief when it seemed to be opening to me the souls of those who were in a close relation to me—when the rational talk, the graceful attentions, the wittily-turned phrases, and the kindly deeds, which used to make the web of their characters, were seen as if thrust asunder by a microscopic vision, that showed all the intermediate frivolities, all the suppressed egoism, all the struggling chaos of puerilities, meanness, vague capricious memories, and indolent make-shift thoughts, from which human words and deeds emerge like leaflets covering a fermenting heap. (*LV*, 13–14)

Latimer's supernormal perception flays the figures around him alive, in order to reveal their inmost thoughts and passions "in all their naked skinless complication"; with the acuity of the microscope, his perceptions unveil the spectacle of their inner lives even as they live them (*LV*, 15). His consciousness, which is coextensive with the narrative itself, vivisects their minds. The surface signs of character and conversation peel back to reveal something deeper: the "chaos" of consciousness, a "fermenting heap" both riotously active and rank-smelling. We can add Latimer's mind to our array of Victorian media systems that include everybody's story: the penny postbag, the telegraph wires, the dialogic novel. But here the unwieldy fusion of direct, personal perception with the all-inclusive objectivity attributed to new media systems makes Latimer's powers a curse.

Elsewhere, Eliot's fiction might assert that knowledge of others increases sympathy for them, but for Latimer, the opposite seems true—or perhaps, for all its accuracy and detail, his awareness of those around him isn't quite knowledge at all. After his initial vision of an unhappy future marriage with a Bertha who is "no longer a fascinating secret, but a measured fact," Latimer complains of the "double consciousness at work within me, flowing on like two parallel streams that never mix" (*LV*, 21)—a version of the epistemological and existential "split" between objective and subjective perspectives.[52] As Helen Small notes, "double consciousness" is a "semi-technical term" from mid-Victorian neurophysiology (as well as from mesmerism)

(*LV*, 94n); the phrase could also describe the treatment of telegraphy as a parallel stream of reality floating under the streets of London.

The final pages of the story reintroduce Charles Meunier, who appears in order to carry out on a human being a physiological experiment he has previously performed on animals. The lady's maid of the imperious Bertha is dying; Meunier proposes to transfuse her arteries with his own blood several minutes after her death, and then to note the effects of the postmortem infusion. "It can do her no harm—will give her no pain," Meunier argues, "for I shall not make it until life is extinct to all purposes of sensation" (*LV*, 39). Momentarily reanimated, and full of a hatred for her mistress that is never explained, the dead woman cries out that Bertha has planned to poison her husband.

A common criticism of "The Lifted Veil" is that the revelatory scientific experiment that ends the tale is irrelevant and unnecessary, since Latimer can read minds.[53] But in fact the story's dénouement can call for a secret to be revealed not by the narrator's own powers but by a gruesome medical experiment—for prescience to give way to the science that has heretofore described it—because the framework of the tale postulates the vivisection of the human mind, the conversion of mental life into so much information, as one of its very données. Like Latimer's mental pictures, experimental physiology makes something internal and personal—Latimer's consciousness, Meunier's blood—a depersonalized medium for distressing but wholly trustworthy information.[54] Not only clairvoyance but also science raises the veil of individual subjectivity in "The Lifted Veil"; both serve as narrative devices that reveal what Evans had missed in Dickens's fiction, "psychological character" and "emotions." As they do so, they highlight and defamiliarize a convention so basic that it is difficult to fully recognize it as such: that realist fiction may without forgoing its realism pretend to give us access to something we never encounter in real life—the unspoken thoughts of others.

When the experiment reaches its revelatory climax, the shocked Meunier "look[s] paralysed" (*LV*, 42). Claude Bernard, a model for Lewes's science (cited, for instance, on the pages before and after Lewes's vision of the human frame "unveiled"), would claim that an experimenting "physiologist . . . a man of science . . . no longer hears the cry of animals, he no longer sees the blood that flows, he sees only his idea and perceives only organisms concealing problems which he intends to solve."[55] That is, a physiologist must regard even the most painful experiment simply as a source of so much data.[56] But perhaps an experiment may yield an unexpected influx of human knowledge where the researcher sought only scientific information. Watching Meunier react to the maid's brief reanimation into hatred and accusation, Latimer concludes dryly that "life for that moment ceased to be a scientific problem to him" (*LV*, 42). "As for me, this scene seemed of one texture with the rest of my existence," asserts Latimer, "and this new revelation was only like an old pain recurring with new circumstances"—further confirmation of the tale's alignment between psychic and scientific disclosure (*LV*, 42). But Meunier's paralysis by unwanted knowledge seems mirrored by Latimer's belated emergence into unprecedented activity. At last, Latimer responds to a dreadful "revelation" as if it offered personal knowledge rather than abstract information; he and Bertha separate, and Latimer becomes a wanderer until his final days. The tale ends with his lonely death from heart trouble—the very scene with which, courtesy of his powers of prevision, the first-person narrative began.

Printed on the Nerves

"The Lifted Veil" appropriates vivisectional language and modern technology in order to figure paranormal thought, but these discourses ultimately help it find similarly estranging possibilities in the original technical medium, writing. Late in the narrative, Latimer meditates on the disconnection between expression and experience: "So much misery—so slow and hideous a growth of hatred and sin, may be compressed into a sentence! And men judge of each other's lives through this summary medium . . . " (*LV*, 34). Even this reflection perversely reinforces the gap between first-person knowledge and verbal representation, offering a platitude that tidily sums up the inadequacy of narrative summarizing. Mapping the gap between information and understanding onto the division between signifier and signified, Latimer's narratorial pronouncements align real knowledge with neurophysiological embodiment: "We learn *words* by rote, but not their meaning; *that* must be paid for with our life-blood, and printed in the subtle fibres of our nerves" (*LV*, 34). Yet this formulation retains a chiasmic complexity. The sentence's opening clause draws an opposition between the outward form of language subject to "rote" learning and "meaning"; the tale has described Latimer's prescient forestalling of his brother's would-be witticisms in similar terms (*LV*, 18). But the passage's final line returns to the reproducible materiality of the modern signifier—print—as a figure for meaning's power to mark our minds and bodies.

"The Lifted Veil" clearly exploits the Victorian fascination with what would soon be termed telepathy. But even as she taps into such cultural fascination, Eliot reworks the topic to highly literary ends. Aware of the future, conscious of the idle thoughts and secret motives of the other characters, Latimer is an audacious but morbid authorial experiment: he is an omniscient narrator who has been given a fictional body and trapped as a character within the story rendered in his voice.[57] "The Lifted Veil" in fact offers the only sustained first-person narrative in Eliot's fiction, as if the unaccustomed horror and melancholy of the tale (Eliot herself called it "outré . . . a *jeu de melancholie*") were concomitant with its uncharacteristic narrative mode.[58] Like Sydney Carton, Latimer dies into the estate of clairvoyant narrator; the first page gives us his prescient view of his death. But with a slow case of "*angina pectoris*" rather than La Guillotine to perform the act, the process becomes more prolonged and painful.

Latimer possesses two modes of uncanny access to information, two parallel powers that might seem to have little inherent connection: he sees the future and he perceives the thoughts in other minds. But this conjunction, the coupling of foresight with insight, follows a specific logic; moreover, it helps identify the mode of the unwritten, latent narrative that has been programmatically transformed into this paranormal tale. For in one highly relevant situation, seeing the future would be substantially equivalent to seeing each among a group of characters made transparent, fully revealed: when reading a conventional fiction of *Bildung* and psychological realism—in particular, when reading a George Eliot novel. When carefully plotted, such a narrative seems to consist of characters encountering each other, slowly revealing themselves, and working out their inner logic: Casaubon's sterile pedantry, Bulstrode's guilt, Dorothea's passion—to cite only a few examples from *Middlemarch*. Latimer's prescience and his knowledge of other characters' minds go together because for Eliot this is how realistic fiction works. By conflating its central character with the medium of realist narration, "The Lifted Veil" becomes a deformation study of literary realism; it turns realism's tales of growth, courtship, and self-revelation into nightmares of narratorial omniscience made real.

"The Natural History of German Life" figures the realist author as half-photographer, half-scientist, a dual status also thrust upon Latimer. Indeed, the tale invokes realism, the rule-bound narration of a recognizable fictional reality in prose, as the sign of Latimer's curse. "The Lifted Veil" systematically opposes poetry, aligned with activity and imagination, to a complex of associations that incorporates passive registration, everyday reality, and mundane prose—an amalgam recognizable as a disenchanted account of realism. Again and again, the story calls up the promise of poetry only to annul it. "You will think, perhaps, that I must have been a poet," ventures Latimer in an address to the reader even before he narrates his earliest extrasensory experience, "[b]ut my lot was not so happy as that" (*LV*, 7). After his first vision, Latimer himself had entertained the possibility:

> No, it was not a dream; was it—the thought was full of tremulous exultation—was it the poet's nature in me, hitherto only a troubled yearning sensibility, now manifesting itself suddenly as spontaneous creation? . . . I did not for a moment believe it was really a representation of that city; I believed—I hoped it was a picture that my newly-liberated genius had painted. . . . (*LV*, 10)

Latimer's attempts to employ these powers "by an exertion of [his] will" fail utterly, yielding mere "prosaic effort," nothing like his vista of Prague (*LV*, 10). Something of the idea that such views might be poetic reveries briefly persists; after his next, equally involuntary vision fades, Latimer is relieved to return to a "scene of simple, waking prose" (*LV*, 12). But, as the passage above suggests, Latimer's visions are no poetry, no paintings by his creative genius, but "real . . . representation[s]"—a phrase that encapsulates the truth of the photograph or the claims of realism. Latimer's abilities are fantastic, but the shock of his perceptions and visions is that they are no fancies but a "superadded consciousness of the actual," stultifyingly real (*LV*, 18).

Within the story, Latimer soon begins receiving credit for what his father calls "poetic nonsense," despite the fact that he neither reveals his powers to others nor writes a single line of poetry (*LV*, 22). Bertha starts carelessly flirting with him, since even "[t]he most prosaic woman likes to believe herself the object of a violent, a poetic passion," and taunts him about what she sarcastically calls his "poetical nature" (*LV*, 16, 17). As the unpoetical Bertha observes when she confesses herself "a heartless girl," "[t]he easiest way to deceive a poet is to tell him the truth" (*LV*, 26). For the first time, her coldly truthful words nearly bring Latimer's unassimilable insights into the texture of his daily life, reviving "for a moment the shadow of my vision [of] the Bertha whose soul was no secret to me" and giving Latimer "a momentary chill of horror" (*LV*, 26). After their marriage, when Latimer's life catches up to that vision of a Bertha whose inner life no longer wears a "veil," Bertha's identification with prose becomes complete: "The terrible moment of complete illumination had come to me, and I saw that the darkness had hidden no landscape from me, but only a blank prosaic wall" (*LV*, 31, 32).

For all their unexplained workings, Latimer's visions and insights are no poetic nonsense but the plainest prose sense. In "The Lifted Veil," even Eliot's sentences and punctuation collude in the merging of prose narrativity and prescience. The sentence "'Well, Latimer, you thought me long,' my father said . . . " occurs first in Latimer's private mental vision of his father's arrival and then, a few dozen lines later, within the outer reality of the tale's plot: "'Well, Latimer, you thought me long,' my father said . . . " (*LV*, 12, original ellipses). Precisely duplicated—we could practically say *reprinted* or *stereotyped* or *photoglyphically engraved*—down to its very ellipsis and bland speaker tag, this early experience of prevision hints that Latimer's powers are a translation of the experience of fictional textuality into life, a schematic inversion of realism's claims to represent life via fictions. As a patently textual effect, the seamless reproduction of Latimer's experience helps to unsettle any fantasy of realism's textual transparency.

The story makes its prose a vehicle for Latimer-like clairvoyance in several ways; it offers readers a painful, microscopic dissection of an unlikable mind (that is, Latimer's) as well as narrated visions that give us the experience of foreknowledge.[59] "The Lifted Veil" not only places Latimer's visions as fragments of the future in its retrospective narrative but also repeatedly incorporates something like foresight within the very texture of its prose. Latimer claims no advance knowledge of his brother's imminent death from a riding accident ("[t]here was no evil in store for *him*," he muses), yet oblique references to the incident creep into his narration of the circumstances that lead up to it (*LV*, 25). Knowing that his brother has gone elsewhere, Latimer visits Bertha at her guardian's house and finds that "[b]y a rare accident she was alone" (*LV*, 25). Later, as he returns home, Latimer sees a man setting off in a hurry and wonders to himself, "Had any accident happened at home?" (*LV*, 27). As it happens, by a rare accident at home—the death of Latimer's brother, her fiancé—Bertha will now be alone and so at liberty to marry him, a destiny Latimer has just inadvertently revealed to her by a "strange, [a] criminal indiscretion" in their conversation (*LV*, 27). Awaiting Meunier's visit, a glum Latimer had hoped that his friend's arrival would bring him "a transient resurrection into a happier pre-existence" (*LV*, 37); this apparently casual anticipation misses the mark by only a single adjective. Conventional foreshadowing indicates realism's assertion of order and logic in the stories it tells, but these subtle verbal accidents and indiscretions hint at something stranger in the weave of the text. Here too, on the smallest level of word choice, "The Lifted Veil" conveys a sense of uncanny access to real truth, connections that reconfigure fiction's usual circuits of meaning.

Flint notes the fissure between subjectivity and embodiment in the story: "[t]he speculative, imaginative, fiction-creating mind . . . has the ability to travel backward and forward in time," "[b]ut the human body has no such ability."[60] Yet in fact, Latimer treats his special perceptions as less a form of fiction-creating authorship than a form of fiction-consuming readership, as if he had simply jumped ahead to a scene that he would soon encounter again in the proper sequence—and in the same printed form.[61] Latimer's untimely visions affect his fictional life little more than they affect our reading; we witness his death in the story's opening pages, but this is hardly a signal to stop reading. Seizing on the informatic possibilities of modern technologies and modes of description, "The Lifted Veil" takes shape around a methodical distortion of realist writing, but its final twist may be the paradigm it offers for realist reading. However much readers may resist identification with the misanthropic, self-pitying Latimer, the text literalizes his powers in our experience of reading "The Lifted Veil" itself. Latimer's vicarious "participation in other people's consciousness" becomes our own, as we gain untimely, repeated glimpses of a set of characters on the page (*LV*, 17).

Long Telegraph Wires

Latimer's consistent, fatal inability to annex his future visions to his present outlook recapitulates the rift between abstract information—even information about inner life and emotions—and embodied understanding, between what is merely known and what is also lived.[62] Likewise, his "microscopic" insight into others' thoughts suggests a conversion of their lived experience into alienated, and alienating, data. The photographic image and the physiological body mark Eliot's willingness to go beyond the humble realism of *Scenes of Clerical Life* or *Adam Bede*, and to imagine the troubling implications of fiction's claims to adapt reality into realistic information. Years later, in *Middlemarch* and *Daniel Deronda*, Eliot would return to similar reference points as markers of both these novels' high realism and the informatic concerns that might modify that realism or point beyond it.

Not until more than a decade after "The Lifted Veil" did Eliot fully combine the discourse of biomedical investigation with her usual subject of provincial life. The most sustained discussion of medical theory and practice in her work is of course her treatment in *Middlemarch* of Tertius Lydgate's struggle to "raise the profession" by importing the most modern techniques of French medicine and anatomy ("diligent application, not only of the scalpel, but of the microscope") to rural England in the 1830s.[63] Mark Wormald has illuminated *Middlemarch*'s discourse of microscopy, emphasizing the presentation of the novel's narrator as "an amateur microscopist."[64] But in a larger sense, scientific devices even stand behind its expressions of its narrative project. Lydgate advocates a "systole and diastole" "in all inquiry," a dialectic of details and relations, whereby the mind of the researcher "must be continually expanding and shrinking between the whole human horizon and the horizon of an object-glass" (*M*, 628); as critics have often recognized, the phrase applies less to Lydgate's medicine than to Eliot's vision. A systole and diastole of inquiry: the phrase describes the ideal rhythm of contraction and expansion between observing the infinitesimal and contemplating the universal, as if the discourse of blood and circulation in "The Lifted Veil" has been generalized to supply the synthesis of broad awareness and local insight that eludes Latimer.[65]

Elsewhere *Middlemarch*'s representation of consciousness links physiology with media in order to treat individual perception and memory abroad in the world. The "impressions" of Rome strike Dorothea "as with an electric shock," presenting a "glut of confused ideas which check the flow of emotion" (*M*, 188). Optics and alienated vision come together courtesy of a media simile for private mental images, the same one used in the "dissolving view" of "The Lifted Veil": "Our moods are apt to bring with them images which succeed each other like the magic-lantern pictures of a doze; and in certain states of dull forlornness Dorothea all her life continued to see the vastness of St. Peter's, the huge bronze canopy . . . the red drapery which was being hung for Christmas spreading itself everywhere like a disease of the retina" (*M*, 188). Jonathan Crary has drawn our attention to the nineteenth century's fascination with the retinal afterimage, a phenomenon that seemed to show the essential subjectivity of vision.[66] Here the movement from exterior appearance to internal perception (from a magic-lantern view to a dozy dream, from a draped chamber to a coating on the retina) becomes pathologically frozen to provide a metaphor for estranged vision and the persistence of memory. In "The Lifted Veil," Latimer's vision of a future Bertha who hates him fades into an afterimage of the emblematic brooch she wears, "the green serpent with the diamond eyes remaining a dark image on the retina" (*LV*, 20).

"If we had a keen vision and feeling of all ordinary human life," observes Eliot in *Middlemarch*'s next paragraph, and some of its most famous lines, "it would be like hearing the grass grow and the squirrel's heart beat, and we should die of that roar which lies on the other side of silence. As it is, the quickest of us walk about well wadded with stupidity" (*M*, 189). The passage accurately describes the plight of Latimer, cursed with an inescapable knowledge of the mundane vanities, anxieties, and tragedies in the mental lives of those around him, deafened by the roar. In fact, "The Lifted Veil" figures the experience of mind-reading in terms that, like its description of the "web" of character, sound like a rehearsal for *Middlemarch*: "It was like a preternaturally heightened sense of hearing, making audible to one a roar of sound where others find perfect stillness" (*LV*, 18).[67] Early in his friendship with Dorothea, Will Ladislaw defines poetry in terms that again link physiology with new media, and that recall Latimer's poetic pretensions in "The Lifted Veil," as well as his sudden visions: a poet needs "a soul in which knowledge passes instantaneously into feeling, and feeling flashes back as a new organ of knowledge. One may have that condition by fits only" (*M*, 218). But Latimer's fits suggest the divergence between a poet's organ of knowledge and a disenchanted medium of information.

Middlemarch's lines about the squirrel's heartbeat touch upon the kinds of observations that nineteenth-century physiologists were making, their developing scientific vision of ordinary life. Not only would the squirrel's heartbeat be audible with a stethoscope, a French invention imported to England by the real-life Lydgates of the 1820s; by Eliot's time, the squirrel's internal pulsations, motions, and secretions had also become graphically recordable by machines and available as quantitative data. Machines and numbers could imbue physiology with an air of techno-scientific objectivity, yet in their limitations, they also suggest the need for the "literature and art" that Lewes considered another source of objective psychological insight. Physiologists could catalog heartbeats but not thoughts, administer electric shocks but not emotional ones; Eliot appropriates the framework of Victorian physiology to go where the science itself could not, to develop her own novelistic techniques for the close analysis of imaginary minds and bodies. At the same time, she suggests in this passage that realism as much as human perception depends on the management of information. No medium holding out the promise—or the threat—of everybody's story can do without a filter.

Daniel Deronda has no Meunier or Lydgate, but it fully exploits the possibilities of imagining fictional psychology along the lines of neurophysiology; indeed, the novel's representation of the dynamic, fluctuating consciousness of Gwendolen Harleth closely follows the language and outlook of physiological experimentation.[68] In what may be that novel's best-known passage, Eliot provides a reflection on its treatment of Gwendolen which is also "in part an *ars poetica*" for the Victorian novel[69]:

> Could there be a slenderer, more insignificant thread in human history than this consciousness of a girl, busy with her small inferences of the way in which she could make her life pleasant?—in a time, too, when ideas were with fresh vigour making armies of themselves, and the universal kinship was declaring itself fiercely: when women on the other side of the world would not mourn for the husbands and sons who died bravely in a common cause, and men stinted of bread on our side of the world heard of that willing loss and were patient: a time when the soul of man was waking to pulses which had for centuries been beating in him unheard, until their full sum made a new life of terror or of joy.
>
> What in the midst of that mighty drama are girls and their blind visions? They are the Yea or Nay of that good for which men are enduring and fighting. In these delicate vessels is borne onward through the ages the treasure of human affections.[70]

As once-"unheard" pulses of the spirit become newly audible, Eliot juxtaposes the systole of female consciousness with the diastole of History,
Gwendolen's story with Daniel's. Here the Clarendon *Daniel Deronda* has
restored the manuscript reading "unheard" in place of other editions' "un-
felt," an emendation confirmed by the connections Eliot and Lewes drew
between the novelist and the listening physiologist.[71] Because women are
the "delicate vessels" that house human sentiment, the "thread" of a young
woman's consciousness provides an appropriate path for the narrative trajec-
tory of the novel.

As one of Eliot's rare fictions with a roughly contemporary setting ("The
Lifted Veil" is another), *Daniel Deronda* includes scattered references to
photography and telegraphy, but its connections to technical media may run
deeper. It features an estate based on Talbot's own Lacock Abbey, famous
from its photographs in *The Pencil of Nature*, and perhaps even appropriates
Talbot himself as something of a model for Deronda's guardian.[72] Daniel
Novak has recently read the novel's typological evacuation of Deronda in
relation to the emerging practice of composite photography, late-Victorian
racial science, and the realist production of abstract likeness.[73] More pointedly, *Daniel Deronda* also includes an entire family of Anglo-Dutch artists,
the Meyricks, whose bland amiability, scrupulous tidiness, and workaday
kindness counterpoint the novel's interest in things that exceed the purview
of their sympathetic understanding: the foreign or exotic (Jews), the world-
historical (Zionism), the sensational (the extravagant misery of Gwendolen Grandcourt). It is hard not to read the trim Meyricks in their tiny
house—they are "all alike small, and so in due proportion to their miniature
rooms"—as a comment on the limitations of an *Adam Bede* realism (*DD*,
180). In the last chapter, for instance, the Meyricks reappear in their obliga-
tory role, to tolerate with cheerful, Bedean magnanimity the appearance
of the "most unpoetic" "Jewish pawnbroker" Ezra Cohen and his family at
"Deronda's little wedding-feast" (*DD*, 362, 753).

In contrast, *Daniel Deronda* seems animated by efforts to comprehend
subjects that fall outside ordinary awareness, or representation in Dutch
paintings, but prove amenable to a realism increasingly concerned with the
relationships between external mimesis, intimate knowledge, and textuality—the same interplay highlighted in "The Lifted Veil." Among such sub-

jects, we can include Gwendolen's tortured consciousness, Daniel's power of sympathetic knowledge, Mordecai's prophetic visions of personal and national destiny. In the weave of Eliot's prose, a fictitious reality becomes infused with truths that overcome the limits of time, space, or individual perspective. As with "The Lifted Veil," the logic of this ambitious and expansive realism, its channeling of human data through narrative writing, reiterates modern inscription systems' fusion of common truth with the sense of transmissions from a far-off realm.

Reading the opening installment of *Daniel Deronda*, one great reader of Eliot recognized this combination, the synthesis that was coming to define the psychic life of information:

> A striking figure in these opening chapters is that of Herr Klesmer, a German music-master, who has occasion to denounce an aria of Bellini as expressing "a puerile state of culture—no sense of the universal." There could not be a better phrase than this latter one to describe the secret of that deep interest with which the reader settles down to George Eliot's widening narrative. The "sense of the universal" is constant, omnipresent. It strikes us sometimes perhaps as rather conscious and over-cultivated; but it gives us the feeling that the threads of the narrative, as we gather them into our hands, are not of the usual commercial measurement, but long electric wires capable of transmitting messages from mysterious regions.[74]

In this passage, Henry James picks up the novel's image of the "thread" as a component of consciousness, an image present in the final pages of the section he had just read (*DD*, 96). But in treating *Deronda* as a work of telegraphic realism, James also consolidated his responses to the novel: Eliot's fiction is "*charged* with reflection and intellectual experience"; the book gives readers "a sort of *lateral extension into another multitudinous world*—a world ideal only in the light" that allows us to see it but "*most real* in its close appeal to our curiosity" (emphasis added).[75] The electric wires figure a novel's sense of astonishing access to a vast world that is laterally distant yet thoroughly real.

By the time James responded to the sublime communications of *Daniel Deronda*, telegraphic wires were becoming a means of everyday commerce, yet by their nature they could still suggest the truthful conduction of displaced realities from an unseen realm. Here James regards the reader as the one who draws together the telegraphic threads of this novel, with its famously disparate plots, but we could also think of this figure assembling the plotlines as a writer or a narrator. As authors from Dickens and Trollope to James start to explore telegraphy as an explicit subject of fiction, the one who holds the threads of reality's stories—and who occupies the medial position where they come together—may also be the telegrapher.

CHAPTER 5

The Telegrapher's Tale

The telegraphic imagination of writers such as Brontë, Gaskell, and Dickens outran the actual progress of the telegraph in England. "The Mid-Victorian city of London" might be "a forest of wires, strung across the rooftops like a tangle of crazy knitting," but throughout the 1850s and 1860s critics complained that the telegraph remained underused and ill understood.[1] Given its "imperfect" "construction" and "too high" "charges," Edward Highton concluded in 1852, it was "no wonder that it has not as yet come into that general and very extended use to which it seems so admirably adapted."[2] "As regards the public, the electric telegraphs of England have been rapidly growing," but "we are still very backward in taking advantage of the facilities they afford," wrote Samuel Smiles a few years later.[3] "The telegraph, as at present existing, is not a popular institution," concurred *All the Year Round* in 1859, reporting on a project "to electrify all London" with a new network of wires for local messages; "[i]ts charges are high; its working is secret and bewildering to the average mind."[4] The speed, simplicity, and low cost of the Penny Post, with its frequent deliveries for urban customers, further discouraged use of the expensive, complex telegraph system.

This situation was changing, however. British telegraph companies handled just over a million private telegrams in 1855 but more than four times as many a decade later.[5] Although the 1866 completion of the transatlantic cable ensured that the telegraph "still retained something of its earlier glamour as 'the wonder of the age,'" it was becoming "an established public service as important as the postal service"—indeed, in Britain the Post Office would soon take over the inland telegraph system.[6] By the century's final decades, an extended, nationalized telegraph network with much lower prices made electric telegraphy a part of everyday life for more and more people in Britain, including writers. In 1877, the editor of the American collection *Lightning Flashes and Electric Dashes: A Volume of Choice Telegraphic Literature, Humor, Fun, Wit and Wisdom* could declare that "the telegraph business of late years has made such rapid progress, and the number of its votaries become so great, that the art seems to demand a literature of its own."[7] In fact, by the time he was writing, the art of telegraphy was already gaining one.

Dickens's memo about telling a story as a telegram describes an idea for a tale he never wrote. But in the 1860s and 1870s, works by Dickens and others begin imagining the fictional possibilities of electric telegraphy. This chapter examines a set of fictional texts that seize on Victorian communication systems not simply as figures, analogues, or inspirations for their representation of reality—as in *The Three Clerks, Jane Eyre, A Tale of Two Cities*, or "The Lifted Veil"—but as a crucial element of the realities they represent. In a sociological sense, these works undoubtedly reflect wider familiarity with the century's new information technologies. They also signal a growing sense of how fiction could exploit the excitement that many readers and writers might feel about them. After watching an otherwise unmemorable dramatic sketch set in a telegraph office during the Crimean War, Dickens conceded that there was "nothing in the piece, but it was impossible not to be moved and excited by the telegraph part of it."[8] Yet this discovery of a new topic for fiction also had critical implications for the nexus between fiction, reality, and information which I have been tracing. Flashing as electricity on the telegraph wires, information could seem to transcend any material basis, to lose its body. But conversely, the promise of technology to relocate human thoughts as information in a physical network might also suggest a material nature for thought itself. The ambiguous properties of electricity—as a bodiless "spirit" endowed with astonishing material powers, and as a physical link between the mechanical and organic worlds—only deepened such dilemmas.

Dickens's *Tale* and Eliot's "Veil" simultaneously express and evade this conflict by spectacularly imagining information as something real that—whatever its nature—lies beyond the normal limits of human minds and bodies. In these works, as in *Jane Eyre*, an unexplained narrative device extends perception, like a new organ of knowledge, an astonishing new medium. In fiction's ability to channel a reality inaccessible in daily life, these works find a virtual medium, a vehicle that evokes the power of modern technologies but which transcends the limitations of any particular medium. As different as they are, the historically grounded *Tale of Two Cities* and the paranormal "Lifted Veil" both conflate the power to transcend material media with writing's practical ability to convey a sense of reality. We might take this conflation, along with the violence that attends the fantasy of transcending matter and bodies, as proof of the works' underlying commitment to realism.

But as they explore ideas about information in tales of information work, a later group of fictions begins to find a divergence between an ideal of disembodied, machinic information and the fact that real human beings are responsible for managing it.[9] Even in the age of the telegraph and photograph, the storage and transmission of information still depended on eyes, ears, heads, hands, and feet. "Every user of the telegraph interacted with particular humans, such as clerks or messengers, in particular spaces"[10]—and information networks seem less intangible once we encounter their workers. By imagining the human dimensions of modern information systems, early tales about telegraphers start to rewire the connections between telegraphy, narrative, and realistic representation. Dickens's "The Signal-Man" envisions a man haunted by mysterious transmissions and represents information as an untimely but accurate ghost; Bracebridge Hemyng's *Telegraph Secrets* imagines the stories a telegraph clerk could tell—and how he might tell them; R. M. Ballantyne's *Post Haste* and *The Battery and the Boiler* present the newly merged post office and telegraph system as a realm of electric adventure. Along with Trollope's "The Telegraph Girl," they also highlight recent social and technical changes in electric telegraphy, including the growing place of women at the nodes of information networks. Such works bring new attention to exactly what fiction's earlier references to electric information tend to disregard: the material properties, and the particular mediations, of all media technologies—including writing itself.

The Ghostly Reality of Information in "The Signal-Man"

By evoking modern media and information, "The Lifted Veil" treats the registration of reality as a kind of haunting; Victorian fantastic fiction could become realism's altered image or uncanny double. Dickens's "The Signal-Man" (1866) imagines the eerie possibilities attending the information systems of the Victorian railway. By the time he wrote the story, Dickens was distressingly well prepared to address these systems' psychic and somatic reverberations. As a railway passenger, he had survived the deadly Staplehurst accident of 1865, in which several coaches of a passenger train plunged from a bridge under repair, a disaster caused by confusion and poor communication on the line. The incident left Dickens physically unhurt—after helping the injured and the dying he even climbed back into his partially derailed carriage and retrieved the manuscript for the latest part of *Our Mutual Friend*—but deeply shaken.

The last of Dickens's ghost stories, and one of his most chillingly effective, "The Signal-Man" first appeared in the Christmas number of *All the Year Round* for 1866, where it formed part of a group of loosely related pieces. The title of the collection, "Mugby Junction," spoofs the name of Rugby Junction, "at the time probably the most well-known junction station in England," as well as suggesting the juxtaposition of stories by various hands.[11] In Dickens's frame story, a lonely middle-aged man aimlessly descends at Mugby, a place full of not only trains but railway information, "[u]nkown languages in the air, conspiring in red, green, and white."[12] As this weary, Clennam-like figure gazes down, it is as if Mugby's "many railway Lines" have been "photographed" upon the "sensitive plate" of his brow, and the rest of this story sustains this interchange between rail lines and lifelines, if in a happier sense (*MJ*, 4). For by exploring the lines from Mugby, he relinquishes the bitterness of his past and finds new connections to the "external world" symbolized by this "Junction of many branches, invisible as well as visible" (*MJ*, 11). This tale follows the broad outlines that the Christmas books had established decades earlier, themes that Dickens often explored in his journals' Christmas issues.[13] In addition to this framing tale, Dickens supplied the comic "Main Line. The Boy at Mugby" and "No. 1 Branch Line. The Signal-Man," while writers from his editorial stable provided the stories for other "lines," most of them centered on the railway: tales of a driver, a clerk on the Travelling Post Office, a railway engineer.

A story of rail accidents mysteriously foretold, "The Signal-Man" draws on Dickens's long-standing interests as well as his recent experiences; long before Staplehurst, he had provided an early literary treatment of death by locomotive in *Dombey and Son*, and had published essays on railway safety in his journals. Dickens's eerie links to railway disasters would only terminate with his death on the fifth anniversary of his accident. But the most compelling recent considerations of "The Signal-Man" have gone much further than simply citing these biographical connections. Jill Matus ties the story to the Victorian discourse of rail trauma, while Norris Pope uses it as a starting point for examining the larger "problems of information management within complex systems"—a topic that Staplehurst and other railway accidents were bringing into public view by the 1860s.[14] These two issues might seem divergent, but my reading will emphasize how the tale suggests the disturbing psychic effects, and even the potential trauma, of modern information.

"The Signal-Man" begins with a line of dialogue without a given speaker, a quotation from no one before us: "Halloa! Below there!" (*MJ*, 20). Here the opening gambit makes an interruptive call for the signalman's attention double as the story's call to its audience. And, like a reader, the signalman seems unable to respond to the call as if it were a real, audible voice. "One would have thought, considering the nature of the ground, that he could not have doubted from what quarter the voice came," muses the anonymous narrator who is also the halloaing speaker; he stands high above a steep railway cutting, shading his eyes with a hand, and addresses the signalman at his lonely post near the tracks and tunnel below (*MJ*, 20).[15] But instead of casting his gaze up toward the sound, the signalman like any reader looks downward: "he turned himself about, and looked down the Line" (*MJ*, 20). The signalman's "remarkable . . . manner" compels the speaker to repeat his cry and to descend into the unearthly landscape in order to converse with him. Even before the main structure of the tale begins—a trio of visits by the narrator to the signalman, "something like a three-act play"—the tale has commenced its drama of displaced signals, a drama that begins and will also end by associating uncanny recognitions with the experience of reading.[16]

During their first conversation, the narrator quizzes the strangely wary signalman about his background and occupation. As he learns, the signalman's task is to link the railway's system of electric telegraphy to the lamps that direct the engines, to provide the interface between weightless, abstract information and the brute reality of the trains. "[A]ctual work—manual labour—he ha[s] next to none"; instead, he simply waits to be "called by his electric bell," sends and receives messages on "a telegraphic instrument with its dial face and needles," and goes out to change the railway signal accordingly (*MJ*, 21). Alone, whiling away his time as he awaits his daily electric summons, he has practiced his arithmetic and even "taught himself a language . . . if only to know it by sight, and to have formed his own crude ideas of its pronunciation, could be called learning it" (*MJ*, 21). Information may seem to transcend any particular sense, and electricity may be perceptible by all the senses alike, as Victorian science writers often noted.[17] But language of course depends on the particular sense modalities of sound and vision; knowing it only by sight is not altogether knowing it, just as pronouncing it in your own way is not speaking it. In a similar fashion, the signalman's equipment seems to send messages to him through an undetermined sense, communications that are not communal. As the narrator converses with him, the signalman efficiently responds to the ordinary messages of his bell and telegraph. But twice during their conversation the signalman looks sharply at the silent electric bell as if it had just rung, then glances out toward the tunnel and his signal lamp.

At their second meeting, the signalman confesses the source of his wariness and agitation: a series of strange messages from a source more mysterious than the electric wires. One night a year before, he had seen a ghostly figure near the tunnel shouting "Halloa! Below there!" and then "Look out! Look out!" (*MJ*, 22). The signalman demonstrates its desperate look and gesture, covering his face with one arm and waving the other in a manner the narrator recognizes as signifying "with the utmost passion and vehemence: 'For God's sake clear the way!'" (*MJ*, 22); Dickens remains sensitive to the telegraphic possibilities of mien and gesture. The spectral figure vanished, and the signalman's anxious electric queries up and down the line revealed nothing wrong. As David Seed points out, this messenger is no chain-rattling ghoul but a "strikingly 'modern'" apparition, one that "is particularly mysterious because it is performing a realistic action without any real context."[18] Carefully described and precisely repeated, the specter's decontextualized actions point to what has been identified as a larger split in the tale: the potential divergence between exactness and the impression of truth.[19] Realism might thrive on an extra detail or two, as Barthes claims, yet it may be undermined by too much information, which brings not just distraction but epistemological unease.

The narrator quickly puts forth an ordinary explanation for this trick played on the signalman's senses: perhaps a "disease of the delicate nerves" of the eye, accompanied by the wind that makes a "wild harp . . . of the telegraph wires"—and which makes telegraphic naïfs think that they are hearing messages (*MJ*, 23). But the signalman continues the story. Within hours of this vision, a terrible accident took place on the line—an accident identifiable with the real-life Clayton Tunnel crash of 1861—and its victims were carried past the ground where the specter stood.[20] Months later, the figure reappeared with its hands covering its face as if in grief; that very day a young woman died on a train as it passed by. Only a bumpkin would confuse an information transfer from distant regions with the sound of wind on wires, but as the signalman tells his tale, "the wind and wires t[ake] up the story with a long lamenting wail" (*MJ*, 23).

And now the figure has returned to the signalman, waving frantically, crying "look out," even making the electric bell sound with a "strange vibration" (*MJ*, 23). But "[w]hat is its warning against?" "Where is the danger?" wonders the signalman (*MJ*, 24). What a sad "irony . . . that the signalman, who is by definition qualified to give and read signals to avert danger from the line, is unable to decode the signals of the spectre."[21] Under such circumstances, how can he carry out his charge, linking shadowy information with physical reality to maintain safety on the line?

> If I telegraph Danger, on either side of me, or on both, I can give no reason for it. . . . I should get into trouble, and do no good. They would think I was mad. This is the way it would work:—Message: "Danger! Take care!" Answer: "What danger? Where?" Message: "Don't know. But for God's sake take care!" They would displace me. What else could they do? (*MJ*, 24)

Reluctantly, the narrator concludes that the signalman must be going mad.

After all, as the *Times* had noted after the Clayton Tunnel disaster, "Your signalmen are not pieces of clockwork . . . ; they are men whose nerves and brains are susceptible of disorder."[22] In 1858 Dickens himself had met a former telegraph worker "afflicted with incurable madness" (he wrote to Wilkie Collins that it might make a good subject for one of Collins's stories).[23] Perhaps the signalman suffers from an immersion in electrical information that has disturbed his connection to the real world; in late nineteenth-century fiction, information workers will regularly suffer from such afflictions. The railway company must be informed lest his illness cause an accident; as Samuel Smiles points out of real-life rail problems, "[w]here railways fail . . . it will usually be found that it is because the men are personally defective."[24] Before the narrator takes such a step, he plans to return with an offer to help the poor signalman consult a doctor.

But what a sight when he comes back the next day: "the appearance of a man" in front of the tunnel, waving just as the signalman had described (*MJ*, 25). It is an engine driver, demonstrating his futile attempts to warn the signalman out of the way as his train came through the tunnel earlier that day. Seeing the signalman on the tracks with his back turned, the driver had shouted "Below there! Look out! Look out! For God's sake clear the way," waving frantically with one arm but covering his face with the other as it became clear that the train would run him down (*MJ*, 25). As it turns out, the signalman saw a portent of his death that was really a reenactment of the way it had already happened, a retrospective miming of his doom, a representation of reality displaced (to use the signalman's term) in time. Like any ghost, the figure in the signalman's mimetic vision channels the past; however, through a Latimer-like temporal dislocation, the specter's past turns out to be the signalman's calamitous future.

As a railway information worker, the signalman had linked the large-scale world of matter and the less tangible world of information. With a gothic elaboration of this role, his tale builds upon the ghostliness of information, its telegraphic sense of abstract truthfulness from unseen regions, facts freed from the constraints of space and time. Elsewhere writers have imagined the scenes of the real world played out on the wire as telegraph messages, but "The Signal-Man" seems to reverse this movement, haunting the signalman in his daily life with an intangible vision modeled on the logic of modern information systems. As in *A Tale of Two Cities* and "The Lifted Veil," this tale makes the signalman's troubled mind and broken body into the ultimate sites for the fatal encounter of reality and information.

Reading "The Signal-Man" as traumatized narrative, Jill Matus points out the story's emphasis not only "on a sense of powerlessness at impending disaster" but also "on the uncoupling of event and cognition, on belatedness, repetitive and intrusive return"—all recognized today as symptoms of trauma.[25] Matus incisively traces the prehistory of trauma through Victorian psychology and railway discourse.[26] But one might also place trauma at the intersection between information and real experience. In trauma, writes Cathy Caruth, an "event is not assimilated or experienced fully at the time, but only belatedly"[27]—a paradigm that marks the untimely information of "The Signal-Man" as well as "The Lifted Veil." If trauma is experience that resists normal integration into psyche and narrative, then information in its abstractness may always harbor the threat of trauma. Furthermore, Caruth points out the troubling literalness of "traumatic dreams and flashbacks," arguing that trauma's "enigmatic core" is that a delay or lack of knowledge nevertheless "remains . . . absolutely *true* to the event"; thus, trauma "is not a pathology," not a "displacement of meaning, but of history itself"[28]—like the displaced history that torments the signalman to death. Realism asks readers to recognize something of their world in the intimate and alienated shape of its prose, and so may always harbor the makings of the uncanny. In its literal repetitions and reenactments, trauma becomes too real to be realistic, but it points out that potential.

The final lines of "The Signal-Man" return to the association the story has drawn between displaced information and reading the narrative itself. "Below there! Look out! Look out! For God's sake clear the way," the driver had shouted, and the narrator pauses to establish the significance of these precise words:

> Without prolonging the narrative to dwell on any one of its curious circumstances more than on any other, I may, in closing it, point out the coincidence that the warning of the Engine-Driver included, not only the words which the unfortunate Signalman had repeated to me as haunting him, but also the words which I myself—not he—had attached, and that only in my own mind, to the gesticulation he had imitated. (*MJ*, 25)

Schematically speaking, all that has happened is that a thought given only to readers in the retrospective first-person narration has been promoted to a place in the tale's outer mimesis.[29] But in the context of the tale, the narrative itself has become untimely information, words with the uncanny accuracy of its ghostly visitations. Like the driver's gestures, the past-tense narrative itself reenacts the eerie death of the signalman. The information exchanges realized by the tale now become part of the signalman's strange ending, an ending that has in various manners been foreseen—by the victim, the terrified driver, and the narrative—but has never actually been seen directly by any of these. It is information that exists outside the normal channels of perception, a vision that retains the untimeliness and brute literalism of trauma.

"The Signal-Man" imagines the properties of immaterial information crossing over to life; it highlights the ghostliness of information freed from time, space, or matter. But as Dickens was envisioning a deadly encounter on the tracks, railway companies were adopting "interlocking" technologies, which connected signaling to switching equipment and thus "linked information and mechanical action into a unified whole."[30] Such devices treated signals not as disembodied, context-free information but as inseparable from the material context that determined their truthfulness. Late in the century, a similar paradigm will emerge in Henry James's telegraphic fiction.

Telegraphing the Story

Other fictional works contemporary to "The Signal-Man" emphasize the more mundane problems of modern information systems. The supposed transparency or neutrality of the electric telegraph helped align telegraphy with fictional truth. Yet when it came to the telegraph, such transparency was a fantasy. To be transmitted, information had to be transcoded into electric impulses, and telegraphic discourse soon developed its own norms based the pricing of language by the word or letter. As telegraphic messages underwent encoding and commodification, they had to pass through another level of mediation: the telegraphists. "Despite the widely expressed optimism that the telegraph would unite humanity, it was only really telegraph operators who were able to communicate with each other directly."[31] And the telegraph's history reveals that the human beings on each end of the wire could play a conspicuous, and sometimes disruptive, role in the process.[32]

Gaskell's "electric telegraph something-or-other" and Dickens's idea of narrating as an "electric message" both disregarded this circumstance, as did even some commentators with more expertise. An early article on the "romance" of the electric telegraph exults "that a person standing in London might hold a conversation with another at Edinburgh, put questions and receive answers, just as if they were seated together in one room."[33] In such fictional and nonfictional accounts of sending telegrams, the machine's real operators do not register. But by the final third of the nineteenth century, the position of the telegrapher begins to offer a subject for fiction.

The shilling- and (thanks to his sojourn across the Atlantic) dime-novelist Bracebridge Hemyng inadvertently highlights the potential obtrusiveness of the telegraph worker in *Telegraph Secrets* (1867), a collection of short stories first published anonymously. (After Hemyng's Jack Harkaway adventure tales made him famous, the book appeared under his name as part of "Diprose's Railway Library," perfect reading for a journey alongside the wires.) "Secresy [*sic*] is . . . an essential element in telegraphic communication," affirm factual reports on the telegraph.[34] But even while emphasizing the confidentiality with which messages are handled, such accounts often suggest that "[c]onsiderable instruction, with some little amusement, might . . . be derived from a perusal of the variegated information, intelligence, and . . . private messages" that flash along it.[35] "Could we but raise the veil of secrecy which . . . we are bound to hold over the correspondence entrusted to us, we could set forth a volume of domestic anxieties, in fragments, which could scarcely be paralleled," affirms the superintendent of a telegraph company.[36] Hemyng takes full advantage of such hints. The episodes in *Telegraph Secrets* purport to be true stories from the life of a telegraph "Station-Master," "occurrences in real life which, by their very nature, are too strange not to be true" but which now appear "wrapped . . . up in the form of narrative" for the delectation of readers.[37]

The telegraphic play between first- and third-person narrative also emerges in *Telegraph Secrets*, in an explicit if clumsy form. The first two stories in Hemyng's collection initially seem written in the third person, complete with the abundant supply of backstory and the reportage of multiple characters' thoughts which indicate narratorial omniscience. But in both texts, a first-person narrator abruptly appears at the end of the story and reveals his connection to the tale—at exactly the moment when secrets are telegraphed: "The telegraph was put into operation, and I transmitted the message which led to Desmond De Vigne's ultimate capture" (from the story "Caught at Last"); or "I was the manipulator who sent the queries flying through sea and air" (in "Odds Against Them") (*TS*, 12, 39). Like realist narration, telegraphy places a shadowy figure at the intersection between sending and receiving its message. In these telegraphic tales, the first-person pronoun and its sudden assertion of narrative identity arrive when the telegrams begin to fly; as a matter of form as well as content, the telegraph becomes a narrative device. The tales in Hemyng's otherwise similar *Secrets of the Dead-Letter Office* (1868) ("By the Author of 'Telegraph Secrets'") confine themselves to the third-person point of view and contain no such narrative fluctuation.

In the second story of *Telegraph Secrets*, the narrator leaves his office in order to personally deliver a telegram to the tale's heroes, and his role continues to increase in subsequent tales, which move more and more decisively into the first person. Perhaps in keeping with its less common use, the telegraph wire furnishes more exotic stories than the idealized Victorian postbag. As the stories progress, the telegrapher-cum-narrator accompanies police detectives to apprehend thieves, forgers, and murderers exposed by telegrams. He reveals his name (he is called "Mr. Mortimer") and even foils an attempt to assassinate the emperor of France (*TS*, 56). Mortimer finds himself able to assist the authorities because he has "for many years past made it a practice to enter all striking telegrams in a book"—documentation that also provides the ostensible origin of *Telegraph Secrets* itself (*TS*, 91). Along with the telegrams he superintends or intercepts, the telegrapher-narrator provides the principle of continuity between the otherwise unconnected tales; his increasing intrusiveness in their action and narration becomes the closest thing to a sustained plot in *Telegraph Secrets*. The characters who send and receive the messages are as oblivious as the inhabitants of Trollope's earth under glass; they treat telegraphy as a transparent, automatic medium, never suspecting that their secrets are also being telegraphed to the authorities, and to readers.

By the final and most outlandish tale in the collection, Hemyng has abandoned any claims to realism or to documentation, and Mortimer has gone from narrator and telegraph worker to private spy. Intrigued by a telegram, Mortimer leaves the telegraph office in the hands of female clerks—a neat summary of the comparative mobility of men and women in telegraphic careers; by this time, women routinely undertook all the tasks performed by men in telegraph offices but were "paid less and had fewer opportunities for advancement."[38] Freed from his desk job, Mortimer masquerades as a valet in order to learn the secret of a telegram sent by a dying gypsy queen who has abducted the woman for whom a rich young man once jilted her. The gypsies, the kidnapped rival, the breathless plot summary: via a wish fulfillment appropriate for a bored clerk, telegrams have taken us far—from the precincts of everyday authenticity deep into the realm of the shilling romance.

Mortimer feels no concern that his extramural impersonations might trouble his employers at the telegraph company, since they know that he is "engaged in the compilation of a book, and wishe[s] to gather materials for it in a legitimate or illegitimate way" (*TS*, 112). In real life, both the plots of these stories and their publication by Mr. Mortimer would have audaciously violated the Telegraph Act of 1863, which established "a penalty not exceeding twenty pounds" for any telegraph worker who delayed a message or divulged its content.[39] Telegraphing secrets left and right, Hemyng's stories might also suggest the desirability of turning the private telegraph networks into a uniform, government-run public service, an effort that began in the year he published his collection. But in Hemyng's imagination, pulling together telegrams, and infiltrating the stories they suggest, justifies itself by becoming a principle of narration and a form of modern authorship. Mid-Victorian novelists could cite or allude to the electric telegraph as a figure for truth at a distance, for the sudden clarity with which fiction sets objects before us, or for the global framework of everyday connection realism presumes. Yet Hemyng's strategy for narrating the telegraph complicates those associations. Placing the telegraphist at the center of its design to reveal sensational secrets, it unravels the web of neutral discourse supposedly woven by the telegraph needles.

Two adventure novels by R. M. Ballantyne put a similar focus on the telegraph, as well as constructing their own alignments between communication technology and narrativity. *Post Haste: A Tale of Her Majesty's Mails* (1880) and *The Battery and the Boiler; or, Adventures in the Laying of Submarine Electric Cables* (1883) display the mixture of raw information and adolescent fantasy that characterizes Ballantyne's novels, works for which the author's research seems to double as a tool for rapid assemblage. Ballantyne's preface to *Post Haste* assures us that the novel is "founded chiefly on facts furnished by the Postmaster Generals' Annual Reports, and gathered . . . at the General Post Office of London and its Branches," and neither book is reluctant to halt its story in order to provide pages of undigested data about the post or telegraph, information about the movement of information.[40] At various points in both works, the provision of facts and figures makes the minds of characters reel, the novels' internal effort to preempt—or at least to acknowledge—the novels' impositions as they suspend narrative development for the sake of mere information. As postal statistics "ke[ep] ringing in his brain," one protagonist of *Post Haste* becomes dazed by "[l]etters, letters, letters!"—an experience that seems partly responsible for his early steps toward youthful dissipation (*PH*, 87, 86). More jocularly, *The Battery and the Boiler* interrupts one character's long lecture on telegraphy with his listener's electrical plea that "my capacity is feeble."[41]

In both novels, the rapid communication supplied by the post and the telegraph also serves as a model for the narrative's ability to overcome space and time. Ballantyne's works are not known for their craft, and both novels move somewhat haphazardly among settings, plotlines, and timelines. But since these novels take shape around widely distributed modern information systems, this very dispersion emphasizes the parallels between their narration and the forms of communication they treat. *Post Haste* opens by following a postal telegram backward from its recipient in western Ireland to its sender in London, and the text remains conscious of the ability of narrative to perform similar operations on geography and temporality; soon afterward, the novel proclaims it "necessary, for the satisfactory elucidation of our tale, that we should go backward a short way in time, and forward a long way into space" (*PH*, 28). *The Battery and the Boiler* makes the analogy explicit. Abruptly ending a chapter in which its young hero joins in the *Great Eastern*'s laying of the Atlantic cable, it offers a telegraphic trope: "But all this we must leave, and carry the reader back to old England faster than the Great Eastern could have rushed—ay, faster than the message on the flashing cable itself could have sped, for mind is more subtle than matter, and thought is swifter than even the Atlantic Telegraph" (*BB*, 118). Nearly three hundred pages later, the novel stops when "the story finds a 'fault,' and the electrical current ends" (*BB*, 399).

FIGURE 5.1. An accident on the Travelling Post Office. Ballantyne, *Post Haste* (1880).

Such easy narrative movements contrast with more ponderous modes of mobility in these novels. Like "The Signal-Man," *Post Haste* treats the railway as the site for a spectacular encounter between information management and the power of steam locomotion. In one high-concept set piece, a wayward piece of equipment on the Travelling Post Office rips open a car, showering the tracks with sorting-clerks and an undifferentiated flow of letters. The narrative has been following a letter through the post, in familiar "Valentine's Day" style, but now suddenly it is lost in the accident—a development in keeping with an emerging emphasis not on the wonders of modern information systems but on their limits and failures.

Telegraph Girls

By the 1870s, the network of "economic cables," the connections "useful to business and private customers" was largely in place, but a new era of imperial telegraph lines laid for essentially "jingoist" or "political reasons" was opening.[42] In line with the real history of late-Victorian telegraphy, the cable crew of *The Battery and the Boiler* moves from connecting Europe and North America to forging undersea links between metropole and Empire, the better to bypass the landlines subject to "unbusiness-like" foreigners (*BB*, 288). "[N]o doubt the lines are all right enough, but the people through whose countries they pass are all wrong"; the result is a "chronic" "telegraphic disease" afflicting imperial communication (*BB*, 296). The threat to the purity of English discourse is explicit, and it is gendered. The cable-laying group journeys to the Indian Ocean only to discover, and to rescue, a beautiful blonde English girl named "Letta" on a pirate island. They try to announce their deeds to their anxious relations back in England, but the telegram they send on the old landline "suffer[s] rather severe mutilation at the hands of the foreigners" and becomes nearly incomprehensible (*BB*, 364).

Foreign interference and noise threaten the integrity of English communication, as well as the novel's internal economy of information; they stop accurate knowledge of the novel's main plotline from reaching the group of characters who remain in England. Only when a lady from Bombay arrives in London to present the astonished family with both "a letter . . . and . . . this dear child, Letta" does the situation become clear to them (*BB*, 367). At the same moment, the lady's dual conveyance of message and child makes apparent the significance of Letta's unusual name. As the heroism of the cable-boys suggests, a British imperial telegraph line will deliver pristine English Lettas from interference by foreign characters. When Letta comes of age, she accepts a telegraphic marriage proposal from one of the cable-layers and journeys with him to India to produce a brood "gifted with galvanic energy and flashing eyes," the offspring of a devoted electrician and the purest English letter (*BB*, 420).

In contrast to the brief "Signal-Man," Ballantyne's courtship plots necessitate a certain attention to female figures in his informatic romances. But the appearance of women in his mail tale *Post Haste* also tracks the new reality of women's information work. As a telegram is "not exactly a letter," so by the 1870s a telegraphist might be not exactly your average male office clerk (*PH*, 7). Tracing a telegram to its sender, *Post Haste* finds the seventeen-year-old May Maylands engaged in her unusual "woman's work," "playing with her pretty little fingers" on the clicking "pianoforte keys" that punch out telegrams to be fed to an automatic telegraph (*PH*, 11). For May is "a female telegraphist in what we may call the literary lungs of London—the General Post-Office at St. Martin's-le-Grand" (*PH*, 13), where by now most of the clerks were women.[43]

During a pause in her work, as May awaits the next message, she turns her mind into a device for experience at a distance, sending it home "to that little cottage by the sea . . . on the west coast of Ireland, with greater speed than ever she flashed those electric sparks which it was her business to scatter broadcast over the land. . . . The mind of May entered through its closed door,—for mind, like electricity, laughs at bolts and bars" (*PH*, 13). Imaginatively released to roam like Dickens's Shadow, May's mind leaves the scenes of the crowded telegram center and "hover[s] over" her far-off Irish "home circle," seeing her mother sewing, watching her younger brothers at play, hearing the sea outside the cottage. The telegraph has offered a parallel for narrative movement and will soon do so again as we follow May's telegram back to Ireland. But this scene also aligns telegraphy with thought itself. Furthermore, it suggests the parallel between May's telegraphic daydreaming and the immersion of the novel's readers in realistic scenes that aren't really there, especially since we have just been asked to envision the same place and characters in our own imaginations.

Figure 5.2. The telegraph office as male preserve. Lardner, *The Electric Telegraph Popularised* (1850). Courtesy of University of Georgia Libraries.

With its references to "woman's work" and introduction of May at a telegraphic "pianoforte," *Post Haste* draws attention to the young woman at the telegraph. For years women had performed telegraph work in Britain; the private companies had started hiring a few women telegraphers as early as the 1850s.[44] An illustration of the instrument room at the Charing Cross Telegraph Office published in 1855 represents it as the kind of "male preserve" that typifies the mid-nineteenth-century office.[45] Yet a revision of the image made just a few years later quietly turns several of the lower clerks into women. Like the fashionable moustache given to the office superintendent, the change not only adds visual interest but also keeps pace with changing social norms. Already by the time of the telegraph system's nationalization in 1870, nearly a third of telegraphers were women.[46] The government's takeover of telegraphy took the process even further, making the feminization of low-level telegraph work into official policy; the Post Office now became "Britain's first major employer of female clerks."[47]

Figure 5.3. The image altered: women in the telegraph office. Shaffner, *The Telegraph Manual* (1859). © British Library Board, All Rights Reserved (1600/712).

Trollope had retired from the Post Office shortly before Parliament nationalized the British telegraph system and merged it into the postal bureaucracy. But for his late short story "The Telegraph Girl" and a companion article called "The Young Women at the London Telegraph Office" (1877), he carefully researched one consequence of this consolidation, the employment of female workers in large processing centers like the one in which May Maylands works. Touring the main telegraph office in London, Trollope was "much struck" by "this branch of female employment"[48]:

Eight-hundred young women at work, . . . earning fair wages at easy work,—work fit for women to do, . . . with leave of absence without stoppage of pay every year, with a doctor for sickness, and a pension for old age and incompetence, . . . with only eight hours of work, never before eight in the morning, and never after eight at night, with female superintendents . . . ! Is not that the kind of institution that philanthropic friends of the weaker sex have been looking for and desiring for years?[49]

After all, opening government postal telegraph work to women would give them a new hold on that "rock of safety to very many men," the civil service. "The Young Women at the Telegraph Office" reveals that Trollope's understanding of government service has hardly changed since his rejection of bureaucratic hard lines in *The Three Clerks*: "There is a security in it, an absence of cruelty, a justice, a clemency leaning a little too much, perhaps, to the side of faulty servants, a philanthropy and consideration forced upon it, both by its magnitude and its publicity" (*YW*). As usual, Trollope's views of the civil service parallel his practice as a novelist. Alter a few incidental words, and this description of the civil service could describe the forbearance with which his fiction generally treats its characters.

But the regular employment of women as telegraphers was far from a matter of philanthropy. Employing women and paying them lower wages supported the great goal of cheaper telegrams. As Rowland Hill in his own retirement recognized, the hiring of "female labour" on fixed-term contracts was an "improvement . . . in the new department of Telegraphy" which could save the office thousands of pounds a year.[50] The special advantage of women was that, in the words of the head of the new telegraph department, they would "solve" the problem of ever-increasing wages based on seniority "by retiring for the purpose of getting married as soon as they get a chance."[51] In 1876 the Post Office adopted a rule that only single women would be hired as clerks, and that any women who married would have to resign; by explicit policy, marriage became both the structural alternative to female telegraph work and its appointed end.[52] The practice of hiring women as telegraphers also provided a foretaste of a turn-of-the-century business world in which inventions such as the first commercial typewriter (1873) and the telephone (1876) would help give rise to a new class of female information workers: type-writers (a word used for both typists and their machines), stenographers, switchboard operators.[53] From the beginning, the Post Office was "mobbed" by female job applicants, part of a rise in the total number of women clerks from 2,000 in 1851 (out of 95,000 clerks in Britain) to 166,000 by 1911 (out of 843,000).[54]

Trollope was certainly intrigued by these rows of women arranged like postal sorting boxes or galvanic batteries. The fictional "Telegraph Girl" suggests how his realist imagination could work outward from the kinds of questions he enumerates in the factual "Young Women at the London

Telegraph Office": who were these young women who found a newer, more technical trade than that of governess or teacher? Were they respectable? For, in Trollope's view,

> that question of character—what we may call respectability—is one much more difficult among women than men, but one which so imperatively demands to be asked and answered. . . . Oh!—if I could only know what those two pretty girls in the distance were talking about!—not from curiosity, but that I might judge somewhat of their inward natures,—whether they were good or bad, happy or unhappy, pure or impure. (*YW*)

And whom—if anyone—might such female telegraph workers marry? After all, women telegraphers "tended to be young" and had to be single.[55] As a handbook from the 1860s notes, updating the romance of the telegraph, it was widely reported that "since the introduction of young ladies to work the Instruments, Telegraphic courtships have, in more than one instance, led to *hymeneal results*."[56]

Lucy Graham in Sophy's World

As it imagines the answers to Trollope's questions, "The Telegraph Girl" will prove something of a signal moment in the history of the connection between fictional realism and electric telegraphy. Like Trollope himself, Lucy Graham—the telegraph girl of the title—is unequivocally a realist. She instantly rejects her roommate Sophy's romantic fantasy that their friend the printing-engineer Mr. Hall might really be "some gentleman in disguise," perhaps in hiding from "paternal tyranny," in favor of the theory that he is simply decent and kind, one of "Nature's gentlemen."[57] Perhaps Sophy is thinking of one of the "telegraphic romances" in which female clerks "meet and marry an eligible bachelor from the upper classes."[58] Trollope clearly means us to find it appropriate, given Sophy's frivolousness and superficiality, that the ultimate object of her affections should be a hairdresser.

The story consistently aligns solid, sensible Lucy with the medium of writing, with words on paper. Having worked in her late brother's bookstore, she is uncommonly literate; "[w]ith English literature she was better acquainted than is usual with young women of her age and class," and she retains a few books as "personal treasures" (*TG*, 355). The story even compares her appearance and clothing to a book with "a good strong binding," one that will "not look disfigured even though a blot of ink should come its way" (*TG*, 356). At home she reads aloud to Sophy, although her companion understands "but little of what was read" and—when Lucy dismisses the fantasy of a highborn Mr. Hall who will fall in love with a telegraph girl—complains that Lucy for "all her reading, kn[ows] nothing of poetry" (*TG*, 361, 363).

Lucy's success as a telegraph worker grows out of her work ethic and this special association with books and reading. So proficient is she at scanning the "little dots and pricks" on her telegraph's paper recording tape that "[n]o one could read and use her telegraphic literature more rapidly or correctly than Lucy Graham" (*TG*, 365). But bookish Lucy is also a worker being edged out by technological change, for the postal "pundits" have introduced a new "system of communicating messages by ear instead of by eye" (*TG*, 365): probably "Bright's Bells" (which turned the left- and rightward movements on Cooke and Wheatstone's needles into ringing bells of different tones) but perhaps the Morse sounder with its clicking dots and dashes.[59] American-style sound-reading had been "brought into use in England [in] about 1875," having gradually overcome "a general prejudice in favour of a recorded message on the paper tape."[60] By the mid-1870s, the visual "alphabet of the wires" struck Trollope as a technology on its way out; "there is less labour and cost" in acoustic telegraphy, he explains, "the clerk receiving the sounds without any interposition of marked paper" (*YW*). In this passage, the advent of sound-based telegraphy inspires a pitiless technical redefinition of writing (as simply "marked paper") and casts it as an "interposition," a mediation and intrusion into the information transfer. Against a competing technology with different properties, the telegraph's writing no longer seems transparent or natural.[61]

As Trollope's story assesses its two female clerks, it also imagines the relationship between a world based on forms of writing and a new order in which alternative modes of communication and storage usurp some of writing's functions. Flighty, flirty, sickly Sophy easily masters sound-reading and is promoted to "the musical box" with a pay raise and better hours (*TG*, 367). This causes "a great separation between the girls," for lacking "musical aptitudes," the levelheaded Lucy cannot accomplish the shift to aurality from literacy (*TG*, 367, 366). Morally flexible and psychologically intuitive, Sophy is "quicker" at her work than Lucy, and Lucy therefore assumes she is "clever" (*TG*, 358). But compared to Lucy, whose only real flaw is her too-rigid adherence to middle-class notions of feminine propriety, Sophy seems at once adept and idle, sharp and strangely "foolish" (*TG*, 365); her qualities appear paradoxical against the norms of Victorian realism and Trollopian good sense. And although Sophy masters a new technology beyond the grasp of hardworking Lucy, her extended sick leave confirms stereotypes about malingering female telegraph clerks (*YW*).[62] How should the character of such a clerk as Sophy be weighed; how might the respectability of such a young woman be measured?

A version of the original telegraphs of the mid-nineteenth century, the machines preferred by Lucy Graham produce "literature." For the realist postmaster Trollope, the Post Office's adoption of more modern acoustic telegraphy signals the technological replacement of literature with something else, something that one does not read but simply "catch" and whose "little tinkling sounds" he can only describe as a sort of music, not a text at all (*TG*, 365–66).[63] Under the circumstances, it seems fortunate for Lucy that the end of the tale brings Valentine's Day to the telegraph office. Defying the letter of official regulations but remaining true to their spirit, Abraham Hall manages to breach the defenses of the telegraph department and propose marriage. He boldly asks to speak to a supervisor, exclaiming that "She is not a prisoner!"—an echo of Trollope's own musings ("The girls, I suppose, are not prisoners") that elaborates the alignment between author, print worker, and bookish telegraphist (*TG*, 378; *YW*). Lucy ends up marrying the printer Mr. Hall and thus necessarily giving up telegraphy for good. A sturdy, generous, self-consciously "independent" heroine finally accepts the statutory alternative to women's telegraph work (*TG*, 355). For Trollope, being realistic also means settling for compromise, a principle that shapes not only the imagined life of the overreaching Alaric Tudor but also the circumscribed possibilities of the irreproachable Lucy Graham.

With the parallel stories of Lucy and Sophy, Trollope suggests that the new world of long-distance communication beyond books, ink, and marks on paper—the age of technologies that separate transmission from recording—might turn out to be Sophy's world. When Sophy stoops to writing notes, Lucy finds them "hard" to interpret because "[s]he writes just as she feels at the moment" (*TG*, 371). Sophy is a sort of vulgar aesthete (thus her attraction to that everyday artist of the ephemeral, a coiffeur), a Paterian impressionist without Pater's asceticism. Her epistolary attempts become a transcription of the thoughts passing through her consciousness, flowing like Pater's impressions—or like the evanescent pulses of acoustic telegraphy. This universe of informatic automatism, intellectual freedom, moral ambiguity, and personal fantasy is a preview of James's *In the Cage*.

The realist narrator may identify with Lucy, but at least by the end of his writing career, Trollope describes his work as more like Sophy's—perhaps fittingly, from a novelist famous for his intuitive rapidity but whose brainpower has sometimes been doubted.[64] In his autobiography (1883), drafted around the same time as "The Telegraph Girl" but published posthumously, Trollope compares the proficient author to a telegraphist at work on an acoustic telegraph, to a Sophy: "His language must come from him as music comes from the rapid touch of the great performer's fingers; as words come from the mouth of the indignant orator; as letters fly from the fingers of the trained compositor; as the syllables tinkled out by little bells form themselves to the ear of the telegraphist" (*A*, 177). "Rapid writing" helps produce "a good and lucid style," "agreeable and easily intelligible to the reader" (*A*, 177, 176). In contrast, "[a] man who thinks much of his words as he writes them will generally leave behind him work that smells of oil" (*A*, 177). The autobiography of a famously fluent novelist turns out to be one more telegrapher's tale.

This use of the telegraph as a model for avoiding the queasy stench of intellection recalls Gaskell, and Trollope's comparison similarly sidesteps questions about the provenance of the message. Musical performance, manual typesetting, sound telegraphy, and even passionate oration—all of these deflect questions of composition. Yet note the compressed genealogy of human language encoded in Trollope's sequence of similes for novel-writing: from "music," spoken "words," and printed "letters" to the tinkling sound of telegraphic "syllables." Trollope updates Gaskell's metaphor for an age of acoustic telegraphy, but he also changes it. The external objects Defoe set out before us are nowhere to be seen; instead we now hear something that sounds like the interaction of autonomic language with automated listening, telegraphic "syllables" that "form themselves to the ear."

The realist telegraph of the 1850s and 1860s was something like Lucy Graham's apparatus, a device that produced telegraphic literature. Conveying words into consciousness through neither speech nor writing, the sounding telegraph does something else. Indeed, it approaches what Friedrich Kittler has identified as a project of the new media technologies of the late nineteenth century: recording or transmitting "sense data" without recourse to the written word.[65] A year before Trollope published "The Telegraph Girl," Alexander Graham Bell tested a device that moved telegraphy even closer toward this incipient ideal; he originally conceived and patented his telephone as an "improvement" to the telegraph.

Later in his autobiography, Trollope imagines the communication between reader and writer as an electric transmission that dispenses with the senses altogether. "The language used should be as ready and as efficient a conductor of the mind of the writer to the mind of the reader as is the electric spark which passes from one battery to [another] battery. In all written matter the spark should carry everything. . . . " (*A*, 235, original brackets). In this passage, observes J. Hillis Miller, "the medium vanishes in its flawless working," an electrical metaphor for Trollope's self-described realism.[66] But as "The Telegraph Girl" indicates, realistically exploring telegraphic discourse was coming to mean investigating the mechanics of telegraphy and imagining the telegraphist. Nineteenth-century realism might start from the premise that the power of writing and other media to overcome space and time trumped the particular effects of their mediations as they channeled reality. But by the final decades of the century, real life itself would have encouraged a growing awareness of the specific properties of different media, of the shaping power of technological mediations, and even of differences within variant forms of the same underlying medium, such as printing telegraphs and acoustic ones.

This greater attention to mediation paralleled—and, as Trollope's fascination with the pretty telegraph girls suggests, might be reinforced by—the new practice of employing women as information workers. If market society tends to obscure the visibility of labor, as Victorian critics from Karl Marx to John Ruskin argue, modern information work "adds another degree of invisibility to the mix": "[t]he virtual characteristics" of information itself as it is "stored, located, duplicated, and exchanged" with such speed and apparent ease.[67] But the feminization of information work might make both information and work peculiarly visible for novelists. For Trollope and company, having young women at the nodes of these technological networks could enhance their appeal for fiction.

Fiction writers from Richardson and Austen to Eliot helped make the development of female subjectivity the quintessential province of the realist novel, but an array of turn-of-the-century works would update this focus for a secretarial age. Late-Victorian fictions as different as Grant Allen's lively new woman novel *The Type-Writer Girl* (1897) and Bram Stoker's *Dracula* (1897) combine attention to new media with an emphasis on the consciousness of the women who help them mediate. From its early years, the promise of the electric telegraph to relocate thought, to externalize the human nervous system, could help encourage renewed attention to the possibilities of representing consciousness in fiction. Now, amid a riot of media even newer than the electric telegraph, these concerns with mental life, mediation, and female subjectivity will coalesce in a work that takes a telegraph girl as the subject not simply for the navigation of a Trollopian marriage plot but for an elaborate Jamesian drama of consciousness. And after more than half a century of connections between new media and realist epistemology, the two can emphatically come together in works that combine an explicit focus on communication technology with a redefinition of realism as a practice of writing.

Cable and Wireless

CHAPTER 6

A Winged Intelligence

Looking back at *In the Cage* (1898), the tale of a young female telegraph worker who becomes obsessed with the coded messages exchanged between two trysting customers, Henry James speculates that its principal "idea" is so evident that it "must again and again have flowered (granted the grain of observation) in generous minds": to wit, "the question of what it might 'mean' . . . for confined and cramped and yet considerably tutored young officials of either sex to be made so free, intellectually, of a range of experience otherwise quite closed to them."[1] After "the spark" of curiosity is aroused in the observing author, the question becomes "an amusement, or an obsession," the spectator echoing the sentiments that the story ascribes to the telegraphist herself (*P*, xix). James concedes that the watcher may be too hasty to attribute such a "critical impulse" to his subject; the tale's "central spirit," the telegraphist, "is, for verisimilitude, I grant, too ardent a focus of divination[,] but without this excess, the phenomena detailed would have lacked their principle of cohesion" (*P*, xix, xxi). Piecing together the story of her customers' affair, the telegraphist applies her insight to bits of information sent by persons who might seem to have little connection to one another; her authorlike critical faculty, her excessive divination, holds the tale together. In fact, "[t]he action of the drama is simply the girl's 'subjective' adventure—that of her quite definitely winged intelligence" (*P*, xxi).

The lovers use the telegraph for secret, virtually instantaneous communication, living out the fifty-year-old visions of telegraphic passion in *Jane Eyre* and early treatments of the technology. Yet by reading and interpreting the messages of Captain Everard and Lady Bradeen, the unnamed telegraphist interposes a level of mediation, a layer that intermingles the materiality of communication, the content of her subjectivity, and the social structures of bureaucracy, class, and gender. James points out that the telegraphist of *In the Cage* has been endowed with the attributes of the "artist" (the quotation marks are his)—and of the novelist (*P*, xix). But she also represents telegraphy not just as a mode of communication but as a social practice, a medium of discourse come to life, an information exchange rendered no longer transparent. *In the Cage* treats the presence of the embodied subject at the nodes of what one might otherwise think would be seamless networks of discourse, the human presence in the informatic machine.

Why should the tale assign its telegraphist the characteristics of a novelist, even at the price of "verisimilitude"? As Chapter 2 showed, the new technology had struck novelists as an apt comparison for their art because it seemed to represent both an essentially neutral medium that kept its mediation to a minimum, and a physical analogue for the many-sided circulation of knowledge and language across a world of causal and cognitive interconnections. In seating the tale's central consciousness within the "cage" of the postal telegraph counter, James literalizes and estranges a medium that had provided Victorian writers with a powerful technological analogue, even a kind of working model, for Victorian realism—an idea that had flowered repeatedly in authorial minds. The image of the telegraph as seized upon by earlier novelists suggested some of the formal and ideological properties of mid-Victorian realism, even the *episteme* supporting the concurrent developments of both telegraphy and realism at midcentury. Recasting the meaning of telegraphy, James discloses his divergences with such predecessors. He explores the telegraph and the realism it resembles with both a turn-of-the-century epistemological skepticism and a greater familiarity with the practice of telegraphy. *In the Cage*'s version of telegraphic realism has much to do with James's notion of realism but also important connections to developments in telegraphy between the 1850s and the 1890s—especially the transition to the sounding telegraph that fiction first noted in Trollope's "The Telegraph Girl."

Telegraphic Connections

It might have been especially tempting for writers to hail the transparency and the community-building possibilities of electric telegraphy in the 1850s, when telegrams were a new medium and too expensive for frequent use by most people, technologically dazzling but with social implications that were still unclear. But the chorus of complaints about the private telegraph companies' high charges and patchwork systems became so strong that in 1868 Parliament voted to nationalize the telegraph companies and fold their operations into the Post Office. The move was virtually unprecedented, "the first case of nationalization in [British] history," and an anomaly in a supposed age of laissez-faire.[2] But the ideology of intercommunication seemed to trump that of economic liberalism as Parliament deemed it necessary to establish "a cheaper, more widely used system of telegraphy."[3] Advocates of the project invoked the Penny Post, and from his retirement Rowland Hill endorsed the incorporation of the telegraph networks into the Post Office, although later he and others felt that the government had paid too much to buy them.[4]

The plan came into effect in 1870, and the price of sending telegrams was immediately reduced; the annual number of telegrams rose from 6.5 million in 1868–69 to nearly 90 million by the turn of the century.[5] But wider use of the telegraph inevitably brought new attention to its flaws. "The wonders of the telegraph have been sufficiently dwelt on," opens "Freaks of the Telegraph," an 1881 *Blackwood's* article by a postal official who was also the son of George Henry Lewes.[6] In contrast to celebrations of the electric Ariel, Charles Lewes describes the device as a mischievous "telegraphic Puck"— after all, it is Shakespeare's Puck who puts the girdle round about the earth in forty minutes. Lewes supplies dozens of examples of misreadings, careless blunders, and messages gone astray—in most cases, not because of mechanical failure but because of errors by customers or telegraphers. "The human element plays so considerable a part in matters telegraphic, that the human propensity to err finds proportionately wide scope," he observes.[7] Rather than guaranteeing neutral discourse, electric telegraphy's very abstraction, immateriality, and lack of context increased its odds of going awry in the hands of concrete, embodied human beings.

Telegraphy had gone from marvel to routine, following a sequence that has helped define technological modernity since the nineteenth century.[8] Hailed as an epoch-making invention at midcentury, the telegraph had become mundane, one of the oldest of the age's new media. By the end of the century, dispatching telegrams was no miraculous experience but "one of the commonest and most taken for granted of London impressions," as James calls it (*P*, xviii); in this tale, the telegraph office occupies "the duskiest corner" of a shabby grocery shop.[9] The final decades of the century introduced an array of newer technologies of transmission and inscription: the telephone, the phonograph and gramophone, the X-ray photograph, the motion picture; in the year he published *In the Cage* James reported having "quite revelled" in a "cinematograph—or whatever they call it" of a prizefight.[10] Most crucial for James's practice of writing was of course the typewriter. Suffering from chronic wrist pain, James bought "an admirable and expensive machine" in 1897 and soon ended up "writing" by dictating to a private typist.[11] Late Jamesian prose takes shape within this system of mediated inscription.

By the time of *The Wings of the Dove* (1902), James claimed that the dictating to a typist was for him "*intellectually*, absolutely identical with the act of writing . . . so that their difference is only material and illusory."[12] But as Mark Seltzer notes, the concurrent developments in technologies of inscription and in James's own habits as a writer could strongly foreground the properties of communication media, even as James carefully disavowed their significance as merely "material."[13] And James was far from the only novelist to react to the new configurations of technology and writing at the turn of the century.[14] *Dracula* invokes a riot of old and new recording technologies (letters, shorthand journals, telegrams, Dr. Seward's phonograph diary) as simultaneously modes of fictional documentation and figures for the novel's own thematics of textuality, secrecy, transmission, and knowledge. As Ivan Kreilkamp has shown, Joseph Conrad's *Heart of Darkness* (1899) responds to the possibilities of "disembodied phonographic language," possibilities that might have been suggested by Conrad's encounter with a technophile and his phonograph.[15]

In contrast to these works, *In the Cage* does not investigate the thematic and formal questions raised by a new medium; rather, it approaches an established one in light of a heightened, turn-of-the-century attention to the properties of recording and transmitting technologies. Carolyn Marvin's study of late nineteenth-century technology suggests that "the introduction of new media is a special historical occasion when patterns anchored in older media . . . are reexamined, challenged, and defended."[16] Although the patterns that Marvin discusses are those of social life, the same argument applies to the entanglement of media technology and literature. In the case of *In the Cage*, James's new attention to the mechanics of telegraphy and to the psychosocial content of the telegraphic exchange indicates how the imaginative possibilities of a medium may change as newer technologies emerge, and suggests the significance of media transitions for literary history.

Telegrams themselves, those tangible products of electric interconnection, are a familiar feature of late nineteenth-century fiction, including James's own; for instance, as plot points and as a technology for intercontinental communication, they feature importantly in his transatlantic novels from *The American* (1876–77) to *The Ambassadors* (1903). In the first chapter of *The Portrait of a Lady* (1881), telegraphy figures as a technology of inscription and compressive encryption, perfectly suited to the peremptory but mystifying messages Mrs. Touchett sends to announce her return to Gardencourt with Isabel Archer in tow. As Ralph tells Lord Warburton:

> [M]y mother has not gone into details. She chiefly communicates with us by means of telegrams, and her telegrams are rather inscrutable. They say women don't know how to write them, but my mother has thoroughly mastered the art of condensation. "Tired America, hot weather awful, return England with niece, first steamer decent cabin." That's the sort of message we get from her—that was the last that came. But there had been another before, which I think contained the first mention of the niece. "Changed hotel, very bad, impudent clerk, address here. Taken sister's girl, died last year, go to Europe, two sisters, quite independent." Over that my father and I have scarcely stopped puzzling; it seems to admit of so many interpretations.[17]

Stunningly, in the thirty-four words of Lydia Touchett's artfully compressed telegrams, James manages to convey not only the character's personal style but also many of the novel's crucial issues. "Taken sister's girl"—"go to Europe"—"quite independent": courtesy of the telegraphic "art of condensation," here is the international theme reiterated with the succinctness of a transatlantic message. Indeed, we should place intercontinental telegraphy in the cultural substrate that permits James to handle that theme as he does. Spurred by his mother's acutely interpretable telegrams, Ralph Touchett adumbrates the questions of Isabel's character and fate that the novel will spend hundreds of pages investigating: "who's 'quite independent,' and in what sense is the term used? . . . is it used in a moral or a financial sense? Does it mean that [she's] been left well off, or that [she] wish[es] to be under no obligations? or does it simply mean that [she's] fond of [her] own way?" (*PL*, 67). Isabel is quite "morally" autonomous and will be left financially well off by the bequest instigated by Ralph—these circumstances are the donnée that allows the drama of Isabel's choices ("Well, what will she *do*?")—and after marriage to Osmond she will learn what it means not to have her own way (*PL*, 51). With a character's jocular sallies at an "inscrutable" telegram, *The Portrait of a Lady* has introduced several of its principal topics and their complexities—beginning with James's international theme and the independences of Isabel Archer, but extending even to concerns such as social snobbery ("insolent clerk") and the aesthetics of interior spaces ("first steamer decent cabin").

In the Cage too treats telegrams as texts that demand intricate interpretation, but it does far more with telegraphy than simply draw upon its compressive effects on language. The central consciousness of the novella belongs to the young telegraphist who begins to take an interest in the affairs of her wealthy customers. Her attention blends obsession, prurience, conscientiousness, and rage—an ambiguous and volatile state resembling that of the governess in *The Turn of the Screw* (1898), a tale to which critics have often compared *In the Cage*.[18] The story's opening sentences incisively conflate her employment, her social status, and her spatial immurement in the post office at Cocker's grocery, coordinating these data as the "position" that gives her a unilateral knowledge of the persons around her:

It had occurred to her early that in her position—that of a young person spending, in framed and wired confinement, the life of a guinea-pig or a magpie—she should know a great many persons without their recognising the acquaintance. That made it an emotion the more lively—though singularly rare and always, even then, with opportunity still very much smothered—to see any one come in whom she knew, as she called it, outside, and who could add something to the poor identity of her function. (*IC*, 835)

"[F]ramed and wired" in place at the counter, the telegraphist is enclosed by a wood and wire "lattice" reminiscent of the telegraphic network, of which her post forms the most prosaic node, as if—through a spectacular metonymic logic—the miles of cable spanning the globe were themselves her "cage."

The situation becomes clearer when the next sentence specifies the workaday "function" that establishes her "poor identity":

Her function was to sit there with two young men—the other telegraphist and the counter-clerk; to mind the "sounder," which was always going, to dole out stamps and postal-orders, weigh letters, answer stupid questions, give difficult change and, more than anything else, count words as numberless as the sands of the sea, the words of the telegrams thrust, from morning to night, through the gap left in the high lattice, across the encumbered shelf that her forearm ached with rubbing. (*IC*, 835)

"[T]hrough the bars of the cage" float money and messages, "numberless" words that must be reckoned before they can enter the system (*IC*, 841). As Jennifer Wicke recognizes, the cage is "a nexus" where acts of "communication" enter a new "grid of social relation."[19] Far from being transparent and idealized, as in the imaginary telegraphy of the mid-Victorians, telegraphic dialogism here is mediated by the postal staff and defined as economic exchange. Were Dickens to "*be*" one of these modern electric messages, he would find that his flight across space began in a decidedly earthbound place, a "smelly shop" where the aromas of "hams, cheese, dried fish, soap, varnish, [and] paraffin" mingle with those of nameless "other solids and fluids" identifiable only by their odors (*IC*, 895, 835). By the 1890s, agitation by postal workers had drawn public awareness to the drudgery of their work, complaints investigated and publicized by the official Tweedmouth Commission (1895–97).[20] Lucy Graham's orderly, protected telegraph center seems luxurious by comparison.

Separated from her customers by a "transparent screen" of glass and wire, James's telegraphist might seem a bit like Carlyle's man in the glass-bell, isolated from social circulation. But in this era of electric information, the world comes to her; she conducts both her professional and her imaginative commerce with human life across the screen's "gap." When her friend Mrs. Jordan accuses her of lacking "imagination," the telegraphist concludes with rueful satisfaction that "people didn't understand her" (*IC*, 838). In fact, contra Mrs. Jordan, "her imaginative life was the life in which she spent most of her time" (*IC*, 838). Despite Gaskell's assurance that the electric telegraph would keep us looking outside instead of inside, the telegraphist's position offers little protection against excessive interiority.

Just as Mrs. Jordan, an impoverished widow with a genteel past, arranges flowers in the houses of wealthy Londoners, so the telegraphist mentally arranges customers: "What *she* could handle freely, she said to herself, was combinations of men and women" (*IC*, 838). With "a certain expansion of her consciousness," the telegraphist experiences "flashes" of "inspiration, divination and interest" about others who scarcely notice her (*IC*, 838). Mrs. Jordan may enter her customers' houses, but the telegraphist believes that she penetrates into their stories, those personal scenes that fill the wires. In the ebb and flow of their words, the telegraphist sees an ocean of vicarious experience: "as the blast of the season roared louder and the waves of fashion tossed their spray further over the counter, there were more impressions to be gathered and really—for it came to that—more life to be led" (*IC*, 839). To live "more life," the telegraphist will maximize the "impressions" from a pulsating flow of secondhand reality. As the example of Trollope's Sophy Wilson hinted, a shrunken Paterism may be an occupational hazard for young women at the telegraph.

Undoubtedly, what shapes the telegraphist's flashes of insight into the lives of her well-to-do clientele is her avid reading of "novels, very greasy, in fine print and all about fine folks," borrowed "at a ha'penny a day"—texts that offer entry into a range of experience to a broad array of the cramped and confined (*IC*, 837). The telegraphist will regularly review the situation of Captain Everard and Lady Bradeen, and eventually her own intrusive part in their drama, in "ha'penny novel" terms. The repeated adjective *fine* "suggests the quality of her aesthetic and moral sensibilities,"[21] but it also indicates the disparity between her reading material and its materiality—the sumptuous subjects of cheap one-volume novels printed in close type—as well as the contrast between the fictions she reads and the one in which she features. Although only thirty-five thousand words long, *In the Cage* first appeared not in the fine print of a magazine or a story collection but in its own volume, generously supplied with large print, wide margins, and two jaunty telegraph poles decorating the British edition's cover.

For the telegraphist, the lovers' telegrams present a coherent, novel-like "reality" that transcends the fragments she encounters in her ordinary life; "[m]ore than ever before it floated to her through the bars of the cage that this at last was the high reality, the bristling truth that she had hitherto only patched up and eked out" (*IC*, 841). As Nicola Nixon observes, the telegraphist "watches for each new telegraphic hint to their story as if it were the next installment of a serialized novel."[22] This paradigm of telegrams coalescing into novels has appeared before—for instance, in the early vision of underground telegraph wires "flowing" with "scenes" of life. Only then the flow of telegraphic scenes seemed to repeat the reality of the scene above for a generalized, Boz-like "ruminating being."[23] Here our observer is carefully defined by class, sex, and occupation, which helps *In the Cage* convey a sense of the imaginative effort necessary to produce the telegraphist's sense of a "prodigious view" of others' lives, to generate a "panorama fed with facts and figures" (*IC*, 846). As she "carr[ies] on the two parallel lines of her contacts in the cage and her contacts out of it," the telegraphic realities and her everyday life come to seem like Latimer's double consciousness: two streams that never meet (*IC*, 859).

What would it take to turn terse, enigmatic telegrams into the kind of narrative in nineteenth-century novels? For one thing, we would need a sense of grammatical and narrative continuity. Such continuity might seem in keeping with the promise of the telegraph to become a new source of connectedness. Yet for the sake of informatic efficiency, the telegraph network also demanded a condensed language that suppressed internal connectives and created a sense of textual discontinuity. If the logic of realism extends the normal cohesion of written prose into a sense of metonymic continuity in the world, as Jakobson argues, the telegraph system creates a rift between the world's interconnectedness and the discontinuities of language. As both Ralph Touchett and Charles Lewes recognize, telegraphic connection could increase the difficulty of interpretation and the likelihood of miscommunication. One journalist claimed that in 1901 the first report of the assassination of an American President—"McKinley shot Buffalo"—had nearly been

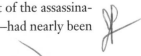

discarded by a Reuters sub-editor in London who grumbled, "These Yanks. They seem to think we're interested in their blooming President's shooting excursions."[24] Despite its promotion as a bringer of intercontinental amity, the Atlantic cable might seem to bear out the only superficially paradoxical observation that "[i]mprovements in communication . . . make for increased difficulties of understanding."[25]

For James's telegraphist, highly conscious of the fragmentariness of tele-gram tales and the scantiness of telegraphic signifiers, imagining the story of Lady Bradeen and Captain Everard means supplying the continuity and the context that would make impressions of their affair into something like a novel's story—a continuity that is notably absent in their telegrams, which supply multiple false identities, terse answers to missing questions, or even raw code. When Everard first visits the telegraphist's window, "her immedi-ate vision of himself ha[s] the effect, while she counted his seventy words, of preventing intelligibility," although she dutifully notes their quantity (*IC*, 843). For Everard's words are "mere numbers"—the modern embodiment of pure information, with no meaning apart from a missing context or a decryption key; they convey "nothing whatever": "no name, . . . no address, . . . no meaning, . . . nothing but a vague, sweet sound and an immense impression" (*IC*, 843). Yet the telegraphist mentally turns this diffusion of useless information into full knowledge: "she had taken it in; she knew ev-erything; she had made up her mind" (*IC*, 843).

The telegraphist protests against those who "show me with as good a conscience as if I had no more feeling than a letter-box" (*IC*, 884). The let-ter-box offered a classic Victorian figure for the multiplicity of discourse on a public communication network, and as it completed the prepayment sys-tem, Trollope's pillar-box also added new privacy to the posting of messages. But *In the Cage* highlights the violation of postal privacy and emphasizes the fungibility of information. Once she becomes involved in the story of Lady Bradeen and Captain Everard, customers handsome enough to recall the characters in her favorite fiction, the telegraphist finds that her interest in their affair "literally . . . ma[kes] up" for the tedium of Cocker's and tempts her to forestall her marriage to the dull grocer Mr. Mudge (*IC*, 838). (The entire tale amounts to a fabulous Jamesian elaboration of the official opposi-tion between women's postal work and marriage.) "[T]hrilling herself" with the thought of what "a bad girl would do" "with such a lot of material," she conjures up "a scene better than many in her ha'penny novels" (*IC*, 866). As she recognizes the scandalous information she has gathered, the telegraphist imaginatively turns it into "material," the hack journalist's or the blackmailer's term for the virtual tangibility achieved by information on the verge of assuming the more material form of prose or money. But of course the telegraph system has already made clear the nature of information as commodified, decontextualized knowledge.

Narrative Telegraphy

Caged at the interchange between the public and the telegraph network, and inspired by her novels, the telegraphist begins by making electrical connections but soon finds herself making intellectual ones:

> There were times when all the wires in the country seemed to start from the little hole-and-corner where she plied for a livelihood, and where, in the shuffle of feet, the flutter of "forms," the straying of stamps and the ring of change over the counter, the people she had fallen into the habit of remembering and fitting together with others, and of having her theories and interpretations of, kept up before her their long procession and rotation. (*IC*, 847)

At the center of the system, the telegraphist works to fit together the endless queue of her clientele and does so in ways suggested by fiction. It is as if, in order to escape her monotonous captivity in the telegraph office, she were attempting to *become* a version of the realist telegraph, the instrument of connection celebrated in Victorian invocations of the telegraphic imaginary. As James's preface indicates, the telegraphist is a "central spirit" who provides "cohesion." What he calls her "winged intelligence"—a phrase that merges her fluttering intellect with the whizzing information on which it goes to work—is also an ironized, subjective version of the electric Ariel's ability to saturate the world with human thought.

In *Thinking in Henry James*, Sharon Cameron demonstrates the opposition in James's work between the idea of consciousness as a product of individual, interior psychology (typically articulated in the New York Edition prefaces) and the more radical possibility that consciousness might be intersubjective or transcendent (usually raised within the fiction itself).

This is exactly the incompatibility over which James frets in his preface to the tale, the problem that "the author" has attributed "rank subtleties" to a specific "soul" unlikely to possess them—a problem that arises from "the author's irrepressible and insatiable, his extravagant and immoral, interest in personal character and in the 'nature' of a mind" (*P*, xx). The author has shared too much of the authorial capacity for scrutinizing consciousness with the very character whose consciousness he scrutinizes. The result of this putative misapportionment is precisely the "winged intelligence," the sovereign consciousness, that seeks an intellectual liberation from the cage of Cocker's. For Cameron, "the novels and Prefaces . . . raise the question of what thinking is, of how it can be made to register, and albeit disconcertingly, of *where* it might do so."[26] *In the Cage*, a tale Cameron does not discuss, provokes similar questions about the registration and dislocation of thinking. Yet it does so not only by formulating complex, intersubjective relationships between characters (as in the fiction Cameron examines) but also by aligning such interrogations with the idea and practice of telegraphy, a technology that promised to register thought across vast distances, to relocate consciousness in the electric pulses of the network.

As both the telegraphic fantasies of earlier novelists and the telegraphist's reading of her story as a novel imply, this alignment between telegraphy and questions of consciousness has much to do with the technology of nineteenth-century fiction. In part, the problem of consciousness which Cameron notes in James simply recasts the novelistic convention of a mobile narrator with selective access to characters' minds (a mode characteristic of Gaskell, most of Eliot and Trollope, and much of Dickens) as no longer merely a habit but now an open question of representing thought. By the late 1890s, this question was much on James's mind. In an 1899 letter to Mary Augusta Ward, that late-Victorian heir to the tradition of Gaskell and Eliot, James argues that the problem is not how many minds a novel seems to penetrate but the coherence of its narrative scheme:

> there are as many magnificent and imperative cases as you like of presenting a thing by "going behind" as many forms of consciousness as you like—all Dickens, Balzac, Thackeray, Tolstoi (save when they use the autobiographic dodge) are huge illustrations of it. . . . [F]or that matter, . . . I "go behind" right and left in "The Princess Casamassima," "The Bostonians," "The Tragic Muse,". . . .

And yet I *must* still add one or two things more. . . . I hold the artist must (infinitely!) know how he is doing it, or he is not doing it at all. . . . he must there choose and stick and be consistent. . . . [27]

Raising this question of consciousness and narrative form to the level of theme, *In the Cage* renders it doubly pressing.

The telegraphist fantasizes that she can see into others but that no one really knows her, a situation that echoes the structure of knowledge and insight in third-person narrative, especially the supervision exercised by the narrators of midcentury realist novels. This translation of narrative convention into a character's consciousness recalls "The Lifted Veil," as do the telegraphist's occasional visions of the future, which resemble special messages from mysterious places. But unlike Latimer's previsions, her fleeting prophetic fancies are often wrong, and her insights into other characters come to seem more and more dubious. By embodying such fantasies of mobile knowledge in the figure of the telegraphist and making her consciousness the center of the tale's character-focalized narration, James places narrative knowledge in the cage; readers are largely confined to the telegraphist's thoughts and perceptions, even as the third-person narrative voice creates a steady sense of irony and distance. The story cages the soul of an "authorial" narrator (who "maintains his own vantage point on the fictional world and its inhabitants"[28]) within the figure of the telegraphist. The makeshift transitions between first- and third-person narrations in Hemyng's telegraph stories have given way to James's self-conscious handling of the same issues in a tale about the same medium.

Through the transparent screen of this narration, James can indicate the "triumphant, vicious feeling of mastery and power" that may inhere in the one-sided knowledge of a shared reality (*IC*, 847). As the telegraphist revels in her awareness of her customers' affair, she comes to consider it ample recompense for the "margin" of "freedom" otherwise "absent" from her work; "[w]ith Captain Everard" she believes she has "simply the margin of the universe" (*IC*, 853, 864). Emphasizing her gender, sexuality, and class position as elements of the telegraphist's psychology and will to knowledge, James suggests some of the real data that the realist narrator function must disavow or neutralize in order to offer a narrative located not in a body so much as within a coherent reticulum of time, space, and meaning.[29]

Crucial to *In the Cage*'s troubling of narrative convention is not only the social situation of the telegraphist as woman and worker but also her particular "position" at the telegraph counter. Several critics have read James's tale of coded interchange and sexual secrecy in a telegraph office in relation to the 1889 Cleveland Street scandal, which revealed that a male brothel in London was supplying its upper-class customers with young telegraph workers.[30] The telegraphist's sense of dual existence as knowing subject and subservient clerk, "the queer extension of her experience" into a "double life" based on knowledge of upper-class sexual scandal, bears out such a field of reference (*IC*, 846). Yet the tale goes far beyond merely using the telegraphist as a figure of scandal, or even of recognizing her tricky location at the interstice between public transactions and private communications.

For *In the Cage* is permeated not simply by a general sense of the telegraphist as a service worker in the late nineteenth century's information economy ("endless right change to make and information to produce," in James's deft summary) but by attention to the specific components, mechanics, and language of telegraphy (*IC*, 844). The telegraphist is "wired" in place at the counter or makes a "ridiculous circuit" to pass by Everard's house on her way home at night (*IC*, 835, 874); again and again, characters "flash" (the verb Dickens used to describe his flight as a telegram) or "dash" (a word that recalls the rhythms of Morse code). In particular, James manages subtly but thoroughly to identify the telegraphist with the device from which she takes her "poor identity" and her designation in the story (*IC*, 835). At work at the counter, she registers the presence of her customers like a sort of hyper-responsive emotional kymograph or seismograph:

> There were those she would have liked to betray, to trip up, to bring down with words altered and fatal; and all through a personal hostility provoked by the lightest signs, by their accidents of tone and manner, by the particular kind of relation she always happened instantly to feel.
>
> There were impulses of various kinds, alternately soft and severe, to which she was constitutionally accessible and which were determined by the smallest accidents. (*IC*, 847)

Not only does this treat the telegraphist as a kind of superfine registering mechanism, "instantly" sensitive to the "lightest signs," but it defines her as "constitutionally accessible" to an alternating series of binary ("soft and severe") "impulses." "The electric telegraph serves us as a new sense," writes Alfred Wallace in an assessment of Victorian technology published in the same year; treating the telegraphist as telegraph, James materializes such general claims and merges them into the realist treatment of a character as part of her environment, a worker as part of her work.[31]

Telegraphic insight may enhance not only the telegraphist's perceptual grasp but even her corporeal reach. When she offers an unsolicited correction to Lady Bradeen's cryptic telegram, it is "as if she had bodily leaped—cleared the top of the cage and alighted on her interlocutress" (*IC*, 871). *Understanding Media* treats technologies as extensions of the human body and sensorium, but long before McLuhan, James suggests a similarly prosthetic view of telegraphy. Picking up the signals like any telegraph, the telegraphist manages in a flash to read the complex, coded relationship between Captain Everard and Lady Bradeen: "The fine, soundless pulse of this game was in the air for our young woman while they remained in the shop" (*IC*, 843). We may recognize *pulse* as a term from Eliot's physiologized fiction, but here it appears as a word that aligns psychology with the rhythmic flows of data on the telegraphic network.

The "soundless" quality of Captain Everard and Lady Bradeen's romance both conveys its furtiveness and marks it as a sort of silent telegraphy. For perhaps the most sustained appropriation of a telegraphic term in the tale involves the "sounder" itself, the business end of the telegraph, the device that is "always going" in Cocker's store. Although Morse had designed his telegraph with a register that recorded its pulses on paper for later translation, telegraphers discovered that they could save time by "sound reading"—by listening to the register's long and short ticks as it received a message.[32] After some initial resistance, telegraph officials came to endorse sound reading, and manufacturers adapted their equipment by replacing the paper register with a "sounder," a simple noise-making device consisting of an electromagnet, armature, and lever.[33] A sort of "reverberator" for telegraphic pulses, to borrow a Jamesian term, the familiar clicking sounder soon became "the universal receiving instrument" of the telegraph even in England, where it gradually displaced the native systems of Cooke and Wheatstone and their successors.[34] Even the doubleness of the telegraphist's life and consciousness has a well-known analogue in acoustic telegraphy. The first sound-reading telegraphers became famous not only for their speed and accuracy but for their ability to converse freely as they attended to the machine.[35] As a telegraph superintendent recalled of one early sound-reader: "He was so poised mentally that he could carry on a conversation while receiving or sending messages without the least apparent disturbance, and was never caught in an error."[36] Attending to her work as her intelligence wings its way to a world of private fantasy, James's telegraphist believes that she possesses the same ability, a hallmark of skilled telegraph workers.

Playing a set of variations on the "sounder," *In the Cage* builds an entire tropology on "sound" in various senses: aurality, articulation, investigation—especially the measurement of depths. As Kipling's paean "The Deep-Sea Cables" (1896) suggests, even this final meaning does not necessarily take us far from telegraphy; the poem highlights the unifying "Power" of the voiceless human words that traverse the silent, soundless deep.[37] Ong argues that "compared to the rest of the senses," sound has a "unique relationship . . . to interiority," since it registers the internal composition of the objects and bodies that produce or transmit it.[38] In this respect, too, the sounding telegraph offers an apt figure for the perception of hidden information, for the telegraphist's sense of penetration into other characters' inner lives.

Although the postal branch in Cocker's only sends telegrams and does not receive them, the sounder dominates the scene of telegraphy. Perhaps as fascinated by acoustic transmission as Trollope was, James identifies the telegraph completely with the sounder. In the story, that device comes synecdochically to stand for the whole apparatus and metonymically to represent the encaged telegraphist who operates it; it occupies "the innermost cell of captivity, a cage within the cage, fenced off from the rest by a frame of ground glass" (*IC*, 840). Sounding the rapid information flows that signal and perform the commerce of modern life, the caged sounder has a symbolic centrality that even the businesslike Mr. Mudge can endorse; he muses, "What did the sounder, as she called it, . . . do but keep the ball going?" (*IC*, 862).

The sounder figures its operator's receptiveness to alternating pulses of soundless signification. And the telegraphist turns out to be as sensitive an instrument as Maisie Farange, the young female center of consciousness in a work James had published a year previously. In fact, a telegraphic trope describes Maisie's desire for shared, silent contact as well. Disunited from her beloved Mrs. Wix by the presence of her stepmother, Maisie misses a mode of communication deeper than words, for "[t]hey had . . . never been so long together without communion or telegraphy."[39] For Maisie as well as for the telegraph's enthusiasts, the phenomenon of telegraphy suggests the fantasy of telepathy, that term coined by analogy with modern media. Even in their foreclosure, the possibilities of psychic "communion or telegraphy" may more generally underwrite the pauses, gaps, interruptions, and sharp intakes of breath that make late Jamesian dialogue—in contrast to the ampleness of James's descriptive prose—seem so telegraphic.

Disconnections

Identifying herself with the telegraph and its network, the telegraphist exults in her position as the coupling that links the couple. Once she perceives the illicit affair between Lady Bradeen and Captain Everard, the telegraphist begins to intrude in it. She corrects Lady Bradeen's coded telegram, an act that would constitute a misdemeanor according to the *General Rules and Regulations for the Guidance of Counter Clerks and Telegraphists of the London Postal Service* (1898); her ladyship leaves in shock when it becomes clear that the telegraphist has been not merely sending her telegrams but also reading and interpreting them.[40] The comparison between the shilling-novelist Hemyng and the guinea-novelist James may seem jarring, but both writers describe the movement between noting unusual telegrams and infiltrating the stories that they hint at, even if only James considers the psychological and ethical implications of the move.

Now the telegraphist begins making her daily circuit past the captain's lodgings. One night she sees him on the street outside; after a pause, he recognizes her and "send[s]" her a laugh "across the way"—a telegraphed greeting that introduces a sustained fantasy of communication deeper than speech (*IC*, 875).[41] During their ensuing conversation, the telegraphist imagines an unspoken connection between the two of them, a soundless mode of transmission, a telegraphy that is also a communion: nothing "vulgarly articulate" leads to the understanding that they will stroll together; she has "an intense desire he should know the type she really was without her doing anything so low as tell him"; the usual relations that an upper-class man might have with a young working woman "were on the mere surface, and *their* relation was behind and below" (*IC*, 876, 877). The telegraphist feels, she tells him, "as if there were something—I don't know what to call it!—between us"—"something unusual and good" (*IC*, 881).

For the Victorians, "[t]he telegraph . . . offered new potentials for making links between bodies and bodies (as in the case of lovers) or spirits and spirits."[42] But James's innovation, and his telegraphist's, is to recognize that the telegraph's real power is to rewire the normal distinctions between bodily and spiritual links and thereby to permit newer, more ambiguous connections between an assortment of minds and bodies. Does the telegraphist dream of seducing Captain Everard, or merely of protecting the privacy of his telegrams and the secrecy of his affair from anyone else? She vows to do "anything" for him, and, with a frisson born of how suggestive this promise "sound[s]," she feels that it is "as if they had been on a satin sofa in a boudoir" (*IC*, 881). "She had never seen a boudoir, but there had been lots of boudoirs in the telegrams" (*IC*, 881).

Soon the telegraphist breaks out to him: "I know, I know, I know!" (*IC*, 885). "Yes," Everard concludes, "that's what's been between us": "everything they had so definitely not named, the whole presence round which they had been circling became a part of their reference, settled solidly between them. It was as if then, for a minute, they sat and saw it all in each other's eyes, saw so much that there was no need of a transition for sounding it at last" (*IC*, 885). The solid, soundless connection between them is the telegraphist's divination and knowledge of the affair. What makes her fantasies of personal telegraphy so ironic is the suggestion that while she conceives of their tie as a high-flown romance, Everard probably believes that she is tactfully threatening blackmail.[43] The telegraphic diffusion of data does not prevent a sublime miscommunication; in fact, it encourages the telegraphist's idea of a relationship that transcends any material framework or social context.

At the seaside with Mr. Mudge for a cheap holiday—a fitting retreat in a tale filled with images of social rising, waves of customers, and currents of information—the telegraphist experiences a sort of Victorian-realist reverie, "seeing many things, the things of the past year, fall together and connect themselves, undergo the happy relegation that transforms melancholy and misery, passion and effort, into experience and knowledge" (*IC*, 888). Briefly, at least, the fragments of life coalesce; informatic impressions seem to become "knowledge." The vision would almost be worthy of *Middlemarch*, were it not for the ironic spin James applies locally by word choice (the blithe and insipid "happy relegation"), and more broadly by deflecting it into the ironized register of his character's thoughts. In the midst of such meditations, the telegraphist's ordinary life in London becomes for her "a far-away story, a picture of another life"—just the relation she once had to her novels and to the lives of her wealthy customers (*IC*, 888).

Strenuously working to convert telegraphic information into firsthand knowledge, the telegraphist imaginatively sets aside the real details of her life. But once she enters the frame of the story she has discovered, misprision fills the space of human interconnection. After her holiday, the telegraphist doesn't see Captain Everard for weeks. When he finally reappears at Cocker's, their encounters become a comedy of ambiguous signs and over-reading. As another clerk waits on him, "nothing passe[s] between" Everard and the telegraphist "but the fulness of their silence," yet she manages to read an elaborate message telegraphed by the series of looks in his eyes: "The look she took from him was his greeting, and the other one a simple sign of the eyes sent her before going out. The only token they exchanged, therefore, was his tacit assent to her wish that, since they couldn't attempt a certain frankness, they should attempt nothing at all" (*IC*, 894). The telegraphist prefers this code to "their former little postal make-believes"; she feels that she has "established on the part of each a consciousness that could end only with death" (*IC*, 894). Even when he leaves the shop, she can "almost hear him, through the tick of the sounder, scatter with his stick . . . the fallen leaves of October"—as if the sounder's clicking were simultaneously the noise his vibrations must overcome and the medium by which they come over (*IC*, 895).

During Everard's subsequent visits to the counter, the telegraphist notices that he seems to be trying to leave her extra money, perhaps as blackmail payments.[44] Pursuing a profounder explanation, she again attempts to read his eyes:

> What was most extraordinary in this impression was the amount of excuse that, with some incoherence, she found for him. He wanted to pay her because there was nothing to pay her for. He wanted to offer her things that he knew she wouldn't take. He wanted to show her how much he respected her by giving her the supreme chance to show *him* she was respectable. Over the driest transactions, at any rate, their eyes had out these questions. (*IC*, 899)

What is most extraordinary about this passage is its trio of middle sentences, the parallel but somewhat contradictory "excuses" that the telegraphist finds for Everard's conduct ("He wanted . . ."). Their anaphora and repeated structure draw attention to the veiled virtuosity here: just as the narrative uses free indirect discourse and psychological narration to present the telegraphist's fictional thoughts from a third-person point of view, this passage uses the same approach recursively, to present Captain Everard's fictitious thoughts from within her point of view—even while the story is narrating her consciousness.

Taken out of context, the three sentences could be a trustworthy transcription of a male character's thoughts and motives; in the story, however, they are an "extraordinary" misreckoning. Yet, on a narratological level, this is the very point at which the telegraphist's thoughts would appear formally to coincide with his. It is as if the narrative were feigning to grant the telegraphist her dream of mental communion with Everard—only in order to reveal it as a chimera. But this remarkable misrecognition is technically congruent with the tale's character-focalized narrative mode. As if beset by such confusions, even as she works so sedulously to manufacture an explanation for Everard's behavior, the telegraphist seeks "the refuge of the sounder"; "to be in the cage had suddenly become her safety, and she was literally afraid of the alternate self who might be waiting outside" (IC, 897, 898).

After entering via telegraphy what she considers the scenes of a real-life novel, the telegraphist loses any secure sense of her role in the story. If the telegraph appealed to the realist imagination by promising to materialize a social structure of connections and exchanges, it also threatened to short-circuit any such stable structure, to become a switchboard for fugitive and unconventional connections. It is this aspect of telegraphy that Deleuze and Guattari highlight in their brief comments on In the Cage: its capacity to map "very different types of relations," from routine personal pairings defined by sex or class, to more elusive "flows" and self-doublings (the telegraphist and Lady Bradeen, the telegraphist with Everard), to still more circuitous and volatile associations.[45] "[T]he telegraphic line is not a symbol, and it is not simple"; ultimately the telegraph steers us toward a line of connection "that is just as real" as those more familiar couples and doubles but which leads to "a kind of absolute deterritorialization."[46] As the telegraph carries out the project of all new nineteenth-century media to annihilate space and time, it becomes a component as well as a model for Deleuze and Guattari's rhizomatic analysis.

In the Cage is hardly *Anti-Oedipus*. It finally closes off these connections, exchanging them for a disillusioned awareness of imperfect information and social separation, a *felix culpa* that permits realist closure. The tale's climax both grants the telegraphist her disillusioned desire to return dealings with her customers to their "proper impersonal basis" and makes her the unexpected human memory bank in the biotechnical assemblage of telegraphic erotics (*IC*, 901). At first she answers the lovers' urgent request for the text of an early telegram with officious detachment; as telegraph manuals warned, the "great drawback" of acoustic telegraphy was "the want of a record" for "*employés*" to consult when questions arose about "telegrams of importance."[47] But in a final display of her mental acumen, the telegraphist manages to recollect the coded message from memory, and thus—in a plot point about which James is deliberately unspecific, one of the codes that is never broken—somehow to save the adulterous couple from exposure.[48]

In the tale's denouement, the telegraphist and her friend Mrs. Jordan reconvene for a final meeting. The text presents their conversation as a comic drama whose evolving suppressions and misunderstandings translate an alternating stream of hauteur and humiliation; as John Carlos Rowe notes in passing, this is a particularly "telegraphic" exchange, elliptical in both its verbal compressions and its circling indirections.[49] Mrs. Jordan had hinted that her employment in upper-class London houses might lead to a match with one of their denizens, and indeed it has. She has become betrothed to a "great and trusted friend" of her employer Lord Rye: a Mr. Drake—who, Mrs. Jordan haltingly admits, is his lordship's butler (*IC*, 912). This shock awakens the telegraphist from her vision of access to the "high reality" that Lady Bradeen's telegrams once suggested: "what our heroine saw and felt for in the whole business was the vivid reflection of her own dreams and delusions and her own return to reality. Reality, for the poor things they both were, could only be ugliness and obscurity, could never be the escape, the rise" (*IC*, 917–18).

To complete the telegraphist's Jamesian disillusionment, Mrs. Jordan also reveals the true state of relations between Captain Everard and Lady Bradeen, Mr. Drake's future employer. And this reality too turns out to be far shabbier than the telegraphist had imagined: after the sudden death of her husband, Lady Bradeen has used the recovered telegram to coerce Captain Everard into marrying her, even though he wished to end their relationship. The telegraphist "had, in the cage, sounded depths, but there was a suggestion here somehow of an abyss quite measureless," an abyss that only recapitulates the chasm that traps "poor things" in "ugliness and obscurity" (*IC*, 920). A "social gulf" now yawns between the telegraphist (affianced to Mr. Mudge, the industrious grocer) and the soon-to-be Mrs. Drake (a servant's wife) (*IC*, 918). In fact, this final gap precisely reiterates the "social . . . gulf" that distinguished the snobbish telegraphist from Cocker's grocery clerks on the tale's very first page (*IC*, 835); far from bridging social separations, telegraphic discourse has left them intact or exacerbated them. Now it is the telegraphist's soundless visions that fall away, and after months of delaying marriage to Mudge, she plans to move up the date. A technology based on coded sounds rather than on written pages, the sounding telegraph has perhaps inevitably failed to offer its operator the "margin" of freedom and knowledge she craved. The separation between the scenes of her life and the boudoir scenes she pictured via telegram is complete.

As James often does, here he stages a character's loss of illusion as an encounter between the seductions of romance and the grounded truths of the real. "The only *general* attribute" of romance, he would argue in the New York Edition's preface to *The American*, is "the kind of experience with which it deals—experience liberated, so to speak; experience disengaged, disembroiled, disencumbered, exempt from the conditions that we usually know to attach to it."[50] This well-known definition of romance as disconnected experience, as imagination liberated from the constraints of real life, is again the telegraphist's winged intelligence, the purely intellectual freedom of this confined young official, her imaginary access to a world of experience otherwise denied her. In Ermarth's terms, gender, sexuality, and the social gulf of class may disturb the consensus necessary to realism in *In the Cage*. But in a larger sense, James hints that the seamless, telegraphic interconnection promised by Victorian realism, like the "fine" society novels that echo it in a vulgarized form, depends on a fantasy of disengaged information recognizable as a covert form of romance.

With an intentionally fanciful figure, James goes on to encapsulate the tethered nature of the realist imagination: "The balloon of experience is in fact of course tied to the earth, and under that necessity we swing, thanks to a rope of remarkable length, in the more or less commodious car of the imagination"; "from the moment that cable is cut we are at large and unrelated" (*IC*, 475). In contrast to the realist's task, "[t]he art of the romancer is . . . insidiously to cut the cable" (*IC*, 475). Perhaps in the cable that keeps things grounded we can perceive an alternative to the telegraph wire that seemed to promise transcendent, disencumbered discourse. The organization of James's figure (a cable fixing a car in space) may even suggest a topological transformation of some familiar terms; in his image it is not the soaring hot-air balloon that represents the "imagination" but the "car" underneath—which we might also call a cage.

No wonder James worries that he has installed in the telegraphist the attributes of the artist and critic. Yet in doing so, he has also developed his critical vision of the relationship between information technology and fictional technique, his own mode of telegraphic realism, a mode more attentive to the properties of media and the realities of mediation. James has used the telegraph far more extensively than his forebears to treat the scripting of private life and consciousness as an act that parallels the conversion of text into telegraphic information. The divergence between the telegraphic realisms of James and earlier writers arises not only from their different ideas about realism but also from changes in the practice of telegraphy: the increased use of the telegraph for everyday communication and the near-universal adoption of the acoustic telegraphy that bewildered solid, reliable Lucy Graham.

As an author who had recently abandoned longhand for dictation to a typist, James might have been especially struck by the use of the sounder in telegraphic transmission, and by the position of the educated young worker who attends it. More than a century after *In the Cage*, we have long become used to the idea of *broadcast*, a perpetual stream of quasi-vicarious communication waiting to be caught by our consciousness. In 1898, only two years after Marconi performed his radio experiments for Post Office officials in London, this sort of experience would have been far more unusual, yet this is something like the telegraphist's "position," both with respect to the messages her customers send and to the sounder, which is always going.

To James, telegraphy is an everyday experience of the modern. It is also an evolving technology whose fictional representation marks the differences between his realism and that of earlier writers who found in telegraphy a figure for their practice. Perhaps telegraphy, like photography, initially seemed to offer nineteenth-century writers a total analogy for the ambitions of realism. However, by the end of the century both technologies had proved not to reproduce a world of consensus, consistency, and neutral truth, but to highlight problems of subjectivism, discontinuity, and mediation. Even a text as apparently straightforward as Thomas Hardy's *A Laodicean* (1881) may hint at such an emerging awareness. In Hardy's novel, the installation of a telegraph line at Stancy Castle represents the encounter of the modern with the medieval, the stated theme of this "story of to-day." But when a forged telegram and an altered photograph condemn the novel's blameless hero, it becomes clear that however modern these technologies are, they may be as likely to mislead as to extend our "direct vision" and our understanding.[51]

In the end, James's telegraphic realism with its epistemological concerns raises new possibilities for fiction and telegraphy. Redistributing space into a network of connections, permitting virtually instantaneous communication across continents and empires, the telegraph "would literally make the world a smaller . . . place" (the adverb is worthy of James),[52] but it would do so in a peculiar way: by collapsing distance into a proximity that was discursive, technologically mediated, and strangely invisible in daily life. For Fredric Jameson, a keynote of modernist writing is its simultaneous feeling of global connection and "spatial disjunction," its sense that the real center always lies elsewhere.[53] Jameson traces this quality to the fact that high modernism arises amid the vast system of imperialism before the Great War, a system whose logic appears everywhere but which is virtually impossible to grasp as a whole. This feeling of immeasurable distance and unseen totality, Jameson claims, underlies even such quietly modernist works as E. M. Forster's *Howards End* (1910), a novel that counters the disorienting ties of global exploitation and control (Mr. Wilcox's "Imperial and West African Rubber Company," or the links materialized by telegrams from across the Empire) with a nostalgic sense of the connections that would allow one to "[l]ive in fragments no longer."[54] Systematically expanded to link continents and empires, the telegraph itself could by the turn of the century suggest the radically decentered possibilities attending the notion that "really . . . relations stop nowhere," as James puts in a famous phrase from the New

York preface to *Roderick Hudson*.[55] Stretched to the breaking point, the realist telegraph may convey the messages of a telegraphic modernism.

The affiliation between telegraphy and the evolving logic of realism confirms that fiction, having long since absorbed the epistle that gave it its Richardsonian form, has by the later nineteenth century not only taken up newer technologies of transmission but developed their implications: as narrative models, chronotopes, and figures for realism's epistemological armature. The confluence represented by telegraphic realism reminds us that technological development flows from the same springs as other cultural productions, including literature. But James's cagey version of telegraphy may also carry a timelier message. Early in the history of the telegraph, promoters hailed its ability to bind the world together with wire webs and instant communication, a vision congruent with the promises of realism at midcentury. Forty years later, James scrutinized the telegraphic muse with a keener sense of telegraphy as social and material practice, and with a more skeptical eye for the claims of a fictional realism that found a counterpart in the telegraph's idealized image.

In his incisive history and critique of communication as a concept, John Durham Peters attempts to counter a "truism that is still very much alive" in the Internet age—and that recalls the telegraphist's sense of consciousness enlarged by telegraphic information: the myth "that the expansion of means leads to an expansion of minds."[56] The era of electric networks may look primitive in our age of electronic interconnection, yet the rhapsodies of its advocates can sound familiar.[57] Like James's telegraphist, we may find that our wired position renders us peculiarly susceptible to certain fantasies: not merely that knowledge might be transparent, but that technology will automatically permit us to transcend our own social and economic rifts. As present-day developments in electronic communication create new fantasies of participation and create new social gulfs, we too might benefit from a margin of the chastened telegraphic realism sounded by *In the Cage*.

When I began writing this book, I coined the term *telegraphic realism* as a heuristic expression of the connections between fiction and the new media technologies of the nineteenth century. Imagine my surprise to find that my shorthand phrase was itself a nineteenth-century invention. In 1886, the American editor and novelist Joseph Kirkland—like Trollope, a realist (and the scion of a mother who turned a failed Midwestern venture into a successful writing career)—sketched out some of the same links: "Photographic exactitude in scene-painting—phonographic literalness in dialogue—*telegraphic realism in narration*—these are the new canons for the art of fiction. Whether this is a novelty or only a restoration, it were bootless to inquire. Kismet—it is fate" (emphasis added).[58] In Kirkland the phrase remains somewhat undefined, but its juxtaposition with photography and sound-recording makes its tenor clear; realistic fiction would have to adjust itself in line with the new media technologies of the age.

Without having heard of Joseph Kirkland, I reproduced his words and much of his meaning—by a novelty, a restoration, or fate. Soon after James wrote *In the Cage*, Kipling would draw on a newer medium to convey the uncanny phenomenon of a verbal link across space and time with no textual source or tangible connection. Kipling calls such concurrence "wireless."

CHAPTER 7

Wireless

In a 1908 letter to Edmund Gosse, Rudyard Kipling complains about the "vice of verbosity" that he believes has "infected" Gosse's prose. Like Gaskell so many years before, Kipling turns to the electric telegraph as a literary corrective, although now against not gloomy introspection but "flowery . . . adjectives" and the "effeminacy" of "wordiness." Indeed, Kipling breezily traces his own writing style (and presumably its manly concision) to his telegraphic tutelage as a journalist in India: "The best training you can get is in writing telegrams. Here a man realises more how far a word can go than in reading any of the famous authors. I am not in debt for style to anything or anybody but the telegraph system."[1]

Rather than emphasizing the electric telegraph as a neutral language machine, Kipling hails the condensed form of the telegram and the commercial "system" that demands payment by the word. His words display a playful condensation of their own. The "man" who "realises" the telegraph system's implications for language (the generic masculine here seems more masculine than generic) simultaneously understands them and makes them real. And by conflating the stylistic condensation of the message with the transmissive power of the medium ("how far a word can go"), Kipling deftly implies that it might be not an electric current so much as the compressed force of the message's brisk language that propels it. On the value of the telegraph, journalist and imperialist would be as one; by the end of the century telegraphy had become indispensable to modern journalism as well as "an essential part of the new imperialism."[2]

For all its jocularity, the outlook of Kipling's letter fits well with familiar attitudes of his fiction and verse: the valuing of action over passive intellection (here, of writing forceful telegrams over "reading . . . famous authors"), the manly submission to rules that are never fully articulated. More implicitly we could also connect telegraphic writing to the terse knowingness of his writing, the "gnomic quality of Kipling's language," and the alluring sense it offers the reader "of being 'in.'"[3] In its necessary concision, a telegram too leaves it to the recipient to fill in its syntactic and semantic gaps. Yet even as Kipling bluffly celebrates the male discipline of telegram-writing, the end of his letter suggests grounds for unease: what might it mean to owe such a vital writerly "debt" as one's "style" not to a human being or a trade but to something as impersonal as a transmission "system"?

If the telegraph seemed powerful when it flashed electric pulses on the network of wires, how potent and strange must a system be that could disseminate invisible, inaudible information through the air; what pressures must it place on style, language, and self-expression. For by the turn of the century, words were coming not just down the wire but also through the luminiferous ether—a phenomenon that Kipling was among the first to consider in fiction. Four years after *In the Cage* treated the interplay between fiction and an established electric communication technology, Kipling published a short story that explored the implications of a much newer medium: wireless telegraphy, the technology that would be officially dubbed *radio* a few years later. *The Progress of Invention* (1900) acclaims wireless as telegraphy's "most modern and startling development," so astounding that "[t]o the average mind [it] is highly suggestive of scientific imposition, so intangible and unknown are the physical forces by which it is rendered possible." "[Y]et this is one of the late achievements of the Nineteenth Century."[4] In Kipling's "'Wireless,'" a tale published in *Scribner's* magazine in 1902 and collected in *Traffics and Discoveries* (1904), a consumptive druggist named

John empties some dull opiate to the drains—and starts channeling Keats. The conjunction between old poetry and new medium lets Kipling imagine the effects on textuality, subjectivity, and the representation of reality, of a technology that dramatically altered not how far a word could go but how it could go so far.

Modern Machinery

Kipling's writing often expresses a fondness for machines, a respect for their ability to carry out their duties without complaint or empty bluster, and a pleasure in the mysteries they present to the uninitiated. In an 1897 animadversion on Kipling's work, Henry James singles out this interest, admitting that he once believed Kipling "perhaps contained the seeds of an English Balzac" but had "quite given that up in proportion as he has come steadily from the less simple in subject to the more simple,—from the Anglo-Indians to the natives, from the natives to the Tommies, from the Tommies to the quadrupeds, from the quadrupeds to the fish, and from the fish to the engines and screws."[5] An inverted hierarchy of complexity terminates in hardware. The quip's chronology is misleading, but James's examples are accurate, especially when it comes to Kipling's mid-1890s transportation tales. His ".007" (1897)—its title must have impressed Ian Fleming more than the story did James—tells the tale of a plucky little engine initiated into the professional life of its fellow trains, while "The Ship That Found Herself" (1895) imagines the conversations among the components of a vessel on its maiden voyage, all the way down to its screw-propeller.

For Kipling, the capacity of modern machines to demand so much technical knowledge surely accounts for much of their attraction.[6] Angus Wilson's verdict on both stories, that they offer "information without the illusion of life," plenty of facts but little reality, seems warranted.[7] Analyzing Kipling's particular "obsession" with transport technologies, Christopher Harvie concedes that "when dealing with technology . . . Kipling tended to be at his most systemic and, inevitably, at his most dogmatic."[8] These stories of transport largely fail to carry technical information into human reality. When Kipling explores another sort of technology for traffic and discovery, the media that transfer knowledge and supply the imaginary transports of storytelling, he achieves a far greater human resonance. Yet surprisingly, in contrast to his personification of engines and screws, Kipling presents these technologies as impersonal and deindividualized.

Appropriately enough, Kipling often takes up the wonders of machinery with the stripped-down, matter-of-fact writing style for which he credited his telegraphic apprenticeship. As Edmund Wilson observes in "The Kipling That Nobody Read," this efficiency in treating the wonders of machinery places the turn-of-the-century Kipling well ahead of the next decade's self-proclaimed Futurists, with their windy tributes to the motorcar. When Kipling's machines talk, they can speak in this voice as well. His poem "The Secret of the Machines" (1911), subtitled "Modern Machinery," celebrates the power and inexorability of machines ("We can neither love nor pity nor forgive / If you make a slip in handling us you die!") in order to make their obvious final "secret" seem strange: that *"for all our power and weight and size / We are nothing more than children of your brain!"* (lines 39–40, 47–48).[9]

The most modern aspect of the poem's machines is that they include not only farm equipment and industrial gear but also media devices:

> Would you call a friend from half across the world?
> If you'll let us have his name and town and state,
> You shall see and hear your crackling question hurled
> Across the arch of heaven while you wait.
> (lines 13–16)

Moreover, the poem suggests that the rise of technological media has allowed machines to assume the roles of authors and audiences ("We can print and plough and weave and heat and light / . . . We can see and hear and count and read and write!"), and implicitly, to reach the consciousness expressed by the poem itself (lines 10–12). The final lines of the poem subsume the power of machines into the power of the human thought that created them. Yet Kipling's refusal to draw distinctions between machines that read and write and those that produce or propel, coupled with his exaggeration of the media machines' achievements, hints at something mechanical within the human, something machinelike in the human "brain" as well as in its offspring. For that matter, T. S. Eliot's professed admiration of Kipling's poems as "'*great* verse'" rather than poetry, highlights the mechanical side of their metrical composition.[10] This trait might seem especially palpable in Eliot's age of recorded sound, broadcast speech, and vers libre—that is, during the era of modern media epitomized by the wireless set.

Marconi Business

Although James Clerk Maxwell had predicted the existence of electromagnetic waves in the 1860s, they remained an unproven hypothesis until Heinrich Hertz demonstrated their presence in 1887. Like Morse, Bell, and Edison a "practician" rather than a scientist or engineer, the young Guglielmo Marconi read about Hertz's work in 1894 and became preoccupied with the possibility of telegraphy via electromagnetic waves.[11] Perhaps because Marconi's amateurism gave him a different frame of reference from the experts', his experiments on his family's estate near Bologna soon began to succeed where others' had failed, and he found himself able to receive Morse-code messages through the air at ever greater distances.[12] Yet he achieved this not by inventing new components or technologies but by rearranging and refining ones that already existed—a situation that soon created doubt about his originality, and later about the validity of his patents. From its earliest days, the medium of wireless telegraphy raised fresh issues of priority and original creation, the very issues that Kipling's "'Wireless'" would highlight.[13]

Since the tale's own explanation of turn-of-the-century wireless telegraphy is more germane, and far more evocative, my treatment of its mechanics will be brief. In standard Hertzian fashion, Marconi's transmitter created bursts of electromagnetic waves when a spark of current flowed across the gap between two charged plates. For his receiver, Marconi adapted an instrument called a Branly tube, a glass tube filled with loose metal filings that would cohere when exposed to a burst of radio waves; this device "passed from resistance to invitation when subjected to an electric impulse from afar."[14] For several years, physicists had used such "coherers" as detectors for Hertzian waves, but Marconi experimented to find the most sensitive kinds of metal filings and reduced the size of the tubes themselves, sometimes making them out of thermometers.[15] He also modified and reconfigured his machines' other components, as well as experimenting with different arrangements of aerials; one of his principal innovations was the "grounded vertical," a tall antenna connected to the earth.[16]

Marconi's devices were inefficient and temperamental. Since the dust in the coherer tended to remain clumped together after each signal, they transmitted messages at a fraction of the speed of late-Victorian wired telegraphy. And because he didn't fully understand the science behind his invention—as yet, no one did—Marconi made elementary mistakes in the early years.[17] Probably the main theoretical problem in early wireless telegraphy was the lack of understanding of tuning, or "syntony," a deficiency that made the effort to establish communication between stations haphazard.[18] Marconi's original spark-gap bursts emitted waves on many frequencies at once, which meant that signals from different transmitters interfered with each other and threatened to create "chaos" on the radio spectrum.[19] But even his early systems could indeed work, at least given enough power for the transmitter and enough fiddling at the receiver.

Possibly rebuffed by Italian officials, or perhaps simply eager to tap into a larger capital market, Marconi took his equipment to England in 1896; thanks to a mother from a wealthy Scots-Irish distilling family, he was well connected in Britain and spoke perfect English. Marconi soon arranged a meeting with William Preece, the Chief Engineer and Electrician of the British Post Office. In keeping with the Post Office's push toward a monopoly over electric media, Preece had long been interested in the possibility of wireless telegraphy and was impressed with the inventor and his machinery. With his imprimatur, the Post Office supported Marconi's work until he received his first patents and founded his private wireless company in 1897.

Marconi's establishment of the company in England placed Britain at the forefront of wireless communication. In the first years of his English work, most of Marconi's experiments took place in hotels on the south coast, first on the Isle of Wight, then in Bournemouth, and finally at the Haven Hotel in Poole, a site that Marconi's company used for decades.[20] The peculiar practice of experimenting in seaside hotels rather than in urban laboratories protected the secrecy of Marconi's designs, but it also indicated one of the primary uses foreseen for wireless telegraphy. For all the cables that now stretched below the ocean, there could be no wired communication at sea. Wireless telegraphy would first see real use as a nautical technology, and Britain's immense maritime involvement would have added to its attraction for Marconi. By the first years of the new century, "Marconi's Wireless Telegraph Company had already won a leading position in ship-to-shore communications in Britain" and was using this position to expand into other markets.[21]

From the start, wireless telegraphy provoked questions of privacy, publicity, and ownership. In fact, the inherent publicness of wireless messages, which might be picked up by anyone with a receiver tuned to some roughly compatible frequency, presented an obstacle to many models for applying and exploiting the technology. "No one wants to pay for shouting to the world," asserted the physicist Oliver Lodge in 1898.[22] Even after the beginnings of continuous-wave transmission and voice communication in the early twentieth century, as well as Lodge's own advances in tuning, the existing model for live voice transmission—the telephone—proved inappropriate precisely because of the greater publicity of what was often called "wireless telephony." Not until a generation later would the establishment of one-way radio broadcasting systems supported by advertising or by governments launch the paradigms for mass broadcast in the twentieth century, turning the publicity of radio, the broadness of its cast, into its greatest asset.

"It's a funny thing, this Marconi business, isn't it?" begins the apothecary John Shaynor, and the rest of Kipling's "'Wireless'" explores the funny business of transmission without a tangible connection.[23] On a chilly night, as Shaynor tends the counter, the narrator and the radiophile young Mr. Cashell gather at old Cashell's chemist shop to try communicating wirelessly with some confederates at Poole. Clearly, we are not far from the milieu of *In the Cage*—even down to the olfactory catalog in the shop's "confused smell of orris, Kodak films, vulcanite, tooth-powder, sachets, and almond-cream" (*W*, 200). A devoted tradesman who slightly resembles Mr. Mudge, Shaynor nonetheless reveals an "interesting . . . mental attitude towards customers" worthy of James's telegraphist: as he proficiently serves them, he is actually working his way through the multivolume "Christy's *New Commercial Plants*," a testament to his narrowness as well as his Kiplingesque regard for occupational knowledge (*W*, 199). Boasting of his ability to "carry as much as half a page of Christie [*sic*] in my head" as he tallies purchases and makes change, Shaynor assures the narrator that he lets his reading go whenever he must fill prescriptions, but he still boasts that he could prepare "the general run of 'em in my sleep, almost" (*W*, 199). Holding a printed text in your head as you sleepwalk through your business: from the start, Kipling's tale hints at the connections it will draw between information transfer, intellection, and automatism.[24]

After Shaynor's girlfriend appears and coaxes Shaynor into coming outside for a walk "round by St. Agnes," the narrator raids the counter and mixes a cocktail of spices, alcohol, and "chloric-ether" (a solution of chloroform) (*W*, 201, 202). Sipping a beaker of this "new and wildish drink," he takes a flask to the young "electrician" working in the back office on a different kind of ether (*W*, 202, 200). Although the narrator—one of Kipling's anonymous first-person tale-tellers—is happy to take advantage of his access to the pharmacopoeia, he has a nonpharmaceutical motive for his visit to Cashell's store on this cold, blustery night. "For reasons of my own," he unhelpfully explains, "I was deeply interested in Marconi's experiments at their outset in England," and so old Cashell (in bed with the flu) has invited him to be present during his nephew's attempts to turn the shop into a temporary "long-range installation" (*W*, 200, 199).

In real life, Kipling's general technical know-how was questionable, for all his love of technology and expert knowledge. He certainly lacked George Eliot's wide scientific awareness or Trollope's specialized professional expertise. When it comes to Kipling's familiarity with Marconism, "'Wireless'" sends out mixed signals. Kipling had met Marconi in 1899, the year he began writing the story, for a meal reminiscent of Dickens's dinner with Rowland Hill half a century earlier. As Kipling recalled their luncheon:

> I got Marconi to talk about wireless, and at the end of an hour I felt that I knew as much about wireless as it was possible for a layman to learn. During the talk I consciously or unconsciously was gathering much material for my story, "'Wireless'", in which I carried the idea of etheric vibrations into the possibilities of thought transference.[25]

Kipling's plain account of his speedy mastery of Marconi's art contrasts with his vagueness here about the workings of his own, but then the genesis of artistic creation, its consciousness or unconsciousness, provides one of the mysteries of the tale.

Several details in the tale demonstrate Kipling's familiarity with turn-of-the-century wireless telegraphy, perhaps even beyond what a lunchtime chat might have offered. Its comparison of the wireless coherer to a thermometer, like young Cashell's attempt to contact a station at Poole, indicates knowledge of Marconi's research. So does the story of a previous experiment that a sniggering Shaynor relays at the opening of the tale: "'the last time they experimented they put the pole on the roof of one of the big hotels here, and the batteries electrified all the water-supply, and'—he giggled— 'the ladies got shocks when they took their baths'" (*W*, 197). Marconi's experiments too took place in seaside hotels, although presumably with less jolting effects. Yet "'Wireless'" suggests a more dubious expertise when it comes to the scientific side of the medium. The story's stress on electromagnetic induction ("it's important to remember that it's an induced current," lectures young Cashell), for instance, may suggest some confusion between Marconi's Hertzian transmission and the earlier, more limited "induction telegraph," a system based on electromagnetic induction rather than wave radiation (*W*, 207).[26]

Clearly, the "voice of the expert" in Kipling's writing is "an artifact," a literary device, a constructed thing.[27] In "'Wireless,'" a lunchtime chat with Marconi is one of the elements from which this voice is constructed. But we could also note how richly "'Wireless'" demonstrates Kipling's ability to exploit the details he picked up, the special skill of the general correspondent or the bluffer—nowhere more so than in the flow of associations that emanate from the tools and jargon of radio transmission. This facility certainly includes the emphasis on "induction," of which "[t]here are a good many kinds," as Cashell gnomically assures the narrator—inducting him into the mysteries of wireless all the while (*W*, 207). When the literary and technological imaginations communicate, their contact doesn't depend on complete mutual understanding—a point echoed in the story itself, which highlights the inductions between plotlines and lifelines that never quite touch.

Whatever the extent of his expertise, Kipling's exposition of the workings of wireless telegraphy captures the satisfaction of the expert revealing the arcana of his trade—and in 1902 most of Kipling's readers would have been encountering a detailed account of wireless for the first time in these pages. Young Cashell points out the various parts of the receiver but pauses when the narrator interrupts with a question about electricity: "what *is* it?"

> "Ah, if you knew *that* you'd know something nobody knows. It's just It—what we call Electricity, but the magic—the manifestations—the Hertzian waves—are all revealed by *this*. The coherer, we call it."

He picked up a glass tube not much thicker than a thermometer, in which, almost touching, were two tiny silver plugs, and between them an infinitesimal pinch of metallic dust. "That's all," he said. . . . "That is the thing that will reveal to us the Powers—whatever the Powers may be—at work—through space—a long distance away." (*W*, 202–3)

Responding to the query, Cashell redirects us from science to technology, from the abstract "*that*" of electricity to the tangible "*this*" of the instrument. The deictic shift likewise moves from the ponderous "It" at large ("Electricity") to the more ponderable "it" at hand ("[t]he coherer"). But in an almost Carlylean sense, the coherer—this smallest imaginable glass tube at the heart of the Marconi receiver—contains mysteries enough.

As Cashell explains it, miles away at Poole, a transmitter will charge a wire with "Hertzian waves which vibrate, say, two hundred and thirty million times a second" (*W*, 208). This electric current creates a magnetic field that will in turn induce electricity to charge another wire within range. The transmitted waves are too weak—the "induction" too faint—to move Cashell's telegraphic sounder, but they are "just" powerful enough to "make that dust cohere" (*W*, 207, 208). While the pinch of metal dust coheres, it allows a far stronger current from the "home battery" in Cashell's receiver to flow, and this internal current makes the sounder tick (*W*, 208). In the model of transmission suggested by Marconi's wireless, a faint and far-off signal activates a capacity that is already there at home; communication happens when some external power lets the receiver complete its own circuit according to a cadence set elsewhere.

With its sprinkling of dust and its electrodes that face without quite touching, the coherer itself provides an image of both the impenetrable mystery and the practical realities of communication. Indeed, we might say that communication can *only* take place across gaps, a precondition that helps create its everyday uncanniness, its inherent aporias, but also its paradoxical prominence as what John Durham Peters calls "a registry of modern longings" for perfect unity and impossible communion.[28] In fact, early wireless telegraphy entailed a succession of gaps, gaps between transmission and reception but also within the coherer and even at the signal's origin: "with a rending crackle there leaped between two brass knobs a spark, streams of sparks, and sparks again" (*W*, 209). Whether to make anything of the fact that Cashell seems to have just transmitted a "W" in International Morse code (·--, perhaps tapping out the first letter in the tale's title?) constitutes the least of the story's mysteries.

Like wired communication before it, wireless telegraphy was in effect digital before it became analog. Marconi's original spark-gap transmitter, the state of the art when he met Kipling, would soon be superseded by continuous-wave systems, which helped permit voice broadcast. Even by 1900, two years before "'Wireless'" appeared, inventors had suggested alternatives to transmission via spark discharge.[29] But for the story, the far-off spark-gap transmitter embodies communication through the void in its very design: in order to broadcast at all, a signal must leap across a breach. In keeping with Peters's call for a pragmatic view of the real-world limits and possibilities of communication, we might note a notorious problem with the coherer. Because its filings remained stuck after every signal, Marconi's receiver had to include a tiny mallet that would automatically tap the coherer after each impulse to make the dust "decohere." This quirk "slowed down receiving speeds . . . severely," and it meant that the receiver could only remain receptive if you overcame its capacity to remember.[30] Kipling does not mention the tapper, but "'Wireless'" will extend the principle of the Marconi coherer—real-time transmission through the ether with no capacity for data storage—as a general theory of textual reproduction.

Keatsian Induction

While young Cashell sets up his experiment in the store's office, the narrator has unwittingly helped to arrange another one in the shop. Returning after that stroll with his sweetheart, Fanny Brand, the ailing Shaynor accepts a glass of the chloroform cocktail after he coughs up some ominous drops of blood. The narrator notices that the blowzy Fanny "distantly resembled the seductive shape on a gold-framed toilet-water advertisement whose charms were unholily heightened by the glare from the red bottle in the window"; "by instinct" he detects that Shaynor has long made the same association and "that the flamboyant thing was to him a shrine" (*W*, 204). Shaynor even begins to cense his altar, treating his cough by burning "Blaudett's Cathedral Pastilles" ("though I'm not a Roman Catholic") beneath the advertising poster (*W*, 204).

As the pastilles release a smell "very like incense" under the "seven-tinted wench with the teeth," Shaynor begins a letter to Fanny but ends up staring absently as "all meaning and consciousness" leave his eyes (*W*, 204–5). As with Jane Eyre's abortive trip to catch the post, an unsent letter leads to a more mysterious mode of communication. A glass of the narrator's potion made the "energetic" Cashell more garrulous (with its tinge of physics, the description is so carefully chosen that Kipling uses it twice) (*W*, 200, 205). But the concoction stupefies Shaynor. As Cashell puts it, "[c]onsumptives go off in those sort of doses very often"—a neat fusion of the cause of his drowsy numbness and its effect (*W*, 207).[31]

Cashell begins his testing in the back room, while Shaynor seems to have sunk Lethe-wards below the poster. But in his daze he begins speaking words. "And threw—and threw—and threw": this incantation sounds out the mystery of the medium in the tale (how it lets messages *through*) before the phrase at last resolves into "And threw warm gules on Madeleine's young breast" (*W*, 210)—and it becomes clear that Shaynor's words come from Keats's "The Eve of St. Agnes" (1820). The narrator confesses his surprise to hear the dutiful druggist apparently quoting Keats yet acknowledges "a certain stained-glass effect of light on the high bosom of the highly-polished picture which might, by stretch of fancy, suggest, as a vile chromo recalls some incomparable canvas, the line he had spoken" (*W*, 211). Likewise, Shaynor's words represent an imperfect reproduction of "The Eve of St. Agnes"; Keats actually wrote, "And threw warm gules on Made*line*'s *fair* breast" (line 218, emphasis added).[32] Shaynor's version of Madeline's name even has an extra *e*, as if a pop of static had been misread as that letter's single Morse dot, a wholly plausible scenario in the early years of wireless.[33]

Approaching the unresponsive Shaynor, the narrator sees that he has filled a page with "half-formed words, sentences, and wild scratches," out of which emerge the lines "—Very cold it was. Very cold / The hare—the hare—the hare— / The birds—," like the needle skipping on a phonograph record, or like someone fixated on the "birds and game" displayed at a neighboring shop (*W*, 211, 200). But finally Shaynor produces "one clear line"—"The hare, in spite of fur, was very cold" (*W*, 211)—a conflation, and stylistic deflation, of the second and third lines of "St. Agnes": "The owl, for all his feathers, was a-cold; / The hare limp'd trembling through the frozen grass" (*ESA*, lines 2–3). By now it seems that Shaynor is not quot-

FIGURE 7.1. Two receivers. Kipling, "'Wireless,'" *Scribner's* (1902). Courtesy of University of Georgia Libraries.

ing the poem so much as composing it, or transcribing it from a live signal source. "Incense in a censer / Before her darling picture framed in gold / Maiden's picture—angel's portrait—" (*W*, 211); compare the end of Keats's first stanza:

> Numb were the Beadsman's fingers, while he told
> His rosary, and while his frosted breath,
> Like pious incense from a censer old,
> Seem'd taking flight for heaven, without a death,
> Past the sweet Virgin's picture, while his prayer he saith.
> (*ESA*, lines 5–9)

Cashell witnesses none of this. But from the next room, "as though in the presence of spirits," he shouts that his receiver too has begun to work: "There's something coming through from somewhere; but it isn't Poole" (*W*, 211–12). Laura Otis documents the interplay between cable telegraphy and Victorian neuroscience, but perhaps this is what happens to the nervous network when electrical communication insidiously cuts the cord: minds and messages enter the ether. From Plato's *pharmakon* to McLuhan's narcosis, the latest medium has often seemed like a new drug.

Like an oblivious, imperfectly tuned Pierre Menard, Shaynor produces the words of an earlier dying consumptive apothecary named John, but with a difference. "The Eve of St. Agnes" treats Porphyro's exploitation of religious legend and its accouterments as tools for seduction—or acquaintance rape. And with its stained-glass bedroom windows, its beadsmen and beldames, its Spenserian stanzas and archaisms, the poem enacts an analogous appropriation of elements from an older literature into decorative trappings for medievalist exoticism; the fact that Keats's poetic language often replicates what were already archaisms in Spenser adds a special coat of instant verdigris. Inspired by an advertisement and the smell of a patent medicine, Shaynor's rendition of the poem takes us from quotation to burlesque, displacing the Beadsman's religious icon with the "darling picture" of a "Maiden"—a poetic pinup. "There's a good deal of *influenza* in town, too, and there'll be a dozen *prescriptions* coming in before morning," Shaynor observed at the beginning of the tale: when a contagious, invisible influence is abroad, there's fore-writing in the air (*W*, 197–98, emphasis added). We know from Keats's example that apothecaries are necessarily Latinists, even though like Keats or Kipling they may not know Homer in the original Greek.[34] And as an early primer on wireless notes, "[t]he French name for induction is *influence*, and this really gives us a very fair idea of what the effect is."[35]

Reaching for a reasonable explanation, the narrator feels a sense of self-division before the spectacle of Shaynor's "machine-like" poetic production or reproduction (*W*, 211)—just the sort of "fractured subjectivity" associated today with modern media, notes Kenneth Rufo.[36] As his "own soul most dispassionately consider[s] [his] own soul" in terror, the narrator's ratiocinating side attempts to offer "encouragement" to his "other self" (*W*, 212). But he hears himself "sounding sentences, such as men pronounce in dreams," a rational-sounding account that is pure fancy:

> If he has read Keats, it proves nothing. If he hasn't—like causes *must* beget like effects. There is no escape from this law. . . . given the circumstances, such as Fanny Brand, who is the key of the enigma, and approximately represents the latitude and longitude of [Keats's fiancée] Fanny Brawne; allowing also for the bright red colour of the arterial blood upon the handkerchief . . . ; and counting the effect of the professional environment, here almost perfectly duplicated—the result is logical and inevitable. As inevitable as induction. (*W*, 212–13)

The "law" of like causes and effects might seem to suggest a deductive logic, but the collected particulars here expose the "inevitable . . . induction" that generates this supposed rule out of the parallels between Shaynor and Keats in the first place.

Under the model of induction, "[n]o intent, no agency, no subject in any strict sense is necessary, since induction occurs on its own account when two objects enter the same field."[37] If logical, psychological, technological, or pharmacological inductions are possible, they become so through the ether of a communal but unconscious causality: "'If he has read Keats it's the chloric-ether. If he hasn't, it's the identical bacillus, or Hertzian wave of tuberculosis, plus Fanny Brand and the professional status which, in conjunction with the main-stream of subconscious thought common to all mankind, has thrown up temporarily an induced Keats'" (*W*, 213). Inevitably, we will learn that the unliterary and unimaginative Shaynor has never heard of Keats, so another kind of causality must obtain. As Bonamy Dobrée recognizes in *Rudyard Kipling: Realist and Fabulist*, the reductive assertion that "like causes must produce like results" offers a wholly "inadequate answer" to the question of causality in the tale.[38] Yet paradoxically, for all these mystical and machinic overtones, we shall see that in literary terms, the tale's technical formula for producing a temporary long-range installation of Keats makes this induction a strangely realistic phenomenon.

Realism Unplugged

Critics have singled out "'Wireless'" for its remarkable evocation of its atmosphere and milieu. "It is seen and felt and heard as few stories are," Randall Jarrell declares, "[o]ne feels after reading this: well, no one ever again will have to describe a drugstore."[39] The dazzling impression of a real setting, an ambience, a mode of late-night conversation—all of this points to the tale's methodical realism. Yet when Shaynor starts channeling Keats, we recognize that the tale's marshalling of realistic particulars has also been a systematic importation of details from Keats's poetry and life history: a frosty night, a consecrated portrait, light through colored glass, the smell of incense; a druggist, a lover named Fanny, a journey in the cold, a cough and a drop of blood. The tale's elaborate descriptions were really Keats's pre-scriptions all along. As in a photomosaic image, the elements of the story that make it seem recognizable and real turn out to be chosen from an artificially constrained palette of appropriations; examined closely, each realistic detail reveals itself as a micro-quotation from that collection. This is a realism not for a postal universe of narrative sorting but for McLuhan's "electrically-configured world" that "force[s] us to move from the habit of data classification to the mode of pattern recognition."[40]

But this elaborate formal exercise also exploits the particular appositeness of "The Eve of St. Agnes" for such an examination of the texture of literary realism. The poem provides an appropriate textual source and literary reference point for "'Wireless'" not only because of its treatment of the movement between dream and reality or its storehouse of physical detail but also because of the poem's skepticism toward idealism and fantasy—what we might recognize as its own poetic realism; the poem highlights the effect of a supposed dream that becomes troublingly real.[41] Moreover, Keats faced criticism and even censorship over one facet of the poem's realism; his publisher balked when he submitted a draft in which the consummation scene was graphic enough to render the poem "unfit for ladies."[42] Although the letters outlining the incident would remain unpublished until the 1920s, Keats's racier versions of the poem had appeared in print by the turn of the century.[43]

Whether or not Kipling knew about the episode, "'Wireless'" discloses the same Foucaultian alignment of sexuality and truth-telling as it reveals the energy source of the home-battery that powers Shaynor's poetic generation and Keats's: thwarted lust. Thanks to multiple transpositions from poetry to the physical and pharmaceutical ether and then to narrative prose, in "'Wireless'" composition becomes decomposition, an unveiling of the components of literary production:

> Followed without a break ten or fifteen lines of bald prose—the naked soul's confession of its physical yearning for its beloved—unclean as we count uncleanliness; unwholesome, but human exceedingly; the raw material, so it seemed to me in that hour and in that place, whence Keats wove the twenty-sixth, seventh, and eighth stanzas of his poem. Shame I had none in overseeing this revelation; and my fear had gone with the smoke of the pastille.
>
> "That's it," I murmured. "That's how it's blocked out. Go on! Ink it in, man. Ink it in!" (*W*, 214)

Shaynor's automatic writing continues, but the story's narration deliberately interrupts the flow of quotation in order to summarize the content of this revelatory "confession." In "'Wireless'" as well as midcentury social realism, a specific combination of narratorial elements helps guarantee truth: a rhetoric of frankness, an acknowledgment of uncomfortable realities—and a readiness to blur the most shocking particulars.

When the realism of "'Wireless'" opens out into fabulism, the story's feel of shoppy authenticity stands disclosed as at the same time a meticulous pastiche made of literary citations from Keats's life and poetry. Kipling builds his workaday setting out of elements borrowed from the poet's biography and from "The Eve of St. Agnes," and these factors in turn—in realistic fashion—shape the carefully contrived response of a particular character to the details given about his social, physical, and psychological environment. At the same time, fictional realism asserts, or assumes, the roots of this individual reaction in general human nature ("the main-stream of subconscious thought common to all mankind"). As with the psychic plot of "The Lifted Veil," the paranormal scheme of "'Wireless'" makes perceptible Victorian realism's assumptions and balancing acts.

The scheme of the tale also clarifies Kipling's subtle departures from Victorian realism, even when his fiction proclaims a sense of unblinkered actuality. Analyzing Kipling in relation to turn-of-the-century sociological theory, Noel Annan points out that Kipling took more interest in Durkheimian social facts, in roles and rituals and group structures, than he did in the details of individual psychological development. "[S]eldom interested in the individual as such," Kipling instead "took the environment as given and noted its effect" on human beings.[44] Press a bit harder on the law of causes and effects, and fictional realism morphs into late nineteenth-century naturalism, a movement with which Kipling flirted in his Indian stories and an early, never-published novel, the vanished *Mother Maturin*.[45] A set of Keatsian circumstances suffices temporarily to "induce" Keats in someone made susceptible by employment, disease, drugs, and sexual desire: with its multiple factors, the narrator's explanatory formula verges on a parody of naturalist determinism ("the identical bacillus, or Hertzian wave of tuberculosis, plus Fanny Brand and the professional status"). The narrator's scientism, and the experimental attitude toward Shaynor that eclipses his interest in the wireless test he has come to see, complete the naturalist paradigm, even if they also mock it.

With the Hertzian waves of the tuberculosis bacillus, explanation may pass into mystification, determinism into mysticism, science into spoof. But the blurred boundaries seem appropriate; after all, the tale explores the fictional representation of reality through its references to a real, new technology that was also astonishing enough to strike many of Marconi's contemporaries as altogether fantastic, and even to bolster the possibilities for telepathy or for contact with the dead.[46] Oliver Lodge, the physicist most responsible for improving wireless tuning, presided over both the British Association for the Advancement of Science and the spiritualist Society for Psychical Research. In fact, Lodge came to regard the electromagnetic ether as the key to psychic experience, the source of continuity in the fabric of the universe, and the deep reality behind the transience of matter.[47] In the 1900 "discourse network," Kittler claims only somewhat hyperbolically, "there is no difference between occult and technological media."[48] In a sense, all "'Wireless'" does is separate the actual communication machinery from the fantasies it provoked, the real ether from the ethereal, and then challenge us to make them cohere.

Like naturalism, realism takes the influence of social station and environment on character and mentality as axiomatic. But in contrast to the offshoot that upsets so many of its equilibria, realism can also maintain the possibility of evading or transcending the absolute logic of such determination: momentarily or in the final pages; through willpower, choice, or sympathy. When it comes to such transcendence, too, "'Wireless'" uses the parallels suggested by new technology to probe the ideology and the limits of nineteenth-century literary realism. James's *In the Cage* traced out the gulf between social demarcation and mental liberation, but it ultimately embraced the possibility of restoring a disillusioned, realistic coherence to the "double life" its heroine thought she could lead (*IC*, 846). And the telegraphist had at least *read* the texts that shaped her fantasies. Her intelligence was winged; Shaynor's is drugged. If James's tale rejects the transcendence selectively endorsed by an earlier mode of realism, Kipling's story orchestrates a version so excessive that—like its adroit looting of a Romantic poem for descriptions of a drugstore—it reveals itself as a brilliant fusion of simulated realism and pure literary fantasy.

In "'Wireless,'" a peculiar conjunction of personal circumstances renders Shaynor temporarily free from just those circumstances. On one level, the tale simply exaggerates the myth of the sensitive artist who rises above life's struggles to travel in realms of poetic gold—a myth that Victorian versions of Keats helped promote.[49] But Shaynor's escape is so complete that it escapes him altogether; he proves as thoroughly unconscious of what he senses as the "frail coil of wire" in the back room (*W*, 202). When Shaynor's intimate fantasies turn out to be distorted scraps of someone else's text, in effect all he can do is take notes "with a clerky air" and a "pen behind his ear" (*W*, 215). The tale creates a high-voltage spark between naturalist determinism and an aesthetic transcendence over time and space so extreme that it too seems parodic. Wireless telegraphy, defined by the connection that isn't there, figures the separation of the knower from the known, of Shaynor's knowledge from Keats's information.

Transmission and the Individual Talent

Only a properly tuned medium can allow such elements to temporarily stick together; as Gillian Beer declares, the "technical word 'coherer' might be the title of Kipling's tale."[50] Within the story, Shaynor acts as Marconi coherer, even down to miming its status as glorified thermometer; the "agony" of poetic reproduction "mount[s]" inside him "like mercury in the tube" (*W*, 217–18). Mercury, the messenger of the gods, was also an essential ingredient in the dust that let the coherer receive its messages.[51] On the level of the tale's discourse rather than its story, however, it is the function of its narrator to act as a coherer—and so necessarily, given the aural dimension of telegraphy and poetry alike, also as co-hearer. Young Mr. Cashell never learns of Shaynor's Keatsian productions; Shaynor misses Cashell's explanations of wireless communication; Shaynor has never read Keats. The witness to parallel stories and texts that never quite touch, the narrator ties them together, physically placed and intellectually equipped to provide the principle of transitory coherence between poetry and radiotelegraphy; "*You* ought to be grateful that you know 'St. Agnes' Eve' without the book," he tells himself (*W*, 213). As he produces such coherence, the nameless first-person narrator functions further to separate the subject from the experience, and the traffic from the discovery.

The anonymous man of letters who narrates Kipling's "'The Finest Story in the World'" (1891) plays a similar role as the literate insider who can identify the sources and assess the quality of a prosaic young man's astonishing vision. That earlier story, which handles many of the same themes as "'Wireless'" but without the wireless connection that could only come later, demonstrates both the consistency of Kipling's interests and the implications of Marconism for them. After hearing the story ideas of a bank clerk and part-time poetaster named Charlie Mears, the older narrator begins to recognize them as not original conceptions but thrilling fragments of Charlie's past lives. These recollections are "absolutely and literally true"—yet the hapless Charlie can neither recognize them as real memories nor reshape them into literature; his banal attempts supplant facticity with clumsy factitiousness.[52] If the narrator can only wring this real-life "material" from Charlie and set it down as his own imaginary story, "the world" will "hail it as an impudent and vamped fiction" (*FS*, 118). Trollope presented his quasi-autobiographical Charley Tudor as a future novelist turning clerkly life into fiction, but thirty-five years later, Kipling's Charlie marks an uncanny separation between office life and the retrieval of the real.

Like "'Wireless,'" "'The Finest Story'" hinges on the interplay between consciousness and creativity, mimesis and poiesis, reality and literary creation. And its narrator too describes Charlie and the extraordinary visions that are so separate from his ordinary life in terms of new media: when he arrives full of "Byron, Shelley, or Keats," Charlie is "as useless as a surcharged phonograph," producing only "a confused tangle of other voices most like the mutter and hum through a City telephone in the busiest part of the day" (*FS*, 119–20). Yet the narrator persists, carefully ascertaining the poetic "medium in which [Charlie's] memory worked best" (Longfellow's "Saga of King Olaf," apparently) before quizzing Charlie on his life as a slave on an ancient galley (*FS*, 121). Soon Charlie is answering his questions "as assuredly as though all his knowledge lay before him on the printed page," although the "medium" of Longfellow impinges enough to revive Charlie's later memories of life as a Viking sailor (*FS*, 126). Appropriately, "'The Finest Story in the World'" soon appeared as one of Kipling's *Many Inventions* (1893), a collection whose title at once cites Ecclesiastes and promotes the author's literary ingenuity as the latest marvel of the Edison Age.

But one day Charlie arrives bearing a medium of his own, a photograph of "a tobacconist's assistant with a weakness for pretty dress," the woman with whom he has just fallen in love (*FS*, 150). In contrast to the unwitting inspiration Shaynor will derive from Fanny Brand and her commercial double, Charlie's love melts away his mystic memories. Fled is that music, and now "the finest story in the world," the story that the narrator dreamed of composing out of Charlie's recollections, will "never be written" (*FS*, 150). "'Wireless'" and "'The Finest Story'" reimagine the relationships between mimesis and mnemonics, the representation of life and the remembrance of it: Charlie remembers past existences but can neither recognize them as life nor shape them into art, while Shaynor channels Keats but will remember nothing of it. Both stories treat metempsychosis as medium-psychosis, a replay of someone's alienated life experience on different psychic channels.[53]

Yet in comparison to the earlier story, "'Wireless'" pays far more mind to the media it engages: their mechanics, properties, and effects. For one thing, like a wireless transmission, the tale seems to take place live; it covers a short interlude during one evening, with a single scene and setting. Schematically, the design of "'Wireless'" simply translates electromagnetic transmission across space into psychic transmission across time. Yet it also reminds us that this latter function is exactly the purpose of writing, nowhere more so perhaps than in Romantic poetry, which encourages the feeling that if we tune in to the text of a Wordsworth or Coleridge, we can start receiving bits of imaginative output. For this reason, Kittler claims that in the Romantic-era "discourse network," "the Book of Poetry became the first medium in the modern sense."[54] As it dreams up a hybrid medium between radio and writing, "'Wireless'" sustains but enriches Kittler's strict "1800/1900" split, mapping it onto a division often explored by Kipling, the generic split between verse and prose.

In contrast to Charlie's uniquely vivid and real story, which remains unwritten except for the fragments anthologized in the tale itself, Shaynor's story has already been written—and it was someone else's story, to boot. For "'Wireless'" takes us from personal transmigration to invisible transmission. With radiotelegraphy diffusing its metaphors on all thematic channels, the story need suggest neither that Shaynor has personally inherited Keats's soul nor that Keats's spirit has temporarily descended to fill Shaynor's body. The absence of a sense of an individual and distinctive spirit seems appropriate. For, as unpredictable as wireless communication could be (as "'Wireless'" appeared, Marconi was tormented by his inability to establish consistent transatlantic contact), wireless telegraphy amounted to a peculiarly impersonal new medium. It couldn't speak with the eerily human voice of the phonograph or telephone, only with pulses of noise or printed markings on a register tape. And even in comparison to cable telegraphy, whose operators claimed they could identify each other by the sound of their personal touch with the manual telegraph key, early wireless would have seemed machinic or cold, since sending code on one of Marconi's early spark-gap transmitters would have been too slow and painstaking to communicate anything like the individual style of wired Morse.

Wireless telegraphy at the turn of the century also lacked the simulated liveliness of its contemporaneous new technology, the moving picture, a contrast at which Kipling hints by juxtaposition. If "'Wireless'" happens live, "Mrs. Bathurst" (1904), which features a central cinematic incident, presents a conversation in one long, uncut take. In this tale that appeared alongside "'Wireless'" in *Traffics and Discoveries*, Emanuel Pyecroft and a group of male acquaintances consider the story of Click Vickery (nicknamed for the ticking made by his ill-fitting false teeth when he speaks). After seeing a "[b]iograph or cinematograph" image of his beloved Mrs. Bathurst walking through Paddington Station, Vickery follows her charismatic figure

off the screen and to his own desertion and death.[55] Elliot Gilbert's classic reading of the tale rightly emphasizes the importance of the cinematic
image, but his treatment of the "moving picture show" as simply Kipling's
"metaphor for life" is misleading.[56] On the contrary, the story depends on
the properties of the medium—its combination of repeatability, verisimilitude, and glamour. Not only does Vickery obsessively attend showings of
the film, only abandoning his post when the show closes, but the tale also
hints that celluloid may enhance Mrs. Bathurst's magnetism. Indeed, with
her uncommon allure, Mrs. Bathurst inadvertently becomes a precocious
movie star and the original "It" girl; years before Elinor Glyn or Clara Bow,
Kipling offers just that nonexplanation of her indefinable personal appeal:
as Pyecroft puts it, "'Tisn't beauty, so to speak, nor good talk necessarily. It's
just It. Some women'll stay in a man's memory. . . . "[57] "It's just It" is also
a quotation from "'Wireless,'" down to its capitalization. Yet when young
Cashell uses the phrase, he's describing not personal magnetism but "what
we call Electricity" (*W*, 202).[58]

In "'Wireless,'" radiotelegraphy has transmitted its distance and abstraction to poetry. Intertextuality becomes not literary allusion so much as
wholesale transposition, with a source text converted from Romantic poetry
into modern data. Two decades before T. S. Eliot's "Tradition and the Individual Talent" (1919), Kipling's prose imagines the impersonality of poetry,
an idea opened to him by what media theorists have recognized as the paradoxical "personalized impersonality" of electrical media.[59] Shaynor in his
drugged semi-consciousness may be supremely sensitive, losing himself to
his material like the "cameleon Poet" Keats describes in a famous letter, yet
Shaynor's sensitivity is less like a poet's than like a modern machine's.[60] The
story highlights the meagerness of his character; we see Shaynor in the passive roles of dutiful employee, compliant boyfriend, and enthralled textbook
reader. Even his deep, uncensored confessions are treated as simple expressions of lust. Perhaps the most unsettling element of "'Wireless'" is that it
presents Shaynor's inner longings as inseparable from his unconscious pla-
giarism of words he has never read and could never intentionally produce;
in Eliot's terms, the poetic expression of Shaynor's personality *is* the escape
from his personality. With Keats's poem, Shaynor's psychology arrives at
an expression as weirdly objective and impersonal as Durkheim's statistical
suicides.

Kipling would later express his view of artistic inspiration to H. R. Haggard, the author of imperial romances and one of the few confidants of Kipling's last decades. In 1918, when Haggard tried to comfort a melancholic Kipling by pointing to Kipling's fame and success as a writer, Kipling

> thrust the idea aside with a gesture of disgust. . . . Moreover he went on to show that anything which any of us did *well* was no credit to us: that it came from somewhere else: "We are only telephone wires." As example he instanced (I *think*) "Recessional" in his own case and "She" in mine. "*You* didn't write 'She' you know," he said; "something wrote it through you!" or some such words.[61]

Many critics have connected the incident to "'Wireless,'" and certainly the use of a modern medium to figure the mysteries of literary creation, to embody its remoteness and impersonality, reveals the same sensibility.[62] But the media metaphors, and the mechanics of transmission they propose, diverge significantly. Conversing with Haggard, Kipling casts literary inspiration as a far-off voice on the telephone, while authors become the "wires" that connect that hidden source with an unseen listener—the reader, who must hold (or must be) the receiver. In this light, Shaynor's *wireless* reception would suggest that there is no author here at all.

The story has often been read as a tale about the mysteries of artistic creation, but Shaynor is not even a figure for the artist who creates without understanding, for he not only doesn't understand but doesn't create. With no wires or authors in sight, Shaynor more closely resembles that staticky receiver, the reader—and reading becomes an unconscious blend of slips and plagiarisms. Likewise, "'Wireless'" reveals a certain affiliation to Kipling's final description of his muse, in *Something of Myself* (1937), as an impersonal "Daemon" whose "peremptory motions" the author could only attend to and recognize.[63] Yet there Kipling contrasts the Daemon's true presence with the mere "'carry-over' or induced electricity" it can leave in its wake; Kipling associates such "induction" with the writing of uninspired tales and sequels after this creature departs.[64] Thirty years after "'Wireless,'" Kipling retains electrical induction as his metaphor for literary creation that isn't creative.

"'Wireless'" etherizes old poetry into new information; the hallucinatory and seductive central medium of Kittler's Romantic discourse network now becomes something impersonal, decontextualized, distanced, subject to interference or noise. The story's very title subtly pushes us beyond individual expression and toward the capacity for words to exist outside any particular consciousness, a property that writing made material, print made mechanical, and wireless telegraphy made ethereal.[65] Kipling often produced story titles wrapped in quotation marks ("'The Finest Story in the World,'" "'Love-o'-Women,'" "'The City of Dreadful Night'"). But only in "'Wireless'" and in the haunting "'They'" (published alongside it in *Traffics and Discoveries*) does a title's terseness and obliqueness create a sense of language alienated from any origin, a quotation disconnected from any source. The word *wireless* provides the story's title, but it never actually appears within the tale. Instead, the word itself comes to us wirelessly, a quotation in no one's voice, letters pulled out of the air.

Under the blazing electric lights of the shop, the world of information becomes a night world. Besides duplicating the setting of "The Eve of St. Agnes," the story's nighttime action confirms the critical opposition between Kipling's day-world of work, men, Englishness, and understated language, and his night-world of vivid expression, women, "sexuality, sleep, and dreams."[66] It picks up a note in Keats's earliest surviving letter to Fanny Brawne: "at night, when . . . the lonely, silent, unmusical Chamber is waiting to receive me as into a Sepulchre, then believe me my passion gets entirely the sway, then I would not have you see those Rapsodies [*sic*] which I once thought it impossible I should ever give way to. . . . "[67] Shaynor too undergoes nocturnal rhapsodies he would never experience in his daytime life. But the night world of "'Wireless'" also parallels both Marconi's experiences with wireless reception and Freud's contemporary explanation of the dream. At night, Marconi and other researchers found, without knowing why, they could receive far-off signals that were impossible to catch during the day, a phenomenon that proved especially significant in attempts to establish transatlantic wireless communication.[68] Perhaps picking up on such nighttime happenings, the engineering professor William Ayrton exulted in the possibility of wireless communication that Marconi's work suggested to him: it seemed "almost like dreamland and ghostland, not the ghostland of the heated imagination cultivated by the Psychical Society, but a real communication from a distance based on true physical laws."[69] In "'Wireless,'" Kipling hints that one name for such nocturnal signals may indeed be dreams. "I suppose I must have been dreaming," Shaynor hazily conjectures when he awakens and leaves his Keatsian "fairyland" (*W*, 218, 216). In placing dreams at the nexus of alphabetic writing and a second, less linear mode, Kipling closely parallels Freud, a writer who also postulates a mind that doesn't always know what it knows, and who treats libidinal energy as the "raw material" (as "'Wireless'" puts it) of the psyche.[70]

Meanwhile, young Cashell awaits those messages from Poole, a real-life station identification that flows into the tale's stream of liquid imagery. The tide hums on the beach; bathwater becomes charged when an antenna is hooked to the plumbing; Shaynor's mercury rises; Fanny Brand recalls an advertisement for toilet-water; ships at sea try to communicate; Keats's Porphyro "melt[s]" into Madeline's "dream" (*ESA*, line 320). Most of all, there are the Hertzian waves, propagated through an imaginary ether that was often figured as a sort of attenuated liquid or gas, "an etheric ocean"; in "'Wireless,'" Jeffrey Sconce concludes, "the sea stands both as a medium and a symbol of separation."[71] If electricity encouraged the idea of information as something fluid yet disembodied, the ether—undetectable because it does not exist—took these traits in an even more radical direction. We never hear the transmissions from Poole, but the name gathers a liquid image into an figure of collection itself, the pool of materials from which Kipling has constructed the story—from the work of one whose name was writ in water—and even the pool of collective psychology, that "main-stream of subconscious thought common to all mankind," through which sentiments propagate unseen.

The suggestion of a psychic ether containing everyone's thoughts and stories may seem an outlandish version of the social postbag, but contemporary discussions of radiotelegraphy would not have placed it far outside the intellectual mainstream. Just a few years before "'Wireless,'" the founder of the Metaphysical Society argued that Marconi's invention offered new evidence for his hypotheses about "Brain-waves," "quasi-magnetic waves of influence which might affect other brains" predisposed to receive them.[72] The trick was to place other brains in syntony, to tune them to the right frequency. In 1901, Marconi explained the need for his new research on syntony in terms that could double as a summary of Kipling's story the next year: "The ether about the English Channel has become very lively, and a non-tuned receiver keeps picking up messages or parts of messages from various sources."[73] Like Marconi as he ramped up his transmitter's voltage for intercontinental communication, the theorist of brain-waves suggests that highly charged emotions will work best to overcome the psychic gaps. But in imagining mental telegraphy, "'Wireless'" suggests an altogether different formula for psychic syntony.

Brand Awareness

Perhaps ideas of human syntony and psychic repetition were in the air. Oscar Wilde's "De Profundis" (written 1896–97) puts it less mystically: "Most people are other people. Their thoughts are someone else's opinions, their lives a mimicry, their passions a quotation."[74] Shaynor begins to doze while starting a letter to Fanny Brand, whom he has just seen, perhaps eager to communicate in writing what he could not express in speech. After producing his final lines from "The Eve of St. Agnes"—he will move on to a short burst from "Ode to a Nightingale" before waking up—Shaynor seems briefly to return to letter-writing:

> Then prose: "It is very cold of mornings when the wind brings rain and sleet with it. I heard the sleet on the window-pane outside, and thought of you, my darling. I am always thinking of you. I wish we could both run away like two lovers into the storm and get that little cottage by the sea which we are always thinking about, my own dear darling. We could sit and watch the sea beneath our windows. It would be a fairyland all of our own—a fairy sea—a fairy sea. . . . " (*W*, 216, original ellipsis)

The passage adapts the last stanzas of "St. Agnes" (the sleet and window-pane passage that Shaynor has already misquoted, the "lovers" who "fled away into the storm," the "elfin-storm from faery land") even as it cannily picks up transitional elements for the coming lines from "Nightingale" (the window and faery land again, the sea) (*ESA*, lines 371, 343). But this note also draws upon Keats's letters to Fanny Brawne, perhaps the most celebrated love letters in the English language.

In fact, Victorians from Matthew Arnold to Coventry Patmore and even A. C. Swinburne greeted the 1878 publication of these letters with disgust—both at the lovestruck Keats and at the book itself, which struck many as an outrageous violation of privacy and propriety.[75] The "'Wireless'" narrator's stance toward Shaynor's "confession" suggests that Kipling might have been more indulgent. He has certainly read the letters. In the letter confessing his nighttime "Rapsodies," Keats writes from a "Cottage" with "a window, looking onto a beautifully hilly country, with a glimpse of the sea"; he is on the Isle of Wight, the future site of Marconi's first wireless station.[76] If not quite "a quotation," Shaynor's passion is at least a plagiarized paraphrase.

In "'Wireless'" the narrator casts Fanny Brawne as the cathected muse for John Keats, and Fanny Brand in the same role for John Shaynor. But the second Fanny has an intermediary with no equivalent in the lives of the first John and Fanny: the image in "the advertisement where the female in the dove-coloured corset had seen fit to put on all her pearls before she cleaned her teeth" (W, 206). As soon as the narrator sees the similarity between Fanny Brand and the advertising poster, he observes that Shaynor has made the same recognition; the connection seems neither arbitrary nor idiosyncratic.

We could describe the psychosocial ether through which these recognitions and transactions occur as *mass culture*, the modern exploitation of mass media technologies as varieties and vectors of mass consumption. When he first hears Shaynor misquoting "The Eve of St. Agnes" in front of his shrine, the narrator admits the likeness between an advertisement bathed in electric light and the original line from Keats, just "as a vile chromo recalls some incomparable canvas" (W, 211). But of course the chromolithograph, another nineteenth-century mass medium, offered a way of reproducing not only magnificent paintings but also colorful advertisements. *Pace* Walter Benjamin, in the age of technical reproducibility, it may not be that art loses its mystical aura so much as that most of the art we see is trying to impart that aura to a tube of toothpaste or a bottle of drugstore perfume.[77] Making an advertising poster into his conscious "shrine" and unconscious "inspiration," Shaynor at once personalizes the enchantment and indicates the strange impersonality of his mediated erotic life (W, 204, 214). Like Porphyro's devious "stratagem" in "The Eve of St. Agnes," an advertisement is a meticulously crafted external fantasy that attempts to melt into our dreams in order to shape and exploit our own desires, to turn our everyday passions into its quotations—not to encompass but to become part of everyone's story (ESA, line 139).

Advertising, mass culture, and wireless telegraphy all mean "shouting to the world," or at least to anyone equipped to receive. Even before the broadcast age, Kipling suggests that when wireless telegraphy multiplies the power and ubiquity of technical reproduction, there's mass culture on every channel. Shaynor's Fanny Brand echoes Keats's Fanny Brawne—as if by a conjugation from present to past—right down to the skepticism with which his male companions treat her. Fanny Brand's name incorporates the fire imagery of "The Eve of St. Agnes" but turns it into a trademark, perhaps even an obscene one. The narrator of "'Wireless'" may register the branding and the coarse pun, even as Fanny's name becomes the most obvious early hint of a Keatsian subtext: "'Fanny *who?*' I said, for the name struck an obscurely familiar chord in my brain" (*W*, 209, emphasis in original). But the latter-day version takes us from the frank physicality encapsulated in the name of Keats's "Fanny Brawne" to the more ambiguous implications of "Fanny Brand."

A dismissive Cashell sums up the second Fanny's attractions by calling her "a great, big, fat lump of a girl," yet for the men in the shop, romantic brawn has become hard to separate from modern brand (*W*, 209).[78] But so has Keats. In the story, the dynamics of mass, commercial culture embody the transmission of culture altogether. When "his work" has been done—the daze work, one could say—Shaynor awakes, and the narrator inquires about his acquaintance with poets (*W*, 214):

> "I meant to ask you if you've ever read anything written by a man called Keats."
>
> "Oh! I haven't much time to read poetry, and I can't say that I remember the name exactly. Is he a popular writer?"
>
> "Middling. I thought you might know him because he's the only poet who was ever a druggist. . . . "
>
> "Indeed. I must dip into him." (*W*, 219)

The description of light reading as partial submersion sustains the tale's liquid imagery and treats culture as an immersive medium: Shaynor has already been dipped into Keats, or Keats has been dipped into him. In comparison to the bestsellers of Kipling, say, the popularity of Keats's texts may register as only "middling," an additional irony that results from applying Shaynor's mass cultural criterion to Keats's art. But under the cover of this incongruity Kipling has imported another term that emphasizes that art's middleness, its mediality.

For Keats too has gone wireless, has become part of late-Victorian mass culture independent of any obvious connection to the eyes or ears of an audience. The Keats that the narrator recognizes has become less potent, less *real* than the Keats that nobody read. The story's adept juxtaposition of mystical and technological media emphasizes the ironies of turn-of-the-century communications; in a wireless age, even the messages not intended for us and the transmissions we never receive go through us, saturate our bodies and brains with unsought information. Perhaps now everyone knows Keats without the book. In the cultural ether, a "medium" as "highly elastic" and "all-pervading" as its suppositious physical counterpart, "The Eve of St. Agnes" jostles with "Kubla Khan" (mentally recited by the tale's narrator) and an advertising picture: a wireless culture can readily carry high poesy on its viewless wings.[79] The postal system provided Carlyle with an image of the world-tissue as collective textual interchange, but wireless transmission suggests a world of stranger and less localized conjunctions.

Before the invention of voice transmission, still less of modern broadcast systems, wireless communication offers a resonant way of figuring the relationships between information and reality in the mediascape of modernity. In the tale, wireless transmission perhaps signals the working of a mass culture ready to disseminate the great works of print culture to a population unconscious of them—but at the price of subtly or manifestly vulgarizing them. Thus, with a wry appropriation that is also a facile reduction of the poem's origins, "The Eve of St. Agnes" becomes an ailing druggist's fevered sex dream. But of course the larger irony here is that "'Wireless'" itself does willfully what it describes as a paranormal phenomenon beyond any conscious will, as the story gamely appropriates Keats's poem for a magazine story named after the latest thrilling gadget.

Failing to channel lines from "Ode to a Nightingale" accurately after several near misses—with his clerkiness and puerile giggles, he "is not rightly tuned"—Shaynor awakes.[80] He is just in time for young Cashell to summon him and the narrator to the back office to hear a "curious performance" on the wireless receiver (*W*, 220). Cashell translates from Morse: ""*K.K.V. Can make nothing of your signals.*"' A pause. '"*M.M.V. M.M.V. Signals unintelligible. Purpose anchor Sundown Bay. Examine instruments to-morrow.*"'" Two ships, "men-o'-war," are "working Marconi signals off the Isle of Wight," attempting in vain to talk to each other" (*W*, 220). "Their transmitters are all right, but their receivers are out of order" (*W*, 220)—realistically enough, since "Marconi's coherer was still a temperamental device, capable of driving shipboard operators in particular to distraction."[81] Miscommunication may be inevitable as these warships try to "talk"; a glance at a compilation of British telegraph codes reveals that, consciously or not, Kipling has given one of them the call letters "MMV," the telegraph code for a Welsh village poignantly called "Mumbles."[82]

"Neither [ship] can read the other's messages," although Cashell's coherer can hear both (*W*, 220). "Perhaps the induction is faulty," Cashell speculates; "perhaps the receivers aren't tuned to receive just the number of vibrations per second that the transmitter sends. Only a word here and there. Just enough to tantalize" (*W*, 220). Words here and there: what a casually powerful summary of the capacities of media to store and transmit language—to collapse physical or temporal remoteness, to tease with the interplay of noise and signal, to map the difference between intimacy and distance ("here" versus "there") onto the crossed lines—or the Morse dash—of a letter *t*. Indeed, the phrase sums up all of this so deftly that Cashell and Kipling use it twice in close succession, both there and here:

> Again the Morse sprang to life.
> "That's one of 'em complaining now. Listen: '*Disheartening—most disheartening.*' It's quite pathetic. Have you ever seen a spiritualistic seance? It reminds me of that sometimes—odds and ends of messages coming out of nowhere—a word here and there—no good at all."
> "But mediums are all impostors," said Mr. Shaynor, in the doorway, lighting an asthma-cigarette. "They only do it for the money they can make. I've seen 'em." (*W*, 220)

If there's something "disheartening" about the partial, fitful achievements of our media, the problem may not just be that we expect too much from communication or from information access. Modern media themselves may seem to dis-hearten us, not only to externalize our selves but also to hint that there was always something external about our inner lives, to cast all our knowledge—most realistically—as potential information.

"[M]ediums are all impostors," Shaynor complains after his internal coherer has passed from invitation back to resistance, echoing the real-life distrust of wireless telegraphy as "scientific imposition." Drawing on the turn-of-the-century overlap between occult and technical media, the druggist's last words dismiss spiritualism, present another moment of dramatic irony, and provide a medium-theory that highlights the role of commerce. With typical unconsciousness, Shaynor also articulates a belief that we must treat warily: that media just *impose*, that they merely place themselves in the gap between sender and receiver. Much in "'Wireless'" contradicts that stance: the tale's attention to imperfect transmission, the separation it orchestrates between a character's words and his consciousness, the deft way in which its impostor-like realism unfolds into something else that was there all along.

Like media and mediums, fictional realism has often stood accused of imposture, of papering over the epistemological gaps between representation and reality, of treating the relationship between language and life as spuriously stable, of suppressing the properties of writing as a medium. But as this study has emphasized, that imposition was always more like transposition or juxtaposition, the sort of movement appropriate to an age that was redefining the properties of writing in line with newer media. To borrow more formulas from "'Wireless,'" "inking it in" has always meant "blocking it out," in every sense of the phrase. Part of the power of realistic writing has turned out to be its shifty power to accommodate the communicational gaps—between media, between the senses, between its communicants.

We hear no more from Shaynor. And as the signal from Poole arrives "at last, clear as a bell," the narrator goes home to bed (*W*, 221). The real world of early wireless, the imaginary reality of fiction, and the ethereal realm of Romantic poetry have come together for a few dozen pages. Here and there, they have cohered—just enough to tantalize. From Penny Post to "'Wireless,'" from Trollope's clerks to Kipling's, reading Victorian fiction in its information ecology has revealed the interchange between media old and new, the print and nonprint information systems that shaped reality as well as changing what one could know about it, and how. By the end of Kipling's story, wireless telegraphy—from spark-gap transmitter to gap-ridden cohearers—looks less like a way of bridging all the gaps than of charging them up and broadcasting them. In this way it resembles the story's formulations of realism and of writing itself. Wireless transmission spreads a communication network across the very web of reality, that fabric that Carlyle's mail call worked so hard to preserve. But as Kipling's "'Wireless'" suggests even more emphatically than Trollope's delivery routes or James's telegraph counter, every network is really just an artfully arranged collection of holes.

Coda: Afterlives of Victorian Information

The English are always degrading truths into facts. When a truth becomes a fact it loses all its intellectual value.

It is a very sad thing that nowadays there is so little useless information.

—OSCAR WILDE, "A FEW MAXIMS FOR THE INSTRUCTION OF THE OVER-EDUCATED"

By the end of the nineteenth century, Wilde could upturn an already familiar complaint about proliferating information into a piece of instant contrarian wisdom. To be sure, this inversion might seem like a clever paradox manufactured in accordance with Wilde's great discovery that the reversal of a cliché also produces a cliché. But as regularly happens with Wilde's best paradoxes, the actual cleverness of the line is the sense it conveys of fortuitous profundity, as if a formulaic reversal has unexpectedly released a truth lying dormant in the truism. When a control revolution can systematically direct flows of information in industry and society, or when a story can assemble its realism from a belletristic storehouse of Keatsiana, surely even recondite or extraneous information stands in some peril of being put to use. In company with Wilde's previous maxim, this lament for useless information hints that unfactual truths might achieve their "intellectual value" by being a kind of useless information—a formulation that resonates with Wilde's most famous aesthetic claims. "[Q]uite useless" is also his most heartfelt, even earnest, description of the status of art.[1]

This book has considered how Victorian culture and literature could explore questions about the nature and use of information as problems of realism, issues of how to represent and interpret knowledge freed from time, space, context, or matter for the purposes of fiction. Plotting a course between truth and fact was always part of the mission, and the intellectual value, of Victorian realism. But Victorian realism could also provide an early paradigm for the mode of belief that made modern information seem real or real enough, a mode that would become more and more important in the coming eras of broadcast and digital media.[2] Attempting to understand the use of apparently superfluous information, Barthes found that a text's haphazard physical detail creates the impression of reality. Yet this paradigm might also suggest that reality consists of whatever could become an extraneous textual detail. Notwithstanding Wilde's quip, perhaps reality itself essentially amounts to useless information.

Older media provide the setting for the development and adoption of new ones, and then they offer a forum in which to understand, appropriate, domesticate, and extend those new media. Thanks to print's ubiquity, cultural centrality, and physical endurance, it is the place to read how deeply new media register for Victorian culture. Within the world of print, realistic fiction was primed to become the century's most wide-ranging response to new media technologies and ideas about information. Emphatically committed not simply to representing a recognizable reality but to reimagining it for large-scale circulation, realistic writing both investigates the possibilities or perils of information and joins modern media in tracing the outlines for an emergent mass culture. When realism quietly reorders the elements of reality to produce the kind of sense that art makes, it may even thematically anticipate the dialectic of randomness and pattern that critics have used to characterize the regime of modern information.[3] In many ways, then, our own encounters with media are part of the afterlife of Victorian information.

Nineteenth-century media from the electric telegraph and daguerreotype to wireless and motion picture supported the idea of information as disembodied knowledge, as fact removed from social, physical, or material context. Paradoxically, for all that it owes to modern media, the concept of information encourages the assumption that the particular medium of inscription or transmission makes no difference, that media do not matter. As Victorian fiction engages with questions of information—its forms and flows, its inscription and circulation, its power and limitations—print culture explores, exploits, and maps out the informatic antinomies of use and uselessness, materiality and transcendence. These engagements with the promises and realities of information come close to the heart of Victorian fiction, and they do not depend upon a clairvoyant protagonist or a telegraphist's romance.

Elizabeth Gaskell's *Cranford* (1851–53) exemplifies the conceptual and practical sense that fiction could make of the possibilities of nineteenth-century information. Conjuring up its quiet village "in possession of the Amazons," *Cranford* suffuses its tales of shabby-genteel "spinsters [and] widows" with a sense of tender comedy and nostalgia for a carefully rendered past.[4] In fact, this tone misleads. *Cranford* is neither so gentle nor so backward-looking. Its first episode kills off Captain Brown, the symbol of masculine modernity, via a cruel conjunction of the modern serial fiction he champions and a new technology he helps bring to Cranford. Engrossed in the latest *Pickwick*, he glances up to see a child playing on the railway tracks and saves her only at the cost of his own life—yet another association between Dickens and railway accidents. Likewise, Gaskell's collection of impressionistic historical detail suggests less a particular point in time to be held in memory than a loose composite of the preceding twenty or thirty years, incorporating even aspects of the 1850s.

One subtle element of the text's modernity emerges during its most extended exercise in intratextual nostalgia. As *Cranford*'s narrator, Mary Smith, watches, the aging spinster Matty Jenkyns casts her old family letters into the fire:

"We must burn them, I think," said Miss Matty, looking doubtfully at me. "No one will care for them when I am gone." And one by one she dropped them into the middle of the fire; watching each blaze up, die out, and rise away, in faint, white, ghostly semblance, up the chimney, before she gave up another to the same fate. The room was light enough now; but I, like her, was fascinated into watching the destruction of those letters, into which the honest warmth of a manly heart had been poured forth. (*C*, 44)

Her father's "honest warmth" blazes again in the fire and then vanishes, briefly raised from metaphorical to literal truth as the conflagration liquidates eighteenth-century epistolarity (the early letters are on sheets of "the old original Post, with the stamp in the corner, representing a post-boy riding for life and twanging his horn") into a less material flow of stories and sentiment (*C*, 47). In essence, however, *Cranford* has hardly annihilated those letters but only signaled a change in their mode of being. As they burn, the text achieves a deft sublation, canceling their physical existence at the moment that it reveals their contents and incorporates those contents into *Cranford*'s narrative itself; the long-frozen flow of manly passions onto paper becomes a new flow of tears from Matty and Mary as well as a flow of nostalgic particulars into the tale. Mimetically destroyed, the letters become diegetically accessible. Surrendering their imaginary physicality, the words diffuse into the text as something more or less than mere letters, a "ghostly semblance" of themselves with far-reaching properties. At the moment of their loss as material objects, the letters of *Cranford* release vicarious history into the text and become information.

Gaskell had not planned, and at first had not written, *Cranford* as a novel at all. After the publication of what are now the work's self-contained first two chapters as a humorous observational piece in *Household Words*, the story somewhat unexpectedly went on, even though Gaskell had already killed off its main characters. In the second installment Mary Smith is "pleasantly surprised" to be invited back to Cranford, and the text launches into a series of longer adventures that permit more sustained and subtle characterization (*C*, 23). Slowly, a series of fictional sketches becomes a novel in serial. Miss Matty's burning letters provide a practical illumination by supplying the retroactive backstory that has become necessary as *Cranford* outgrows its literary and material limitations of format, length, and genre. "It seemed curious that I should never have heard of [Matty's] brother before," muses Mary Smith as the letters reveal the unsuspected existence of Peter Jenkyns, a signal development in the novel's plot (*C*, 46).

There are no electric telegraphs in Cranford, although the intersection of railway and serial fiction that dooms Captain Brown hints at telegraphy's union of networked machinery and fragmented, sequential prose. Yet Gaskell's text assumes, and exploits, the ambiguities of information. In the material, metaphysical, and narratological transformation of old letters into new information, *Cranford* provides a fitting image of Victorian fiction's fascination with the transitions between the old medium of writing and the newer forms that promised at once to annihilate it and to extend its power. Matty burns the letters out of fear that when she dies they will lose their familial context and their archivist, and this action lets them enter the new context of the developing narrative. But the text also imagines putting information to use in ways that go beyond this pragmatic delivery of story elements into its narrative discourse.

The disappearance of young Peter Jenkyns was attended by dead letters and postal setbacks: a note from his mother that never reached him, returned sealed and never opened until the day it joined the others in the fire; a letter from the captain whose ship would take Peter on his journey toward the East, a letter so delayed by the vagaries of the pre–Rowland Hill post that it reached his parents only after he had departed. As Mary Smith has warned us, letters bear "much the same relation to personal intercourse that . . . books of dried plants . . . do to the living and fresh flowers in the lanes and meadows" (*C*, 23). But when Matty loses her savings, the comparative desiccation of letters allows Mary to compose a carefully oblique note to the long-lost Peter, who just might be the kindly "Aga Jenkyns" whom another character has met in India. Thanks no doubt to an avoidance of much context or too much information, Mary's letter "to the Aga Jenkyns . . . should affect him, if he were Peter, and yet seem a mere statement of dry facts if he were a stranger" (*C*, 127); like Gaskell's fictional telegraph, this message will put objects, not feelings, before any other reader. Without telling Matty, Mary transcribes the "very queer" Indian address and drops the letter in the box of a receiving-house:

> and then for a minute I stood looking at the wooden pane, with a gaping slit which divided me from the letter, but a moment ago in my hand. It was gone from me like life—never to be recalled. It would get tossed about on the sea, and stained with sea-waves perhaps; and be carried among palm-trees, and scented with all tropical fragrance;—the little piece of paper, but an hour ago so familiar and commonplace, had set out on its race to the strange wild countries beyond the Ganges! But I could not afford to lose much time on this speculation. (*C*, 127)

With a mortal finality, the letter leaves *Cranford*'s meticulously detailed world of "familiar and commonplace" objects to venture where the novel assuredly will not. The moment it passes through the gap into the collection box, it enters an imperial information network whose brisk automatism lets it "race" toward its destination through the most generically exotic imaginary scenes. No intangible puff of pure information, "the little piece of paper" will retain its material integrity, even if it incorporates the traces of its journey as scents and stains.

Only a "slit" connects the place of the real world and the space of the information network, but it is a "gaping" one created to accommodate writing. In the novel's final pages, the power of modern information systems returns in a more tangible form. For the letter to India finally recalls to Cranford life no ghost or post but a flesh-and-blood brother. With Mary's letter, a piece of writing achieves far-reaching significance by allying itself with a vast Victorian information system that is both separated from ordinary life and coupled to it at all points, from an English village to India. By this point in *Cranford*, the arrival of Peter is rather unnecessary, since Matty's friends have contrived a way for her to live by means of surreptitious charity and the sale of tea. Readers have often considered the development as either a belated reassertion of male control or the private fantasy of an author whose real brother was lost at sea many years before. But the development also embodies a novelist's imagination of information and its networks, as Mary Smith turns vicarious, dematerialized information into Victorian writing that effectively recovers the content of that information—a letter that vanquishes space and time to materialize Peter Jenkyns. As the novel nears its end, the afterlife of information provides a note of extravagant, gratuitous closure.

The power of Victorian information systems connects Cranford to "Chunderabaddad," domestic fiction to the imperial order, everyday life to unreserved wish-fulfillment (*C*, 110). As I have argued, such power also links our own age to the nineteenth century. Our fascination with a realm of immaterial information that we take for a truthful fiction represents the most enduring afterlife of Victorian information.

Notes

INTRODUCTION

1. Dickens, *Letters*, 4:472–73.

2. The editors of Dickens's letters can only speculate that the enterprise discussed in the passage "may have had some connection with the 'electric telegraph' referred to" in correspondence between Paxton and his wife. Dickens, *Letters*, 4:473n. But their speculation is confirmed and clarified by Charles West, who recounts the involvement of Dickens and Paxton in West's plans for an Anglo-French cable, including their provision of letters of introduction for Captain Tayler, the group's negotiator in Paris. C. West, *Story of My Life*, 15–22.

3. Dickens, *Letters*, 4:470.

4. Ibid., 4:486. For another editorial plan for news by rail, see ibid., 4:487–88.

5. Archer, *Guide to the Electric Telegraph*, 17.

6. Ackroyd, *Dickens*, 487–88. On Dickens and free flows, see also Trotter, *Circulation*.

7. See Byrn, *Progress of Invention*; and Wallace, *Wonderful Century*. In keeping with an age of invention, the Victorians developed much of the modern sense of the word *technology* itself. Marsden and Smith, *Engineering Empires*, 3; see also G. Wilson, *What Is Technology?*

8. Bright, Preface to *The Electric Telegraph*, vi.

9. Quoted in Solymar, *Getting the Message*, 81.

10. For instance, work by Nancy Armstrong, Jay Clayton, Lisa Galvan, Jennifer Green-Lewis, Ivan Kreilkamp, Laura Otis, John Picker, and Leah Price has contributed to Victorian studies' turn to media over the past decade.

11. Welsh, *George Eliot and Blackmail*, v.

12. I. Williams, *Realist Novel in England*, x; Levine, *Realistic Imagination*.

13. Ong, *Orality and Literacy*, 117–35; B. Anderson, *Imagined Communities*, 22–26.

14. Davis, *Factual Fictions*, 212.

15. "Romance of the Electric Telegraph," 296; G. Wilson, "The Electric Telegraph" 459.

16. Wallace, *Wonderful Century*, 16.

17. Kittler, *Discourse Networks*, 369. Kittler takes the term from Freud's paranoid memoirist Schreber.

18. Ibid., 5.

19. Shelley, *Frankenstein*, 75, 74, 79.

20. Jay Clayton argues that Kittler's neglect of transmission technologies such as the telegraph and telephone reflects his emphasis on data storage over communication as he explores media's inscriptive power. *Charles Dickens*, 65–70. That is, Kittler seems to follow the century's typical treatment of electrical communication as nonmaterial. In contrast, I will show that late-Victorian fiction can offer an ample sense of such transmission as material practice and bodily discipline.

21. In this larger recognition I depart from the objective of a study such as Lawrence Rothfield's *Vital Signs*, which aims "to give a more local precision to the 'real' of the realistic novel" by analyzing issues of medical and novelistic representation in nineteenth-century fiction (xii). For a fascinating examination of the relationships between popular science, industrial publishing, and the development of a mass readership in early Victorian England, see Secord, *Victorian Sensation*.

22. On the Gutenberg era as information age, see Linstone, *Challenge of the Twenty-first Century*, 164; on the age of Diderot, see Headrick, *When Information Came of Age*.

23. By 1897, the British Patent Office awarded as many patents each year as had been granted during the two centuries of the original system abolished in 1852. Mitchell, *British Historical Statistics*, 438–49. Dickens, who served on a patent reform committee, assails the burdensome older system in "A Poor Man's Tale of a Patent" (1850) and *Little Dorrit* (1855–57). See Boehm, *British Patent System*, 21. Rigorously applying the Victorian ideal of open information, many free traders advocated abolishing patents altogether, deeming them a state-sponsored monopoly on technical knowledge. Coulter, *Property in Ideas*, 73–100. On the literary history of intellectual property in the nineteenth century, see Pettit, *Patent Inventions*.

24. Headrick, *When Information Came of Age*, vii.

25. Mitchell, *British Historical Statistics*, 12–13, 563–64, 566.

26. "The first thirty-five years of the nineteenth century introduced more radical changes in book production than the previous 350." Patten, *Charles Dickens*, 55. For an overview of the nineteenth century's industrialization of writing, see Martin, *History and Power of Writing*, 397–462.

27. Frankel, "Blue Books," 310, 308.

28. Benjamin, "Work of Art," 237.

29. Thorburn and Jenkins, "Introduction," 11.

30. Siskin, *Work of Writing*, 11.

31. Ong, *Orality and Literacy*, 144–55.

32. Kieve, *Electric Telegraph*, 64–65; Gitelman, *Scripts, Grooves*, 192.

33. Bagehot, "Sir Robert Peel," 254–55.

34. See Garrett, *Victorian Multiplot Novel*.

35. Otis's *Networking* shows that the network model provided the Victorians with a powerful paradigm for the relationships between coordinated parts, even when they enlisted the model to support conflicting theories.

36. Dickens, *Hard Times*, 151.

37. Nunberg, "Farewell to the Information Age," 111.

38. Dickens, *Hard Times*, 220.

39. Nunberg, "Farewell to the Information Age," 111. Citing Austen and Emerson, Nunberg speculatively traces *information*'s modern significance to the now-obsolete meaning of *information* as education or *Bildung* (113). Welsh points out the English legal definition of *information* as legal accusation, a meaning that bolsters his association between a rising information culture and blackmail. *George Eliot and Blackmail*, 43n22.

40. *Information* comes to connote a fluid version of what Mary Poovey calls the "modern fact," a datum (ideally associated with a number) awarded a discursive truthfulness beyond rhetoric or contingency—which then makes it available for argument. Poovey, *History of the Modern Fact*. On the ascendance of numbers from the seventeenth century to the Victorians, see I. Cohen, *Triumph of Numbers*.

41. Schaffer, "Babbage's Intelligence: Calculating Engines," 204. Examining the discourse of "intelligence" in the factory movement and Babbage's calculating engines, Simon Schaffer argues that "[i]n early nineteenth-century Britain the word *intelligence* simultaneously embodied the growing system of social surveillance and the emerging mechanization of natural philosophies of mind."

42. Dickens, *Bleak House*, 12.

43. Brown and Duguid, *Social Life of Information*, 119, 120.

44. Ibid., 120.

45. Smith, *Society for the Diffusion*, 5.

46. Rauch, *Useful Knowledge*, 2. On the S.D.U.K.'s embodiment of larger cultural attitudes toward knowledge-work, see Rauch, *Useful Knowledge*, 40–46.

47. See Hampton, *Visions of the Press*, 32–34, 54–55; Curran, "Ugly Face of Reform."

48. Croker, "Post-office Reform," 532.

49. See Brand, *Media Lab*, 202–7, 211–19.

50. Rauch, *Useful Knowledge*, 14–15, 39.

51. Froude, "On Progress," 374.

52. Ibid., 374–75.

53. Richards, *Imperial Archive*, 5.

54. Keep, "Blinded by the Type," 153.

55. Ibid., 153.

56. The distinction between knowledge (internalized, contextual) and informa-

tion (disembodied, fragmented) may seem overly humanistic or sentimental. In fact, either term may be misleading; a fuller model might treat media, minds, and bodies as intertwined aspects of our systems for producing, managing, and acting on representations of what we can know. In any case, the relationships between knowledge and information in these senses—between embodied experience and external data— arise as central and complex issues in much of the fiction this book discusses.

57. Seltzer, *Bodies and Machines*, 196n57; see also Seltzer, "Graphic Unconscious."

58. Reddy, "Conduit Metaphor"; Peters, *Speaking into the Air*, 65.

59. Dickens, *Hard Times*, 48.

60. Barthes, "Reality Effect," 14.

61. Bill Brown notes the barometer's ability "to materialize (to signify indexically)" the "absent presence" of atmospheric pressure, which makes it odd that the device should appear as Barthes's example of an "empty—or emptied—sign." *Material Unconscious*, 16.

62. Schivelbusch, *Railway Journey*, 187.

63. Beniger, *Control Revolution*, 245.

64. Shannon, "Mathematical Theory," 379.

65. Hayles, *How We Became Posthuman*, 18.

66. Pierce, *Introduction to Information Theory*, 20.

67. G. Wilson, *Progress of the Telegraph*, 1; Byrn, *Progress of Invention*, 15.

68. Boole, *Investigation of the Laws*, 1.

69. Negroponte, *Being Digital*, 12, 13.

70. On Carlyle's and Babbage's views of miracles, as well as Carlyle's skepticism about Babbage's engine, see Schaffer, "Babbage's Intelligence by Simon Schaffer."

71. Babbage, *Ninth Bridgewater Treatise*, 5–8; see also Swade, "It Will Not Slice," 44–46.

72. Babbage, *Ninth Bridgewater Treatise*, 8.

73. Ibid., 36–37.

74. See Dickens, "Birmingham and Midland Institute," 399. John Picker intriguingly explores the resonance of Babbage's claims in relation to the discourses of propagation in Dickens's *Dombey and Son* (1846–48). *Victorian Soundscapes*, 15–40.

75. See Schaffer, "Babbage's Intelligence: Calculating Engines."

76. Babbage, *Ninth Bridgewater Treatise*, 36.

77. Wheeler, *Death and the Future Life*, 112, 113.

78. See J. Miller, Introduction to *Bleak House*.

Chapter 1

1. On Carlyle's dislike of novels, and realist fiction's paradoxical debt to his work, see Schor, "Stupidest Novel."

2. Carlyle, *Sartor Resartus*, 185. Hereafter cited in the text as *SR*.

3. Citations of the text refer to the unpaginated advertisement in *Nicholas Nickleby*'s thirteenth number, as reprinted in facsimile by Scolar Press. Some advertisements appear in a different order or with variant illustrations in various copies of *Nickleby*; see Slater, *Composition and Monthly Publication*. The pamphlet version of Cole's dialogue departs from the text squeezed into the back of Dickens's serial in many minor ways; see Cole, *Report of a Scene*.

4. Fryer and Ackerman, *Reform of the Post Office*, 1:xl.

5. Ibid., 1:xli; Robinson, *British Post Office*, 281n15; Patten, *Charles Dickens*, 99.

6. Yeazell, "Why Political Novels," 143, 127.

7. Muir, *Postal Reform*, 11.

8. Robinson, *British Post Office*, 195.

9. Cole, *Fifty Years*, 44.

10. Baines, *Forty Years*, 1:115.

11. Robinson, *British Post Office*, 201.

12. Hoag and Hallett, *Proportional Representation*, 164.

13. Fryer and Akerman, *Reform of the Post Office*, 1:xxiv; Robinson, *British Post Office*, 261.

14. Hoag and Hallett, *Proportional Representation*, 167.

15. Babbage, *Economy of Machinery*, 101, 191–92; see I. Hill, "Charles Babbage," 3–10.

16. R. Hill, *Post Office Reform*, 10. Hereafter cited in the text as *POR*. Citations refer to the so-called second edition of *Post Office Reform* (February 1837) as reprinted in Fryer and Akerman, *Reform of the Post Office*. Hill had circulated a "private and confidential" first edition to government officials a month earlier.

17. Coase, "Rowland Hill." As Coase notes, Hill's original plan distinguished between the "primary distribution" that cheaply moved correspondence between postal towns and the more variable "secondary distribution" that might be needed to complete its journey. In order to simplify the plan, Hill abandoned the distinction (432).

18. Beniger, *Control Revolution*, 15.

19. R. Hill and G. Hill, *Life of Sir Rowland Hill*, 1:246; Robinson, *British Post Office*, 262.

20. Robinson, *British Post Office*, 273.

21. Great Britain, *First Report*, 13.

22. On the "rhizomatic network of the mails" and the "erotic possibilities" that arise in a system "with an inlet and outlet at every address in the nation," see John Durham Peters, *Speaking into the Air*, 173. Examining the affective arguments for postal reform, Eileen Cleere analyzes penny postage as a measure that promised to strengthen familial ties but also threatened to remap them in unpredictable ways. Cleere, *Avuncularism*, 202.

23. Great Britain, *Second Report*, 140.

24. Great Britain, *First Report*, 383.

25. Ashurst, *Facts and Reasons*, 128.

26. Ibid., 128.

27. A. Briggs, Preface to *Reform of the Post Office*, ix; Porter, *Progress of the Nation*, 716.

28. Great Britain, *First Report*, 18, 228, 381.

29. Quoted in R. Hill and G. Hill, *Life of Sir Rowland Hill*, 1:349.

30. Robinson, *British Post Office*, 297.

31. Quoted in Goodwyn, *Royal Reform*, 33n1.

32. Daunton, *Royal Mail*, 25–35.

33. Hey, *Rowland Hill*, 13, 82; Robinson, *British Post Office*, 353–54; Farrugia, *Letter Box*, 145–54.

34. Dickens, "Curious Misprint," 419.

35. R. Hill and G. Hill, *Life of Sir Rowland Hill*, 1:258.

36. Henry Cole, for one, regarded uniformity as an "unanswerable" principle, the "keystone of Rowland Hill's great discovery." Cole, *Fifty Years*, 47. See also Coase, "Roland Hill," 433–35.

37. Lewis Carroll would jocularly elucidate the need for extra stamps in *Eight or Nine Wise Words about Letter-Writing* (1890), a guide written to accompany "The Wonderland Postage-Stamp Case." The Penny Post could support not only literature but also literary merchandising.

38. Pam Morris argues that the goal of envisioning social inclusiveness shapes fiction and political discourse from the 1840s to 1860s. She speculatively links the growth of letter-writing to the adoption of "sincerity as the appropriate mode of correspondence between those whose relations were neither intimate nor hierarchical." Morris, *Imagining Inclusive Society*, 44.

39. Waverton, *People's Letter Bag*, iv.

40. See Downs, Introduction to *Familiar Letters*.

41. Cochrane-Baillie, "Royal Mail," 617.

42. Thomas, "Queer Job for a Girl," 54.

43. Daunton, *Royal Mail*, 80.

44. Altick, *English Common Reader*, 170–71.

45. Robinson, *British Post Office*, 315. The benefits of cheap uniform postage would eventually be extended to international and imperial mail, by the Universal Postal Union (1875) and by a late-Victorian crusade for reduced imperial postage (letter rates were cut to 2.5 pence in 1890 and a penny in 1911) (397–402, 423–24).

46. Favret, *Romantic Correspondence*, 207.

47. R. Hill and G. Hill, *Life of Sir Rowland Hill*, 1:385.

48. Staff, *Penny Post*, 93.

49. Quoted in Evans, *Mulready Envelope*, 28.

50. Quoted in R. Hill and G. Hill, *Life of Sir Rowland Hill*, 394n.

51. Patten, *Charles Dickens*, 46. The format was distinctive enough that Dickens

was "livid" upon hearing about a plan by the publisher of *Sketches by Boz* to reissue it "in the same format [as *Pickwick*], twenty monthly numbers, with the same green wrappers"—and a new wrapper cover by Cruikshank (38). On other novelists' largely unsuccessful attempts to exploit the characteristic serial format in which Dickens published *Pickwick*, *Nickleby*, and most of their successors, see Sutherland, *Victorian Fiction*, 86–113.

52. Dickens, *Nicholas Nickleby*, 19–20:x.

53. Robinson, *British Post Office*, 315.

54. Goodwyn, *Royal Reform*, 55.

55. Quoted in Wears, *Mulready Envelope*, 33.

56. Evans, *Mulready Envelope*, 44.

57. Robinson, *British Post Office*, 315; R. Hill and G. Hill, *Life of Sir Rowland Hill*, 1:395.

58. Quoted in R. Hill and G. Hill, *Life of Sir Rowland Hill*, 1:393. For an engaging history of postal reform, postage stamps, postcards, and philately, see A. Briggs, *Victorian Things*, 290–328.

59. Quoted in J. Forster, *Life of Charles Dickens*, 2:419–20.

60. Ibid., 2:420.

61. Ibid., 2:421.

62. Lohrli, *Household Words*, 23.

63. Stone, Introduction to *Uncollected Writings*, 1:12.

64. Jaffe, *Vanishing Points*, 15.

65. Stone, Introduction to *Uncollected Writings*, 1:53.

66. Dickens, "Preliminary Word," 1.

67. Dickens and Wills, "Valentine's Day at the Post-Office," 70. Hereafter cited in the text as *VD*.

68. Keirstead, "Going Postal," 93; Bowen, *Other Dickens*, 54–57.

69. Perry, *Victorian Post Office*, 3.

70. Stone, Introduction to *Uncollected Writings*, 1:18. Furthermore, Hill had expanded postal duties to include carrying even larger journals, so that by 1850 "[a]t the end of every month the sorting tables at the Post-office [were] like publishers' counters, from the number of quarterlies, monthlies, magazines, and serials." Wynter, "Post-Office," 228.

71. Smyth, *Sir Rowland Hill*, 163–64n.

72. Dickens, *Pickwick Papers*, 44.

73. Clayton, *Charles Dickens*, 4.

74. Spufford, "Difference Engine," 290; see Head, "Mechanism of the Post-Office."

75. Commenting on this scene, David Trotter notes Dickens's fascination with "the flow of information" in the 1850s, an interest that also shapes *A Tale of Two Cities*. Trotter, *Circulation*, 102.

76. Levine, *Realistic Imagination*, 56.

77. Croker, "Post-office Reform," 532.

78. Head, "Mechanism of the Post-Office," 86.

79. Dickens and Wills, "Post-Office Money-Orders," 398.

80. Trollope, *Autobiography*, 88. Hereafter cited in the text as *A*.

81. For an overview of the work of the surveyors, the *"corps d'elite* of Post Office provincial organization" over more than two centuries, see Foxell and Spafford, *Monarchs of All*, 3.

82. See Super, *Trollope at the Post Office*, 26–28.

83. Hill minimized Trollope's achievement, citing his own early interest in letter-boxes. R. Hill and G. Hill, *Life of Sir Rowland Hill*, 1:417. Yet Trollope not only made the suggestion independently but also convinced the Post Office to act on it. As both acknowledged, the British pillar-box was inspired by similar boxes in France. See Farrugia, *Letter Box*, 25–29, 117–22.

84. Siegert, *Relays*, 110.

85. Baines, *Forty Years*, 1:258; Daunton, *Royal Mail*, 282; Perry, *Victorian Post Office*, 17.

86. R. Hill, "Circular to Surveyors."

87. Fryer and Akerman, *Reform of the Post Office*, 1:261, 303, 315.

88. Baines, *Forty Years*, 1:134.

89. Trollope's *Autobiography* reveals his pride in the prose of his surveyors' reports; he felt that their direct style offended office sensibilities because they had "no savour of red-tape" (135). No one else has been able to find any record of disfavor— or much to distinguish his reports' prose. On the contrary, in *The Reasonable Man*, Coral Lansbury argues that Trollope's adoption of the Post Office's stripped-down style helped instill the plainness, particularity, and regimentation that distinguish his novel-writing.

90. Super, *Trollope at the Post Office*, 87.

91. Trollope, *Marion Fay*, 543.

92. For a reading of the novel in the light of the movement for civil service reform, and Trollope's hostility to it, see Shuman, *Pedagogical Economies*, 76–122. For Shuman, the novel "demonstrates the connection between Trollope's opposition to Northcote-Trevelyan and his rejection" of the "construction of interiority" and "self-integration" as practiced by other canonical realist writers (89).

93. Bareham, "Patterns of Excellence," 67.

94. See Lukács, especially "Realism in the Balance"; Ermarth, *Realism and Consensus*; Kearns, *Nineteenth-Century Literary Realism*; Levine, *Realistic Imagination*.

95. James, *Partial Portraits*, 122.

96. Trollope, *Three Clerks*, 1. Hereafter cited in the text as *TC*.

97. Clark, *Language and Style*, 134.

98. Hey, *Rowland Hill*, 56; Farrugia, *Sir Rowland Hill*, 13.

99. By the mid-1850s, Surbiton was experiencing rapid growth as well as a specu-

lative market in land for house-building; its character was already "residential," in contrast to the "trading community" of nearby Kingston. Richardson, *Surbiton*, 18.

100. James, *Partial Portraits*, 122.

101. Pearson, "'The Letter Killeth,'" 397; E. Moody, "Partly Told in Letters," 5.

102. E. Moody, "Partly Told in Letters," 12.

103. Hall, Introduction to *The Three Clerks*, xii.

104. Lansbury, *Reasonable Man*, 224.

105. Bareham, "Patterns of Excellence," 64; Goodlad, *Victorian Literature*, 138.

106. Herbert, "Trollope and the Fixity," 230; Kendrick, *Novel-Machine*, 86. Lauren Goodlad argues that *The Three Clerks*, at one with the civil service reforms it opposes, participates in a "discourse of character" as "stationary" and treats gentlemanliness as the ineffable ideal. Goodlad, *Victorian Literature*, 130.

107. apRoberts, *Trollope*, 36, 125. D. A. Miller's mordant reading of discord and tolerance in *Barchester Towers* (1857) recasts such Trollopian traits in more skeptical terms. See *Novel and the Police*, 107–45.

108. Mattelart, *Networking the World*, 5.

109. Trimming *The Three Clerks* for one-volume publication, Trollope excised several dozen passages, including the one that contains this sentence.

110. Elizabeth Epperly sums up *The Three Clerks* as "a lengthy exploration" of each clerk's understanding of *excelsior*, but in fact the novel extends the motto to descriptions of an heiress's dream of marriage to a good dancer and a barmaid's vision of marriage as social mobility. Epperly, *Patterns of Repetition*, 5; Trollope, *Three Clerks*, 318, 319.

111. Bareham, "Patterns of Excellence," 58, 74.

112. Polhemus, *Changing World*, 9.

113. Lansbury, *Reasonable Man*, 89.

114. Kincaid, *Novels of Anthony Trollope*, 15–23, 71–74.

115. Ibid., 60.

116. D. Miller, *Novel and the Police*, 117.

117. Ibid., 128.

118. More recently, critics such as Lauren Goodlad have urged us "beyond the Panopticon" so central to much Foucaultian critique as we seek to understand the dynamics of control in Victorian society and literature. *Victorian Literature*, 1; see also Foucault, *Discipline and Punish*, 195–228. Goodlad persuasively refutes the recourse to Foucault's "panopticism" as a general account of power and governance in Victorian Britain, but despite her consideration of Trollope and *The Three Clerks*, she disregards local systems of surveillance within institutions such as the General Post Office at St. Martin's-le-Grand, or Millbank Prison, the Bentham-designed penitentiary in which Trollope places Alaric Tudor.

119. Kendrick, *Novel-Machine*, 50.

CHAPTER 2

1. Hubbard, *Cooke and Wheatstone*, 14.
2. Fahie, *History of Electric Telegraphy*.
3. Finlaison, *Some Remarkable Applications*, 100.
4. On German contributions to the electric telegraph's early history, see Otis, *Networking*, 125–27, 131–32.
5. Hubbard, *Cooke and Wheatstone*, 94–96, 118–25.
6. Kieve, *Electric Telegraph*, 36. Amused congressmen suggested setting aside half of the funds sought by Morse for experiments in "the science of mesmerism"—a joke that confirms the cultural association between electromagnetism and animal magnetism. Harlow, *Old Wires*, 85.
7. Smiles, Preface to *George and Robert Stephenson*, xiii.
8. Quoted in Schivelbusch, *Railway Journey*, 38.
9. Hubbard, *Cooke and Wheatstone*, 113.
10. Headrick, *When Information Came of Age*, 205.
11. James Carey, "Technology and Ideology," 204.
12. Lardner, *Electric Telegraph Popularised*, ¶1.
13. Dickens, *Letters*, 1:359; Dickens, *Nicholas Nickleby*, 19–20:viii.
14. Head, *Stokers and Pokers*, 125.
15. Dickens, *Sketches by Boz*, 96.
16. James Carey, "Technology and Ideology," 203.
17. R. Williams, *Keywords*, 72.
18. Porter, *Progress of the Nation*, 292.
19. Wallace, *Wonderful Century*, 19.
20. For the most thorough examination of long-distance signaling before the electric telegraph, see Holzmann and Pehrson, *Early History*.
21. Siegert, *Relays*, 103.
22. G. Wilson, "Electric Telegraph," 467; C. Walker, *Electric Telegraph Manipulation*, 35.
23. Wark, "Telegram from Nowhere," 31.
24. On the Crippen case and its importance in the history of wireless, see Early, "Technology, Modernity."
25. "Few Weeks from Home," 209.
26. Ong, *Orality and Literacy*, 136.
27. Dodwell, *Illustrated Hand Book*, 5; Progress, *Electric Telegraph*, 69.
28. This mytheme exists in any number of similar forms; for further versions, see *Anecdotes of the Electric Telegraph*, 39, 92; Baines, *Forty Years*, 1:284–86, 291; Ballantyne, *Battery and the Boiler*, 210–12; Head, *Stokers and Pokers*, 126–27; Highton, *Electric Telegraph*, 138; Progress, *Electric Telegraph*, 68, 77; "Romance of the Electric Telegraph," 306–7; Wynter, "Electric Telegraph," 145–46. Predictably, an American version includes an old "colored woman" in the role of telegraphic naïf. Clippinger,

Sam Johnson, 95. On the significance of mythemes, see Lévi-Strauss, *Structural Anthropology*, 206–31.

29. The complete relinquishment of Morse code for significant applications took place only in the late 1990s. See "SOS, RIP."

30. Hayles, *How We Became Posthuman*, 246.

31. Ibid., 50.

32. G. Wilson, "Electric Telegraph," 444; see also G. Wilson, *Electricity*, 16.

33. Lodge, *Modern Views*, 12–13.

34. Ibid., 300.

35. Sconce, *Haunted Media*, 27.

36. Briggs and Maverick, *Story of the Telegraph*, 14, 13; Garfield, "Dr. Samuel F. B. Morse," 2:28.

37. Garvey, *Silent Revolution*, 7.

38. Dickens, "Birmingham and Midland Institute," 404.

39. James Carey, "Technology and Ideology," 204.

40. Brontë, *Jane Eyre*, 419. Hereafter cited in the text as *JE*.

41. Head, *Stokers and Pokers*, 115.

42. Troup, "Literary Register," 348.

43. *Hand Book to the Electric Telegraph*, 5, 11.

44. C. Walker, *Electric Telegraph Manipulation*, 106; *Anecdotes of the Electric Telegraph*, 66.

45. G. Wilson, *Progress of the Telegraph*, 48–49.

46. Sutherland, *Is Heathcliff a Murderer?*, 61.

47. Gaskell, *Life of Charlotte Brontë*, 319.

48. Winter, *Mesmerized*, 55. Lardner held that "animal magnetism straddled the mental and the physical," notes Winter, a belief that echoes Victorian discussions of electricity (52).

49. On mesmeric influence and social cohesion, see ibid., 307–43.

50. Nancy Armstrong notes that by announcing its departures from realism, a text such as *Jane Eyre* could still "carr[y] on the work of Victorian realism." *Fiction in the Age of Photography*, 169. Armstrong points to the beginning of the Thornfield section of the novel, but we could analyze Jane's long-distance communication with Rochester in the same terms.

51. Yeazell, "More True Than Real," 141.

52. Fahie, *History of Electric Telegraphy*, 101–3.

53. Progress, *Electric Telegraph*, 12.

54. Ibid., 68.

55. Sconce, *Haunted Media*, 7.

56. Booth, *Uniformity of Time*, 5, 15.

57. Ibid., 12.

58. Bagwell, *Transport Revolution*, 112–13. On the telegraph and the standardization of time, see also Morus, "'Nervous System of Britain,'" 464–70.

59. "Romance of the Electric Telegraph," 298.

60. Booth, *Uniformity of Time*, 11, 12.

61. B. Anderson, *Imagined Communities*, 25. Anderson finds a similar vision in modern nationalism, which imagines the nation as a single social "organism moving calendrically through . . . time" (26). If vernacular print literature helps produce this image, the simultaneity evoked by the telegraph and standard time helps materialize the vision of the nation as a group of people united in a shared relationship to the march of time.

62. Booth, *Uniformity of Time*, 14.

63. Head, *Stokers and Pokers*, 128.

64. Ibid., 128, 129.

65. Levine, *Realistic Imagination*, 188.

66. In the 1840s and 1850s, "the telegraph was seen as producing a particular kind of intimacy," even while it permitted the "levelling" of knowledge across societies. Morus, "'Nervous System of Britain," 459, 463. As one writer claimed in 1852, "[i]ts mission appears to be to make human intercourse more intimate, and its own uses more cosmopolitan." Archer, *Guide to the Electric Telegraph*, 2.

67. Several of Brontë's letters to Heger convey more anguish, but one from 24 July 1844 suggests its author's failure to know a medium. It does so through the classic media effect of a slip of the pen, turning Heger's letters into the writer himself: "je tacherai de ne plus être égoïste et tout regardant *vous* letters comme un des plus grand bonheurs que je connais j'attendrai patiemment pour en recevoir . . . " ("I will try not to be egotistical anymore, and although I regard *you* letters as one of the greatest pleasures I know, I will wait patiently to receive them . . . ") (my emphasis). Brontë, *Letters*, 1:355. As if soliciting the kind of correction *Villette* would eroticize, Brontë begins the letter's next paragraph with her fear of forgetting the French she studied with Heger ("*Je crains beaucoup d'oublier français*") (1:355, original emphasis).

68. For a bracing analysis of Jane's omissions and prevarications, see Sternlieb, "*Jane Eyre*: 'Hazarding Confidences.'"

69. Peters, *Speaking into the Air*.

70. Investigating *Jane Eyre*'s dynamics of readerly address, Garrett Stewart demonstrates how the novel exploits the properties of written prose as a medium, most notably its call for readers to replicate it as subvocalized language. Stewart, *Dear Reader*, 242–49.

71. For an analysis of *Jane Eyre*'s treatment of the reader as confidante, a summary of how feminist readers have responded to this call, and reflections on how and why it might be resisted, see Kaplan, "Girl Talk."

72. Sternlieb, "*Jane Eyre*: 'Hazarding Confidences,'" 458.

73. Kreilkamp, *Voice and the Victorian*, 123, 126.

74. Levine, *Realistic Imagination*, 184.

75. Kreilkamp, *Voice and the Victorian*, 138.

76. Gaskell, *Letters*, 541.

77. Typically Gaskell's critics use ellipses to excise her metaphors of corporeal interiority and electric telegraphy altogether. See, for instance, Carse, "Penchant for Narrative," 32; Croskery, "Mothers without Children," 208.

78. McLuhan, *Understanding Media*, 23, 30.

79. Ibid., 8.

80. Levine, *Realistic Imagination*, 12.

81. See Nagel, *View from Nowhere*.

82. Dickens, *Charles Dickens' Book*, 19.

83. Hollingshead, "Right through the Post," 190.

84. Dickens, *Bleak House*, 272.

85. Ermarth, *Realism and Consensus*, 194.

86. Ibid., 196–97.

87. Ibid., 196.

88. Lukács, "Realism in the Balance," 38.

89. Bright, Preface to *The Electric Telegraph*, v.

90. Garvey, *Silent Revolution*, 103.

91. On the first, malfunctioning cable laid between Europe and North America, see Gordon, *Thread across the Ocean*, 121–41; as well as Blondheim's more skeptical account in *News over the Wires*, 110–14.

92. *Hand Book to the Electric Telegraph*, 21–22.

93. Quoted in Brett, *Oceanic Electric Telegraph*, 67, 69. After publishing an earlier piece satirizing the prospect of Anglo-French telegraphy, *Punch* printed a poem and a full-page cartoon treating the new submarine cable in a similarly awestruck and reverent vein. Compare "Chit-Chat by Telegraph" to "Mermaid's Last New Song"; Leech, "Effect of the Submarine Telegraph."

94. See Horne, "The Great Peace-Maker."

95. Briggs and Maverick, *Story of the Telegraph*, 11, 22, 12, 14.

96. Morus, "Electric Ariel," 341. See Dodwell, *Illustrated Hand Book*, 3–4; Lardner, *Electric Telegraph Popularised*, ¶11; "Romance of the Electric Telegraph," 296; Wallace, *Wonderful Century*, 21; Wynter, "Electric Telegraph," 119.

97. Briggs and Maverick, *Story of the Telegraph*, 12.

98. "Moral Influence of the Telegraph," 240. On Garfield's assassination and the late nineteenth-century media ecology, see Menke, "Media in America."

99. Carmichael, *Law Relating to the Telegraph*, 41.

100. Wark, "All That Is Solid," 22.

101. On the "production of abstract space" in nineteenth-century Britain, see Poovey, *Making a Social Body*, 25–54.

102. Jakobson, "Two Aspects of Language," 111.

103. Bakhtin, *Dialogic Imagination*, 84.

104. P. West, "'By Magnetic Telegraph.'"

105. Quoted in Stephens, *History of News*, 258.

106. Allan, *News Culture*, 16.

107. Quoted in Blondheim, *News over the Wires*, 195.

108. Quoted in Read, *Power of News*, 106.

109. Stephens, *History of News*, 253.

110. James Carey, "Technology and Ideology," 211.

111. Schudson's work casts doubt on any simple relationship between use of the telegraph and the norm of objectivity. For one thing, he notes that newspaper writing remained effusive and emotional (by modern standards) through the end of the century, which contradicts telegraphic journalism's supposed emphasis on unadorned fact. Schudson, "Objectivity Norm," 158–59; see also Schudson, *Power of News*, 67–68; and *Discovering the News*, 4–5.

112. Nagel, *View from Nowhere*, 63.

113. Matheson, "Birth of News Discourse," 566.

114. Quoted in Read, *Power of News*, 107.

115. Dickens, "Newsvendors' Benevolent Institution," 339.

116. Wynter, "Who Is Mr. Reuter?" 243, 245.

117. Macaulay, *History of England*, 1:26.

118. Macaulay, *Letters*, 4:2.

119. Levine, *Dying to Know*, 8.

120. Space and time were hardly annihilated, as nineteenth-century technophiles liked to claim, but for the classic account of their modern transformations, see Kern, *Culture of Time and Space*.

121. McLuhan, *Gutenberg Galaxy*, 28; Ong, *Orality and Literacy*, 135.

122. McLuhan, *Gutenberg Galaxy*, 253.

123. Many works from these decades reveal a similar play with narrative point of view. In addition to the famous double narration of *Bleak House*, consider Thackeray's adoption of Pendennis as narrator for *The Newcomes*; the emergence of "Mary Smith" from the anonymity of the essay in Gaskell's *Cranford*; the massing of multiple narratives in the service of a total view of the crime in Collins's *The Moonstone*; the peculiar ventriloquism of Kingsley's Cockney poet in *Alton Locke*; the disappearing first-person narrator of Eliot's *The Mill on the Floss*. In such works at least, the novel's point of view might seem not so fixed.

124. Gitelman and Pingree, "Introduction," xii.

125. Levine, *Realistic Imagination*, 18.

CHAPTER 3

1. Bolter and Grusin, *Remediation*, 26–28.

2. I concur with other critics in considering Lukács's understanding of realism, and its concern with presenting a society's total structure of relations, more convincing than his critique of modernism. Identifying modernism with an "expressionism" fixated on the fragmentation of market society, Lukács treats it as an intensified liter-

ary naturalism. See "Realism in the Balance." For Lukács's related attack on naturalism's mania for disconnected detail, see "Narrate or Describe?"

3. Bolter and Grusin use the term *translucent* differently; for them, it describes digital texts (such as CD-ROM encyclopedias) that purport to enhance older forms without challenging their practices of representation. *Remediation*, 46.

4. See Lukács, *Historical Novel*.

5. Scott, *Redgauntlet*, 236.

6. Ibid., 410n46.

7. For an analysis of *Redgauntlet*'s use of letters in the service of its domestication of revolution, see Watson, *Revolution and the Form*, 149–53.

8. Scott, *Redgauntlet*, 141.

9. Langan, "Understanding Media in 1805," 141.

10. Dickens, *Tale of Two Cities*, 5. Hereafter cited in the text as *TTC*.

11. For influential interpretations of the novel's vision of history—as an elemental, inhuman force, or as at once continuous and catastrophically violent—see Alter, "Demons of History"; Rignall, "Dickens and the Catastrophic Continuum."

12. Dickens, *Letters*, 9:145.

13. On Dickens's understanding of social welfare and misery as the result of "a system of flows and stoppages," see Trotter, *Circulation*, 104.

14. Robinson, *British Post Office*, 125; Foxell and Spafford, *Monarchs of All*, 25; Robinson, *British Post Office*, 126.

15. Baines, *Track of the Mail-Coach*, 283. Baines notes the early opposition to the railway by residents of "the district traversed by the Dover mail" (79).

16. Dickens, *Pickwick Papers*, 582. This real-life "Pickwick also worked for the Post Office, providing teams which carried the Bristol-Oxford Mail between Bristol and Bath." Vale, *Mail-Coach Men*, 170–71. On the post in *Pickwick*, a text fascinated by "the paper, marks, traces, messengers, and vehicles of circulation," see Bowen, *Other Dickens*, 53. Bowen treats "The Tale of the Bagman's Uncle" as a stranger reiteration of *Pickwick*'s thematics of writing and death, posting and ghosting.

17. De Quincey, "English Mail Coach," 193.

18. Ibid., 224.

19. G. Walker, *Haste, Post, Haste!* 199; Robinson, *British Post Office*, 140. See also Vale, *Mail-Coach Men*, 48.

20. Clear, *John Palmer*, 17.

21. Foxell and Spafford, *Monarchs of All*, 30.

22. Garvey, *Silent Revolution*, 51.

23. Jackman, *Development of Transportation*, 324.

24. Clear, *John Palmer*, 17; Robinson, *British Post Office*, 137–38.

25. G. Walker, *Haste, Post, Haste!* 189.

26. Harper, *Dover Road*, 36. Coincidentally, Shooter's Hill was also the site of some of the eighteenth-century electrical experiments that inspired the invention of Britain's first electric telegraph. Ronalds, *Electrical Telegraph*, 3.

27. Robinson, *British Post Office*, 245.

28. Harper, *Stage-Coach and Mail*, 2:149.

29. G. Walker, *Haste, Post, Haste!* 206, 208.

30. Had Dickens needed a fresh reminder of the tendency of the informatic imaginary to outpace the capacities of real media, the fate of the transatlantic cable completed in August 1858 would have offered one. Its establishment provoked widespread public exultation on both sides of the Atlantic over the power of technology and the peaceful reintegration of Britain and the United States; its feeble operation and mysterious failure after only a few weeks brought intercontinental dismay.

31. Dunn, "Tale for Two Dramatists," 121.

32. Tambling, *Dickens, Violence*, 137.

33. Baldridge makes a case for the centrality of this passage, which other critics have found "problematic" or "anomalous." "Alternatives to Bourgeois Individualism," 636. For Baldridge, the passage articulates a critique of liberal individuality that contrasts it with the modes of communality associated with the Revolution, even though the novel will demonize them. I agree that *A Tale of Two Cities* is deeply concerned with the relations of selves to history, but I see more complexity in the novel's exploration of how subjectivity may or may not register to other subjects or upon the pages of history.

34. Rignall, "Dickens and the Catastrophic Continuum," 577.

35. Gallagher, "Duplicity of Doubling," 141.

36. Dickens's fascination with dead bodies, distilled in the irresistible pull that the Paris Morgue exerts over the Uncommercial Traveller, is well known. For the most extensive and contextual examination of his fiction's treatment of death, see Sanders, *Charles Dickens*. Although Andrew Sanders spends only a few pages on *A Tale of Two Cities*, his suggestive remarks about resurrection and "the mysteries of the psyche" support several of my readings (168–69). Albert Hutter raises parallel points but adds an important insight; the "Night Shadows" passage describes people as dead and separate, yet it affirms a "narrational" connection that makes "author and reader . . . for the moment, resurrectionists." Hutter, "Novelist as Resurrectionist," 19. For a consideration of the interplay in Dickens's work between living characters and corpses, effigies, or dummies, see John Carey, *Violent Effigy*, 80–104.

37. Sterne, *Audible Past*, 43.

38. See for instance G. Lewes, "Dickens in Relation."

39. Furthermore, Phiz's illustrations depict Madame Defarge as "a strong, dark-haired version of Lucie." Hutter, "Nation and Generation," 457. For a detailed consideration of Lucie and Madame Defarge as doubles, see Schor, *Dickens*, 89–90.

40. Headrick, *When Information Came of Age*, 186.

41. Ibid., 188–89.

42. Forgetting may be one of the great unremembered themes of the Victorian historical novel, a paradox supported by Nicholas Dames's reading of Eliot's *Romola*

(1863) as an example of the amnesiac orientation he finds in novels from Austen to Eliot. *Amnesiac Selves*, 206–35.

43. Marshall McLuhan and Eric McLuhan, *Laws of Media*.

44. John, *Spreading the News*, 86.

45. Headrick, *When Information Came of Age*, 194; see Marsden and Smith, *Engineering Empires*, 181–85.

46. Carlyle, *French Revolution*, 2:373. Hereafter cited in the text as *FR*.

47. Headrick, *When Information Came of Age*, 202. For considerations of the place of the optical telegraph in the histories of communication and information, see Holzmann and Pehrson, *Early History*, 47–94; Headrick, *When Information Came of Age*, 181, 193–202.

48. Alexander, *Plan and Description*, 8.

49. Back in 1816, Francis Ronalds had been discouraged from pursuing his groundbreaking experiments in telegraphy via frictional electricity by the British Admiralty's curt rebuff *"that telegraphs of any kind were then wholly unnecessary, and that no other than the one then in use would be adopted."* Ronalds, *Electrical Telegraph*, 24n. See Coe, *Telegraph*, 14.

50. Dickens, *Pickwick Papers*, 513, 793, 700.

51. Once more, Dickens has elaborated a hint provided by Carlyle's *French Revolution*. "Delay, and still delay!" complain his denizens of Saint-Antoine as they start to rise "unexpectedly, like an Enceladus, living-buried," and return to the world to seek "Revenge" (*FR*, 1:215, 216).

52. McLuhan, *Understanding Media*, 22–32.

53. "With Carton . . . Dickens comes closest to creating something like the mystery and opacity of individuality that he refers to in the 'Night Shadows' meditation," Rignall concedes, "but only up to a point, since in the final scenes of the character's transformation there is a movement back towards conventional coherence and transparency." "Dickens and the Catastrophic Continuum," 583. As I indicate, whatever coherence and transparency Carton gains at the end of the *Tale* is clearly not the conventional province of third-person characters. For a remarkable, sustained reading of the novel's last scene, see Stewart, *Death Sentences*, 83–97. Closely analyzing the grammar and syntax of its language, Stewart treats it as the culmination of the novel's images of death by drowning.

54. Baldridge, "Alternatives to Bourgeois Individualism," 145.

55. Orwell, "Charles Dickens," 24–25.

56. On the *Tale*'s refusal of the theatrical in favor of the novelistic, see Gallagher, "Duplicity of Doubling," 140–42.

57. Solymar, *Getting the Message*, 69–70.

58. Nunberg, "Farewell to the Information Age," 120.

59. Levine, *Dying to Know*, 150. *Dying to Know* does not mention *A Tale of Two Cities* or the knowing, dying protagonist of "The Lifted Veil" but includes readings of objectivity and self-abnegation in *Our Mutual Friend* and *Daniel Deronda*.

60. Nunberg, "Farewell to the Information Age," 121.

61. Carton's "prophecy must envisage Paris of the 1840s," Tambling notes with brisk literalism; "if so, its projection of tranquillity is strikingly inaccurate." *Dickens, Violence,* 153.

62. Carton's last "thoughts are couched like all fiction in the self-confirming authority of pure invention." Stewart, *Death Sentences,* 92.

CHAPTER 4

1. McLuhan, *Understanding Media,* 3.

2. Otis, *Networking,* 11. See also Morus, "'Nervous System of Britain,'" 470–75.

3. Winter, *Mesmerized,* 120.

4. Smee, *Electro-Biology,* 49, 46. Smee was best known for inventing a high-power battery.

5. G. Lewes, *Physiology of Common Life,* 2:14.

6. On Lewes's rejection of the telegraph and embrace of the network as a model for nervous physiology, see Otis, *Networking,* 69–78.

7. G. Lewes, *Study of Psychology,* 14. Lewes contends that we must understand physiology and psychology, nerves and neuroses, as the objective and subjective presentations of the same phenomena, a position now known as dual-aspect monism. "Mental and physical processes," then, "are simply different aspects of one and the same series of psychophysical events." Wozniak, *Mind and Body,* 12; see especially G. Lewes, *Physical Basis of Mind,* 376–98.

8. G. Lewes, *Study of Psychology,* 99.

9. Ibid., 98.

10. Highton, *Electric Telegraph,* 178.

11. N. Armstrong, *Fiction in the Age of Photography,* 115, 298n22.

12. See Bowers, *Sir Charles Wheatstone,* 46–54.

13. Silverman, *Lightning Man,* 189–91, 195–200.

14. Eastlake, "Photography," 465. On the photograph and electric telegraph as complementary inventions, and the involvement of Morse with both, see also Levinson, *Soft Edge,* 37, 48–54, 59.

15. Gitelman aptly links mid-nineteenth-century physiological measurement to new media in their implications for textuality: "Incidents as fleeting as the pulsations of the heart and activities as evanescent as the private use of electrical current were captured, registered, metered, and read in new mechanical ways. . . . Many [of the resulting products], like the grooved surfaces of phonograph records, provoked explicit questions about textuality, about how some inscriptions might or might not be like texts." *Scripts, Grooves,* 3.

16. Eliot, "Natural History of German Life," 271. Hereafter cited in the text as *NH.*

17. Collins, Introduction to *Dickens*, 6. Collins's collection includes five pieces published between 1845 and 1857 (including Marian Evans's) which compare Dickens's work to photographic technologies. On photography and *Little Dorrit*, see Marsh, "Inimitable Double Vision," 266–68.

18. Eliot, *Adam Bede*, 223–24.

19. Monika Brown notes that by the time of *Adam Bede*, "'Dutch painting' was already an established code for certain features of realistic novels as well as a tool for explaining 'how to read' new works"—and, I would add, how to read a new medium. "Dutch Painters," 155.

20. The familiarity of "The Open Door" persists. Green-Lewis includes it in her informal "top twenty (or so)" of widely reproduced Victorian photographs. "At Home," 63.

21. Talbot, *Pencil of Nature*, plate 6.

22. Quoted in Newhall, Introduction to *The Pencil of Nature*.

23. Jeffrey, *Photography*, 24.

24. Marien, *Photography*, 74.

25. Green-Lewis, *Framing the Victorians*, 4, 31. Even for Talbot, photography's "over-riding objective" was finally not to create art but "to record information." Ward, "William Henry Fox Talbot," 24.

26. Eliot, "Lifted Veil," 3. Hereafter cited in the text as *LV*.

27. Wolfreys, *Victorian Hauntings*, 92.

28. Susan Reynolds points out that Latimer's narrative of his actual, physical visit to Prague echoes Eliot's enthusiastic diary entries of July 1858 "almost word for word"; with some puzzlement, she can only blame the darkness of his earlier prophetic vision on Eliot's personal difficulties since her visit. "The Most Splendid City," 230.

29. "Photographic Print," 162.

30. "Mr. Fox Talbot's New Discovery," 25; see also "Our Photoglyphic Transparencies."

31. Buckland, *Fox Talbot*, 112.

32. Ostroff, "Photomechanical Process," 125.

33. Buckland, *Fox Talbot*, 116, 115.

34. C. Armstrong, *Scenes in a Library*, 4, 17.

35. Arnold, *William Henry Fox Talbot*, 137; see also fig. 21.

36. "Photographic Print," 163.

37. Buckland, *Fox Talbot*, 89.

38. Green-Lewis, "Not Fading Away," 579.

39. Nagel, *View from Nowhere*, 110.

40. Barthes, *Camera Lucida*, 26, 27.

41. See N. Armstrong, *Fiction in the Age of Photography*, 77; Levinson, *Soft Edge*, 46.

42. Eastlake, "Photography," 454.

43. Ibid., 466.

44. Eliot, *Letters*, 3:307.

45. Critics have long recognized the tale's epistemological concerns. In one of the earliest analyses of the story, U. C. Knoepflmacher argues that "[f]ar from being a curious anomaly, 'The Lifted Veil' is as central to a century obsessed with epistemology as it is to the preoccupations of its author." *George Eliot's Early Novels*, 159–60.

46. For an account of Lewes's involvement with vivisection and the Victorian controversy over animal experimentation, see Menke, "Fiction as Vivisection," 622–27.

47. Foucault, *Birth of the Clinic*, 170.

48. Ibid., 166.

49. On the importance of devices such as the kymograph (for measuring and charting internal flows), "the recording device that more than any other can be identified with nineteenth-century physiology," see Bynum, *Science and the Practice of Medicine*, 98–99. For a fascinating account of the rise of scientific "self-recording devices" and their links to nineteenth-century epistemologies of science, information, and language, see Brain, "Representation on the Line."

50. Flint, "Blood, Bodies," 458. Flint offers a detailed reading of "The Lifted Veil" in relation to the physiology of blood. Although the paranormal and pseudo-scientific aspects of the tale have received much comment, she claims, "the relationship between *The Lifted Veil* and more mainstream science is much closer" than most critics have recognized (461).

51. G. Lewes, *Physiology of Common Life*, 1:271.

52. Nagel, *View from Nowhere*, 88.

53. James, "Lifted Veil," 131; Mudford, Introduction to *Silas Marner*, xxxi.

54. The scene also recalls the most notorious photograph of late 1858, Henry Peach Robinson's "Fading Away." This elaborately staged (and photographically reassembled) scene of a young woman on her deathbed proved so striking, and controversial, that "copies of the photograph were displayed in the shop windows of print sellers throughout the country." Harker, *Henry Peach Robinson*, 27.

55. Bernard, *Introduction to the Study*, 103.

56. Zola would later invoke Bernard's experimental medicine as the explicit model for a hard-nosed, clinical naturalism. See Rothfield, *Vital Signs*, 123–29.

57. In a related vein, Terry Eagleton argues that the story dramatizes the fantasies of omniscience common to Victorian science, realism, and market society. "Knowledge and Power." Sandra Gilbert and Susan Gubar make some similar remarks, but in order to support their broader thesis, they directly identify the rueful possessor of omniscience with an immured and evasive Eliot. *Madwoman in the Attic*, 475–76. Rosemarie Bodenheimer's comments provide the subtlest exploration of the tale in relation to the painful unveiling of Eliot's pseudonymous authorship in 1859. *Real Life of Mary Ann Evans*, 134–36.

58. Eliot, *Letters*, 3:41. Eliot places the essays and sketches of *The Impressions of Theophrastus Such* (1878), her final book, more or less in the first-person voice of Theophrastus.

59. On Latimer as a medium—Spiritualist as well as technical—and on narration as mediation in "The Lifted Veil," see Galvan, "Narrator as Medium."

60. Flint, "Blood, Bodies," 460.

61. Charles Swann too recognizes that Latimer's situation is "comparable to that of a reader and re-reader of a story." "Déjà Vu, Déjà Lu," 53.

62. Ben Underwood's unpublished paper "Living Textually" helped clarify this point for me.

63. Eliot, *Middlemarch*, 91, 146. Hereafter cited in the text as *M*. For extended readings of the ties between Lydgate's medical theory and Eliot's realism, see Tambling, "*Middlemarch*, Realism"; Rothfield, *Vital Signs*, 84–119.

64. Wormald, "Microscopy and Semiotic," 518.

65. Neil Hertz has noted *pulse* as a keyword elsewhere in Eliot's fiction, a figure for "the disparity between the grand motions of Nature or History and the restricted circle of concerns and fragile consciousness of individual characters," especially young women. "George Eliot's Pulse," 37. With its overtly physiological language, this passage suggests that the pulse touches on a larger complex of associations identifying Eliot's novelistic techniques with the sort of physiological measurement they invoke and surpass.

66. See Crary, *Techniques of the Observer*.

67. For an exploration of *Middlemarch* as "a story of sympathy, networks, and communication, [with] the movement of information . . . at the heart of its famous metaphorical web," see Otis, *Networking*, 93.

68. See Menke, "Fiction as Vivisection."

69. Brooks, *Body Work*, 248.

70. Eliot, *Daniel Deronda*, 109. Hereafter cited in the text as *DD*.

71. Picker offers an extended consideration of the place of the acoustic in *Deronda*. *Victorian Soundscapes*, 91–108.

72. McCormack, "George Eliot, Julia Cameron," 177.

73. Novak, "A Model Jew."

74. James, "*Daniel Deronda*," 93.

75. Ibid., 92–93.

CHAPTER 5

1. Hubbard, *Cooke and Wheatstone*, 145.

2. Highton, *Electric Telegraph*, 7.

3. Smiles, *Life of George Stephenson*, 538.

4. Hollingshead, "House-Top Telegraphs," 107.

5. J. Anderson, *Statistics of Telegraphy,* 109.

6. Shiers, Introduction to *The Electric Telegraph.*

7. Johnston, *Lightning Flashes,* 3.

8. Dickens, *Letters,* 8:12.

9. Otis has elaborated an allied concern in several telegraphers' stories from the *Lightning Flashes* anthology. In these works, as in lectures by the physicist and physiologist Hermann von Helmholtz, she finds a growing "awareness of bodies and machines as closely related communications devices, and of the shortcomings of each." "Other End," 184; see also *Networking,* 136–46. In contrast, Katherine Stubbs points out the temporary freedom from gendered embodiment that such fiction could imagine, especially fiction by women telegraphists. "Telegraphy's Corporeal Fictions."

10. Downey, "Virtual Webs," 224–25.

11. N. Pope, "'The Signalman' and Information Problems," 436.

12. Dickens et al., "Mugby Junction," 2. Hereafter cited in the text as *MJ.*

13. See Glancy, "Dickens and Christmas."

14. Matus, "Trauma, Memory"; N. Pope, "'The Signalman' and Information Problems," 448.

15. The tale hints that the unnamed narrator might be the Clennam-esque protagonist from the "Mugby Junction" frame story; the narrator is "a man who had been shut up within narrow limits all his life, and who, being at last set free, had a newly-awakened interest in these great works" (*MJ,* 21). Indeed, some critics assume the identity of the characters or view the narrator as simply "a modified form of the anonymous traveller" in "Mugby." Glancy, "Dickens and Christmas," 71; Seed, "Mystery in Everyday Things," 48. But the placement of the eerie "Signal-Man" *after* the happy ending of the frame story, and the fact that none of the other "branch" stories allude to the frame at all, make this identification less likely. Seizing on the narrator's ambiguous identity, another critic speculates that he may even be the soul of the signalman, released by death but returned for another of the tale's backward hauntings. Stahl, "Source and Significance," 99–100. The signalman tells the narrator that he is "doubtful [uncertain] whether I had seen you before," a feeling that readers may share (*MJ,* 21).

16. Bonheim, "Principle of Cyclicity," 381.

17. At high intensity, electricity "is cognisable by all the senses," points out an 1849 essay on the telegraph. "It addresses the eye by a spark or lightning-flash; the ear by its snap or thunder; the nostrils by a peculiar indescribable odour which it develops; the tongue by an equally peculiar taste which it occasions; and the organs of touch by its characteristic shock." G. Wilson, "Electric Telegraph," 444.

18. Seed, "Mystery in Everyday Things," 54.

19. Day, "Figuring out the Signalman," 29–30.

20. N. Pope, "'The Signalman' and Information Problems," 441.

21. Mengel, "Structure and Meaning," 276.

22. Quoted in N. Pope, "'The Signalman' and Information Problems," 447.

23. Dickens, *Letters*, 8:505.

24. Smiles, Preface to *George and Robert Stephenson*, xi

25. Matus, "Trauma, Memory,"414.

26. On railway accidents, technology, and the history of shock, see also Schivelbusch, *Railway Journey*, 135–60.

27. Caruth, Introduction to *Trauma*, 4.

28. Ibid., 5.

29. The words also recall the signalman's hypothetical telegrams of vague warning: "for God's sake take care!" (*MJ*, 24). See Bonheim, "Principle of Cyclicity," 385.

30. N. Pope, "'The Signalman' and Information Problems," 458.

31. Standage, *Victorian Internet*, 145.

32. See Morus, "Electric Ariel," 368–71.

33. "Romance of the Telegraph," 296.

34. "Electric Telegraph," 408.

35. Head, *Stokers and Pokers*, 127–28.

36. C. Walker, *Electric Telegraph Manipulation*, 91.

37. Hemyng, *Telegraph Secrets*, 1. Hereafter cited in the text as *TS*.

38. Jepsen, *My Sisters Telegraphic*, 37.

39. Telegraph Act (1863), 26 & 27 Vict. c. 112; see Carmichael, *Law Relating to the Telegraph*, 43–44.

40. Ballantyne, *Post Haste*, iii. Hereafter cited in the text as *PH*.

41. Ballantyne, *Battery and the Boiler*, 33. Hereafter cited in the text as *BB*.

42. Headrick, *Tools of Empire*, 162.

43. Beauchamp, *History of Telegraphy*, 72.

44. Jepsen, *My Sisters Telegraphic*, 8.

45. Davies, *Woman's Place*, 27.

46. Jepsen, *My Sisters Telegraphic*, 59.

47. Lowe, *Women in the Administrative Revolution*, 17.

48. Trollope, *Letters*, 2:706.

49. Trollope, "Young Women at the Telegraph Office." Hereafter cited in the text as *YW*.

50. R. Hill and G. Hill, *Life of Sir Rowland Hill*, 2:403, 403n.

51. Quoted in Daunton, *Royal Mail*, 217.

52. Ibid., 219–20. For a more detailed analysis of the relationship of postal work to marriage, see Thomas, "Queer Job for a Girl." Thomas analyzes same-sex partnership and postal work in Trollope's "Telegraph Girl" and Eliza Lynn Linton's new woman novel *The Rebel of the Family* (1880).

53. On the cultural history of women's information work, see Davies, *Woman's Place*; Keep, "Blinded by the Type," "Cultural Work," and "Exhibiting the Telegraph Girl"; as well as the analyses of the gendered information systems of 1900 in Kittler, *Discourse Networks* and *Gramophone, Film, Typewriter*.

54. Zimmeck, "Jobs for the Girls," 164, 154. Jane Lewis's statistics suggest an even greater shift, from only 279 women clerks in England and Wales in 1861 (out of a total of about 92,000 clerks) to nearly 125,000 in 1911 (out of 686,000). "Women Clerical Workers," 34. As Lewis notes, changing census categories make comparisons difficult, but the trend is clear.

55. Jepsen, *My Sisters Telegraphic*, 60.

56. Dodwell, *Illustrated Hand Book*, 38–39.

57. Trollope, "Telegraph Girl," 362, 363. Hereafter cited in the text as *TG*.

58. Jepsen, *My Sisters Telegraphic*, 40.

59. See Dodwell, *Illustrated Hand Book*, 43.

60. "Our Postal Telegraphs," 512.

61. In fact, the telegraph's "writing" itself could provoke questions about the nature of reading. Morse's printing telegraph was meant to be read by sight, but a description of it from the 1850s notes that the "impressions" it leaves resemble not ordinary writing so much as "raised printing for the blind." Turnbull, *Lectures on the Telegraph*, 51.

62. See Jepsen, *My Sisters Telegraphic*, 103–4.

63. The association between women's information work and music persisted in the next decades, as writers compared typewriters to pianos in order to explain women's special aptitude as typists. Keep, "Blinded by the Type," 155.

64. James would later moderate the tone of his response to Trollope, if not altogether his sentiments, but his early review of *The Belton Estate* found it "a *stupid* book. . . . essentially, organically, consistently stupid," "without a single idea." James, *Critical Muse*, 58.

65. Kittler, *Discourse Networks*, 229.

66. J. Miller, *Ethics of Reading*, 90.

67. Downey, "Commentary," 249.

Chapter 6

1. James, Preface to *In the Cage*, xviii, xix. Hereafter cited in the text as *P*.

2. Perry, "Rise and Fall," 416.

3. Carmichael, *Law Relating to the Telegraph*, 53; see Telegraph Act (1868), 31 & 32 Vict. c. 110. Perry offers the most thorough consideration of the history and importance of the state's takeover of inland telegraphy; see especially "Rise and Fall."

4. Baines, *Forty Years*, 1:300; S. Montefiore, *Electric Telegraph Reform*, 5; R. Hill and G. Hill, *Life of Sir Rowland Hill*, 2:250–51.

5. Perry, "Rise and Fall," 422.

6. C. Lewes, "Freaks of the Telegraph," 468.

7. Ibid., 468.

8. See Gunning, "Re-Newing Old Technologies," 41.

9. James, *In the Cage*, 835. Hereafter cited in the text as *IC*.

10. Quoted in Edel, *Life of Henry James*, 4:175.

11. Ibid., 4:176. Pamela Thurschwell provides a fascinating examination of the psychodynamics of dictation—in *In the Cage*, for James and his typists, and beyond the grave. *Literature, Technology, and Magical Thinking*, 86–114.

12. Quoted in Edel, *Life of Henry James*, 5:127.

13. Seltzer, *Bodies and Machines*, 195–96n57. Seltzer suggests that James "powerfully registers that radical recompositions of writing and information-technologies at the turn of the century" as Jamesian "'psychology,' a psychology inseparable from the writing of writing." Specifically, Seltzer cites James's explorations of "the materiality of information-processing and technologies of communication (*In the Cage*, for example), the corporeality of thinking and speaking (*What Maisie Knew*, for example), the psychophysics, and pathologization, of reading and writing (*The Turn of the Screw*, for example)" (197n57).

14. See Seltzer, "Graphic Unconscious," 25–27.

15. Kreilkamp, *Voice and the Victorian*, 179–205.

16. Marvin, *When Old Technologies Were New*, 4.

17. James, *Portrait of a Lady*, 67. Hereafter cited in the text as *PL*.

18. While Heath Moon compares the "romantic Toryism" of the telegraphist and of the governess, Janet Gabler-Hover reads *In the Cage* as a ghost story. Moon, "More Royalist," 31; Gabler-Hover, "Ethics of Determinism," 265–68. John Carlos Rowe has used the two enigmatically similar tales to set each other off, contrasting the antiquarian trappings of *The Turn of the Screw* (governesses in isolated country houses) with the modern scene of *In the Cage* (communication workers in turn-of-the-century London). *Other Henry James*, 155–56, 162.

19. Wicke, "Henry James's Second Wave," 146–47.

20. See Nixon, "Reading Gaol," 189; A. Moody, "Harmless Pleasure of Knowing," 55.

21. Aswell, "James's *In the Cage*," 376.

22. Nixon, "Reading Gaol," 190.

23. Head, *Stokers and Pokers*, 125.

24. Quoted in Read, *Power of News*, 107.

25. Innis, *Bias of Communication*, 28.

26. Cameron, *Thinking in Henry James*, 42.

27. James, *Letters*, 4:110, 111.

28. Cohn, "Optics and Power," 14.

29. On the importance of the telegraphist's marginal sexual and class status in the tale, and her desire for a "margin" of freedom or control, see Wicke, "Henry James's Second Wave"; Bauer and Lakritz, "Language, Class, and Sexuality."

30. Savoy, "'In the Cage' and the Queer Effects," 290–92; Stevens, "Queer Henry in the Cage," 128–31. Savoy also considers *In the Cage* in light of Oscar Wilde's 1895

trials, a consideration extended into a reading of the tale as a response to "The Ballad of Reading Gaol" (1897) by Nixon, "Reading Gaol."

31. Wallace, *Wonderful Century*, 19.

32. See Coe, *Telegraph*, 66.

33. F. Pope, *Modern Practice*, 138.

34. Coe, *Telegraph*, 71. Jay Clayton considers *In the Cage* and other works in relation to the specifically acoustic nature of telegraphy and argues that the aurality of the sounding telegraph makes it anomalous ("odd" or "queer") in light of the "disembodiment" usually associated with modern technologies. "Voice in the Machine," 226–29. Clayton raises fascinating points, but I think that James's tale provokes more far-reaching questions about the relationships between disembodied knowledge and the form and ideology of fiction. For an expanded version of Clayton's analysis of sound telegraphy, now coupled with reflections on Austen's *Mansfield Park* (1814) and the semaphore telegraph, see *Charles Dickens*, 50–80.

35. Harlow, *Old Wires*, 216–27.

36. Reid, *Telegraph in America*, 187.

37. Kipling, *Complete Verse*, 173.

38. Ong, *Orality and Literacy*, 71.

39. James, *What Maisie Knew*, 226–27.

40. "Telegrams are to be regarded as strictly confidential communications.... Any Officer who forges, or wilfully and without due authority, alters, a telegram ... shall, whether he had or had not an intent to defraud, be guilty of a misdemeanor; and shall be liable on summary conviction to a fine not exceeding ten pounds; and, on conviction on indictment, to imprisonment, with or without hard labour, for a period not exceeding twelve months." *General Rules and Regulations*, ¶15.

41. Jill Galvan points out that these fantasies of wordless communication both sustain the telegraphist's feelings of psychic rapport with the aristocracy and attempt to circumvent "the story's telegraphic logic, which equates language with money." "Class Ghosting," 302.

42. Peters, *Speaking into the Air*, 147.

43. Nixon, "Reading Gaol," 192.

44. The unspoken topos of the telegraphist's sexualized negotiation of privacy, publicity, and money is prostitution, that infamous second job of telegraph boys. Savoy, "'In the Cage' and the Queer Effects"; Nixon, "Reading Gaol."

45. Deleuze and Guattari, *Thousand Plateaus*, 196.

46. Ibid., 197.

47. Sabine, *History and Progress*, 59

48. Ralf Norrman delineates the deep irony of the situation: Everard and Lady Bradeen are "saved" by a mistake in the telegram's code—probably the same mistake that the telegraphist thought she was correcting earlier in the tale. "Intercepted Telegram Plot." As Katherine Hayles points out, the fact "[t]hat the climax depends upon a mistake in the coding sequence, not simply on ambiguities in language, indi-

cates that . . . the story, like the yearnings of the protagonist, locates itself within the regime of information." "Escape and Constraint," 241.

49. Rowe, *Other Henry James*, 159.

50. James, *Critical Muse*, 474. Recognizing the telegraphist's dreams of "romantic disengagement," Nixon applies this passage both to the telegraphist and the fantasies of transcendence in "The Ballad of Reading Gaol." "Reading Gaol," 196.

51. Hardy, *Laodicean*, 320. For a different consideration of telegraphy in *A Laodicean*, see Clayton, *Charles Dickens*, 70–73. The plot of the forged postmark in Trollope's *John Caldigate* (1878–79) offers another contemporary exploration of the nontransparency of a supposedly neutral information system.

52. Morus, "Electric Ariel," 341.

53. Jameson, "Modernism and Imperialism," 51.

54. E. Forster, *Howards End*, 195. Elsewhere Jameson indicates that this world-situation and the spatial mapping that accompanies it represent a point of continuity, not rupture, between turn-of-the-century realism and modernism, especially in the work of writers such as Gide, Conrad, and James. "Cognitive Mapping," 350.

55. James, *Critical Muse*, 452.

56. Peters, *Speaking into the Air*, 29.

57. See Standage, *Victorian Internet*, 194–98.

58. Kirkland, "Tolstoi, and the Russian Invasion," 81.

CHAPTER 7

1. Kipling, *Letters*, 3:329.

2. Headrick, *Tools of Empire*, 163.

3. Trilling, "Kipling," 115.

4. Byrn, *Progress of Invention*, 26.

5. James, *Letters*, 4:70.

6. A stationmaster who often saw Kipling during his years in Vermont, the period when he wrote many of his machinic tales, recalled him as having "the darndest mind," always "want[ing] to know everything about everything"; "I never saw a man so hungry for information." Quoted in Carrington, *Rudyard Kipling*, 220.

7. A. Wilson, *Strange Ride*, 186.

8. Harvie, "'Sons of Martha,'" 269–70.

9. Kipling, *Complete Verse*, 733–34.

10. T. Eliot, "Rudyard Kipling," 39.

11. Hong, *Wireless*, 25.

12. Hong argues that Victorian physicists overemphasized the relationship of "Hertzian" waves to optics, since visible light was the most familiar part of the electromagnetic spectrum. See *Wireless*, 2–9. In contrast, Marconi's point of reference, like Kipling's, was the telegraph system; for instance, he began grounding the transmitter and receiver, an innovation imported from wired telegraphy (17–23).

13. Rival claimants to the discovery of wireless telegraphy would include an international cast that sounds almost like a group out of Kipling, most notably the Russian Aleksander Popov, the Indian Jagadish Chandra Bose, and the Englishman Oliver Lodge. See Lochte, "Invention and Innovation." For an analysis of the early controversies, and a detailed assessment of the contributions of Marconi and Lodge, see Hong, *Wireless*.

14. Iles, *Flame, Electricity*, 219.
15. Weightman, *Signor Marconi's Magic Box*, 18.
16. Aitken, *Syntony and Spark*, 193; see also Hong, *Wireless*, 21, 194–96.
17. Garratt, *Early History of Radio*, 75–87.
18. Jolly, *Marconi*, 97.
19. Lochte, "Invention and Innovation," 98.
20. Jolly, *Marconi*, 50, 99.
21. Aitken, *Syntony and Spark*, 143.
22. Quoted in Jolly, *Marconi*, 58.
23. Kipling, "'Wireless,'" 197. Hereafter cited in the text as *W*.
24. Shaynor's methods as a reader also parallel accounts of Kipling's practice as a writer. An acquaintance recalled an incident in the 1890s when Kipling

> answered my query as to what he had been at work on with the information that he had just completed a long ballad. I asked to see it.
> "Oh, I can't show it to you now," he explained, "for it isn't written down yet. But I've got it all in my head and I'll say it to you if you like."
> When I assured him that this was exactly to my liking, he began to recite "McAndrew's Hymn" [1893]. . . .

Matthews, "'I've Got It All in My Head,'" 140–41. After hearing Kipling spontaneously deliver the poem, a Calvinistic reflection on steamship engineering, his listener shyly asked Kipling whether all the "technicalities" were correct (141).

25. Clemens, "Chat with Rudyard Kipling," 241.
26. The induction telegraph featured long parallel plates or wires that could register a signal sent along nearby telegraph cables without a physical connection and had a maximum range between several feet and several miles. Edison devised an induction telegraph for trains, and Preece experimented with a similar device before and during his work with Marconi. Weightman, *Signor Marconi's Magic Box*, 62–64.

27. E. Gilbert, *Good Kipling*, 125.
28. See Peters, *Speaking into the Air*, 2. Today, the coherer may also strike us as an image of a synapse, in which neurons reach toward each other without touching, so that the electrochemical transmission between them must occur across the gap. Although the mechanics of neuronal transmission remained unknown until the twentieth century, Otis points out that the speculations of late nineteenth-century neurologists anticipated such discoveries. *Networking*, 67.

29. Dunsheath, *History of Electrical Engineering*, 272.

30. Aitken, *Syntony and Spark*, 147. As Timothy Campbell notes, wireless transmission depends on the coupling of a receiver and headset to a sensitive operator "capable of copying without understanding" of "surrendering himself to what has already been selected, combined, and transmitted." Campbell describes the mental state produced by wireless as "delirium." *Wireless Writing*, 3, 13.

31. The pun, or misprint, is absent from the version of the tale in *Scribner's*.

32. Keats, "Eve of St. Agnes." Hereafter cited in the text as *ESA*.

33. In early 1903, this very mistake would turn a transatlantic birth announcement sent to the Marconi engineer Richard Vyvyan into something stranger. A message sent as "Jan. 3rd. Wife of R. N. Vyvyan—a daughter" became "Jane 3rd Wife of . . . " (emphasis added). Jolly, *Marconi*, 131.

34. See Kipling, "Uses of Reading," 62.

35. Bottone, *Wireless Telegraphy*, 8.

36. Rufo, "Ghosts in the Medium," 25.

37. Ibid., 24. As Luckhurst shows, Victorian psychic researchers eagerly seized upon physical phenomena such as electromagnetic induction to justify theories of mental transmission—and electric communications themselves were sometimes explained by analogy with telepathic transfer. Luckhurst, *Invention of Telepathy*, 75–92.

38. Dobrée, *Rudyard Kipling*, 25.

39. Jarrell, Introduction to *The English*, xi, xii.

40. McLuhan and Fiore, *Medium Is the Massage*, 63.

41. See Stillinger, "Hoodwinking of Madeline."

42. Quoted in Stillinger, *Reading "The Eve of St. Agnes,"* 22.

43. Ibid., 29.

44. Annan, "Kipling's Place," 347, 328.

45. Seymour-Smith, *Rudyard Kipling*, 65, 77.

46. See Sconce, *Haunted Media*, 69–91; Thurschwell, *Literature, Technology, and Magical Thinking*, 30–31; Knowles, "Wireless Telegraphy and 'Brain-waves.'"

47. On Lodge's ethereal theories, see Luckhurst, *Invention of Telepathy*, 90–91; as well as Lodge, *Continuity* and *Ether of Space*. Late in his life, Lodge's linked beliefs in spiritualism and ether became virtually a creed: as his preface to *Ether and Reality* puts it, "the material and the spiritual worlds . . . together seem to constitute the Universe. The Ether of Space is the connecting link" (vii). In *My Philosophy*, Lodge recognizes that "the Ether pervaded all my ideas, both of this world and the next" (5). Kipling's sister Alice was a medium who worked with the Society for Psychical Research; for readings of "'Wireless'" in relation to the Society's concerns, see Thurschwell, *Literature, Technology, and Magical Thinking*, 29–31; Luckhurst, *Invention of Telepathy*, 178.

48. Kittler, *Discourse Networks*, 229.

49. For instance, Frank Lentricchia traces turn-of-the-century American critics' construction of a Keats who rejected "the world and the body in the world" and whose name "signif[ied] freedom from bourgeois economic contamination." *Ariel and the Police*, 160, 161.

50. Beer, "'Wireless,'" 156.

51. Hong, *Wireless*, 19.

52. Kipling, "'Finest Story in the World,'" 118. Hereafter cited in the text as *FS*.

53. Kipling offers similar media analogies for realist invention and psychic experience in his autobiography. An early tale comes to him "stereoscopically clear"; later, although he disavows belief in "psychic" experience, Kipling recounts having had a dream about an incident that only happened later, a Latimer-like glimpse of "an unreleased roll of my life-film." *Something of Myself*, 43, 125, 126.

54. Kittler, *Discourse Networks*, 115.

55. Kipling, "Mrs. Bathurst," 328.

56. E. Gilbert, *Good Kipling*, 97.

57. Kipling, "Mrs. Bathurst," 325.

58. For discussions of Kipling's "Mrs Bathurst" and the "It" of sex appeal in the age of cinema, see Daly, *Literature, Technology, and Modernity*, 68–109. Daly also mentions the electrical "It" of "'Wireless'" (76).

59. Gozzi, "Paradoxes of Electric Media," 128.

60. Keats, *Letters*, 1:387.

61. Quoted in M. Cohen, *Rudyard Kipling*, 100.

62. T. S. Eliot echoes this conversation as he describes Kipling's most uncanny trait as a writer: "a queer gift of second sight, of transmitting messages from elsewhere, a gift so disconcerting when we are made aware of it that henceforth we are never sure when it is *not* present." "Rudyard Kipling," 25. Marconi's daughter glimpsed a comparable self-understanding in the inventor: "He thought of himself, I believe, as a scientific vessel, a human instrument, chosen by a higher power." Marconi, *My Father*, 85–86.

63. Kipling, *Something of Myself*, 68.

64. Ibid., 68, 111.

65. For the most influential account of the new kinds of consciousness encouraged by writing and print, see Ong, *Orality and Literacy*, especially 78–179.

66. J. Montefiore, "Day and Night," 122.

67. Keats, *Letters*, 2:122.

68. Jolly, *Marconi*, 117–18.

69. Quoted in "Syntonic Wireless Telegraphy," *Electrical Review*, 820. The version of Ayrton's comments published in another engineering journal omits the mention of the Psychical Society, a reference that might have been his swipe at Lodge. "Syntonic Wireless Telegraphy," *Engineering Magazine*.

70. *The Interpretation of Dreams* (1900) too presents dreams as medium-events. In his best-known account of the strange division between a dream's manifest content and the latent thought behind it, Freud describes them as "like two versions of the same subject-matter in two different languages. Or, more properly, the dream-content seems like a transcript of the dream-thoughts into another mode of ex-

pression"—"a pictographic script," perhaps, or "a rebus." Freud, *Interpretations of Dreams*, 4:276. In 1907 Freud cited Kipling as one of his favorite writers. Jones, *Life and Works*, 3:422.

71. Sconce, *Haunted Media*, 63, 70.

72. Knowles, "Wireless Telegraphy and 'Brain-waves,'" 858. Knowles's conjectures, first published in 1869 and later revived for the Marconi era, originally took the then-new "3,000 miles of Atlantic wire" as inspiration for long-range thought transfer (863). Our ghosts and spirits reliably materialize around our media.

73. Quoted in "Syntonic Wireless Telegraphy," *Engineering Magazine*, 596.

74. Wilde, "De Profundis," 169.

75. See Keats, *Letters*, 1:4–7.

76. Ibid., 2:122–23.

77. Benjamin, "Work of Art."

78. On the intertwined histories of advertising and literature from Dickens to Joyce, see Wicke, *Advertising Fictions*.

79. Bottone, *Wireless Telegraphy*, 9; Albery, "Hertzian Waves," 28.

80. Tompkins, *Art of Rudyard Kipling*, 93.

81. Aitken, *Syntony and Spark*, 187.

82. Mackay, *Telegraphic Codes*, 50.

Coda

1. Wilde, "Preface."

2. For an analysis of mass communication along similar lines, see Luhmann, *Reality of the Mass Media*.

3. Hayles, *How We Became Posthuman*, 25–28. Hayles explores the intriguing suggestion of twentieth-century information theory that information itself may correspond both to pattern and to randomness.

4. Gaskell, *Cranford*, 1, 64. Hereafter cited in the text as *C*. On modernity and women's writing in *Cranford*, see Schor, *Sheherezade in the Marketplace*, 83–119. My analysis complements Schor's discussion of the "mediatory power of letters" in Gaskell's novel (110).

Works Cited

Ackroyd, Peter. *Dickens*. London: Sinclair-Stevenson, 1990.

Aitken, High G. J. *Syntony and Spark: The Origins of Radio*. New York: Wiley, 1976.

Albery, Richard H. "Hertzian Waves and Wireless Telegraphy." In *Proceedings of the Warrington Literary and Philosophical Society*, 1904–1905–1906, 1–28. Warrington, UK: Mackie, 1906.

Alexander, William. *Plan and Description of the Original Electromagnetic Telegraph*. London: Longman, 1851.

Allan, Stuart. *News Culture*. 2nd ed. Buckingham, UK: Open Univ. Press, 2004.

Allen, Grant [Olive Pratt Rayner, pseud.]. *The Type-writer Girl*. 1897. Edited by Clarissa J. Suranyi. Peterborough, Ont.: Broadview, 2004.

Alter, Robert. "The Demons of History in Dickens' *Tale*." *Novel* 2 (1969): 135–42.

Altick, Richard Daniel. *The English Common Reader: A Social History of the Mass Reading Public, 1800–1900*. Chicago: Univ. of Chicago Press, 1957.

Anderson, Benedict. *Imagined Communities: Reflections on the Origin and Spread of Nationalism*. Rev. ed. London: Verso, 1991.

Anderson, James. *Statistics of Telegraphy*. London, 1872.

Anecdotes of the Electric Telegraph. The London Anecdotes. London: Bogue, [1848].

Annan, Noel. "Kipling's Place in the History of Ideas." *Victorian Studies* 3 (1960): 323–48.

apRoberts, Ruth. *Trollope: Artist and Moralist*. London: Chatto, 1971. Also published as *Moral Trollope*. Athens: Ohio State Univ. Press, 1971.

Archer, Charles Maybury. *Guide to the Electric Telegraph*. London: Smith, 1852.

Armstrong, Carol M. *Scenes in a Library: Reading the Photograph in the Book, 1843–1875*. Cambridge, MA: MIT Press, 1998.

Armstrong, Nancy. *Fiction in the Age of Photography: The Legacy of British Realism*. Cambridge, MA: Harvard Univ. Press, 1999.

Arnold, H. J. P. *William Henry Fox Talbot: Pioneer of Photography and Man of Science*. London: Hutchinson Benham, 1977.

Ashurst, W. H. *Facts and Reasons in Support of Mr. Rowland Hill's Plan for a Universal Penny Postage*. 2nd ed. London: Hooper, 1838.

Aswell, E. Duncan. "James's *In the Cage*: The Telegraphist as Artist." *Texas Studies in Literature and Language* 8 (1966): 375–84.

Babbage, Charles. *The Economy of Machinery and Manufactures*. 1832. Vol. 8 of *The Works of Charles Babbage*. Edited by Martin Campbell-Kelly. 11 vols. New York: New York Univ. Press, 1989.

———. *The Ninth Bridgewater Treatise: A Fragment*. 1837. 2nd ed. Vol. 9 of *The Works of Charles Babbage*. Edited by Martin Campbell-Kelly. 11 vols. New York: New York Univ. Press, 1989.

Bagehot, Walter. "The Character of Sir Robert Peel." *National Review* 3 (July 1856): 146–74. Reprinted in *The Collected Works of Walter Bagehot*, 15 vols., edited by Norman St. John Stevas, 3:241–71. London: Economist, 1965–86.

Bagwell, Philip S. *The Transport Revolution*. 2nd ed. London: Routledge, 1988.

Baines, F. E. *Forty Years at the Post-Office*. 2 vols. London: Bentley, 1895.

———. *On the Track of the Mail-Coach*. London: Bentley, 1895.

Bakhtin, M. M. *The Dialogic Imagination*. Edited by Michael Holquist. Translated by Caryl Emerson and Michael Holquist. Austin: Univ. of Texas Press, 1981.

Baldridge, Cates. "Alternatives to Bourgeois Individualism in *A Tale of Two Cities*." *SEL: Studies in English Literature, 1500–1900* 30 (1990): 633–54.

Ballantyne, R. M. *The Battery and the Boiler; or, Adventures in the Laying of Submarine Electric Cables*. London: Nisbet, 1883.

———. *Post Haste: A Tale of Her Majesty's Mails*. London: Nisbet, 1880.

Bareham, Tony. "Patterns of Excellence: Theme and Structure in *The Three Clerks*." In *Anthony Trollope*, edited by Tony Bareham, 54–80. London: Vision, 1980.

Barthes, Roland. *Camera Lucida: Reflections on Photography*. 1980. Translated by Richard Howard. New York: Noonday Press, 1981.

———. "The Reality Effect." In *French Literary Theory Today: A Reader*, edited by Tzvetan Todorov, translated by R. Carter, 11–18. Cambridge: Cambridge Univ. Press, 1982.

Bauer, Dale M., and Andrew Lakritz. "Language, Class, and Sexuality in Henry James's 'In the Cage.'" *New Orleans Review* 14.3 (Fall 1987): 61–69.

Beauchamp, Ken. *History of Telegraphy*. London: Institute of Electrical Engineers, 1999.

Beer, Gillian. "'Wireless': Popular Physics, Radio, and Modernism." In Spufford and Uglow, *Cultural Babbage*, 149–66.

Bell, Alexander Graham. "Improvement in Telegraphy." United States Patent 174,465, issued 7 March 1876.

Beniger, James R. *The Control Revolution: Technological and Economic Origins of the Information Society*. Cambridge, MA: Harvard Univ. Press, 1986.

Benjamin, Walter. "On the Mimetic Faculty." In *Reflections*, edited by Peter Demetz, translated by Edmund Jephcott, 333–36. New York: Schocken, 1978.

———. "The Work of Art in the Age of Mechanical Reproduction." In *Illumina-*

tions, edited by Hannah Arendt, translated by Harry Zohn, 217–51. New York: Schocken, 1969.

Bernard, Claude. *An Introduction to the Study of Experimental Medicine*. 1865. Translated by Henry Copley Greene. New York: Dover, 1957.

Blondheim, Menahem. *News over the Wires: The Telegraph and the Flow of Public Information in America, 1844–1897*. Cambridge, MA: Harvard Univ. Press, 1994.

Bodenheimer, Rosemarie. *The Real Life of Mary Ann Evans: George Eliot, Her Letters and Fiction*. Ithaca, NY: Cornell Univ. Press, 1994.

Boehm, Klaus, in collaboration with Aubrey Silberston. *The British Patent System: I. Administration*. Cambridge: Cambridge Univ. Press, 1967.

Bolter, Jay David, and Richard Grusin. *Remediation: Understanding New Media*. Cambridge, MA: MIT Press, 2000.

Bonheim, Helmut. "The Principle of Cyclicity in Charles Dickens' 'The Signalman.'" *Anglia: Zeitschrift für Englische Philologie* 106 (1988): 380–92.

Boole, George. *An Investigation of the Laws of Thought*. London: Macmillan, 1854.

Booth, Henry. *Uniformity of Time: Considered Especially in Reference to Railway Transit and the Operations of the Electric Telegraph*. London: Weale; Liverpool: Baines, 1847.

Bottone, S. R. *Wireless Telegraphy and Hertzian Waves*. 4th ed. London: Whittaker, [1910].

Bowen, John. *Other Dickens: Pickwick to Chuzzlewit*. Oxford: Oxford Univ. Press, 2000.

Bowers, Brian. *Sir Charles Wheatstone FRS, 1820–1875*. London: Institute of Electrical Engineers/Science Museum, 2001.

Brain, Robert M. "Representation on the Line: Graphic Recording Instruments and Scientific Modernism." In Clark and Henderson, *From Energy to Information*, 155–77.

Brand, Stewart. *The Media Lab: Inventing the Future at MIT*. New York: Viking, 1987.

Brett, John W. *On the Origin and Progress of the Oceanic Electric Telegraph*. London: Johnson, 1858.

Briggs, Asa. Preface to Fryer and Akerman, *Reform of the Post Office*, 1:ix.

———. *Victorian Things*. 1988. Rev. ed. Stroud: Sutton, 2003.

Briggs, Charles F., and Augustus Maverick. *The Story of the Telegraph: And a History of the Great Atlantic Cable*. New York: Rudd and Carleton, 1858.

Bright, Edward B. Preface to *The Electric Telegraph*, by Dr. Lardner, revised by Edward B. Bright, v–vi. London: Walton, 1867.

Brontë, Charlotte. *Jane Eyre*. 1847. Edited by Margaret Smith. Oxford: World's Classics/Oxford Univ. Press, 2000.

———. *The Letters of Charlotte Brontë*. Edited by Margaret Smith. 3 vols. Oxford: Clarendon Press, 1995–2004.

Brooks, Peter. *Body Work: Objects of Desire in Modern Narrative*. Cambridge, MA: Harvard Univ. Press, 1993.

Brown, Bill. *The Material Unconscious: American Amusement, Stephen Crane, and the Economies of Play*. Cambridge, MA: Harvard Univ. Press, 1996.

Brown, John Seely, and Paul Duguid. 2000. *The Social Life of Information*. Boston: Harvard Business School, 2002.

Brown, Monika. "Dutch Painters and British Novel-Readers: *Adam Bede* in the Context of Victorian Cultural Literacy." *Victorians Institute Journal* 18 (1990): 113–33.

Buckland, Gail. *Fox Talbot and the Invention of Photography*. Boston: Godine, 1980.

Bynum, W. F. *Science and the Practice of Medicine in the Nineteenth Century*. Cambridge: Cambridge Univ. Press, 1994.

Byrn, Edward M. *The Progress of Invention in the Nineteenth Century*. New York: Russell and Russell, 1900. Facsimile reprint. N.p.: Russell and Russell, 1970.

Cameron, Sharon. *Thinking in Henry James*. Chicago: Univ. of Chicago Press, 1989.

Campbell, Timothy C. *Wireless Writing in the Age of Marconi*. Minneapolis: Univ. of Minnesota Press, 2006.

Carey, James W. "Technology and Ideology: The Case of the Telegraph." In *Communication as Culture: Essays on Media and Society*, 201–30. Boston: Unwin Hyman, 1989.

Carey, John. *The Violent Effigy: A Study of Dickens' Imagination*. London: Faber, 1973.

Carlyle, Thomas. *The French Revolution: A History*. 1837. Edited by K. J. Fielding and David Sorensen. Oxford: World's Classics/Oxford Univ. Press, 1989.

———. *Sartor Resartus*. 1833–34. Edited by Kerry McSweeney and Peter Sabor. Oxford: World's Classics/Oxford Univ. Press, 1987.

Carmichael, Evelyn G. M. *The Law Relating to the Telegraph, the Telephone, and the Submarine Cable*. London: Knight, 1904.

Carrington, Charles. *Rudyard Kipling: His Life and Work*. London: Macmillan, 1953.

Carroll, Lewis. *Eight or Nine Wise Words about Letter-Writing*. Oxford: Emberlin, 1890.

Carse, Wendy K. "A Penchant for Narrative: 'Mary Smith' in Elizabeth Gaskell's *Cranford*." *Journal of Narrative Technique* 20 (1990): 318–30.

Caruth, Cathy. Introduction to *Trauma: Explorations in Memory*, edited by Cathy Caruth, 3–12; 151–57. Baltimore: Johns Hopkins Univ. Press, 1996.

"Chit-Chat by Telegraph." *Punch* 18 (1850): 13.

Clark, John W. *The Language and Style of Anthony Trollope*. London: Deutsch, 1975.

Clarke, Bruce, and Linda Dalrymple Henderson, eds. *From Energy to Information: Representation in Science and Technology, Art, and Literature*. Stanford, CA: Stanford Univ. Press, 2002.

Clayton, Jay. *Charles Dickens in Cyberspace: The Afterlife of the Nineteenth Century in Postmodern Culture*. Oxford: Oxford Univ. Press, 2003.

———. "The Voice in the Machine: Hazlitt, Hardy, James." In *Language Machines: Technologies of Literary and Cultural Production*, edited by Jeffrey Masten, Peter Stallybrass, and Nancy Vickers, 209–32. New York: Routledge, 1997.

Clear, Charles R. *John Palmer, Mail Coach Pioneer*. London: Blandford/Postal History Society, 1955.

Cleere, Eileen. *Avuncularism: Capitalism, Patriarchy, and Nineteenth-Century British Culture*. Stanford, CA: Stanford Univ. Press, 2004.

Clemens, Cyril. "A Chat with Rudyard Kipling." 1941. In *Kipling: Interviews and Recollections*, edited by Harold Orel, 2:239–44. 2 vols. Totowa, NJ: Barnes & Noble, 1983.

[Clippinger, John Albert]. *Sam Johnson: The Experience and Observations of a Railroad Telegraph Operator*. New York: Johnston, 1878.

Coase, R. H. "Rowland Hill and the Penny Post." *Economica*, n.s., 6 (1939): 423–39.

[Cochrane-Baillie, A. D. R. W.]. "The Royal Mail." Rev. of *The Royal Mail: Its Curiosities and Romance*, by James Wilson Hyde. *Blackwood's Magazine* 137 (May 1885): 617–30.

Coe, Louis. *The Telegraph: A History of Morse's Invention and Its Predecessors in the United States*. Jefferson, NC: McFarland, 1993.

Cohen, I. Bernard. *The Triumph of Numbers: How Counting Shaped Modern Life*. New York: Norton, 2005.

Cohen, Morton, ed. *Rudyard Kipling to Rider Haggard: The Record of a Friendship*. London: Hutchinson, 1965.

Cohn, Dorrit. "Optics and Power in the Novel." *New Literary History* 26 (1995): 3–20.

Cole, Henry. *Fifty Years of Public Work of Sir Henry Cole, K. C. B.* 2 vols. London: Bell, 1884.

———. *A Report of a Scene at Windsor Castle Respecting the Uniform Penny Postage*. London: Hooper, 1839.

Collins, Philip. Introduction to *Dickens: The Critical Heritage*, edited by Philip Collins, 1–26. New York: Barnes & Noble, 1971.

Coulter, Moureen. *Property in Ideas: The Patent Question in Mid-Victorian Britain*. Kirksville, MO: Thomas Jefferson Univ. Press, 1991.

Crary, Jonathan. 1990. *Techniques of the Observer: On Vision and Modernity in the Nineteenth Century*. Cambridge, MA: MIT Press, 1992.

[Croker, J. W.] "Post-office Reform." *Quarterly Review* 64 (October 1839): 513–74.

Croskery, Margaret Case. "Mothers without Children, Unity without Plot: *Cranford*'s Radical Charm." *Nineteenth-Century Literature* 52 (1997): 198–220.

Curran, James. "The Ugly Face of Reform." In *Power without Responsibility: The Press, Broadcasting, and New Media in Britain*, by James Curran and Jean Seaton, 18–23. 6th ed. London: Routledge, 2003.

Daly, Nicholas. *Literature, Technology, and Modernity, 1860–2000*. Cambridge: Cambridge Univ. Press, 2004.

Dames, Nicholas. *Amnesiac Selves: Nostalgia, Forgetting, and British Fiction,* 1810–1870. Oxford: Oxford Univ. Press, 2001.

Daunton, M. J. *Royal Mail: The Post Office since* 1840. London: Athlone, 1985.

Davies, Margery W. *Woman's Place Is at the Typewriter: Office Work and Office Workers,* 1870–1930. Philadelphia: Temple Univ. Press, 1982.

Davis, Lennard J. *Factual Fictions: The Origin of the English Novel.* New York: Columbia Univ. Press, 1983.

Day, Gary. "Figuring out the Signalman: Dickens and the Ghost Story." In *Nineteenth-Century Suspense: From Poe to Conan Doyle,* edited by Clive Bloom, Brian Docherty, Jane Gibb, and Keith Shand, 26–45. London: Macmillan, 1988.

Deleuze, Gilles, and Félix Guattari. *A Thousand Plateaus: Capitalism and Schizophrenia.* 1980. Translated by Brian Massumi. Minneapolis: Univ. of Minnesota Press, 1987.

De Quincey, Thomas. "The English Mail-Coach, or the Glory of Motion." 1849. In *Confessions of an English Opium-Eater and Other Writings,* edited by Grevel Lindoop, 183–233. Oxford: World's Classics/Oxford Univ. Press, 1985.

Dickens, Charles. "Birmingham and Midland Institute: Annual Inaugural Meeting: Birmingham, 27 September 1869." In *The Speeches of Charles Dickens,* edited by K. J. Fielding, 397–408. Oxford: Clarendon Press, 1960.

———. *Bleak House.* 1852–53. Edited by George Ford and Sylvère Monod. New York: Norton, 1977.

———. *Charles Dickens' Book of Memoranda: A Photographic and Typographic Facsimile of the Notebook Begun in January* 1855. Transcribed and annotated by Fred Kaplan. New York: New York Public Library, 1981.

———. "Curious Misprint in *The Edinburgh Review.*" 1857. In *"Gone Astray" and Other Papers from* Household Words, 1851–59, vol. 3 of *Dickens' Journalism,* edited by Michael Slater, 413–20. London, Dent, 1998.

———. *Hard Times.* 1854. Edited by Fred Kaplan and Sylvère Monod. 3rd ed. New York: Norton, 2001.

———. *The Letters of Charles Dickens.* Pilgrim ed. Edited by Madeline House, Graham Storey, and Kathleen Tillotson. 12 vols. Oxford: Clarendon Press, 1965–2002.

———. *The Life and Adventures of Nicholas Nickleby.* 20 numbers. London: Chapman and Hall, 1838–39. Facsimile reprint. Menston: Scolar, 1972–73.

———. "Newsvendors' Benevolent Institution, 9 May 1865." In *The Speeches of Charles Dickens,* edited by K. J. Fielding, 337–42. Oxford: Clarendon Press, 1960.

———. *The Pickwick Papers.* 1836–37. Edited by Robert L. Patten. London: Penguin Books, 1986.

[———]. "A Preliminary Word." *Household Words* 1 (30 March 1850): 1–2.

———. *Sketches by Boz.* 1836, 1837. Edited by Dennis Walder. London: Penguin Books, 1995.

―――. *A Tale of Two Cities.* 1859. Edited by Richard Maxwell. London: Penguin Books, 2003.

―――. *The Uncollected Writings of Charles Dickens, Household Words* 1850–59. Edited by Harry Stone. 2 vols. Bloomington: Indiana Univ. Press, 1968; London: Allen Lane/Penguin Books, 1969.

Dickens, Charles, Andrew Halliday, Charles Collins, Hesba Stretton, and Amelia B. Edwards. "Mugby Junction." Special issue. *All the Year Round* 16 (Christmas 1866): 1–48.

Dickens, Charles, with W. H. Wills. "Post-Office Money-Orders." *Household Words* 5 (20 March 1852), 1–5. Reprinted in Dickens, *Uncollected Writings*, 2:392–400.

―――. "Valentine's Day at the Post-Office." *Household Words* 1 (30 March 1850), 6–12. Reprinted in Dickens, *Uncollected Writings*, 1:69–84.

Dobrée, Bonamy. *Rudyard Kipling: Realist and Fabulist.* London: Oxford Univ. Press, 1967.

Dodwell, Robert. *An Illustrated Hand Book to the Electric Telegraph.* 2nd ed. London: Lemare, [1862].

Downey, Gregory. "Commentary: The Place of Labour in the History of Information-Technology Revolutions." In *Uncovering Labour in Information Revolutions, 1750–2000,* edited by Aad Blok and Gregory Downey. Supplement 11 to *International Review of Social History* 48 (2003): 225–61.

―――. "Virtual Webs, Physical Technologies, and Hidden Workers: The Spaces of Labor in Information Internetworks." *Technology and Culture* 42 (2001): 209–35.

Downs, Brian W. Introduction to *Familiar Letters on Important Occasions,* by Samuel Richardson, ix–xxvi. London: Routledge, 1928.

Dunn, Richard J. "A Tale for Two Dramatists." *Dickens Studies Annual* 12 (1983): 117–24.

Dunsheath, Percy. *A History of Electrical Engineering.* London: Faber, 1962.

Eagleton, Terry. "Knowledge and Power in 'The Lifted Veil.'" *Literature and History,* 2nd ser., 9 (1983): 52–61.

Early, Julie English. "Technology, Modernity, and 'the Little Man': Crippen's Capture by Wireless." *Victorian Studies* 39 (1996): 309–37.

[Eastlake, Elizabeth]. "Photography." *Quarterly Review* 101 (April 1857): 442–68.

Edel, Leon. *The Life of Henry James.* 1953–72. 5 vols. New York: Avon Books, 1978.

"The Electric Telegraph." *Fraser's Magazine* 49 (April 1854): 401–11.

Eliot, George [Marian Evans]. *Adam Bede.* 1859. Edited by Stephen Gill. London: Penguin Books, 1985.

―――. *Daniel Deronda.* 1874–76. Edited by Graham Handley. Oxford: Clarendon Press, 1984.

―――. *Essays of George Eliot.* Edited by Thomas Pinney. New York: Columbia Univ. Press; London: Routledge and Kegan Paul, 1963.

―――. *The George Eliot Letters.* Edited by Gordon S. Haight. 9 vols. New Haven, CT: Yale Univ. Press, 1954–78.

———. "The Lifted Veil." 1859. In *The Lifted Veil; Brother Jacob*, edited by Helen Small, 1–43. Oxford: World's Classics/Oxford Univ. Press, 1999.

———. *Middlemarch*. 1871–72. Edited by David Carroll. Oxford: Clarendon Press, 1986.

[———]. "The Natural History of German Life." *Westminster Review* 66 (1856): 51–79. Reprinted in Eliot, *Essays*, 266–99.

[———]. "Silly Novels by Lady Novelists." *Westminster Review* 66 (1856): 442–61. Reprinted in Eliot, *Essays*, 300–24.

Eliot, T. S. "Rudyard Kipling." 1941. Introduction to *A Choice of Kipling's Verse*, 7–40. Garden City, NY: Anchor-Doubleday, 1962.

———. "Tradition and the Individual Talent." 1919. In *The Sacred Wood*, 47–59. London: Methuen, 1960.

Epperly, Elizabeth R. *Patterns of Repetition in Trollope*. Washington, DC: Catholic Univ. of America Press, 1989.

Ermarth, Elizabeth Deeds. *Realism and Consensus in the English Novel: Time, Space and Narrative*. 1983. Edinburgh: Edinburgh Univ. Press, 1998.

Evans, Edward B. *A Description of the Mulready Envelope and of Various Imitations and Caricatures of Its Design*. London: Gibbons, 1891.

Everdell, William R. *The First Moderns: Profiles in the Origins of Twentieth-Century Thought*. Chicago: Univ. of Chicago Press, 1997.

Fahie, J. J. *A History of Electric Telegraphy to the Year* 1837. London: Spon, 1884.

Farrugia, Jean Young. *The Letter Box: A History of Pillar and Wall Boxes*. Fontwell, UK: Centaur, 1969.

———. *Sir Rowland Hill: Reformer Extraordinary, 1795–1879, Some Notes on His Life and Work*. London: National Postal Museum, 1979.

Favret, Mary A. *Romantic Correspondence: Women, Politics, and the Fiction of Letters*. Cambridge: Cambridge Univ. Press, 1993.

"A Few Weeks from Home. The Electric Telegraph." *Chambers Edinburgh Journal* 9 (25 July 1840): 209–10.

Finlaison, John. *An Account of Some Remarkable Applications of the Electric Fluid to the Useful Arts by Mr. Alexander Bain*. London: Chapman, 1843.

Flint, Kate. "Blood, Bodies, and *The Lifted Veil*." *Nineteenth-Century Literature* 51 (1997): 455–73.

Forster, E. M. *Howards End*. 1910. New York: Vintage, 1989.

Forster, John. *The Life of Charles Dickens*. 3 vols. London: Chapman and Hall, 1872–74.

Foucault, Michel. *The Birth of the Clinic: An Archaeology of Medical Perception*. Translated by A. M. Sheridan Smith. New York: Vintage, 1994.

———. *Discipline and Punish: The Birth of the Prison*. Translated by Allen Sheridan. New York: Pantheon, 1977.

Foxell, J. T., and A. O. Spafford. *Monarchs of All They Surveyed: The Story of the Post*

Office Surveyors. London: Published for the Postmaster-General by Her Majesty's Stationery Office, 1952.

Frankel, Oz. "Blue Books and the Victorian Reader." *Victorian Studies* 46 (2004): 310–18.

Freud, Sigmund. *The Interpretation of Dreams.* 1900, 1930. Vols. 4–5 of *The Standard Edition of the Complete Psychological Works of Sigmund Freud.* Translated by James Strachey. 24 vols. London: Hogarth/Institute of Psycho-Analysis, 1953–74.

———. "The Uncanny." 1919. In *The Standard Edition of the Complete Psychological Works of Sigmund Freud*, translated by James Strachey, 17:219–52. 24 vols. London: Hogarth/Institute of Psycho-Analysis, 1953–74.

Froude, James Anthony. "On Progress." 1870. In *Short Studies on Great Subjects*, 2:351–96. 2nd ser. 3 vols. London: Longmans, 1878.

Fryer, Gavin, and Clive Akerman, eds. *The Reform of the Post Office in the Victorian Era and Its Impact on Social and Economic Activity.* 2 vols. London: Royal Philatelic Society, 2000.

Gabler-Hover, Janet. "The Ethics of Determinism in Henry James's 'In the Cage.'" *The Henry James Review* 13 (1992): 253–74.

Gallagher, Catherine. "The Duplicity of Doubling in *A Tale of Two Cities.*" *Dickens Studies Annual* 12 (1983): 125–45.

Galvan, Jill. "Class Ghosting 'In the Cage.'" *The Henry James Review* 22 (2001): 297–306.

———. "The Narrator as Medium in George Eliot's 'The Lifted Veil.'" *Victorian Studies* 48 (2006): 240–48.

Garfield, James Abram. "Dr. Samuel F. B. Morse." In *The Works of James Abram Garfield*, 2 vols., edited by Burke A. Hinsdale, 2:26–29. Boston: Osgood, 1882.

Garratt, G. R. M. *The Early History of Radio: From Faraday to Marconi.* London: Institute of Electrical Engineers, 1994.

Garrett, Peter K. *The Victorian Multiplot Novel: Studies in Dialogical Form.* New Haven, CT: Yale Univ. Press, 1980.

Garvey, Michael Angelo. *The Silent Revolution; Or, The Future Effects of Steam and Electricity upon the Condition of Mankind.* London: Cash, 1852.

Gaskell, Elizabeth. *Cranford.* 1851–53. Edited by Elizabeth Porges Watson. Oxford: World's Classics/Oxford Univ. Press, 1980.

———. *The Letters of Mrs Gaskell.* Edited by J. A. V. Chapple and Arthur Pollard. Cambridge, MA: Harvard Univ. Press, 1967.

———. *The Life of Charlotte Brontë.* 1857. Edited by Elisabeth Jay. London: Penguin Books, 1997.

General Rules and Regulations for the Guidance of Counter Clerks and Telegraphists of the London Postal Service. London: Eyre and Spottiswoode for Her Majesty's Stationery Office, 1898.

Gilbert, Elliot L. *The Good Kipling: Studies in the Short Story.* Athens: Ohio Univ. Press, 1970.

Gilbert, Sandra M., and Susan Gubar. *The Madwoman in the Attic: The Woman Writer and the Nineteenth-Century Literary Imagination.* 1979. New Haven, CT: Yale Univ. Press, 1984.

Gitelman, Lisa. *Scripts, Grooves, and Writing Machines: Representing Technology in the Edison Era.* Stanford, CA: Stanford Univ. Press, 1999.

Gitelman, Lisa, and Geoffrey B. Pingree. "Introduction: What's New about New Media?" In Gitelman and Pingree, *New Media*, xi–xxii.

———, eds. *New Media, 1740–1915.* Cambridge, MA: MIT Press, 2003.

Glancy, Ruth F. "Dickens and Christmas: His Framed-Theme Tales." *Nineteenth-Century Fiction* 35 (1980): 53–72.

Goodlad, Lauren M. E. *Victorian Literature and the Victorian State: Character and Governance in a Liberal Society.* Baltimore: Johns Hopkins Univ. Press, 2003.

Goodwyn, Charles W. *Royal Reform: Postal Reform, 1837–1841, as Reflected in the Royal Philatelic Collection.* Bristol, UK: Stuart Rossiter Trust, 1999.

Gordon, John Steele. *A Thread across the Ocean: The Heroic Story of the Transatlantic Cable.* New York: HarperCollins-Perennial, 2003.

Gozzi, Raymond, Jr. "Paradoxes of Electric Media." *EME: Explorations in Media Ecology* 3 (2004): 127–30.

Great Britain. House of Commons. Select Committee on Postage. *First Report from the Select Committee on Postage,* 4 April 1838.

———. *Second Report from the Select Committee on Postage,* 1 August 1838.

Green-Lewis, Jennifer. "At Home in the Nineteenth Century: Photography, Nostalgia, and the Will to Authenticity." *Nineteenth-Century Contexts* 22 (2000): 51–75.

———. *Framing the Victorians: Photography and the Culture of Realism.* Ithaca, NY: Cornell Univ. Press, 1996.

———. "Not Fading Away: Photography in the Age of Oblivion." *Nineteenth-Century Contexts* 22 (2001): 559–85.

Gunning, Tom. "Re-Newing Old Technologies: Astonishment, Second Nature, and the Uncanny in Technology from the Previous Turn-of-the-Century." In *Rethinking Media Change: The Aesthetics of Transition,* edited by David Thorburn and Henry Jenkins, 39–60. Cambridge, MA: MIT Press, 2003.

Hall, N. John. Introduction to *The Three Clerks,* by Anthony Trollope, vii–xvii. London: Folio Society, 1992.

Hampton, Mark. *Visions of the Press in Britain, 1850–1950.* Urbana: Univ. of Illinois Press, 2004.

Hand Book to the Electric Telegraph. 2nd ed. London: Scales; Clark, 1847.

Hardy, Thomas. *A Laodicean; Or, the Castle of the De Stancys: A Story of To-Day.* 1881. Oxford: World's Classics/Oxford Univ. Press, 1991.

Harker, Margaret F. *Henry Peach Robinson: Master of Photographic Art, 1830–1901.* Oxford: Blackwell, 1988.

Harlow, Alvin F. *Old Wires and New Waves: The History of the Telegraph, Telephone, and Wireless.* New York: Appleton, 1936.

Harper, Charles G. *The Dover Road: Annals of an Ancient Turnpike.* 1895. 2nd ed. London: Palmer, 1922.

————. *Stage-Coach and Mail in Days of Yore.* 2 vols. London: Chapman, 1903.

Harris, Stanley. *The Coaching Age.* London: Bentley, 1885.

Harvie, Christopher. "'The Sons of Martha': Technology, Transport, and Rudyard Kipling." *Victorian Studies* 20 (1977): 269–82.

Hayles, N. Katherine. "Escape and Constraint: Three Fictions Dream of Moving from Energy to Information." In Clarke and Henderson, *From Energy to Information,* 235–54.

————. *How We Became Posthuman: Virtual Bodies in Cybernetics, Literature, and Informatics.* Chicago: Univ. of Chicago Press, 1999.

[Head, Francis Bond]. "Mechanism of the Post-Office." *Quarterly Review* 87 (1850): 69–115.

————. *Stokers and Pokers, or, the London and North-Western Railway, the Electric Telegraph, and the Railway Clearing-House.* London: Murray, 1849.

Headrick, Daniel R. *The Tools of Empire: Technology and European Imperialism in the Nineteenth Century.* New York: Oxford Univ. Press, 1981.

————. *When Information Came of Age: Technologies of Knowledge in the Age of Reason and Revolution,* 1700–1850. Oxford: Oxford Univ. Press, 2000.

[Hemyng, Bracebridge.] *Secrets of the Dead-Letter Office: By the Author of "Telegraph Secrets."* London: Clarke, [1868].

[————]. *Telegraph Secrets: By a Station-Master.* London: Clarke, [1867]. Reprinted as *Telegraph Secrets.* By Bracebridge Hemyng. Diprose's Railway Library. London: Diprose & Bateman, [1877].

Herbert, Christopher. "Trollope and the Fixity of the Self." *PMLA* 93 (1978): 228–39.

Hertz, Neil. "George Eliot's Pulse." *differences* 6 (1994): 28–45.

Hey, Colin G. *Rowland Hill: Victorian Genius and Benefactor.* London: Quiller, 1989.

Highton, Edward. *The Electric Telegraph: Its History and Progress.* 2nd ed. London: John Weale, 1852.

Hill, I. D. "Charles Babbage, Rowland Hill, and Penny Postage." *Postal History International* 2 (1973): 3–10.

Hill, Rowland. "Circular to Surveyors, 1847, 1855." Royal Mail Archive, London. POST 68/433.

————. *Post Office Reform: Its Importance and Practicability.* 1837. Reprinted in Fryer and Akerman, *Reform of the Post Office,* 1:1–46.

Hill, Rowland, and George Birkbeck Hill. *The Life of Sir Rowland Hill and the History of Penny Postage.* 2 vols. London: De la Rue, 1880.

Hoag, Clarence Gilbert, and George Hervey Hallett Jr. *Proportional Representation.* New York: Macmillan, 1926.

[Hollingshead, John]. "House-Top Telegraphs." *All the Year Round* 2 (26 Nov. 1859): 106–9.

[———]. "Right through the Post." *All the Year Round* 1 (18 June 1859): 190–92.

Holzmann, Gerard J., and Björn Pehrson. *The Early History of Data Networks.* Los Alamitos, CA: IEEE Computer Society, 1995.

Hong, Sungook. *Wireless: From Marconi's Black-Box to the Audion.* Cambridge, MA: MIT Press, 2001.

[Horne, R. H.] "The Great Peace-Maker: A Sub-Marine Dialogue." *Household Words* 3 (14 June 1851): 275–77.

Hubbard, Geoffrey. *Cooke and Wheatstone and the Invention of the Electric Telegraph.* London: Routledge, 1965.

Hutter, Albert D. "Nation and Generation in *A Tale of Two Cities.*" *PMLA* 93 (1978): 448–62.

———. "The Novelist as Resurrectionist: Dickens and the Dilemma of Death." *Dickens Studies Annual* 12 (1983): 1–39.

Iles, George. *Flame, Electricity, and the Camera: Man's Progress from the First Kindling of Fire to the Wireless Telegraph and the Photography of Color.* New York: Doubleday, 1900.

Innis, Harold A. *The Bias of Communication.* 1951. Toronto: Univ. of Toronto Press, 1964.

Jackman, W. T. *The Development of Transportation in Modern England.* 1916. 3rd ed. London: Cass, 1966; New York: Kelley, 1968.

Jaffe, Audrey. *Vanishing Points: Dickens, Narrative, and the Subject of Omniscience.* Berkeley and Los Angeles: Univ. of California Press, 1991.

Jakobson, Roman. "Two Aspects of Language and Two Types of Aphasic Disturbances." In *Language in Literature,* edited by Krystyna Pomorska and Stephen Rudy, 95–114. Cambridge, MA: Belknap/Harvard Univ. Press, 1987.

James, Henry. *The Critical Muse: Selected Literary Criticism.* London: Penguin Books, 1987.

[———]. "*Daniel Deronda.*" *The Nation,* 24 Feb. 1876, 131. Reprinted in *A Century of George Eliot Criticism,* edited by Gordon S. Haight, 92–93. Boston: Houghton Mifflin, 1965.

———. *In the Cage.* 1898. In *Complete Stories, 1892–1898,* 835–923. New York: Library of America, 1996.

———. *Letters.* Edited by Leon Edel. 4 vols. Cambridge, MA: Belknap/Harvard Univ. Press, 1974–84.

[———]. "'The Lifted Veil' and 'Brother Jacob.'" *The Nation* (25 April 1878), 277. Reprinted in *A Century of George Eliot Criticism,* edited by Gordon S. Haight, 130–31. Boston: Houghton Mifflin, 1965.

———. *Partial Portraits.* London: Macmillan, 1888.

———. *The Portrait of a Lady.* 1881. Edited by Geoffrey Moore. London: Penguin Books, 1986.

———. Preface to *What Maisie Knew; In the Cage; The Pupil*, 11:v–xxii. New York ed. New York: Scribner's, 1908.

———. *What Maisie Knew*. 1897. London: Penguin Books, 1985.

Jameson, Fredric. "Cognitive Mapping." In *Marxism and the Interpretation of Culture*, ed. Cary Nelson and Lawrence Grossberg, 347–57. Urbana: Univ. of Illinois Press, 1988.

———. "Modernism and Imperialism." In *Nationalism, Colonialism, and Literature*, 43–66. Minneapolis: Univ. of Minnesota Press, 1990.

Jarrell, Randall. Introduction to *The English in England: Short Stories by Rudyard Kipling*, v–xv. 1963. Gloucester, UK: Peter Smith, 1972.

Jeffrey, Ian. *Photography: A Concise History*. New York: Oxford Univ. Press, 1981.

Jepsen, Thomas C. *My Sisters Telegraphic: Women in the Telegraph Office, 1846–1950*. Athens: Ohio Univ. Press, 2000.

John, Richard R. *Spreading the News: The American Postal System from Franklin to Morse*. Cambridge, MA: Harvard Univ. Press, 1995.

[Johnston, William John, ed.] *Lightning Flashes and Electric Dashes: A Volume of Choice Telegraphic Literature, Humor, Fun, Wit and Wisdom*. New York: Johnston, 1877.

Jolly, W. P. *Marconi*. London: Constable, 1972.

Jones, Ernest. *The Life and Works of Sigmund Freud*. 3 vols. New York: Basic Books, 1953–57.

Kaplan, Carla. "Girl Talk: *Jane Eyre* and the Romance of Women's Narration." *Novel* 30 (1996): 5–31.

Kearns, Katherine. *Nineteenth-Century Literary Realism: Through the Looking-Glass*. Cambridge: Cambridge Univ. Press, 1996.

Keats, John. "The Eve of St. Agnes." 1820. In *The Poems of John Keats*, edited by Jack Stillinger, 299–318. Cambridge, MA: Belknap/Harvard Univ. Press, 1978.

———. *The Letters of John Keats, 1814–1821*. Edited by Hyder Edward Rollins. 2 vols. Cambridge, MA: Harvard Univ. Press, 1958.

Keep, Christopher. "Blinded by the Type: Gender and Information Technology at the Turn of the Century." *Nineteenth-Century Contexts* 23 (2001): 149–73.

———. "The Cultural Work of the Typewriter-Girl." *Victorian Studies* 40 (1997): 401–26.

———. "Exhibiting the Telegraph Girl." Paper presented at the annual convention of the Modern Language Association, New Orleans, 30 December 2001.

Keirstead, Christopher M. "Going Postal: Mail and Mass Culture in *Bleak House*." *Nineteenth-Century Studies* 17 (2003): 91–106.

Kendrick, Walter M. *The Novel-Machine: The Theory and Fiction of Anthony Trollope*. Baltimore: Johns Hopkins Univ. Press, 1980.

Kern, Stephen. *The Culture of Time and Space, 1880–1920*. Cambridge, MA: Harvard Univ. Press, 1983.

Levine, George. *Dying to Know: Scientific Epistemology and Narrative in Victorian England.* Chicago: Univ. of Chicago Press, 2002.

———. "George Eliot's Hypothesis of Reality." *Nineteenth-Century Fiction* 35 (1980): 1–28.

———. *The Realistic Imagination: English Fiction from Frankenstein to Lady Chatterley.* Chicago: Univ. of Chicago Press, 1981.

Levinson, Paul. *The Soft Edge: A Natural History and Future of the Information Revolution.* London: Routledge, 1997.

Lévi-Strauss, Claude. *Structural Anthropology.* Translated by Claire Jacobson and Brooke Grundfest Schoepf. New York: Basic Books, 1963.

[Lewes, Charles Lee]. "Freaks of the Telegraph." *Blackwood's Magazine* 129 (1881): 468–78.

Lewes, George Henry. "Dickens in Relation to Criticism." *Fortnightly Review* 17 (1872): 141–54.

———. *The Physical Basis of Mind.* Ser. 2 of *Problems of Life and Mind.* Boston: Houghton, 1877.

———. *The Physiology of Common Life.* 2 vols. Edinburgh and London: Blackwood, 1859–60.

———. *The Study of Psychology: Its Object, Scope, and Method.* Ser. 3, vol. 1 of *Problems of Life and Mind.* Boston: Houghton, 1879.

Lewis, Jane E. "Women Clerical Workers in the Late Nineteenth and Early Twentieth Centuries." In *The White-Blouse Revolution: Female Office Workers since 1870,* edited by Gregory Anderson, 27–47. Manchester, UK: Manchester Univ. Press, 1988.

Linstone, Harold A., with Ian I. Mitroff. *The Challenge of the Twenty-first Century: Managing Technology and Ourselves in a Shrinking World.* Albany: State Univ. of New York Press, 1994.

Lochte, Robert Henry. "Invention and Innovation of Early Radio Technology." *Journal of Radio Studies* 7 (2000): 93–116.

Lodge, Oliver. *Continuity: The Presidential Address to the British Association, Birmingham 1913.* London: Dent, 1913.

———. *Ether and Reality: A Series of Discourses on the Many Functions of the Ether of Space.* 1925. London: Hodder and Stoughton, 1930.

———. *The Ether of Space.* New York: Harper, 1909.

———. *Modern Views of Electricity.* London: Macmillan, 1889.

———. *My Philosophy: Representing My Views on the Many Functions of the Ether of Space.* London: Benn, 1933.

Lohrli, Anne. *Household Words: A Weekly Journal, 1850–59, Conducted by Charles Dickens.* Toronto: Univ. of Toronto Press, 1973.

Lowe, Graham S. *Women in the Administrative Revolution: The Feminization of Clerical Work.* Toronto: Univ. of Toronto Press, 1987.

Luckhurst, Roger. *The Invention of Telepathy, 1870–1901.* Oxford: Oxford Univ. Press, 2002.

Luhmann, Niklas. *The Reality of the Mass Media.* Trans. Kathleen Cross. Stanford, CA: Stanford Univ. Press, 2000.

Lukács, Georg. *The Historical Novel.* 1937. Translated by Hannah and Stanley Mitchell. Lincoln: Univ. of Nebraska Press, 1983.

———. "Narrate or Describe?" 1936. In *Writer and Critic and Other Essays,* edited and translated by Arthur Kahn, 110–48. London: Merlin, 1970.

———. "Realism in the Balance." 1938. Translated by Rodney Livingstone. In *Aesthetics and Politics,* by Theodor Adorno, Walter Benjamin, Ernst Bloch, Bertolt Brecht, and Georg Lukács, 28–59. London: Verso, 1980.

Macaulay, Thomas Babington. *The History of England from the Accession of James the Second.* 1848–61. Edited by Charles Harding Firth. 6 vols. London: Macmillan, 1913.

———. *The Letters of Thomas Babington Macaulay.* Edited by Thomas Pinney. 6 vols. Cambridge: Cambridge Univ. Press, 1974–81.

Mackay, James. A. *Telegraphic Codes of the British Isles, 1870–1924.* Dumfries, UK: n.p., 1981.

Marconi, Degna. *My Father, Marconi.* London: Frederick Miller, 1962.

Marien, Mary Warner. *Photography: A Cultural History.* New York: Abrams, 2002.

Marsden, Ben, and Crosbie Smith. *Engineering Empires: A Cultural History of Technology in Nineteenth-Century Britain.* Basingstoke, UK: Palgrave, 2005.

Marsh, Joss Lutz. "Inimitable Double Vision: Dickens, *Little Dorrit*, Photography, Film." *Dickens Studies Annual* 22 (1993): 239–82.

Martin, Henri-Jean. *The History and Power of Writing.* 1988. Translated by Lydia G. Cochrane. Chicago: Univ. of Chicago Press, 1994.

Marvin, Carolyn. *When Old Technologies Were New: Thinking About Electric Communication in the Nineteenth Century.* New York: Oxford Univ. Press, 1988.

Matheson, Donald. "The Birth of News Discourse: Changes in News Language in British Newspapers, 1880–1930." *Media, Culture, and Society* 22 (2000): 557–73.

Mattelart, Armand. *Networking the World, 1794–2000.* 1996. Translated by Liz Carey-Libbrecht and James A. Cohen. Minneapolis: Univ. of Minnesota Press, 2000.

Matthews, Brander. "'I've Got It All in My Head.'" 1917. In *Kipling: Interviews and Recollections,* edited by Harold Orel, 1:139–41. 2 vols. Totowa, NJ: Barnes & Noble, 1983.

Matus, Jill. "Trauma, Memory, and Railway Disaster: The Dickensian Connection." *Victorian Studies* 43 (2001): 413–36.

Maxwell, James Clerk. "On Governors." 1868. In *The Scientific Letters and Papers of James Clerk Maxwell,* edited by P. M. Harman, 2:105–20. 3 vols. Cambridge: Cambridge Univ. Press, 1990–2002.

McCormack, Kathleen. "George Eliot, Julia Cameron, and William Henry Fox Talbot: Photography and *Daniel Deronda.*" *Word & Image* 12 (1996): 175–79.

McLuhan, Marshall. *The Gutenberg Galaxy: The Making of Typographic Man.* 1962. Toronto: Univ. of Toronto Press, 1965.

———. *Understanding Media: The Extensions of Man.* 1964. Cambridge, MA: MIT Press, 1994.

McLuhan, Marshall, and Quentin Fiore. *The Medium Is the Massage.* New York: Bantam Books, 1967.

McLuhan, Marshall, and Eric McLuhan. *Laws of Media: The New Science.* Toronto: Univ. of Toronto Press, 1988.

Mengel, Ewald. "The Structure and Meaning of Dickens's 'The Signalman.'" *Studies in Short Fiction* 20 (1983): 271–80.

Menke, Richard. "Fiction as Vivisection: G. H. Lewes and George Eliot." *ELH* 67 (2000): 617–53.

———. "'Framed and Wired': Teaching 'In the Cage' at the Intersection of Literature and Media." *The Henry James Review* 25 (2004): 33–43.

———. "Media in America, 1881: Garfield, Guiteau, Bell, Whitman." *Critical Inquiry* 31 (2005): 638–64.

———. "Telegraphic Realism: Henry James's *In the Cage.*" *PMLA* 115 (2000): 975–90.

"The Mermaid's Last New Song." *Punch* 19 (1850): 116.

Miller, D. A. *The Novel and the Police.* Berkeley and Los Angeles: Univ. of California Press, 1988.

Miller, J. Hillis. *The Ethics of Reading: Kant, de Man, Eliot, Trollope, James, and Benjamin.* New York: Columbia Univ. Press, 1987.

———. Introduction to *Bleak House,* by Charles Dickens, edited by Norman Page, 11–34. Harmondsworth, UK: Penguin Books, 1971.

Mitchell, B. R. *British Historical Statistics.* Cambridge: Cambridge Univ. Press, 1988.

Montefiore, Janet. "Day and Night in Kipling." 1978. In *Arguments of Heart and Mind: Selected Essays, 1977–2000,* 112–23. Manchester, UK: Manchester Univ. Press, 2002.

Montefiore, Sidney. *Electric Telegraph Reform: Being a Plan for the Combination of the Telegraph with the Post-Office in the United Kingdom.* Melbourne: Tait, 1866.

Moody, Andrew J. "'The Harmless Pleasure of Knowing': Privacy in the Telegraph Office and Henry James's 'In the Cage.'" *The Henry James Review* 16 (1995): 53–65.

Moody, Ellen. "Partly Told in Letters." *Trollopiana* 48 (February 2000): 4–31.

Moon, Heath. "More Royalist Than the King: The Governess, the Telegraphist, and Mrs. Gracedew." *Criticism* 24 (1982): 16–35.

"The Moral Influence of the Telegraph." *Scientific American* 15 October 1881, 240.

Morris, Pam. *Imagining Inclusive Society in Nineteenth-Century Novels: The Code of Sincerity in the Public Sphere*. Baltimore: Johns Hopkins Univ. Press, 2004.

Morus, Iwan Rhys. "The Electric Ariel: Telegraphy and Commercial Culture in Early Victorian England." *Victorian Studies* 39 (1996): 339–78.

———. "'The Nervous System of Britain': Space, Time, and the Electric Telegraph in the Victorian Age." *British Journal for the History of Science* 22 (2000): 455–75.

"Mr. Fox Talbot's New Discovery: Photoglyphic Engravings." *The Photographic News: A Weekly Record of the Progress of Photography* (24 September 1858), 25–26.

Mudford, Peter. Introduction to *Silas Marner; The Lifted Veil; Brother Jacob*, by George Eliot, edited by Peter Mudford, xix–xxxii. London: Everyman/Dent, 1996.

Muir, Douglas N. *Postal Reform and the Penny Black: A New Appreciation*. London: National Postal Museum, 1990.

Nagel, Thomas. *The View from Nowhere*. New York: Oxford Univ. Press, 1986.

Negroponte, Nicholas. *Being Digital*. New York: Knopf, 1995.

Newhall, Beaumont. Introduction to Talbot, *Pencil of Nature*, n. pag.

Night Mail. Directed by Basil Wright and Henry Watt. General Post Office Film Unit, 1936.

Nixon, Nicola. "The Reading Gaol of Henry James's *In the Cage*." *ELH* 66 (1999): 179–201.

Norrman, Ralf. "The Intercepted Telegram Plot in Henry James's 'In the Cage.'" *Notes and Queries*, n.s., 24 (1977): 425–27.

Novak, Daniel. "A Model Jew: 'Literary Photographs' and the Jewish Body in *Daniel Deronda*." *Representations* 85 (Winter 2004): 58–97.

Nunberg, Geoffrey. "Farewell to the Information Age." In *The Future of the Book*, edited by Geoffrey Nunberg, 103–38. Berkeley and Los Angeles: Univ. of California Press, 1996.

Ong, Walter. *Orality and Literacy: The Technologizing of the Word*. London: Routledge, 1982.

Orwell, George. "Charles Dickens." In *Inside the Whale and Other Essays*, 9–85. London: Victor Gollancz, 1940.

Ostroff, Eugene. "The Photomechanical Process." In *Henry Fox Talbot: Selected Texts and Bibliography*, edited by Mike Weaver, 125–30. Boston: Hall, 1993; Oxford: Clio, 1992.

Otis, Laura. *Networking: Communicating with Bodies and Machines in the Nineteenth Century*. Ann Arbor: Univ. of Michigan Press, 2001.

———. "The Other End of the Wire: Uncertainties of Organic and Telegraphic Communication." *Configurations* 9 (2001): 181–206.

"Our Photoglyphic Transparencies." *The Photographic News: A Weekly Record of the Progress of Photography* (12 Nov. 1858), 109.

"Our Postal Telegraphs." *The Engineer* (18 Dec. 1891), 491–513.

Patten, Robert L. *Charles Dickens and His Publishers*. Oxford: Clarendon Press, 1978.

Pearson, David. "'The Letter Killeth': Epistolary Purposes and Techniques in *Sir Harry Hotspur of Humblethwaite*." *Nineteenth-Century Fiction* 37 (1982): 396–418.

Perry, C. R. "The Rise and Fall of Government Telegraphy in Britain." *Business and Economic History* 26 (1977): 416–25.

———. *The Victorian Post Office: The Growth of a Bureaucracy*. Woodbridge, UK: Royal Historical Society/Boydell, 1992.

Peters, John Durham. *Speaking into the Air: A History of the Idea of Communication*. Chicago: Univ. of Chicago Press, 1999.

Pettit, Claire. *Patent Inventions: Intellectual Property and the Victorian Novel*. Oxford: Oxford Univ. Press, 2004.

"Photographic Print." *All the Year Round* 1 (11 June 1859): 162–64.

Picker, John M. *Victorian Soundscapes*. Oxford: Oxford Univ. Press, 2003.

Pierce, John R. *An Introduction to Information Theory: Symbols, Signals, and Noise*. 2nd ed. New York: Dover, 1980.

Polhemus, Robert M. *The Changing World of Anthony Trollope*. Berkeley and Los Angeles: Univ. of California Press, 1968.

Poovey, Mary. *A History of the Modern Fact: Problems of Knowledge in the History of Wealth and Society*. Chicago: Univ. of Chicago Press, 1998.

———. *Making a Social Body: British Cultural Formation, 1830–1864*. Chicago: Univ. of Chicago Press, 1995.

Pope, Franklin Leonard. *Modern Practice of the Electric Telegraph*. 15th ed. New York: Van Nostrand, 1899.

Pope, Norris. "Dickens's 'The Signalman' and Information Problems in the Railway Age." *Technology and Culture* 42 (2001): 436–61.

Porter, G. R. *The Progress of the Nation in Its Various Social and Economic Relations, from the Beginning of the Nineteenth Century*. New ed. London: Murray, 1847.

Price, Leah. *The Anthology and the Rise of the Novel, from Richardson to George Eliot*. Cambridge: Cambridge Univ. Press, 2000.

Progress, Peter (pseud.). *The Electric Telegraph*. London: R. Yorke Clarke, 1847.

Rauch, Alan. *Useful Knowledge: The Victorians, Morality, and the March of Intellect*. Durham, NC: Duke Univ. Press, 2001.

Read, Donald. *The Power of News: The History of Reuters*. 2nd ed. Oxford: Oxford Univ. Press, 1999.

Reddy, Michael J. "The Conduit Metaphor." In *Metaphor and Thought*, edited by Andrew Ortony, 284–324. Cambridge: Cambridge Univ. Press, 1979.

Reid, James D. *The Telegraph in America: Its Founders, Promoters, and Noted Men*. New York: Derby, 1879.

Reynolds, Susan. "'The Most Splendid City in Germany?': George Eliot and Prague." *Contemporary Review* 282 (April 2003): 228–31.

Richards, Thomas. *The Imperial Archive: Knowledge and the Fantasy of Empire.* London: Verso, 1993.

Richardson, Rowley W. C. *Surbiton: Thirty-Two Years of Local Self-Government, 1855–1887.* Surbiton, UK: Bull, 1888.

Riffaterre, Michael. *Fictional Truth.* Baltimore: Johns Hopkins Univ. Press, 1990.

Rignall, J. M. "Dickens and the Catastrophic Continuum of History in *A Tale of Two Cities.*" *ELH* 51 (1984): 575–87.

Robinson, Howard. *The British Post Office: A History.* Princeton, NJ: Princeton Univ. Press, 1948. Westport, CT: Greenwood, 1970.

"The Romance of the Electric Telegraph." *New Monthly Magazine,* n.s., 89 (1850): 296–307.

Ronalds, Francis. *Descriptions of an Electrical Telegraph, and of Some Other Electrical Apparatus.* London: Hunter, 1823.

Rothfield, Lawrence. *Vital Signs: Medical Realism in Nineteenth-Century Fiction.* Princeton, NJ: Princeton Univ. Press, 1992.

Rowe, John Carlos. *The Other Henry James.* Durham, NC: Duke Univ. Press, 1998.

Rufo, Kenneth. "Ghosts in the Medium: The Haunting of Heidegger's Technological Question." *EME: Explorations in Media Ecology* 4 (2005): 21–48.

Sabine, Robert. *The History and Progress of the Electric Telegraph.* 2nd ed., with additions. London: Virtue, 1869.

Sanders, Andrew. *Charles Dickens: Resurrectionist.* New York: St. Martins, 1982.

Savoy, Eric. "'In the Cage' and the Queer Effects of Gay History." *Novel* 28 (1995): 284–307.

Schaffer, Simon. "Babbage's Intelligence by Simon Schaffer." [Expanded version of "Babbage's Intelligence: Calculating Engines and the Factory System."] 1998–99. The Hypermedia Research Centre, University of Westminster. http://www.hrc.wmin.ac.uk/theory-babbagesintelligence.html.

———. "Babbage's Intelligence: Calculating Engines and the Factory System." *Critical Inquiry* 21 (1994): 203–27.

Schivelbusch, Wolfgang. *The Railway Journey: Trains and Travel in the Nineteenth Century.* 1978. Translated by Anselm Hollo. Oxford: Blackwell, 1980.

Schor, Hilary M. *Dickens and the Daughter of the House.* Cambridge: Cambridge Univ. Press, 1999.

———. *Scheherezade in the Marketplace: Elizabeth Gaskell and the Victorian Novel.* New York: Oxford Univ. Press, 1992.

———. "The Stupidest Novel in London: Thomas Carlyle and the Sickness of Victorian Fiction." *Carlyle Studies Annual* 16 (1996): 117–31.

Schudson, Michael. *Discovering the News: A Social History of American Newspapers.* New York: Basic Books, 1978.

———. "The Objectivity Norm in American Journalism." *Journalism* 2 (2001): 149–70.

———. *The Power of News.* Cambridge, MA: Harvard Univ. Press, 1995.

Sconce, Jeffrey. *Haunted Media: Electronic Presence from Telegraphy to Television*. Durham, NC: Duke Univ. Press, 2000.

Scott, Walter. *Redgauntlet*. 1824. Edited by Kathryn Sutherland. Oxford: World's Classics/Oxford Univ. Press, 1985.

Secord, James A. *Victorian Sensation: The Extraordinary Publication, Reception, and Secret Authorship of "Vestiges of the Natural History of Creation."* Chicago: Univ. of Chicago Press, 2000.

Seed, David. "Mystery in Everyday Things: Charles Dickens' 'Signalman.'" *Criticism* 23 (1981): 42–57.

Seltzer, Mark. *Bodies and Machines*. New York: Routledge, 1992.

———. "The Graphic Unconscious: A Response." *New Literary History* 26 (1995): 21–28.

Seymour-Smith, Martin. *Rudyard Kipling*. London: Macdonald/Queen Anne, 1989.

Shaffner, Taliaferro P. *The Telegraph Manual: A Complete History and Description of the Semaphoric, Electric and Magnetic Telegraphs of Europe, Asia, Africa, and America*. New York: Pudney, 1859.

Shannon, C. E. "A Mathematical Theory of Communication." *Bell System Technical Journal* 27 (1948): 379–423, 623–56.

Shelley, Mary. *Frankenstein*. 1818. Edited by J. Paul Hunter. New York: Norton, 1996.

Shiers, George. Introduction to *The Electric Telegraph: An Historical Anthology*, edited by George Shiers, n. pag. New York: Arno, 1977.

Shuman, Cathy. *Pedagogical Economies: The Examination and the Victorian Literary Man*. Stanford, CA: Stanford Univ. Press, 2000.

Siegert, Bernhard. *Relays: Literature as an Epoch of the Postal System*. 1993. Translated by Kevin Repp. Stanford, CA: Stanford Univ. Press, 1999.

Silverman, Kenneth. *Lightning Man: The Accursed Life of Samuel F. B. Morse*. New York: Knopf, 2003.

Siskin, Clifford. *The Work of Writing: Literature and Social Change in Britain, 1700–1830*. Baltimore: Johns Hopkins Univ. Press, 1998.

Slater, Michael. *The Composition and Monthly Publication of "Nicholas Nickleby."* Menston, UK: Scolar, 1972.

Smee, Alfred. 1849. *Principles of the Human Mind, Deduced from Physical Laws, Together with a Lecture on Electro-Biology, or, The Voltaic Mechanism of Man*. South Bend, IN: And Books, 1980.

Smiles, Samuel. *The Life of George Stephenson, Railway Engineer*. 4th ed. London: Murray, 1857.

———. Preface to *The Life of George Stephenson and of His Son Robert Stephenson*, iii–xxxi. New York: Harper, 1868.

Smith, Harold. *The Society for the Diffusion of Useful Knowledge, 1826–1846: A Social and Bibliographical Evaluation*. Halifax, Nova Scotia: Dalhousie Univ. Libraries and Dalhousie Univ. School of Library Service, 1974.

Smyth, Eleanor C. *Sir Rowland Hill: The Story of a Great Reform, Told by His Daughter.* London: Unwin, 1907.

Solymar, Laszlo. *Getting the Message: A History of Communications.* Oxford: Oxford Univ. Press, 1999.

"... --- ... . ---. (SOS, RIP)." *Economist.* North American ed. 23 January 1999, 71–73.

Spufford, Francis. "The Difference Engine and *The Difference Engine.*" In Spufford and Uglow, *Cultural Babbage,* 266–90.

Spufford, Francis, and Jenny Uglow, eds. *Cultural Babbage: Technology, Time, and Invention.* London: Faber, 1996.

Staff, Frank. *The Penny Post, 1680–1918.* London: Lutterworth, 1964.

Stahl, John Daniel. "The Source and Significance of the Revenant in Dickens's 'The Signal-Man.'" *Dickens Studies Newsletter* 11 (1980): 98–101.

Standage, Tom. *The Victorian Internet: The Remarkable Story of the Telegraph and the Nineteenth Century's Online Pioneers.* London: Weidenfield & Nicolson, 1998.

Stephen, James Fitzjames. "The License of Modern Novelists." *Edinburgh Review* 106 (July 1857): 124–56.

Stephens, Mitchell. *A History of News: From the Drum to the Satellite.* New York: Viking, 1988.

Sterne, Jonathan. *The Audible Past: Cultural Origins of Sound Reproduction.* Durham, NC: Duke Univ. Press, 2003.

Sternlieb, Lisa. "*Jane Eyre*: 'Hazarding Confidences.'" *Nineteenth-Century Literature* 53 (1999): 452–79.

Stevens, Hugh. "Queer Henry In the Cage." In *The Cambridge Companion to Henry James,* edited by Jonathan Freedman, 120–38. Cambridge: Cambridge Univ. Press, 1998.

Stewart, Garrett. *Dear Reader: The Conscripted Audience in Nineteenth-Century British Fiction.* Baltimore: Johns Hopkins Univ. Press, 1996.

———. *Death Sentences: Styles of Dying in British Fiction.* Cambridge, MA: Harvard Univ. Press, 1984.

Stillinger, Jack. "The Hoodwinking of Madeline: Skepticism in 'The Eve of St. Agnes.'" 1961. In *The Hoodwinking of Madeline and Other Essays on Keats's Poems,* 67–93. Urbana: Univ. of Illinois Press, 1971.

———. *Reading "The Eve of St. Agnes": The Multiples of Complex Literary Transaction.* New York: Oxford Univ. Press, 1999.

Stoker, Bram. *Dracula.* 1897. Edited by A. N. Wilson. Oxford: World's Classics/ Oxford Univ. Press, 1983.

Stone, Harry. Introduction to *The Uncollected Writings of Charles Dickens, Household Words,* 1850–59, by Charles Dickens, edited by Harry Stone, 1:3–68. 2 vols. Bloomington: Indiana Univ. Press, 1968; London: Allen Lane/Penguin Books, 1969.

Stubbs, Katherine. "Telegraphy's Corporeal Fictions." In Gitelman and Pingree, *New Media*, 91–111.

Super, R. H. *Trollope at the Post Office*. Ann Arbor: Univ. of Michigan Press, 1981.

Sutherland, John. *Is Heathcliff a Murderer? Great Puzzles in Nineteenth-Century Fiction*. Oxford: World's Classics/Oxford Univ. Press, 1996.

———. *Victorian Fiction: Writers, Publishers, Readers*. 1995. Basingstoke, UK: Palgrave Macmillan, 2006.

Swade, Doron. "'It Will Not Slice a Pineapple': Babbage, Miracles, and Machines." In Spufford and Uglow, *Cultural Babbage*, 34–51.

Swann, Charles. "Déjà Vu, Déjà Lu: 'The Lifted Veil' as an Experiment in Art." *Literature and History*, 1st ser., 5 (1979): 40–57.

"Syntonic Wireless Telegraphy." *Electrical Review* 38 (1901): 820.

"Syntonic Wireless Telegraphy." *The Engineering Magazine* 21 (1901): 595–98.

Talbot, William Henry Fox. *Henry Fox Talbot: Selected Texts and Bibliography*. Edited by Mike Weaver. Boston: Hall, 1993; Oxford: Clio, 1992.

———. *The Pencil of Nature*. 1844–46. Facsimile reprint. New York: Da Capo, 1969.

Tambling, Jeremy. *Dickens, Violence, and the Modern State: Dreams of the Scaffold*. Basingstoke, UK: Macmillan; New York: St. Martin's, 1995.

———. "*Middlemarch*, Realism, and the Birth of the Clinic." *ELH* 57 (1990): 939–60.

Thomas, Katie-Louise. "A Queer Job for a Girl: Women Postal Workers, Civic Duty, and Sexuality, 1870–80." In *In a Queer Place: Sexuality and Belonging in British and European Contexts*, edited by Kate Chedgzoy, Emma Francis, and Murray Pratt, 50–70. Aldershot, UK: Ashgate, 2002.

Thorburn, David, and Henry Jenkins. "Introduction: Towards an Aesthetics of Transition." In *Rethinking Media Change: The Aesthetics of Transition*, edited by David Thorburn and Henry Jenkins, 1–16. Cambridge, MA: MIT Press, 2003.

Thurschwell, Pamela. *Literature, Technology, and Magical Thinking, 1880–1920*. Cambridge: Cambridge Univ. Press, 2001.

Tompkins, J. M. S. *The Art of Rudyard Kipling*. London: Methuen, 1959.

Trilling, Lionel. "Kipling." 1943. In *The Liberal Imagination: Essays on Literature and Society*, 114–24. Garden City, NY: Anchor/Doubleday, 1957.

Trollope, Anthony. *An Autobiography*. 1883. Edited by Michael Sadleir and Frederick Page. Oxford: World's Classics/Oxford Univ. Press, 1989.

———. *John Caldigate*. 1878–79. Edited by N. John Hall. Oxford: World's Classics/Oxford Univ. Press, 1993.

———. *The Letters of Anthony Trollope*. Edited by N. John Hall. 2 vols. Stanford, CA: Stanford Univ. Press, 1983.

———. *Marion Fay*. 1881–82. Edited by Geoffrey Harvey. Oxford: World's Classics/Oxford Univ. Press, 1992.

———. *The New Zealander*. Edited by N. John Hall. Oxford: Clarendon Press, 1972.

———. "The Telegraph Girl." 1877. In *Later Short Stories*, edited by John Sutherland, 354–85. Oxford: World's Classics/Oxford Univ. Press, 1995.

———. *The Three Clerks*. 1858. Edited by Graham Handley. Oxford: World's Classics/Oxford Univ. Press, 1989.

———. "The Young Women at the Telegraph Office." 1877. In *Miscellaneous Essays and Reviews*, n. pag. New York: Arno, 1981.

Trotter, David. *Circulation: Defoe, Dickens, and the Economies of the Novel*. Basingstoke, UK: Macmillan, 1988.

Troup, George. "Literary Register: Jane Eyre." Rev. of *Jane Eyre: An Autobiography*, by Currer Bell [Charlotte Brontë]. *Tait's Edinburgh Magazine*, n.s., 15 (May 1848): 346–48.

Turnbull, Laurence. *Lectures on the Electro-Magnetic Telegraph, with an Historical Account of Its Rise and Progress*. Philadelphia: Barnard, 1852.

Underwood, Ben. "Living Textually: George Eliot's 'The Lifted Veil' as an Experiment on Readers." Unpublished essay, 2004.

Vale, Edmund. *The Mail-Coach Men of the Late Eighteenth Century*. London: Cassell, 1960.

Walker, Charles V. *Electric Telegraph Manipulation: Being the Theory and Plain Instructions in the Art of Transmitting Signals to Distant Places, As Practised in England*. London: George Knight, 1850.

Walker, George. *Haste, Post, Haste! Postmen and Post-roads through the Ages*. London: Harrap, 1938.

Wallace, Alfred Russel. *The Wonderful Century: Its Successes and Its Failures*. London: Swan Sonnenschein, 1898.

Ward, John. "William Henry Fox Talbot." In *Printed Light: The Scientific Art of William Henry Fox Talbot and David Octavius Hill with Robert Adamson*. By John Ward and Sara Stevenson, 9–27. Edinburgh: Her Majesty's Stationery Office, 1986.

Wark, McKenzie. "All That Is Solid Melts into Airwaves." *Angelaki* 4.2 (September 1999): 19–23.

———. "Telegram from Nowhere." In *Mutations*, edited by Rem Koolhaas, Stefano Boeri, Sanford Kwinter, Nadia Tazi, and Hans-Ulrich Obrist, 30–39. Barcelona: Actar; Bordeaux: Arc en rêve centre d'architecture, 2000.

Watson, Nicola J. *Revolution and the Form of the British Novel, 1790–1825: Intercepted Letters, Interrupted Seductions*. Oxford: Clarendon Press, 1994.

Waverton, William. *The People's Letter Bag and Penny Post Companion*. 2nd ed. London: Darton and Clark, [1840].

Wears, T. Martin. *The History of the Mulready Envelope*. Bury St. Edmund's, UK: Nunn/Stamp Collectors' Journal, 1886.

Weightman, Gavin. *Signor Marconi's Magic Box*. Cambridge, MA: Da Capo Press, 2003.

Welsh, Alexander. *George Eliot and Blackmail*. Cambridge, MA: Harvard Univ. Press, 1985.

[West, Charles?]. *The Story of My Life, by the Submarine Telegraph*. London: West, 1859.

West, Peter H. "'By Magnetic Telegraph': The Production of Authenticity in the Mexican War." Paper presented at the annual convention of the Modern Language Association, New York, 30 December 2002.

Wheeler, Michael. *Death and the Future Life in Victorian Literature and Theology*. Cambridge: Cambridge Univ. Press, 1990.

Wicke, Jennifer. *Advertising Fictions: Literature, Advertisement, and Social Reading*. New York: Columbia Univ. Press, 1988.

———. "Henry James's Second Wave." *The Henry James Review* 10 (1989): 146–51.

Wilde, Oscar. "De Profundis (Epistola: In Carcere et Vinculis)." 1905/1949. In *De Profundis and Other Writings*, 97–210. London: Penguin Books, 1986.

———. "A Few Maxims for the Instruction of the Over-Educated." 1894. In *Oscar Wilde*, 571–72. Oxford Authors. Oxford: Oxford Univ. Press, 1989.

———. Preface to *The Picture of Dorian Gray*. 1891. In *Oscar Wilde*, 48. Oxford Authors. Oxford: Oxford Univ. Press, 1989.

Williams, Ioan. *The Realist Novel in England: A Study in Development*. London: Macmillan, 1974; Pittsburgh: Univ. of Pittsburgh Press, 1975.

Williams, Raymond. *Keywords: A Vocabulary of Culture and Society*. Rev. ed. London: Fontana, 1988.

Wilson, Angus. *The Strange Ride of Rudyard Kipling*. New York: Viking, 1977.

Wilson, Edmund. "The Kipling That Nobody Read." 1941. In *The Wound and the Bow*, 105–81. New York: Oxford Univ. Press, 1947.

Wilson, George. *Electricity and the Electric Telegraph: Together with the Chemistry of the Stars*. London: Longman, 1852.

[———]. "The Electric Telegraph." *Edinburgh Review* 90 (Oct. 1849): 434–72.

———. *The Progress of the Telegraph, Being the Introductory Lecture on Technology for 1858–59*. Cambridge: Macmillan, 1859.

———. *What Is Technology? An Inaugural Lecture Delivered at the University of Edinburgh on November 7, 1855*. Edinburgh: Sutherland, 1855.

Winter, Alison. *Mesmerized: Powers of Mind in Victorian Britain*. Chicago: Univ. of Chicago Press, 1998.

Wolfreys, Julian. *Victorian Hauntings: Spectrality, Gothic, the Uncanny and Literature*. New York: Palgrave, 2002.

Wormald, Mark. "Microscopy and Semiotic in *Middlemarch*." *Nineteenth-Century Literature* 50 (1996): 501–24.

Wozniak, Robert H. *Mind and Body: René Descartes to William James*. Washington, DC: National Library of Medicine/American Psychological Association, 1992.

[Wynter, Andrew]. "The Electric Telegraph." *Quarterly Review* 95 (June 1854): 118–64.

[———]. "The Post-Office." *Fraser's Magazine* 41 (February 1850): 224–32.

[———]. "Who Is Mr. Reuter?" *Once a Week* 4 (23 February 1861): 243–46.

Yeazell, Ruth Bernard. "More True Than Real: Jane Eyre's 'Mysterious Summons.'" *Nineteenth-Century Fiction* 29 (1974): 127–43.

———. "Why Political Novels Have Heroines: *Sybil, Mary Barton*, and *Felix Holt*." *Novel* 18 (1985): 126–44.

Young, Paul. "Media on Display: A Telegraphic History of American Cinema." In Gitelman and Pingree, *New Media*, 229–64.

Zimmeck, Meta. "Jobs for the Girls: The Expansion of Clerical Work for Women, 1850–1914." In *Unequal Opportunities: Women's Employment in England, 1800–1918*, edited by Angela V. John, 153–77. London: Blackwell, 1986.

Index

Adam Bede (Eliot), 139, 160
advertising, 34–35, 227, 244
afterimage, 158
Allen, Grant, 188
Alter, Robert, 269n11
Anderson, Benedict, 6, 266n61
Annan, Noel, 234
apRoberts, Ruth, 62
Armstrong, Carol, 142
Armstrong, Nancy, 137, 144, 265n50
Auden, W. H., 52
Autobiography (Trollope), 60–61, 64, 66, 186–87, 262n89
automata, 117–18
Ayrton, William, 241

Babbage, Charles: and Dickens, 25, 76; *Economy of Machinery and Manufactures*, 39; *Ninth Bridgewater Treatise*; 24–25, 258n70; and postal system, 37
Bagehot, Walter, 15
Bakhtin, Mikhail, 95
Baldridge, Cates, 270n33
Ballantyne, R. M.: *The Battery and the Boiler*, 176, 178–79; *Post Haste*, 175–80
Barthes, Roland, 20, 146, 169, 250, 258n61
Battery and the Boiler (Ballantyne), 176, 178–79
Beer, Gillian, 235
Bell, Alexander Graham, 82, 187
Beniger, James, 20, 28, 38
Benjamin, Walter, 1, 13, 244
Bentham, Jeremy, 25
Bernard, Claude, 149, 151–52, 274n56

Birkbeck, George, 39
Bleak House (Dickens), 17, 26, 49, 90
Bodenheimer, Rosemarie, 274n57
body: and the electric telegraph, 76, 82, 88–89, 96, 98, 205, 208, 278n61; flows of, 137, 274n49; gestures of, as communication, 125–26, 129, 168; and information, 130–32, 137, 149, 168, 242, 250; and narration, 113; as network, 15, 66–67, 134–36, 148; and writing, 10–11, 130–32, 149, 152, 156. *See also* nervous system; physiology
Bolter, Jay David, 5, 103–4, 269n3
books as media. *See* print
Boole, George, 23
Booth, Henry, 83
Bowen, John, 50, 269n16
Brand, Stewart, 17, 39
"Bridge over the River Moldau" (Talbot, Clouzard/Soulier), 142–44
Briggs, Asa, 39
Briggs, Charles, 92
broadcast, 213, 223, 244–46. *See also* wireless telegraphy
Brontë, Charlotte, 266n67; *Jane Eyre*, 9, 59, 77–88, 265n50, 266n68, 266nn70–71
Brown, Bill, 258n61
Brown, Hablot Knight ("Phiz"), 45–48, 120
Brown, Monika, 273n19
bureaucracy, 10, 20, 56–58. *See also* civil service; information workers; Post Office

Calculating Engine (Babbage), 24–25
Cameron, Sharon, 201–2
Campbell, Timothy, 282–83n30
Carey, James, 70
Carlyle, Thomas, 24, 108, 114, 258n70; *The French Revolution*, 124–25, 127, 129–30, 271n51; and the postal system, 32–33, 35–36; *Sartor Resartus*, 31–33, 35–36, 66; and Victorian fiction, 31
Carroll, Lewis (Charles Dodgson), 260n37
Caruth, Cathy, 171
Chappe, Claude, 124–25
chronotope, 95
circulation, 20, 66–67, 106, 157. *See also* flow
civil service, 57, 65, 182, 197, 262n92, 263n106. *See also* information workers; Post Office
Clark, Latimer, 137
Clayton, Jay, 51, 256n20, 280n34
Cleere, Eileen, 259n22
Cleveland Street scandal, 204
Coase, R. H., 259n17
Cole, Henry, 34–36, 259n3, 260n36
communication, 10, 12, 27–28, 200; as conduit, 19–20; by gesture, 125–26, 129, 168; history, 62, 72–73; in *In the Cage* (James), 197; in *Jane Eyre* (Brontë), 84–87; in *A Tale of Two Cities* (Dickens), 112–19; in "'Wireless'" (Kipling), 226. *See also* Claude Shannon; *and specific media*
Conrad, Joseph, 194–95
consciousness: in *In the Cage* (James), 201–3, 213; in "The Lifted Veil" (Eliot), 136, 150–51; in *Middlemarch* (Eliot), 157–61; and new media 7, 187–88. *See also* subjectivity
control revolution, 20, 28, 38
Cooke, William Fothergill, 68–69. *See also* electric telegraph
Cranford (Gaskell), 251–54
Crary, Jonathan, 158
Crippen, Hawley Harvey, 73, 264n24
Cruikshank, George, 44–45

Daguerre, Louis, 137
Daily News (ed. Dickens), 1–2
Daly, Nicholas, 284n58
Dames, Nicholas, 270–71n42

Daniel Deronda (Eliot), 159–61
Davis, Lennard, 6
"Deep-Sea Cables" (Kipling), 206
Deleuze, Gilles, 210–11
"De Profundis" (Wilde), 243
De Quincey, Thomas, 110
Dickens, Charles: and Anglo-French telegraph proposal, 1–3, 255n2; and Babbage, 25, 76; *Bleak House*, 17, 26, 49, 90; *Daily News*, 1–2; *Dombey and Son*, 2–3, 258n74; George Eliot critiques, 138–39; first publication, 50; *Hard Times*, 15–16, 18–19, 49, 108; and Rowland Hill, 5, 33, 41, 50; *Household Words*, 47–50, 92, 252; *Little Dorrit*, 41, 90, 138–39; *Nicholas Nickleby*, 34, 45–46, 71; *Pickwick Papers*, 50, 110, 125, 251, 269n16; "Postal Money Orders," 53; and Post Office, 5, 50–53, 269n16; and railway, 2–3, 76–77, 166–72, 251; on Reuter, 97; and serial fiction, 108, 260–61n51; "The Signal-Man," 166–72; *Sketches by Boz*, 71–72, 114; *A Tale of Two Cities*, 16, 90, 105–23, 126–33; on telegraphs, 76, 90–92, 97, 125–26, 164; "Valentine's Day at the Post-Office," 50–53, 261n75
Dobrée, Bonamy, 231
Dombey and Son (Dickens), 2–3, 258n74
Dracula (Stoker), 10, 188, 194
Durkheim, Émile, 234, 239

Eagleton, Terry, 274n57
Early, Julie English, 264n24
Eastlake, Elizabeth, 137, 146
Economy of Machinery and Manufactures (Babbage), 39
electricity, 68, 226–27; history, 136–37; as human, 22–23; as shock, 78, 81, 165; as spirit, 75–76, 80, 165. *See also* electric telegraph; nervous system
electric telegraph, 6, 14, 19, 70, 81, 137; acoustic, 184–87, 205–6, 211–13; Anglo-French, 1–2, 92, 130, 255n2, 267n93; and bodies, 76, 82, 88–89, 96, 98, 205, 208, 278n61; and communication, 70, 74–75; and deterritorialization, 210–11; Dickens and, 1–3, 76, 90–92, 97, 125–26, 164, 255n2; errors, 193–94; Gaskell and, 88–90; history, 68–73, 81, 91–94,

123, 163–64, 180–81, 193–94, 264n4, 264n6, 271n49; as human, 22–23; and information, 75–76, 98, 242; in *In the Cage* (James), 192–95, 197–213; and intimacy, 84, 208, 266n66; and *Jane Eyre* (Brontë), 79–84; and journalism, 1–2, 95–100, 199–200, 268n111; Kipling and, 217–18; law and regulation, 93, 175, 182, 207; G. H. Lewes and, 135–36; in London, 5, 70–71, 163, 181, 194; and lovers, 83–84, 183, 192, 211–12; and narration, 90–92, 95, 173–74, 176, 199, 201, 203–5; needle, 73, 80, 97; and nervous system, 135; and new media, 13; and objectivity, 90, 95–97, 123, 268n111; optimism about, 92–93; and realism, 70–71, 88–95, 161, 175, 183–86, 192–93, 201, 212–15; and textuality, 12, 73–74; and time, 82–84, 265n58, 266n61; transatlantic, 92, 176, 267n91, 270n30; as transmitting thought, 7, 69, 82, 92, 187, 202; as virtual orality, 8, 80, 87. *See also* electricity; information workers; network; wireless telegraphy
Electro-Biology (Smee), 135
Eliot, George (Marian Evans): *Adam Bede*, 139, 160; *Daniel Deronda*, 159–61; on Dickens, 138–39; "The Lifted Veil," 14, 105, 134–35, 137–38, 140–42, 144–56, 158, 161; *Middlemarch*, 15, 157–59; "The Natural History of German Life," 14, 138–39; on photography, 146; and realism, 14, 138–39, 153–55, 160–61; "Silly Novels by Lady Novelists," 14
Eliot, T. S., 220–21, 239
embodiment. *See* body
"English Mail-Coach" (De Quincey), 110
Epperly, Elizabeth, 263n110
Ermarth, Elizabeth, 26, 91, 93, 146, 212
ether, chloric (chloroform), 224
ether, luminiferous, 11, 76, 234, 242
"Eve of St. Agnes" (Keats), 228–230, 232–33, 241–46
Everdell, William, 21

fact: and electric telegraph, 95; in *Hard Times* (Dickens), 15, 18–19, 257n40; in *Household Words* (Dickens), 50; and photography, 146

Favret, Mary, 44
"'Finest Story in the World'" (Kipling), 236–37
Flint, Kate, 149, 274n50
flow: in the body, 137, 274n49; Dickens and, 2, 19, 52, 112, 261n75, 269n13; of electricity, 75–76, 80; and ether, 242; of information, 10, 19–21, 75–76, 206, 242, 261n75; of letters, 52; in "The Lifted Veil" (Eliot), 142, 149–51; and mesmerism, 80; of reality, 137, 144–45; of telegrams, 71–72, 198, 205; in *The Three Clerks* (Trollope), 62–64; in "'Wireless'" (Kipling), 242; of writing, 185–86. *See also* circulation; physiology
Forster, E. M., 214
Foucault, Michel, 65–66, 149, 233, 263n118
Frankenstein (Shelley), 7–8
"Freaks of the Telegraph" (C. Lewes), 193–94
The French Revolution (Carlyle), 124–25, 127, 129–30, 271n51
Freud, Sigmund, 241–42, 284–85n70
Froude, James Anthony, 18

Gallagher, Catherine, 115
Galvan, Jill, 275n59, 280n41
Galvani, Luigi, 136
Garvey, Michael Angelo, 107, 111
Gaskell, Elizabeth: *Cranford*, 251–54; on the electric telegraph, 88–90
gesture, as communication, 125–26, 129, 168, 171
Gilbert, Elliot, 239
Gilbert, Sandra, 274n57
Gitelman, Lisa, 272n15
Goodlad, Lauren, 263n106, 263n118
Gosse, Edmund, 217
gramophone. *See* phonograph
Green-Lewis, Jennifer, 140, 145, 273n20
Grusin, Richard, 5, 103–4, 269n3
Guattari, Félix, 210–11
Gubar, Susan, 274n57

Haggard, H. R., 240
Hall, N. John, 60
Hard Times (Dickens), 15–16, 18–19, 49, 108
Hardy, Thomas, 214
Hawthorne, Nathaniel, 66

Hayles, N. Katherine, 5, 75–76, 280–81n48, 285n3
Head, Francis Bond, 70–71, 83–84
Headrick, Daniel, 9
Heart of Darkness (Conrad), 194–95
Hemyng, Bracebridge, 173–75, 203, 207
Hertz, Heinrich, 221
Hertz, Neil, 275n65
Hill, Rowland, 36–39; and Dickens, 5, 33, 41, 50; and electric telegraph, 182, 193; and Post Office, 40–42, 261n70; *Post Office Reform*, 35–38, 259nn16–17; and railway, 59; and S.D.U.K., 17, 37; and Trollope, 55–56, 65, 262n83. *See also* Penny Post; Post Office
History of England (Macaulay), 97–98
Hollingshead, John, 90
Hong, Sungook, 281n12, 282n13
Household Words (ed. Dickens), 47–50, 92, 252
Howards End (Forster), 214
Hunt, Leigh, 17
Hutter, Albert, 270n36, 270n39

imperialism, 47, 178–79, 254
information, 4, 6; as abstract, 16, 18–19, 156–57, 170, 200, 240; as analog, 22–24; and the body, 130–32, 137, 149, 168, 242, 250; as electricity, 75–76, 98, 242; as fluid, 19–21, 75–76, 242; history, 9–10, 16, 75, 257nn39–40; versus knowledge, 16–18, 146–47, 150–52, 158, 200–201, 208–9, 235, 257–58n56; management of, 10, 21, 25, 158–59, 167; and materiality, 11, 22, 74–77, 90, 131–32, 165, 169–70, 250; and newspapers, 96–97; and realism, 18, 99, 132–33, 138, 159, 183–84, 212–13, 250–52; and subjectivity, 116–18, 130–32, 150–51, 240; and trauma, 167, 171–72; useless, 18, 200, 249–50; Victorian versus modern, 21–25; wants to be free, 17–18, 39, 137. *See also* electric telegraph; fact; flow; objectivity
information theory, 22–23
information workers, 165, 168–75, 186–87, 191, 197, 206–7; women, 174, 179–83, 187–88. *See also In the Cage* (James); Post Office
intelligence, 16–18, 98, 257n41. *See also* information; knowledge

In the Cage (James), 191–213, 223, 235
intimacy, long-distance, 82–88

Jaffe, Audrey, 49, 114
Jakobson, Roman, 95, 199
James, Henry: on George Eliot, 161; *In the Cage*, 191–213, 223, 235; on Kipling, 219; and media, 194–95; *The Portrait of a Lady*, 195–96; on realism and romance, 212–13; on Trollope, 57, 278n64; *The Turn of the Screw*, 196; *What Maisie Knew*, 206–7
Jameson, Fredric, 214
Jane Eyre (Brontë), 9, 59, 77–88, 265n50, 266n68, 266nn70–71
Jarrell, Randall, 232
Jenkins, Henry, 13
John Caldigate (Trollope), 56
journalism, 1–3, 95–100, 199–200, 268n111

Kaplan, Cora, 266n71
Keats, John, 228–39, 241–46
Keep, Christopher, 18, 278n63
Kern, Stephen, 268n120
Kincaid, James, 65
Kipling, Rudyard: "The Deep-Sea Cables," 206; and electric telegraph, 217–18; "'Finest Story in the World,'" 236–37; on inspiration, 240; and Marconi, 5, 224; and media, 220, 237; "Mrs. Bathurst," 238–39; and realism, 232–35; "Secret of the Machines," 220; *Something of Myself*, 240; and telephone, 240; and transportation, 219; "'Wireless,'" 218–19, 221–48; and wireless telegraphy, 5, 216, 220, 224–26
Kirkland, Joseph, 215–16
Kittler, Friedrich, 5, 7–8, 21, 187, 234, 238, 256n20
Knight, Charles, 37–39
Knoepflmacher, U. C., 274n45
knowledge, 16–18, 146–47, 158; taxes on, 17. *See also* information; Society for the Diffusion of Useful Knowledge
Kreilkamp, Ivan, 87, 194–95

Langan, Celeste, 106
Lansbury, Coral, 61, 64, 262n89
Laodicean (Hardy), 214

Lardner, Dionysius, 39, 70–71, 81, 265n48
Leech, John, 47
letter-boxes, 55, 262n83
letters: in *Cranford* (Gaskell), 251–54, guides to writing, 42; of Keats, 233, 239, 241, 243–44; in *Post Office Reform* (Hill), 37; as representation of society, 42–43; in "Right Through the Post" (Hollingshead), 90; in *Sartor Resartus* (Carlyle), 31–33, 35–36, 66; in *A Tale of Two Cities* (Dickens), 121–23; in Trollope's fiction, 59–60, 186; in "Valentine's Day at the Post-Office" (Dickens and Wills), 51–53; in "'Wireless'" (Kipling), 228, 243
Levine, George: on death and knowledge, 131, 271n59; on realism, 7, 26, 52, 84, 87, 89, 100, 104
Levinson, Paul, 272n14
Lévi-Strauss, Claude, 74–75, 265n28
Lewes, Charles, 193–94
Lewes, George Henry, 135–36, 147–49, 151, 159–60
"Lifted Veil" (Eliot), 14, 105, 134–35, 137–38, 140–42, 144–56, 158, 161
Lightning Flashes and Electric Dashes, 164
Little Dorrit (Dickens), 41, 90, 138–39
Lodge, Oliver, 75–76, 223, 234
Longfellow, Henry Wadsworth, 62–63, 237
Luckhurst, Roger, 82, 283n47
Lukács, George, 91, 104, 105, 268–69n2

Macaulay, Thomas Babington, 97–98
magic lantern, 141, 157
mail coach, 109–12
Marconi, Guglielmo, 5, 221–25, 238, 241–42, 244. *See also* wireless telegraphy
Marion Fay (Trollope), 56
Marvin, Carolyn, 195
mass culture, 244–46, 250
materiality: of communication, 113, 165; and electric telegraph; 74–77, 264–65n28; and information 11, 22, 74–77, 90, 131–32, 165, 169–70, 250–52; of thought, 165; of writing, 152, 155–56, 198–99, 252–54. *See also* body
Mattelart, Armand, 15
Matus, Jill. 167, 171

Maverick, Augustus, 92
Maxwell, James Clerk, 20, 221
McLuhan, Marshall, 5; on electric media, 89, 232; on media as extensions, 134–35, 205; on media as hot and cold, 89, 127; media laws, 124; on print, 89, 99
measurement, standardized, 62. *See also* time, standardized
media: and bodies; 10–11, 98; in *Jane Eyre* (Brontë), 84; and language, 247; in "The Lifted Veil" (Eliot), 152–56; new nineteenth-century, 4, 10, 103, 184–87, 194–95, 250; realism and, 18–19, 103–4, 250; in systems, 8, 13, 138, 150; in *A Tale of Two Cities* (Dickens), 116–18, 123. *See also* McLuhan; *and specific media*
media ecology, 12; nineteenth-century, 11–13, 18–19, 187
mediation, 84, 89. *See also* communication; intimacy; media
memory: and historical fiction, 270–71n42; in *In the Cage* (James), 211; in "The Lifted Veil" (Eliot), 141–42; in *Middlemarch* (Eliot), 158; and photography, 145; in *A Tale of Two Cities* (Dickens), 120–23; in "'Wireless'" (Kipling), 227, 236–37
mesmerism, 80–81, 135, 264n6, 265nn48–49
Middlemarch (Eliot), 15, 157–59
Miller, D. A., 65–66, 263n107
Miller, J. Hillis, 26, 187
modernism, 21, 28, 214–15
Moody, Ellen, 59
Morris, Pam, 260n38
Morse code, 265n29, 283n33; and information theory, 22; in "'Wireless'" (Kipling), 226–27
Morse, Samuel F. B., 68–69, 81–82, 137, 205
Morus, Iwan Rhys, 265n58, 266n66
motion pictures, 194, 238–39
"Mrs. Bathurst" (Kipling), 238–39
"Mugby Junction" (ed. Dickens), 166–72
Mulready, William, 43
Mulready envelope, 43–45
mytheme, of electric telegraph, 74–75, 264–65n28

Nagel, Thomas, 145

narrators, 25–26, 268n123; in *In the Cage* (James), 202–3, 210; James on, 202–3; in *Jane Eyre* (Brontë), 76, 78, 84, 86–87; in "The Lifted Veil" (Eliot), 153–54; and new media, 86, 99–100, 173–75, 203; in *A Tale of Two Cities* (Dickens), 114–15, 133; in *Telegraph Secrets* (Hemyng), 173–75; Trollope's, 59; in "'Wireless'" (Kipling), 224, 231, 236
"Natural History of German Life" (Eliot), 14, 138–39
naturalism, 234–35, 274n56
Negroponte, Nicholas, 23
nervous system, 15, 66–67, 69, 134–36, 145, 147–50
network, 21, 257n35; body as, 15, 66–67, 134–36, 168; as collection of holes, 248; electric telegraph, 77, 91, 94–95, 134–36; postal, 32–33, 41, 43, 54, 66, 259n22; and realism, 91, 248; society as, 15, 66, 91; wireless telegraphy as, 248. *See also* electric telegraph; nervous system; Post Office
newspapers. See *Daily News*; journalism
Nicholas Nickleby (Dickens), 34, 45–46, 71
Night Mail, 52
Ninth Bridgewater Treatise (Babbage), 24–25, 258n70
Nixon, Nicola, 199
Norrman, Ralf, 280n48
Northcote-Trevelyan Report, 57, 262n92
Novak, Daniel, 160
Nunberg, Geoffrey, 15, 130, 257n39

objectivity, 89–90, 95–97, 105, 123, 130–33, 136–37, 150, 268n111
Ong, Walter, 5, 6, 13, 99, 206. *See also* orality
optical telegraph, 72, 123–27
orality, 8, 80, 87
Orwell, George (Eric Blair), 128
Otis, Laura, 15, 135, 230, 257n35, 264n4, 275n67, 276n9, 282n28

Palmer, John, 111
Pamela (Richardson), 42
Panopticon, 25, 52
patents, 256n23
Pater, Walter, 186, 198
Paxton, Joseph, 1–2, 255n2

Pearson, David, 59
Pencil of Nature (Talbot), 139–40
Penny Black, 47
Penny Post, 6, 27, 33–43, 51–53. *See also* Rowland Hill; Post Office
People's Letter Bag and Penny Post Companion (Waverton), 42
Peters, John Durham, 85–86, 215, 226–27, 259n22
Phiz (Hablot Knight Browne), 45–48, 120
phonograph, 10–11, 117, 194, 237
photoglyphic process (Talbot), 142–44
Photographic News, 142–45
photography, 10–11, 14, 137–47, 160
physiology, 135–37, 147–52, 158–59, 274n49. *See also* body; nervous system
Physiology of Common Life (G. H. Lewes), 135–36, 147–49
Picker, John, 258n74, 275n71
Pickwick Papers (Dickens), 50, 110, 125, 251, 269n16
pillar-boxes, 55, 262n83
Poovey, Mary, 257n40, 267n101
Pope, Norris, 167
Porter, G. R., 39, 72
Portrait of a Lady (James), 195–96
postage stamp, 38, 47
"Postal Money Orders" (Dickens and Wills), 53
postal reform. See Henry Cole; Rowland Hill; Penny Post
Post Haste (Ballantyne), 175–80
Post Office, 5–6; as bureaucracy, 50, 56–58, 64; Carlyle and, 32–33, 35–36; and electric telegraph, 180–81, 193; and Empire, 44, 47; growth, 9–10, 43; Rowland Hill and 40–42, 261n70; history, 35–36, 180–81, 193, 222; and lovers, 53, 259n22; as network, 32–33, 41, 43, 54, 66, 259n22; in *Post Haste* (Ballantyne), 175–80; as society's image, 32–33; Trollope and, 54–56, 64–65; in "Valentine's Day at the Post Office" (Dickens and Wills), 50–53; and wireless telegraphy, 222. *See also* letters; Rowland Hill; Penny Post
Post Office Reform (Hill), 35–38, 259nn16–17
Prague, 141–46, 273n28
Preece, William, 222

preprocessing, 38, 58–59
Problems of Life and Mind (G. H. Lewes),
    136
process articles, 49–50, 90, 144. *See also*
    "Valentine's Day at the Post-Office"
    (Dickens and Wills)
print, 3–4, 6, 28; and Brontë, 87;
    combines storage and transmission,
    10–11; and George Eliot, 138, 152–56;
    and new media, 10–11, 13, 82, 87, 89,
    246, 250; and photography, 142–44;
    and realism, 11, 13–14, 87, 99–100,
    133, 138; technologies of, 10–11, 36,
    142–44, 256n26. *See also* textuality;
    writing
publishing, 256n26. *See also* print

"Queen Victoria and the Uniform Penny
    Postage" (Cole), 34–35, 259n3

radio. *See* Marconi; wireless telegraphy
railway, 110; Dickens and, 2–3, 76–77,
    166–72, 251; and electric telegraph,
    69–70; Hill and 59; and time-keeping,
    82–83; Travelling Post Office, 52, 90,
    177–78
Rauch, Alan, 17, 257n46
realism; 6, 9, 28, 104, 154, 248; as analog,
    26; as anticipating new media, 13, 82;
    and Babbage, 25–26; and Brontë, 81,
    84; critical accounts of, 7, 13, 17, 26,
    87, 89, 91, 93, 95, 99, 104, 144, 146,
    265n50, 268–69n2; and Dickens, 49,
    53, 118, 132–33, 165, 169, 171; and
    electric telegraph, 70–71, 88–95, 161,
    175, 183–86, 192–93, 201, 212–15;
    and George Eliot, 14, 138–39, 153–55,
    160–61; and Gaskell, 89–90; and
    information, 18, 99, 132–33, 138,
    159, 183–84, 212–13, 250; and James,
    192–93, 203–5, 211–15; and Kipling,
    232–35; and metaphor or metonym,
    26, 66, 95; of photography, 137–40,
    145–46; and postal reform, 41; and the
    Post Office, 53; and print textuality,
    11, 13–14, 87, 99–100, 133, 138; and
    Trollope, 56–57, 59–60, 66, 183–86,
    262n92; and the Victorian media
    ecology, 12–13, 18–19, 187. *See also*
    reality effect
reality effect, 20, 146, 169, 250

Redgauntlet (Scott), 105–6
remediation, 103–4
Reuter, Paul Julius, 97
Reuters, 96–97, 200
Reynolds, Susan, 273n28
Richards, Thomas, 18
Richardson, Samuel, 42
Riffaterre, Michael, 26
"Right Through the Post"
    (Hollingshead), 90
Rignall, J. M., 115, 269n11, 271n53
Robinson, Henry Peach, 274n54
Roland, Jeanne-Marie Phlipon, 129–30
romanticism, 7–8, 237–38
Ronalds, Francis, 271n49
Rothfield, Lawrence, 256n21
Rowe, John Carlos, 211
Rufo, Kenneth, 231

Sanders, Andrew, 270n36
Sartor Resartus (Carlyle), 31–33, 35–36,
    66
Schaffer, 257n41, 258n70
Schivelbusch, Wolfgang, 20
Schor, Hilary, 258n1, 270n39, 285n4,
    270n39, 285n4
Sconce, Jeffrey, 76, 82, 242
Scott, Walter, 105–6
"Secret of the Machines" (Kipling), 220
Seed, David, 168–69
Seltzer, Mark, 19, 194, 279n13
Shannon, Claude, 22–23
Shelley, Mary, 7–8
ships, 219, 246–47
Shooter's Hill, 111–12, 269n26
Shudson, Michael, 268n111
Shuman, Cathy, 262n92
Shuttleworth, Sally, 147, 149
Siegert, Bernhard, 55, 73
"Signal-Man" (Dickens), 166–72
Siskin, Clifford, 13
Sketches by Boz (Dickens), 71–72, 114
Smee, Alfred, 135
Smiles, Samuel, 170
Society for the Diffusion of Useful
    Knowledge (S.D.U.K.), 17–18, 37,
    257n46
Something of Myself (Kipling), 240
sound, 79–80, 117, 158–59, 167–69,
    184–85, 205–6, 236. *See also* electric
    telegraph; orality; phonograph;
    telephone

speed: of electric telegraph, 92–93, 96, 127, 179; of information, 23, 27; in *A Tale of Two Cities* (Dickens), 105–11, 126–27; of transportation, 105–11

spirits, 108, 208. *See also* electricity; telepathy

spiritualism, 82, 234, 247. *See also* mesmerism; telepathy

Spufford, Francis, 51

stamp, postage, 38, 47

standardization: of measurement, 62; of time, 82–84. *See also* preprocessing

Steinheil, Rudolf, 73

Stephen, James Fitzjames, 41

Sternlieb, Lisa, 86–87, 266n68

Stewart, Garrett, 266n71, 271n53, 272n62

Stoker, Bram, 10, 188, 194

Stone, Harry, 49–50

Stubbs, Katherine, 276n9

subjectivity: in *Daniel Deronda* (Eliot), 159–61; and the electric telegraph, 95, 201; in "The Lifted Veil" (Eliot), 137, 150–51, 156; and new media, 188, 201, 231, 240; in *A Tale of Two Cities* (Dickens) 106–7, 115–19, 122–23, 130–32. *See also* consciousness; narrators; objectivity

Super, R. H., 56

Sutherland, John, 80, 261n51

sympathy, 74, 80–81, 87. *See also* mesmerism; spiritualism; telepathy

Talbot, William Henry Fox, 139–40, 142–44, 146, 160

Tale of Two Cities (Dickens), 16, 90, 105–23, 126–33

Tambling, Jeremy, 272n62

Tawell, John, 73, 89

telegrams: expense, 70–76; fragmentation of, 199; in James, 195–96; in newspapers, 95–97. *See also* electric telegraph; *In the Cage* (James)

telegraph. *See* electric telegraph; optical telegraph; wireless telegraphy

"Telegraph Girl" (Trollope), 182–86

Telegraph Secrets (Hemyng), 173–75, 203, 207

telegraphers. *See* information workers

telepathy, 82, 153, 155, 207, 234, 242–43. *See also In the Cage* (James); "The

Lifted Veil" (Eliot); "'Wireless'" (Kipling)

telephone, 5, 7, 77, 82, 187, 223, 237, 240

textuality: and electric telegraph, 12, 73–74; and new media, 10–13; and orality, 87. *See also* print; writing

Thomas, Katie-Louise, 43, 277n52

Thomson, William, Baron Kelvin, 92

Thorburn, David, 13

Three Clerks (Trollope), 54–65, 262n92

Thurschwell, Pamela, 279n11, 283n47

time, standardized, 82–84, 265n58, 266n61

trains. *See* railway

transportation, 9, 72, 74, 108–9, 112, 127–28, 219. *See also* mail coach; railway; ships; speed

trauma, 167, 171–72

Travelling Post Office, 52, 90, 177–78

Trollope, Anthony: *Autobiography*, 60–61, 64, 66, 186–87, 262n89; and Rowland Hill, 55–56, 65, 262n83; *John Caldigate*, 56; and letter boxes, 55, 262n83; *Marion Fay*, 56; on postal network; 54; as postal official, 54–55, 262n89; "The Telegraph Girl," 182–86; *Three Clerks*, 54–65, 262n92; "The Young Women at the London Telegraph Office," 181–83

Trotter, David, 261n75, 269n13

Troup, George, 79–80

Turn of the Screw (James), 196

Tweedmouth Commission, 197

typewriter, 14, 194

Type-Writer Girl (Allen), 188

"Valentine's Day at the Post-Office" (Dickens and Wills), 50–53, 261n75

Victoria, Queen, 34–35, 39–40

vivisection. *See* Claude Bernard; G. H. Lewes; physiology

voice. *See* orality

Volta, Alessandro, 68, 136

voting reform, 36–37

Walker, Charles, 93–94

Wallace, Alfred Russel, 7, 72, 204–5

Wallace, Robert, 38–39

Wark, McKenzie, 73, 94

Watson, Nicola, 269n7

Waverton, William, 42

Welsh, Alexander, 5–6

What Maisie Knew (James), 206–7
Wheatstone, Charles, 68–69, 73–74, 80–81. *See also* electric telegraph
Wicke, Jennifer, 197, 279n29, 285n78
Wilde, Oscar, 243, 249–50
Williams, Raymond, 72
Wills, W. H., 50–53
Wilson, Edmund, 220
Wilson, George, 75, 80
Winter, Alison, 80–81, 265nn48–49
"'Wireless'" (Kipling), 218–19, 221–48
wireless telegraphy, 5–7; and "brain-waves," 242–43; and broadcast, 223, 244–46; Dr. Crippen and, 73; versus electric telegraph, 222, 238; history, 218, 221–23, 227; impersonality,

238; mechanics, 225–27; versus postal system, 246. *See also* Marconi; "'Wireless'" (Kipling)
Wolfreys, Julian, 141
Wozniak, Robert, 272n7
writing: and the body, 10–11, 130–32, 149, 152, 156; flow of, 185–86; and newer media, 10–11, 89, 183–84, 237, 248, 253; as technology, 8, 118, 121–22, 129, 152–56. *See also* print; textuality

Yates, Edmund, 55
Yeazell, Ruth Bernard, 34–35, 81
"Young Women at the London Telegraph Office" (Trollope), 181–83